Bloom's Modern Critical Views

African American Poets:
Wheatley-Tolson
Edward Albee
American and Canadian
Women Poets,
1930–present
American Women
Poets, 1650–1950
Maya Angelou
Asian-American Writers
Margaret Atwood
Jane Austen
James Baldwin
Honoré de Balzac
Samuel Beckett
Saul Bellow
The Bible
William Blake
Jorge Luis Borges
Ray Bradbury
The Brontës
Gwendolyn Brooks
Elizabeth Barrett
Browning
Robert Browning
Italo Calvino
Albert Camus
Lewis Carroll
Willa Cather
Cervantes
Geoffrey Chaucer
Anton Chekhov
Kate Chopin
Agatha Christie
Samuel Taylor
Coleridge
Joseph Conrad
Contemporary Poets
Stephen Crane
Dante
Daniel Defoe
Don DeLillo
Charles Dickens
Emily Dickinson
John Donne and the
17th-Century Poets
Fyodor Dostoevsky
W.E.B. Du Bois

George Eliot
T. S. Eliot
Ralph Ellison
Ralph Waldo Emerson
William Faulkner
F. Scott Fitzgerald
Sigmund Freud
Robert Frost
Johan Wolfgang von
Goethe
George Gordon, Lord
Byron
Graham Greene
Thomas Hardy
Nathaniel Hawthorne
Ernest Hemingway
Hispanic-American
Writers
Homer
Langston Hughes
Zora Neale Hurston
Aldous Huxley
Henrik Ibsen
John Irving
Henry James
James Joyce
Franz Kafka
John Keats
Jamaica Kincaid
Stephen King
Rudyard Kipling
Milan Kundera
D. H. Lawrence
Ursula K. Le Guin
Sinclair Lewis
Bernard Malamud
Christopher Marlowe
Gabriel García Márquez
Cormac McCarthy
Carson McCullers
Herman Melville
Arthur Miller
John Milton
Molière
Toni Morrison
Native-American
Writers
Joyce Carol Oates

Flannery O'Connor
Eugene O'Neill
George Orwell
Octavio Paz
Sylvia Plath
Edgar Allan Poe
Katherine Anne Porter
J. D. Salinger
Jean-Paul Sartre
William Shakespeare:
Histories and Poems
William Shakespeare:
Romances
William Shakespeare:
The Comedies
William Shakespeare:
The Tragedies
George Bernard Shaw
Mary Wollstonecraft
Shelley
Percy Bysshe Shelley
Alexander
Solzhenitsyn
Sophocles
John Steinbeck
Tom Stoppard
Jonathan Swift
Amy Tan
Alfred, Lord Tennyson
Henry David Thoreau
J. R. R. Tolkien
Leo Tolstoy
Mark Twain
John Updike
Kurt Vonnegut
Alice Walker
Robert Penn Warren
Eudora Welty
Edith Wharton
Walt Whitman
Oscar Wilde
Tennessee Williams
Thomas Wolfe
Tom Wolfe
Virginia Woolf
William Wordsworth
Richard Wright
William Butler Yeats

Modern Critical Views

NATIVE-AMERICAN WRITERS

Edited and with an introduction by
Harold Bloom
Sterling Professor of the Humanities
Yale University

CHELSEA HOUSE PUBLISHERS
Philadelphia

© 1998 by Chelsea House Publishers, a subsidiary of
Haights Cross Communications.

Introduction © 1998 by Harold Bloom

Printed and bound in the United States of America

10 9 8 7 6 5 4

∞ The paper used in this publication meets the minimum
requirements of the American National Standard for
Permanence of Paper for Printed Library Materials,
Z39.48-1984

Library of Congress Cataloging-in-Publication Data

Native American Writers / edited and with an introduction
by Harold Bloom.
        p.   cm.—(Modern critical views)
     Includes bibliographical references and index.
     ISBN 0-7910-4785-7 (hc)
     1. American literature—Indian authors—History and
criticism.
I. Bloom, Harold. II. Series.
PS153.I52N387   1998
810.9'897—dc21   97-51447
                                                       CIP

Contents

Editor's Note   ix

Introduction   1
  Harold Bloom

Words and Place: A Reading of *House Made of Dawn*   5
  Lawrence J. Evers

Alienation and Broken Narrative in *Winter in the Blood*   25
  Kathleen M. Sands

An Act of Attention: Event Structure in *Ceremony*   35
  Elaine Jahner

"He Had Never Danced With His People":
Cultural Survival in John Joseph Mathews's *Sundown*   45
  Louis Owens

Ancient Children at Play—Lyric, Petroglyphic,
and Ceremonial   57
  Kenneth M. Roemer

Textual Perspectives and the Reader in
The Surrounded   73
  James Ruppert

The Dialogic of Silko's *Storyteller*   83
  Arnold Krupat

Reading Narrated American Indian Lives:
Elizabeth Colson's *Autobiographies of
Three Pomo Women*   95
    Greg Sarris

The Rebirth of Indian and Chinese Mythology
in Gerald Vizenor's *Griever: An American
Monkey King in China*   127
    Cecilia Sims

Alienation and the Female Principle in
Winter in the Blood   135
    A. Lavonne Ruoff

Fighting for Her Life: The Mixed-Blood
Woman's Insistence Upon Selfhood   151
    Janet St. Clair

The New "Frontier" of Native American
Literature: Dis-Arming History with
Tribal Humor   161
    Kimberly M. Blaeser

To Be There, No Authority to Anything:
Ontological Desire and Cultural and Poetic
Authority in the Poetry of Ray A. Young Bear   175
    Robert Dale Parker

The Indian Historical Novel   195
    Alan Velie

"Where, Then, Shall We Place the Hero of
the Wilderness?" William Apess's Eulogy on
King Philip and Doctrines of Racial Destiny   211
    Anne Marie Dannenberg

"My People . . . My Kind": Mourning Dove's *Cogewea,
the Half-blood* as a Narrative of Mixed Descent   227
    Martha L. Viehmann

Dead Voices, Living Voice: On the Autobiographical
Writing of Gerald Vizenor   243
   Arnold Krupat

Comic Liberators and Word-Healers: The
Interwoven Trickster Narratives of Louise Erdrich   259
   Jeanne Rosier Smith

Chronology   277

Contributors   285

Bibliography   289

Acknowledgments   295

Index   299

Editor's Note

This book brings together a representative selection of the better critical essays available on Native American writers. My Introduction concerns itself with Nineteenth-Century versions of American Indian poetry, so as to help provide some background for the interpretation of modern Native American literature. I have concentrated upon songs of the Ghost-Dance.

The chronological sequence of criticism begins with Lawrence J. Evers' reading of Navarre Scott Momaday's *House Made of Dawn*. Evers finds in the novel a profound "sense of place" (D.H. Lawrence's term) and a remarkable renewal of oral narrative traditions, culminating in Abel's ceremonial dawn-race.

James Welch's *Winter in the Blood* is seen by Kathleen M. Sands as ironic parables that teach the painful acceptance of the present, while Elaine Jahner interprets Leslie Silko's *Ceremony* as a training in modes of attentiveness.

Cultural survival is emphasized by Louis Owens as the central theme and purpose of John Joseph Matthews's *Sundown*, after which Kenneth M. Roemer returns us to Scott Momaday, whose *The Ancient Child* is expounded in terms of the Navajo idea of harmonic play.

James Ruppert examines D'Arcy McNickle's *The Surrounded* in the light of Wolfgang Iser's work on the implied reader, while Leslie Silko's autobiographical *Storyteller* is considered by Arnold Krupat, who employs the critical perspectives of Mikhail Bakhtin.

Elizabeth Colson's *Autobiographies of Three Pomo Women* is analyzed by Greg Sarris, who judges that Colson did not fully consider her own relation to the women she interviewed, after which Cecilia Sims uncovers the theme of the trickster in Gerald Vizenor's *Griever*.

We return to Welch's *Winter in the Blood* with A. Lavonne Ruoff's meditation upon the book's portraits of female suffering, a subject amplified in

Janet St. Clair's account of mixed-blood woman's survival in novels by Louise Erdrich, and several other recent Native American writers.

Kimberly M. Blaeser studies "survival humor" in Native American literature, while Robert Dale Parker seeks the sources of poetic authority in the work of Ray A. Young Bear.

For Alan Velie, the radical differences between the historical novels of Gerald Vizenor and James Welch are subsumed by their common concern for preserving Native American concepts.

William Apess's *Eulogy on King Philip* is interpreted by Anne Marie Dannenberg as a complex alliance between the quest for Native American rights and the Abolitionist cause, after which Mourning Dove's novel, *Cogewea, The Half-Blood*, is seen by Martha L. Viehmann as the transition to a new kind of western romance that permits the Native-American perspective to emerge.

The autobiographical writings of Gerald Vizenor are praised by Arnold Krupat as exemplary instances of a mixed-blood writer fully realizing his own identity. This book then concludes with Jeanne Rosier Smith's sustained meditation upon Louise Erdrich's mastery of the image of the trickster, particularly in the feminist revisionism with which Erdrich has transformed that ancient image.

Introduction

The Sioux Outbreak of 1890 took part of its origin in the Ghost-Dance religion. James Mooney, whose 1896 account of that event and that faith included his versions of Ghost-Dance songs, prefaced his translations with a useful summary both of doctrine and of the lyrics:

> The great underlying principle of the ghost dance doctrine is that the time will come when the whole Indian race, living and dead, will be reunited upon a regenerated earth, to live a life of aboriginal happiness, forever free from death, disease, and misery. On this foundation each tribe has built a structure from its own mythology, and each apostle and believer has filled in the details according to his own mental capacity or ideas of happiness, with such additions as come to him from the trance . . . The differences of interpretation are precisely such as we find in Christianity, with its hundreds of sects and innumerable shades of individual opinion. The white race, being alien and secondary and hardly real, has no part in this scheme of aboriginal regeneration, and will be left behind with the other things of earth that have served their temporary purpose, or else will cease entirely to exist.

> There is no limit to the number of these songs, as every trance at every dance produces a new one, the trance subject after regaining consciousness embodying his experience in the spirit world in the form of a song, which is sung at the next dance and succeeding performances until superseded by other songs originating in the same way. Thus, a single dance may easily result in twenty or thirty new songs. While songs are thus born and die, certain ones which appeal especially to the Indian heart . . . live

1

and are perpetuated. There are also with each tribe certain songs which are a regular part of the ceremonial, as the opening song and the closing song, which are repeated at every dance. Of these the closing song is the most important and permanent. In some cases certain songs constitute a regular series, detailing the experiences of the same person in successive trance visions.

Mooney's versions of the Ghost-Dance songs are now most readily available in John Hollander's superb Library of America anthology, *American Poetry: The Nineteenth Century*, Volume Two. Shamanistic and wonderfully expressive, the songs have a pathos and intensity that testify to the awesome power of the Ghost-Dance religion. Invoking the Father and the Morning Star, the songs celebrate the faithful who "have danced until daylight," and then call out to the coming whirlwind. The Sioux, with marvelous poignancy, associate the arrival of the ghost-warriors with the return of the buffalo, decimated by white slaughterers. Repetition is employed with skill and a fine control of visual perspective in one of the Sioux Ghost-Dance chants:

The whole world is coming,
A nation is coming, a nation is coming,
The Eagle has brought the message to the tribe.
The father says so, the father says so.

Over the whole earth they are coming.
The buffalo are coming, the buffalo are coming,
The Crow has brought the message to the tribe,
The father says so, the father says so.

A Kiowa song catches something of the same ethos of expectation:

The spirit army is approaching,
The spirit army is approaching,
The whole world is moving onward,
The whole world is moving onward,
See! Everybody is standing watching,
See! Everybody is standing watching,
Let us all pray,
Let us all pray.

Franz Boas, reporting in 1897 on the Secret Societies of the Kwakiutl Indians, gives us a version of a Ghost-Dancer's song very different from the apocalyptic expectations of the Sioux:

> You sent us everything from out of the under world, ghosts!
>   who take away man's senses.
> You heard that we were hungry, ghosts!
>   who take away man's senses.
> We shall receive plenty from you, ghosts!
>   who take away man's senses.

Here we are beyond the hopes that fed the Sioux Outbreak, and are held instead by the implicit despair of a shamanism that surrenders perception in a desperate exchange for sustenance. The polarities of the Ghost-Dance songs are part of the heritage of modern Native-American literature. So far, that literature is stronger in narrative, particularly autobiographical fiction, than it is in poetry. But the poets who will return to their own equivalents of the Ghost-Dance songs now begin to develop, and the apocalyptic intensity of the heroic Sioux Outbreak will find further literary expression and fulfillment.

LAWRENCE J. EVERS

Words and Place: A Reading of House Made of Dawn

In order to consider seriously the meaning of language and of literature,
we must consider first the meanings of the oral tradition.

Native American oral traditions are not monolithic, nor are the traditions with which Momaday works in *House Made of Dawn*—Kiowa, Navajo, and Towan Pueblo. Yet, there are, he suggests, "common denominators." Two of the most important of these are the native American's relations to the land and his regard for language.

By imagining who and what they are in relation to particular landscapes, cultures and individual members of cultures form a close relation with those landscapes. Following D. H. Lawrence and others, Momaday terms this a "sense of place." A sense of place derives from the perception of a culturally imposed symbolic order on a particular physical topography. A superb delineation of some such symbolic order is offered by Tewa anthropologist Alfonso Ortiz in his study *The Tewa World* from which the following prayer is taken:

> Within and around the earth, within and around the hills, within and
> around the mountains, your authority returns to you.

The Tewa singer finds in the landscape which surrounds him validation for his own song, and that particular topography becomes a cultural landscape,

From *Western American Literature* 11. © 1985 by Andrew Wiget.

at once physical and symbolic. Like Ko-sahn, Momaday's grand- mother, the native American draws from it "strength enough to hold still against all the forces of chance and disorder."

The manner in which cultural landscapes are created interests Momaday, and the whole of his book *The Way to Rainy Mountain* may be seen as an account of that process. During their migration journey the Kiowa people "dared to imagine and determine who they were. . . . The journey recalled is among other things the revelation of one way in which these traditions are conceived, developed, and interfused in the human mind." The Kiowa journey, like that recounted in emergence narratives of other tribes, may be seen as a movement from chaos to order, from discord to harmony. In this emergence the landscape plays a crucial role, for cultural landscapes are created by the imaginative interaction of societies of men and particular geographies.

In the Navajo emergence narrative, for example, First Man and First Woman accompanied by Coyote and other actors from the animal world journey upward through four underworlds into the present Fifth World. The journey advances in a series of movements from chaos to order, and each movement takes the people toward greater social and symbolic definition. The cloud pillars of the First World defined only by color and direction become in the Fifth World the sacred mountains of the four directions, the most important coordinates in an intricate cultural geography. As with the Tewa and the Kiowa, that cultural landscape symbolizes the Navajo concep- tion of order, the endpoint of their emergence journey. Through the emer- gence journey, a collective imaginative endeavor, the Navajos determined who and what they were in relation to the land. The extraordinary interest in geography exhibited in Navajo oral literature then may be seen as an effort to evoke harmony in those narratives by reference to the symbolic landscape of the present world. Significantly, a major test theme in Navajo oral litera- ture requires identification of culturally important geographic features. Consider the Sun's test of the Hero Twins in one of the final episodes in the emergence narrative:

> He asked them to identify various places all over the surface of the earth.
>
> He asked, "Where is your home?" The boys knew where their home was.
>
> They pointed out Huerfano Mountain and said that was where they lived.
>
> The Sun next asked, "What mountain is that in the East?"

"That's *Sis Naajiní* (Blanca Peak)," replied the boys.

"What mountain is down here below us?"

"That's *Tsoodzi* (Mount Taylor)," said the boys.

"What mountain is that in the West?"

That's *Dook'o'oosííd* (San Francisco Peak)."

"Now, what mountain is that over in the north?"

"Those are the *Dibé Nitsaa* (La Plata Mountains)."

> Because all the boys' answers were correct, the Sun said goodby to them as they were lowered down to the earth at the place called *Tó Sidoh* (Hot Springs).

Through their knowledge of the Navajo cultural landscape the Twin proved who and what they were to the Sun.

The pattern of the emergence narrative—a journey toward order symbolized by a cultural landscape—is repeated in Navajo chantway rituals. A patient requires a chantway ritual when his life is in some way out of order and harmony. In order for that harmony to be restored he must be taken through a ritual re-emergence journey paralleling that of the People. It is important to note the role of the singer and his ritual song here, for without songs there can be no cure or restoration of order. Through the power of the chanter's words the patient's life is brought under ritual control, and he is cured.

We come round, then, to another of the "common denominators" Momaday finds in oral traditions: attitude toward language. Of Kiowa oral tradition Momaday writes: "A word has power in and of itself. It comes from nothing into sound and meaning; it gives origin to all things." It is this concept, remarkably like one text version of the Navajo origin giving "One Word" as the name of the original state of the universe, which forms the center of Tosamah's sermon on St. John's gospel in the novel. But more germane to our discussion of oral tradition generally is the related notion that "by means of words can a man deal with the world on equal terms." It is only through words that a man is able to express his relation to place Indeed, it is only through shared words or ritual that symbolic landscapes are able to exist. So it is that the Tewa singer, the Navajo chanter, and the Kiowa "man of words" preserve their communities through their story and song. Without them there would be no community. One contemporary Navajo medicine man suggests that loss of ceremonial words will signal the end of the world: "The medicine men who have knowledge in the Blessing Way (*Hozho ji*) will all evidently be lost. The words to the song will vanish from their memory, and they will not know how to begin to sing."

In this context we can better appreciate Abel's dilemma in *House Made of Dawn*. As Momaday suggests: "One of the most tragic things about Abel, as I think of him, is his inability to express himself. He is in some ways a man without a voice. . . . So I think of him as having been removed from oral tradition."

II

House Made of Dawn opens and closes with the formulaic words which enclose all Jemez pueblo tales—*dypaloh* and *qtsedaba*, placing it consciously in that oral tradition. As many oral narratives, the novel is shaped around a movement from discord to harmony and is structurally and thematically cyclic. The prologue is dominated by the race, a central theme in the novel as Momaday has suggested:

> I see [*House Made of Dawn*] as a circle. It ends where it begins and it's informed with a kind of thread that runs through it and holds everything together. The book itself is a race. It focuses upon the race, that's the thing that does hold it all together. But it's a constant repetition of things too.

Parsons tells us that racing is a conspicuous feature of Jemez ceremonialism. The winter race Abel runs in the prologue and at the end of the novel is the first race in the Jemez ceremonial season, an appropriate ceremonial beginning. But the race itself may be seen as a journey, a re-emergence journey analogous to that mentioned in connection with Navajo and Kiowa oral tradition. Indeed, the language echoes a Navajo re-emergence song sung in the Night Chant, from which the title of the book is taken.

These journey and emergence themes begin to unfold in the following scene as Francisco goes in his wagon to meet the bus returning Abel to Walatowa after WWII. The wagon road on which he rides is parallel to the modern highway on which Abel rides. The two roads serve as familiar metaphors for the conflicting paths Abel follows in the novel, and Momaday reinforces the conflict by parallel auditory motifs as well. As the wagon road excites in Francisco memories of his own race "for good hunting and harvests," he sings good sounds of harmony and balance. At the same time the recurrent whine of tires on the highway is constantly in the background until "he heard the sharp wheeze of the brakes as the big bus rolled to a stop in front of the gas pump. . . ." (p. 13) The re-emergence theme is suggested in the passage by the presence of the reed trap (p. 10)—recalling the reed of emergence, and the fact that Abel returns "ill" (p. 13). He is drunk, of course, but he is also ill, out of balance, in the manner of a patient in a Navajo chantway.

Abel's genealogy, the nature of his illness, and its relation to the auditory motifs mentioned above are further defined in the seven fragments of memory he experiences as he walks above the Cañon de San Diego in the first dawn following his return. At the same time these fragments establish a context for Abel's two prominent encounters in Part I with Angela Grace St. John and with the albino Juan Reyes Fragua.

Abel's genealogy is complicated. He did not know who his father was. "His father was a Navajo, they said, or a Sia, or an Isleta, an outsider anyway," which made Abel "somehow foreign and strange" (p. 15). The ties Abel does have to Walatowa are through his mother whose father, Francisco—both sacristan and kiva participant—is the illegitimate son of the consumptive priest Fray Nicolas V. (p.184). Through Francisco, Abel is a direct descendant of the Bahkyush, a group of Towan-speaking pueblos who immigrated to Jemez in the mid-nineteenth century. He is a "direct [descendant] of those men and women who had made that journey along the edge of oblivion" (p. 19), an experience which gave them a "tragic sense." Abel, as his Bahkyush ancestors, is on just such a "journey along the edge of oblivion" in the novel.

Abel's journey in Part I is a journey of return to Walatowa and his illness is most explicitly related to a WWII experience. At the end of his seven memory fragments in the first dawn of his return Abel recalls:

> This—everything in advance of his going—he could remember whole and in detail. It was the recent past, the intervention of days and years without meaning, of awful calm and collision, time always immediate and confused, that he could not put together in his mind. (p. 25)

In the confusion of war among soldiers who recognized him only as a "chief" speaking in "Sioux or Algonquin or something" (p. 108), Abel lost both the sense of place which characterized his tribal culture and the very community which supports that sense of place. "He didn't know where he was, and he was alone" (p. 26). Incredibly, he doesn't even recognize the earth: "He reached for something, but he had no notion of what it was; his hand closed upon the earth and the cold, wet leaves" (p. 26).

Mechanical sounds are associated with Abel's disorientation. The "low and incessant" (p. 26) sound of the tank descending upon him reaches back in the novel to the "slow whine of tires" Francisco hears on the highway and looks ahead to the sound of Angela's car intruding on his vision in the first dawn above the valley as it creeps along the same highway toward the Jemez church (p. 27). These are the same mechanical sounds Abel tried "desperately to take into account" as the bus took him away to the war—again on the same highway (p. 25). They are the sounds that reminded him as he left the pueblo to go to war that "the town and the valley and the hills" could no longer center him, that he was now "centered upon himself" (p. 25).

That Angela Grace St. John, the pregnant wife of a Los Angeles physician who comes to Walatowa seeking a cure for her own ailments, will become an obstacle in Abel's re-emergence journey is first suggested by the extensive auditory motifs of Part I. Yet her perceptions of his problems and of the Indian world generally have earned the sympathy of some readers. Perhaps her most seductive perception is that of the significance of the corn dancers at Cochiti Pueblo:

> Their eyes were held upon some vision out of range, something away in the end of distance, some reality that she did not know, or even suspect. What was it that they saw? Probably they saw nothing after all, . . . nothing at all. But then that was the trick, wasn't it? To see nothing at all, . . . nothing in the absolute. To see beyond the landscape, beyond every shape and shadow and color, *that* was to see nothing. That was to be free and finished, complete, spiritual. . . . To say "beyond the mountain," and to mean it, to mean, simply, beyond everything for which the mountain stands of which it signifies the being. (pp. 37–38)

As persuasive as Angela's interpretation of the Cochiti dancers may seem, it is finally a denial of the value of the landscape which the novel celebrates. Angela's assumption that the Cochiti dancers possess a kind of Hindu metaphysics which rejects phenomena for noumena is a projection of her own desires to reject the flesh. Her attitude toward the land is of a piece with her attitude toward her own body: "she could think of nothing more vile and obscene than the raw flesh and blood of her body, the raveled veins and the gore upon her bones" (p. 36). We become almost immediately aware of the implications of that denial she craves in two following scenes—the *corre de gaio* and Abel's second reflection on the Cañon de San Diego.

We view the *corre de gaio* through Angela who again projects feelings about her own existence on the ceremony. For Angela the ceremony like herself is "so empty of meaning . . . and yet so full of appearance" (p. 43). Her final impression of the ceremony is sexual. She senses some "unnatural thing" in it and "an old fascination returned upon her" (p. 43). Later she remarks of the ceremony: "Like this, her body had been left to recover without her when once and for the first time, having wept, she had lain with a man" (p. 45). In the albino's triumph and Abel's failure at the *corre de gaio* she finds sexual pleasure.

The etiological legend of Santiago (St. James) and the rooster is told by Fr. Olguin appropriately enough for his "instinctive demand upon all histories to be fabulous" (p. 68). The legend explains the ceremonial game which follows in the novel. Just as the sacrifice of the rooster by Santiago produced cultivated plants and domesticated animals for the Pueblo people, so too does ritual re-enactment of the sacrifice promote fertility at Walatowa. While ethnographers suggest that the *corre de gaio* is of relatively minor ceremonial importance in Pueblo societies, in the context of the novel the rooster pull affords Abel his first opportunity to re-enter the ceremonial functions of the village. It is, we are told, the first occasion on which he has taken off his uniform. Though the ceremony itself seems efficacious, as rain follows in the novel, Abel is "too rigid" and "too careful" (p. 42) at the game and fails miserably.

Abel's failure at the rooster pull demonstrates his inability to reenter the ceremonial life of the village, as he realizes in his second reflection at dawn, July 28, 1945. The section opens with an explicit statement of the relation of the emergence journey and the landscape: "The canyon is a ladder to the plain" (p. 54), and is followed by a description of the ordered and harmonious existence of life in that landscape. Each form of life has its proper space and function in the landscape, and by nature of that relation is said to have "tenure in the land" (p. 56). Similarly, "man came down the ladder to the plain a long time ago. It was a slow migration . . ." (p. 56). Like the emergency journeys of the Kiowa and the Navajo mentioned earlier, the migration of the people of Walatowa led to an ordered relation to place which they express in their ceremonial life. As Abel walks in this landscape in the dawn he is estranged from the town and the land as well. "His return to the town had been a failure" (pp. 56–7) he realizes because he is no longer attuned to its rhythms. He has no words to express his relation to the place. He is "not dumb," but "inarticulate" (p. 57).

Despite his inarticulateness, the rhythm and words are still there "like memory, in the reach of his hearing" (p. 57). We recall that on July 21, seven days before, "for a moment everything was all right with him" (p. 32). Here however;

He was alone, and he wanted to make a song out of the colored canyon, the way the women of Torre6n made songs upon their looms out of colored yarn, but he had not got the right words together. It would have been a creation song; he would have sung lowly of the first world, of fire and flood, and of the emergence of dawn from the hills. (p. 57)

Abel is at this point vaguely conscious of what he needs to be cured. He needs a re-emergence. He needs words, ceremonial words, which express his relation to the cultural landscape in which he stands. He needs to feel with the Tewa singer quoted earlier his authority return to him. But here out of harmony with himself and his community he needs most of all the kind of re-emergence journey offered in a Navajo chantway.

Significantly, the passage closes, as did the dawn walk of July 21, with an emblem of Angela St. John intruding on Abel's vision: "the high white walls of the Benevides house" (p. 58). The house itself is another symbol of Angela's denial of the land or more particularly the landscape of the Cañon de San Diego. In contrast to Francisco and the other native residents of Walatowa who measure space and time by reference to the eastern rim of the canyon, Angela measures hers in relation to this "high, white house:"

She would know the arrangement of her days and hours in the upstairs and down, and they would be for her the proof of her being and having been. (p. 53)

His re-entry into the village spoiled, Abel turns not to the ceremonial structure of the pueblo for support but to Angela. And it is the Benevides house, not the land, which provides "the wings and the stage" for their affair (p. 53). Abel's first sexual encounter with Angela is juxtaposed in the novel with Francisco's encounter with the albino witch in his cornfield. Indeed, Angela, who "keened" to the unnatural qualities of the albino during the *corre de gaio*, echoes the auditory symbols of evil mentioned earlier. Just as Nicolas *teah-whau* "screamed" at him (p. 15), and the moan of the wind in the rocks (p. 16) frightened him earlier, as Angela and Abel make love "she wanted to scream" and is later "moaning softly" (p. 62).

Earlier in his life Abel found physical regeneration through a sexual experience with Fat Josie (pp. 93, 106–7). His affair with Angela has just the opposite effect. Lying physically broken on the beach in Part II Abel reflects:

He had loved his body. It had been hard and quick and beautiful; it had been useful, quickly and surely responsive to his mind and will. . . . His body, like his mind, had turned on him; it was his enemy. (p. 93)

The following couplet in the text implicates Angela in this alienation:

> Angela put her white hands to his body.
> Abel put his hands to her white body. (p. 94)

Later Abel tells Benally that "she [Angela] was going to help him get a job and go away from the reservation, but then he got himself in trouble" (p. 161). That "trouble" derives in part from Abel's separation from his land.

Auditory symbols follow Abel directly from his affair with Angela to the climactic scene of Part I, the killing of the albino. Just before the murder the albino laughs "a strange, inhuman cry" (p. 77). Like the sound of Nicolas *teah-whau* it is "an old woman's laugh" that issues from a "great, evil mouth" (p. 77). At the very scene of the murder the only sound that breaks the silence is "the moan of the wind in the wires" (p. 77).

That Abel regards the albino as evil, as a witch (*sawah*), is clear enough even without the explicit statements of Father Olguin, Tosamah, and Benally later (pp. 94–5, 136–7). Moreover, it is clear at the time of the murder that Abel regards the albino as a snake. He feels "the scales of the lips and the hot slippery point of the tongue, writhing" (p. 78). But that Abel is "acting entirely within the Indian tradition" when he kills the albino is wrong.

Abel's compulsion to eradicate the albino-snake reveals an attitude toward evil more akin to the Christian attitude of Nicolas V.: "that Serpent which even is the One our most ancient enemy" (p. 50). The murder scene is rife with Christian overtones. The killing takes place beneath a telegraph pole which "leaned upon the black sky" (p. 77); during the act "the white hands still lay upon him as if in benediction" (p. 78); and after the albino's death "Abel knelt" and noticed "the dark nails of the hand seemed a string of great black beads" (p. 79). Abel appears to kill the albino then as a frustrated response to the White Man and Christianity, but he does so more in accordance with Anglo tradition than Indian tradition. Indeed, he has been trained in the Army to be a killer.

We recall here that the murder takes place squarely in the middle of the fiesta of Porcingula, the patroness of Walatowa, and that a central part of the ceremony on that feast is a ritual confrontation between the Pecos bull and the "black-faced children, who were the invaders" (p. 73). Parsons describes the bull-baiting at Jemez during the fiesta of Porcingula, August 1, 1922, as follows:

> An hour later, "the Pecos bull is out," I am told and hasten to the Middle. There the bull-mask is out playing, with a following of about a

dozen males, four or five quite young boys. They are caricaturing Whites, their faces and hands painted white; one wears a false mustache, another a beard of blond hair. "U.S.A." is chalked on the back of their coat or a cross within a circle. . . . They shout and cry out, "What's the matter with you boy?" or more constantly "*Muchacho! Muchacho!*"

. . . .

The bull antics are renewed, this time with attempts of his baiters to lassoo. Finally they succeed in dragging him in front of their house, where he breaks away again, to be caught again and dragged into the house. From the house a bugler steps out and plays "Wedding Bells" and rag-time tunes for the bull-baiters to dance to in couples, "modern dances," ending up in a tumble. Two by two, in their brown habit and sandalled feet, four of the Franciscan Fathers pass by. It grows dark, the bugler plays "taps" and this burlesque, reaching from the Conquistadores to the Great War, is over for the night.

The very day then that Abel kills the albino the community from which he is estranged could have provided him with a way of ritually confronting the white man. Had his return not been a failure, he might have borne his agony, as Francisco had "twice or three times" (p. 76), by taking the part of the bull. "It was a hard thing," Francisco tells us, "to be the bull, for there was a primitive agony to it, and it was a kind of victim, an object of ridicule and hatred" (p. 75). Hard as that agony was, Abel as Francisco before him might have borne it with the support of his community. Separated from that community, he acts individually against evil and kills the white man.

Momaday forces us to see the murder as more complicated and subtle in motivation despite Benally's sympathetic reflections on the realities of witchery (p. 137), Tosamah's reference to the murder as a legal conundrum (p. 136), and Abel's own statement that the murder was "not a complicated thing" (p. 95). Death has not been a simple thing for Abel to cope with earlier in the novel, as shown by his emotional reactions to the deaths of the doe (pp. 16–17), the rabbit (p. 22), the eagle (pp. 24–25), as well as the deaths of his brother Vidal and his mother. More to the point is the fact that the White Man Abel kills is, in fact, a white Indian, an albino. He is the White Man in the Indian; perhaps even the White Man in Abel himself. When Abel kills the albino, in a real sense he kills a part of himself and his culture which he can no longer recognize and control. That that part should take the shape of a snake in his confused mind is horribly appropriate given the long association of the Devil and the snake in Christian tradition (cf. Fray Nicolas V.) and the subsequent Puritan identification of the American Indians as demonic snakes and witches in so much of early American literature. In orthodox Pueblo belief the snake and the powers with which it is associated are accepted as a necessary part of the cosmic order: "The Hebrew view of the serpent as the embodiment of unmitigated evil is never elaborated among the Pueblos; he is too often an ally for some desired end."

Yet, the whiteness of the albino suggests something more terrible than evil to Abel. As the whiteness of the whale does to Ishmael, it suggests an emptiness in the universe, a total void of meaning. It is an emblem complementary to Angela's philosophizing over the Cochiti dancers. The albino confronts Abel with his own lack of meaning, his own lack of a sense of place.

This reading is reinforced by the poignant final scene in Part I. Francisco stands alone in his corn field demonstrating the very sense of place Abel has lacked on his return. We recall that in this very field Francisco too had confronted evil in the shape of the albino, but that he responded to the confrontation very differently:

> His acknowledgement of the unknown was nothing more than a dull, intrinsic sadness, a vague desire to weep, for evil had long since found him out and knew who he was. He set a blessing upon the corn and took up his hoe. (p. 64)

Because of Abel's act, Francisco is for the first time separated from the Walatowa community. He stands muttering Abel's name as he did in the opening of the chapter, and near him the reed trap—again suggesting the reed of emergence—is empty.

III

Part II of the novel opens with Abel lying broken, physically and spiritually, on the beach in Los Angeles. Like the helpless grunion with whom he shares the beach, he is out of his world. Abel's problem continues to be one of relating to place. As in Part I at Walatowa he fails to establish a sense of place in Los Angeles because of a failure to find community. Not only is he separated from other workers at the factory, but even Tosamah and the Indian men at the Silver Dollar reject Abel. That rejection is a major cause of Abel's second futile and self-destructive confrontation with evil in the person of Martinez, a sadistic Mexican policeman. The pattern of the second confrontation is a repetition of the first. Just as Abel kills the albino at Walatowa after he has failed to find community there, so too he goes after

Martinez, also perceived as a snake (*culebra*), after he has failed utterly to find community in Los Angeles. Implication of Anglo society in this failure is again explicit and powerful, as Abel has been sent to Los Angeles by the government on its Relocation Program after serving time in prison for killing the albino.

On the beach Abel "could not see" (p. 92). This poverty of vision, both physical and imaginative, is akin to the inability of one-eyed Father Olguin to "see" and is related to Abel's prison experience: "After a while he could not imagine anything beyond the walls except the yard outside, the lavatory and the dining hall—or even walls, really" (p. 97). Yet it is by the sea that Abel gains the insight required to begin his own re-emergence. For the first time he asks himself "where the trouble had begun, what the trouble was" (p. 97), and though he still cannot answer the question consciously, his mind turns again to the mechanical auditory images noted earlier:

> The bus leaned and created; he felt the surge of motion and the violent shudder of the whole machine on the gravel road. The motion and the sound seized upon him. Then suddenly he was overcome with a desperate loneliness, and he wanted to cry out. He looked toward the fields, but a low rise of the land lay before them. (p. 97)

The bus takes Abel out of a context where he has worth and meaning and into a context where "there were enemies all around" (p. 98). From the cultural landscape of the Cañon de San Diego to the beach where "the world was open at his back (p. 96), Abel's journey has taken him, as his Bahkyush ancestors, to "the edge of oblivion": "He had been long ago at the center, had known where he was, had lost his way, had wandered to the end of the earth, was even now reeling on the edge of the void" (p. 96). On the beach, then, Abel finally realizes that "he had lost his place" (p. 96), a realization accompanied by the comprehension of the social harmony a sense of place requires. Out of his delirium, as if in a dream, his mind returns to the central thread of the novel, the race, and here at last Abel is able to assign meaning to the race as a cultural activity:

> The runners after evil ran as water runs, deep in the channel, in the way of least resistance, no resistance. His skin crawled with excitement; he was overcome with longing and loneliness, for suddenly he saw the crucial sense in their going, of old men in white leggings running after evil in the night. They were whole and indispensable in what they did; everything in creation referred to them. Because of them, perspective,

proportion, design in the universe. Meaning because of them. They ran with great dignity and calm, not in hope of anything, but hopelessly; neither in fear nor hatred nor despair of evil, but simply in recognition and with respect. Evil was. Evil was abroad in the night; they must venture out to the confrontation; they must reckon dues and divide the world. (p. 96)

We recall that as Abel killed the albino "the terrible strength of the hands was brought to bear only in proportion as Abel *resisted them*" (p. 78, emphasis added). The murder is an expression of Abel's disharmony and imbalance. As Abel here realizes "evil is that which is ritually not under control. In the ceremonial race, not in individual resistance, the runners are able to deal with evil.

Tosamah's description of the emergence journey and the relations of words and place serve as a clue to Abel's cure, but the role he plays in Abel's journey appears as ambiguous and contradictory as his character. He is at once priest and "clown" (p. 165). He exhibits, often on the same page, remarkable insight, buffoonery, and cynicism. He has then all the characteristics of Coyote, the trickster figure in native American mythologies. Alternately wise and foolish, Coyote in native American oral tradition is at once a buffoon and companion of the People on their emergence journey. As Coyote, a member of "an old council of clowns" (p. 55), the Right Reverend John Big Bluff Tosamah speaks with a voice "full of authority and rebuke" (p. 55). As Coyote, "he likes to get under your skin; he'll make a fool out of you if you let him" (p. 165). Note how Momaday describes Tosamah:

> He was shaggy and awful-looking in the thin, naked light; big, lithe as a cat, narrow-eyed, suggesting in the whole of his look and manner both arrogance and agony. He wore black like a cleric; he had the voice of a great dog. (p. 85)

The perspective Tosamah offers Abel and the reader in the novel derives not so much from his peyote ceremonies, for which Momaday seems to have drawn heavily on La Barre's *The Peyote Cult*, but rather from the substance of the two sermons he gives. The second sermon, "The Way to Rainy Mountain," which Momaday has used in his book by the same title and several other contexts, addresses the relation of man, land, community, and the word. In it Tosamah describes the emergence of the Kiowa people as "a journey toward the dawn" that "led to a golden age" (p. 118). It was a journey which led the Kiowa to a culture which is inextricably bound to the land of the southern plains. There, much in the manner of Abel looking over the Cañon de San Diego in Part I, he looks out on the landscape at dawn and muses: "your imagination comes to life, and this, you think, is where Creation was begun" (p. 117). By making a re-emergence journey, Tosamah is able to feel a sense of place.

That coherent native relation to the land described so eloquently by Tosamah is counterpointed in the novel not only by Abel's experiences but also by the memories of Milly, the social worker who becomes Abel's lover in Los Angeles. Milly, like Tosamah, is from Oklahoma. There her family too had struggled with the land, but "at last Daddy began to hate the land, began to think of it as some kind of enemy, his own very personal and deadly enemy" (p. 113). Even viewed in the dawn her father's relation to the land was a despairing and hopeless one:

> And every day before dawn he went to the fields without hope, and I watched him sometimes saw him at sunrise far away in the empty land very small on the skyline turning to stone even as he moved up and down the rows. (p. 113)

The contrast with Francisco, who seems most at home in his fields, and with Tosamah, who finds in that very landscape the depth of his existence is obvious. The passage also recalls Angela's denial of the meaning of the land and Abel's own reflections on "enemies."

In his first sermon in the novel, Tosamah addresses the crucial role of words and the imagination in the re-emergence process. The sermon is a bizarre exegesis of St. John's gospel which compares Indian and Anglo attitudes toward language. As participants in oral traditions, Indians, Tosamah tells us, hold language as sacred. They have a childlike regard for the mysteries of speech. While St. John shared that sensibility, he was also a white man. And the white man obscures the truth by burdening it with words:

> Now, brothers, and sisters, old John was a white man, and the white man has his ways. Oh gracious me, he has his ways. He talks about the Word. He talks through it and around it. He builds upon it with syllables, with prefixes and suffixes, and hyphens and accents. He adds and divides and multiplies the Word. And in all of this he subtracts the Truth. (p. 87)

The white man may indeed, Tosamah tells us, in a theory of verbal overkill that is wholly his own, "perish by the Word" (p. 89).

Words are, of course, a problem for Abel. On the one hand, he lacks the ceremonial words—the words of a Creation song—which properly express his relation to community and place. He is inarticulate. On the other he is plagued by a surfeit of words from white men. The bureaucratic word of the social worker's forms effectively obscure his real problems. At the murder trial, he thinks: "Word by word by word these men were disposing of him in language, *their* language, and they were making a bad job of it (p. 95). Again when Benally takes him to the hospital after the beach scene bureaucratic words get in the way. Indeed, Benally perceives Abel's central problem as one of words, as he equates finding community with having appropriate words:

> And they can't help you because you don't know how to talk to them. They have a lot of words, and you know they mean something, but you don't know what, and your own words are no good because they're not the same; they're different, and they're the only words you've got. . . . You think about getting out and going home. You want to think you belong someplace, I guess. (p. 144)

Tosamah perceives a similar dislocating effect of words on Abel though he relates it to religion. Scorning his inarticulateness and innocence he sees Abel as caught in "the Jesus scheme" (p. 136). Beyond his sermons there is a special irony in the fact that Tosamah doesn't understand Abel and his problems, for he is described several times in Part II as a "physician." Though they put Abel's problems in a broader and clearer perspective, Tosamah's words are of little use to Abel.

IV

Part III is told from the point of view of Ben Benally, a relocated Navajo who befriends Abel in Los Angeles. Roommates in Los Angeles, Ben and Abel share many things in their backgrounds. On his one visit to Walatowa, Benally finds the landscape there similar to that in which he grew up. Like Abel he was raised in that landscape without parents by his grandfather. Benally even suggests that he is somehow related to Abel since the Navajos have a clan called Jemez, the name of Abel's pueblo. Moreover, we recall that Abel's father may have been a Navajo, and that Francisco regards the Navajo children who come to Walatowa during the Fiesta of Porcingula as "a harvest, in some intractable sense the regeneration of his own bone and blood" (p. 72). This kinship gives Benally special insight into Abel's problems and strengthens his role as Night Chanter.

Benally's childhood memories of life with his grandfather near Wide Ruins reveal a sense of place very like that Abel groped for on his return to Walatowa:

> And you were little and right there in the center of everything, the sacred mountains, the snow-covered mountains and the hills, the gullies and the flats, the sundown and the night, everything—where you were little, where you were and had to be. (p. 143)

Moreover, this sense of place gives him words: ". . . you were out with the sheep and could talk and sing to yourself and the snow was new and deep and beautiful" (p. 142).

In Los Angeles, however, Benally's sense of place is lost in his idealism and naïveté. Return to the reservation seems a pale option to the glitter of Los Angeles. "There would be nothing there, just the empty land and a lot of old people, going noplace and dying off" (p. 145). Like Milly, Benally believes in "Honor, Industry, the Second Chance, the Brotherhood of Man, the American Dream. . ." (p. 99). Theirs is a 50s American Dream of limitless urban possibilities. Benally believes you can have anything you want in Los Angeles and that "you never have to be alone" (p. 164). Yet in the very scene following his reflection on this urban cornucopia, we find Benally excluded even from the community of The Silver Dollar, counting his pennies, unable to buy a second bottle of wine. Idealism obscures Benally's vision, even as Tosamah's cynicism obscures his.

Nevertheless, Benally is the Night Chanter, the singer who helps restore voice and harmony to Abel's life. In the hospital having realized the significance of the runners after evil, Abel asks Benally to sing for him:

> "House made of dawn." I used to tell him about those old ways, the stories and the songs, Beautyway and Night Chant. I sang some of those things, and I told him what they meant, what I thought they were about. (p. 133)

The songs from both the Beautyway and the Night Chant are designed to attract good and repel evil. They are both restorative and exorcising expressions of the very balance and design in the universe Abel perceived in the runners after evil. Ben's words from the Night Chant for Abel are particularly appropriate, since the purpose of the Night Chant is to cure patients of insanity and mental imbalance. The structure and diction of the song demonstrate the very harmony it seeks to evoke. Dawn is balanced by evening light, dark cloud and male rain by dark mist and female rain. All things are in balance and control, for in Navajo and Pueblo religion good is control. Further note that a journey metaphor is prominent in the song ("may I walk. . . .") and that the restorative sequence culminates with "restore my voice for me." Restoration of voice is an outward sign of inner harmony. Finally, note that the song begins with a culturally significant geographic reference: *Tségihi*. One of its central messages is that ceremonial words are bound efficaciously to place. No matter how dislocated is Benally or idiosyncratic his understandings of Navajo ceremonialism, the songs he sings over Abel clearly serve a restorative function.

Angela also visits Abel in the hospital and offers him words. She tells Abel the story her son likes "best of all" (p. 169). It is a story about "a young Indian brave," born of a bear and a maiden, who has many adventures and finally saves his people. Benally marvels at the story which reminds him of a similar story from the Mountain Chant told to him by his grandfather. Yet unlike the Navajo legend and the Kiowa bear legend told by Tosamah earlier (pp. 120–21), both etiological legends tied firmly to cultural landscapes, Angela's story is as rootless as a Disney cartoon. Abel seems to realize this, if Benally does not, for he does not respond to Angela. Benally couldn't tell what he was thinking. He had turned his head away, like maybe the pain was coming back, you know (p. 170). Abel refuses to play Angela's game a second time.

V

Part IV opens with a description of a grey, ominous winter landscape. Olguin is reflecting on his seven years' service at Walatowa. He claims to have grown "calm with duty and design," to have "come to terms with the town" (p. 174). Yet he remains estranged from the village; it is not his place. He measures his achievement in the language of commerce, noting with his predecessor Nicolas V what good works "accrued to his account" (p. 174). Like Angela who was offended that Abel "would not buy and sell" (p. 35), Olguin seeks to at least make good the "investment" of his pride.

Whereas Abel looks to Benally's Night Chant for restoration Olguin seeks and claims to find restoration from the journal of Nicolas. In that same journal we recall Nicolas V himself sought restoration of his Christian God:

When I cannot speak thy Name, I want Thee most to restore me.

Restore me! Thy spirit comes upon me & I am too frail for Thee! (p. 48)

The passage leaves off in a fit of coughing and seems a singularly ineffectual request.

At the same time Abel sits with his dying grandfather. Though Francisco's voice had been strong in the dawn, it now grows weaker and fades as it has on each of the six days since Abel's return to Walatowa. The few words Francisco does speak, in Towa and Spanish, juxtapose in the manner of Parts I and II the memory fragments which Abel seeks to order in his own mind. Francisco is here, as Momaday suggests, "a kind of reflection of, Abel." The passage translates:

> Little Abel . . . I'm a little bit of something . . . Mariano . . . cold . . . he gave up . . . very, very cold . . . conquered . . . aye [exclamation of pain], Porcingula . . . how white, little Abel . . . white devil . . . witch . . . witch . . . and the black man . . . yes . . . many black men . . . running, running . . . cold . . . rapidly . . . little Abel, little Vidal . . . What are you doing? What are you doing?

As the seventh dawn comes these words grow into coherent fragments in Francisco's memory and serve as a final statement of the realizations about the relation of place, words, and community Abel has had earlier in the novel.

Each of the fragments is a memory of initiation. In the first Francisco recalls taking Abel and Vidal to the ruins of the old church near the Middle to see "the house of the sun."

> They must learn the whole contour of the black mesa. They must know it as they knew the shape of their hands, always and by heart. . . . They must know the long journey of the sun on the black mesa, how it rode in the seasons and the years, and they must live according to the sun appearing, for only then could they reckon where they were, where all things were in time. (p. 177)

This is the sense of place Abel lost in "the intervention of days and years without meaning, of awful calm and collision, time always immediate and confused" (p. 25). As he is instructed to know the shape of the eastern mesa like his own hands, it is appropriate that in the *corre de gaio* the albino should first attack his hands (p. 44), that in the murder scene (and Abel's memory of it) hands should be so prominent (pp. 77–79, 94), and finally that as he lies on the beach after Martinez's brutal beating of his hands, Abel should think of Angela's effect on him in terms of hands (p. 94). The relation to place taught him by Francisco is broken by each, as are his hands. Now through Francisco's memory Abel is re-taught his ordered relation to place and how it is expressed in "the race of the dead" (pp. 185–86). Abel similarly participates in Francisco's memories of his initiation as a runner (in the race against Mariano pp. 187–88), as a dancer (from which he gained the power to heal pp. 186–87), as a man (with Porcingula, "the child of the witch" pp. 184–85), and as a hunter (as he stalks the bear pp. 178–84).

All signs then point to a new beginning for Abel as he rises February 28, the last day of the novel. His own memory healed by Francisco's, for the first time in the novel he correctly performs a ceremonial function as he prepares Francisco for burial and delivers him to Father Olguin. He then joins the ashmarked runners in the dawn. Momaday comments on that race in his essay "The Morality of Indian Hating:"

> The first race each year comes in February, and then the dawn is clear and cold, and the runners breathe steam. It is a long race, and it is neither won nor lost. It is an expression of the soul in the ancient terms of sheer physical exertion. To watch those runners is to know that they draw with every step some elementary power which resides at the core of the earth and which, for all our civilized ways, is lost upon us who have lost the art of going in the flow of things. In the tempo of that race there is time to ponder morality and demoralization, hungry wolves and falling stars. And there is time to puzzle over that curious and fortuitous question with which the people of Jemez greet each other.

That very question—"Where are you going?"—must ring in Abel's ears as he begins the race. The time and direction of his journey are once again defined by the relation of the sun to the eastern mesa, "the house made of dawn." Out of the pain and exhaustion of the race, Abel regains his vision: "he could see at last without having to think" (p. 191). That vision is not the nihilistic vision of Angela—"beyond everything for which the mountain stands." Rather, Abel's "last reality" in the race is expressed in the essential unity and harmony of man and the land. He feels the sense of place he was unable to articulate in Part I. Here at last he has a voice, words and a song. In beauty he has begun.

KATHLEEN M. SANDS

Alienation and Broken Narrative in
Winter in the Blood

The narrator of James Welch's *Winter in the Blood* suffers the malaise of modern man; he is alienated from his family, his community, his land, and his own past. He is ineffective in relationships with people and at odds with his environment, not because he is deliberately rebellious, or even immaturely selfish, but because he has lost the story of who he is, where he has come from.

Welch's narrator is an American Indian, but one who suffers more than the tensions of living on the margins of conflicting societies. He is an Indian who has lost both tribal identification and personal identity because he is cut off from the tradition of oral narration which shapes consciousness, values, and self-worth. He is a man whose story is confused, episodic, and incomplete because he has never received the story of those who came before and invested the landscape and the people with significance and meaning. Storytelling keeps things going, creates a cultural matrix that allows a continuum from past to present and future; but for the deliberately nameless narrator of *Winter in the Blood*, there is no past, no present, and certainly no future, only the chaos of disconnected memories, desperate actions, and useless conversation.

His dilemma is clear from the beginning of the novel. Welch is blunt as he reveals the barrenness of the narrator's perceptions of himself and his environment. As he walks toward his mother's ranch the narrator reflects, "Coming home was not easy anymore" (p. 2). The land he crosses is empty and abandoned: "the Earthboys were gone" (p. 1). The ranch buildings have

Reprinted from the *American Indian Quarterly* by permission of the University of Nebraska Press. © 1978 University of Nebraska Press.

caved in. Even at this own ranch, there is a sense of emptiness, especially in his relationships with his family: "none of them counted; not one meant anything to me. And for no reason. I felt no hatred, no love, no guilt, no conscience, nothing but a distance that had grown through the years" (p. 2). In fact, he reveals he no longer has feelings even about himself.

There is little for him to feel but pain. His injured knee aches; he is bruised and hung over; his woman has run off, taking his rifle and razor; his mother is abrupt and self-concerned; his ancient grandmother is silent. His memories give him no comfort: his father drunk and grotesquely frozen to death, his brother mangled on the road, his own bitter realization that his red skin, not his skill, had been the reason he got a job in the Tacoma hospital. Memory fails him totally as the events of the past stream through his mind in a nightmare collage. The story of his life is disordered, chaotic, and finally, to him, meaningless. As the narratives are broken, so is the man.

Welch develops the intensity of the narrator's sense of dislocation and alienation through the episodic nature of the narrative. In the first encounter between Lame Bull and the narrator, they recall a flood on the stream where the narrator is fishing. Lame Bull insists that it occurred when the narrator was not much more than a gleam in his father's eye. The narrator counters, "I remember that. I was almost twenty" (p. 8). The story is brief and terse; conflicting versions result in separation of the men rather than a sharing of a common event. The story does not work because it does not grow out of a shared perception. Other such episodes in the novel demonstrate the emptiness and distance created by separate stories or conflicting versions of the same one. Teresa and the narrator tell variants of the story of Amos, the one duck that survived the neglected water tub. Teresa's version is skeletal and the narrator becomes confused, mixing up Amos and the turkey. The retelling of the events creates confusion rather than clarity. Then, when the narrator asks his mother why his father stayed away so much, she is defensive and abrupt, switching the focus of the discussion to a recollection of First Raise's death. The narrator admits limply that he has little recollection of the event. The episode results not in shared grief or comfort but in Teresa's accusing her son of being a drifter too. The narrator is alienated again: "I never expected much from Teresa and I never got it. But neither did anybody else. Maybe that's why First Raise stayed away so much" (p. 21). This is a bitter resolution to the question which prompted the brief story.

The stories that might make the narrator understand his family and his history are either incomplete or contradictory. They increase his discomfort, frustrating his attempts to confirm his past and create a continuity of events from which to operate in the present. Even when recollections from the family past nudge his memories to the surface, he is unable to patch together satisfactory narratives within his own mind: "Memory fails" (p. 19).

The one story that he does recall, as he sits in the living room facing his grandmother, is her story. Memory does not fail the narrator here as he recalls in rich detail the circumstances of the telling and the events of the narrative: "When the old lady had related this story, many years ago, her eyes were not flat and filmy; they were black like a spider's belly and the small black hands drew triumphant pictures in the air" (p. 36). Traditional story-telling devices are themselves memorable to the narrator: gesture, animation, drama. And as Welch spins out the memory in the narrator's mind, he enriches the language with detailed images and melodious rhythms. The narrator's memories take on the color, logical sequence, and vitality of the traditional tale, all stylistic characteristics which are deliberately absent from the disturbing episodes which create conflict and further alienate the narrator. In recalling his grandmother's story of her youth he is struck with a kind of awe because "she revealed a life we never knew, this woman who was our own kin" (p. 34). He is caught up in the mystery of the past, in a yearning to know the complete story, and in a fear that he might lose what part of it he still holds. The memory is incomplete but it is not cause for confusion or recrimination. It is the single intact thread in the torn fabric of his history. It holds a promise of some continuity with the past, of pride in his Blackfeet ancestry. His grandmother, however, is silent now, lost in her own memories and physical frailties, and the narrator's memories of the story she told years before slip away, too fleeting to affect the practiced chaos of his life.

When the narrator heads for town, his confusion and misdirection intensify even more: "Again I felt that helplessness of being in a world of stalking white men. But those Indians down at Gable's were no bargain either. I was a stranger to both and both had beaten me" (p. 120).

The structure of the novel reflects the increased sense of disorientation in the terseness of the language and the separation of incidents. As the narrator's life lacks motivation, direction, continuity, the novel apparently does too. This merging of narrative and form allows the structure of the work to carry the theme as effectively as the narration itself. The airplane man becomes a key figure in the effectiveness of the episodic technique. He is a man with no past, no identity, no future, and, more importantly, no story to tell. "Well, that's another story," he says (p. 45), but he never tells the story. His hints and contradictions only puzzle the narrator further. The airplane man is the radical extreme of disorientation, dislocation, distrust, disillusionment, and disgust. The narrator is mildly fascinated by his wild plots, but he is also repulsed, instinctively aware of the severity of the man's disorder. The appearance of the airplane man marks the narrator's most frustrating and isolated period in the novel, so that even his encounters with women are without intimacy or emotion. They provide drunkenness without relief or elation, fights without victory. And all the while there are snatches of stories, traces of memories. The incompleteness of the stories and memories that disturbed him acutely at home has intensified so that life becomes a confusing and sterile nightmare: "There were the wanted men with ape faces, cuffed sleeves and blue hands. They did not look directly into my eyes but at *my mouth, which was dry and hollow of words.* They seemed on the verge of performing an operation. Suddenly a girl loomed before my face, slit and gutted like a fat rainbow, and begged me to turn her loose, and I found my own guts spilling from my monstrous mouth. Teresa hung upside down from a wanted man's belt, now my own belt, crying out a series of strange warnings to the man who had torn up his airplane ticket" (p. 52 italics added). The nightmare goes on; images and stories melt into one incomprehensible vision of chaos and mute desperation. The elements of a dozen stories have merged into a bizarre and terrifying reality that follows the narrator from sleep into consciousness. Not until the airplane man is arrested, still without having told his story or revealed his identity, has the narrator had enough of the town, and of himself: "I wanted to lose myself" (p. 125).

The time he has spent in the towns has not been without some benefit, however, for it is there that he is confronted again and again with the memory of his brother's death. The story of Mose's death is crucial to his confrontation with his personal past and the landscape that defines him. The story unfolds slowly in his mind. It is too painful to recall at once, so he pieces it together slowly. It too is episodic, but as with his grandmother's story, it is set apart from the alien world of the present by a detailed narrative and a richness of style absent from the action concerned with his search for his girl friend. The story, however, is left unfinished in the city. Not until the narrator returns to the reservation and cleanses himself of the town dirt and corruption can he face the pain of the remembered sequence of events that preceded Mose's death.

The final episode in the story is precipitated by two events that enable the narrator to complete the story. First, his grandmother has died during his absence and he shares the task of digging her grave with Lame Bull. As they rest he notices the grave of his father, with its headstone which tells only part of a story: "A rectangular piece of granite lay at the head of the grave. On it were written the name, John First Raise, and a pair of dates between which he had managed to stay alive. It said nothing about how he had liked to fix machines and laugh with the white men of Dodson, or how he came to be frozen stiff as a plank in the borrow pit by Earthboy's"(p. 137).

First Raise had been a man who told stories. Granted, they were stories to entertain the white men in the bars, but he had one story which had given him hope, a reason to live from year to year. Every fall he had planned to go hunting, had made elaborate preparations in his mind, and had told his sons of the deer he would shoot. It was a story to live on, but no gravestone could carry First Raise's story. That was up to the narrator. And Mose, the only other man the narrator was not alienated from, did not even have a grave marker. All that was left was the narrator's memory. Awareness of the grave and his recollection of the bone-chilling cold of winter send his memory back over the last few minutes of his brother's life. Even then, so close to the end, the memory breaks off as the narrator walks out to look at his brother's unmarked grave, returns to the house, picks up the nearly-full bottle of wine, and goes to the corral to saddle Bird. Then, as though some unconscious understanding of the power of the story still permeates his mind, he invents a story for Bird, surmising the terror the horse must have felt when it had been broken, empathizing with the animal fear and sympathizing with the age and loyalty of the animal, which in its terror of man had been conquered only by its comprehension of death: "You ran and ran for what must have seemed like miles, not always following the road, but always straight ahead, until you thought your heart would explode against the terrible constriction of its cage. It was this necessity, this knowledge of death, that made you slow down to a stiff-legged trot, bearing sideways, then a walk, and finally you found yourself standing under a hot sun in the middle of a field of foxtail and speargrass, wheezing desperately to suck in the heavy air of a summer's afternoon . . . A cow horse" (pp. 145–46). In the invention of the story, Bird, the same horse he was riding when his brother was struck and killed, is forgiven for its part in the death through the narrator's comprehension of its instinctive acceptance of its role as cow horse: "No, don't think it was your fault—when that calf broke, you reacted as they trained you." The forgiveness allows the narrator to resume and complete Mose's story, "I didn't even see it break, then I felt your weight settle on your hind legs" (p. 146). At last there is no blame. He has forgiven the horse, helpless to reverse its instincts, and he has forgiven himself in the process. Finally, he can grieve: " 'What use,' I whispered, cried for no one in the world to hear, not even Bird, for no one but my soul, as though the words would rid it of the final burden of guilt, and I found myself a child again" (p. 146). A burden does remain, but it is the burden of grief, not guilt; the story has created a catharsis. The pain has been confronted and endured, and again, in the eloquence of the language and the merging of emotion, landscape, and tragedy, Welch has demonstrated that this story, as the story of his grandmother's youth, is essential to the narrator's comprehension of himself and his relationship to all that is past. The narrator's telling of his brother's death has been long and painful, a kind of logo-therapy, at least in part curative of the alienation and bitterness and distance he feels. True, the tears he sheds are solitary, but they are a demonstration of feeling for his brother, and more importantly, for himself.

Having unburdened himself, the narrator moves on toward the isolated cabin Yellow Calf inhabits to tell the blind Indian of his grandmother's death. He had been there twice before, once when he was a child, riding behind First Raise through a snow storm, and again before his trip to town. The first trip had seemed significant at the time, but his understanding of it was incomplete. He had known the old man was important, but he had been too young then to ask the right questions. The questions had lingered all those years though, and now on the third visit, he begins, "Did you know her at all?" (p. 151). Slowly, with prompting from the narrator, Yellow Calf tells the story of the bitter winter, the starvation, the shunning of the then–beautiful young wife of Standing Bear, the bad medicine the people associated with her after the chief's death. Finally, with the right questions, Yellow Calf tells how someone became her hunter and protector. The half-formed questions that the narrator has carried over two decades are suddenly answered. At the end of Yellow Calf's story, he thinks for a moment and in that moment the old horse farts: "And it came to me, as though it were riding one moment of the gusting wind, as though Bird had had it in him all the time and had passed it to me in that one instant of corruption. 'Listen, old man' I said. 'It was you— you were old enough to hunt!" (p. 158). Now he knows: Yellow Calf and his grandmother were both Blackfeet; for twenty-five years they had met and loved; Teresa was their child; he was their grandson. The story that his grandmother had told meshed with the one completed by Yellow Calf, and with the completion the narrator knows himself.

The narrator laughs at Bird's fart, at the revelation of truth, at the amazing simplicity of the mystery of his beginnings which had eluded him for so long: "I began to laugh, at first quietly, with neither bitterness nor humor. It was the laughter of one who understands a moment in his life, of one who has been let in on the secret through luck and circumstance" (p. 158). Yellow Calf joins in the laughter, the laughter of relief that the story is finished and the mystery revealed, that he has lived long enough to pass his memory on to his grandson. It is the mutual laughter of the understanding of just one moment in time, but it is a beginning.

The story has done more than give the narrator a personal identity. It has given him a family, a tribal identity. It has invested the land with history and meaning, for Yellow Calf still lives in that place of the bitter winter, dwelling in harmony with the earth. The old man makes explicit the continuity of human history and the land: "Sometimes in the winter, when the wind has packed the snow and blown the clouds away, I can still hear the muttering of the people in their tepees. It was a very bad time" (p. 153). But it was also a memorable time, a time of such suffering that the land has taken on a sacred meaning for the old hunter, and in turn for the young man. The oral tradition of the people has been passed on to the alienated, isolated Blackfeet man and given him a continuity of place and character. The images that have lived for decades in the old man's mind have been transferred to the younger man: "And so we shared this secret in the presence of ghosts, in wind that called forth the muttering tepees, the blowing snow, the white air of the horses' nostrils. The cottonwoods behind us, their dead white branches angling to the threatening clouds, sheltered these ghosts as they had sheltered the camp that winter. But there were others, so many others" (p. 159). The story merges the past with the present, and the language is detailed and descriptive, at times poetic, meant to make the images indelible in the narrator's mind. Like his grandmother's story, Yellow Calf's story is "literary" in style. This rich style is used by Welch only in the two complete narrations in the novel, Mose's story and the combined stories of the old ones.

The two most important narratives in the novel come to completion in one day, both of them on the land where they began in real experience, and they offer the narrator a balanced and curative release of both tears and laughter, a sense of harmony with the earth, and an understanding of himself. But the reintegration of man into family, society, and the land is not accomplished in a moment, not even a moment of intense revelation; the rent fabric of life is not so easily repaired. Even as the secret of Yellow Calf is revealed, the narrator realized "there were others, so many others" (p. 159) . Yet that very realization is in itself a sign of insight, and what he has learned gives him the capacity for imagination for the first time in the novel: "I tried to imagine what it must have been like, the two of them, hunter and widow. If I was right about Yellow Calf's age, there couldn't have been more than four or five years separating them . . . It seemed likely that they had never lived together (except perhaps that first winter out of need). There had never been any talk, none that I had heard . . . So for years the three miles must have been as close as an early morning walk down this path I was now riding" (pp. 160–61). His imagination crosses the boundaries of time, but it is linked to the land as he ponders the knowledge he has gained: "It was a good time for odor. Alfalfa, sweet and dusty, came with the wind, above it the smell of rain. The old man would be lifting his nose to this odor, thinking of other things, of those days he stood by the widow when everyone else had failed her. So much distance between them, yet they lived only three miles apart. But what created this distance? And what made me think that he was Teresa's father? After all, twenty-five years had passed between the time he had become my grandmother's hunter and Teresa's birth. They could have parted at any time. But he was the one. I knew that. The answer had come to me as if by instinct, . . . as though it was his blood in my veins that had told me" (p. 160). Inevitably there must be doubts left for the narrator, but one crucial question had been asked and firmly answered, opening the possibility for reintegration. If Yellow Calf and his grandmother had closed the distance, perhaps his feelings of distance from his family, his past, his people, his land were not unconquerable.

Two events at the end of the novel demonstrate the positive effect of the narrator's new comprehension of himself and his place within the social and physical environments. As he returns to the ranch, he is met by family friends who have come ostensibly to offer condolences but really to question him about the woman who had run away from him. In response to the query the narrator invents a story, saying that his "wife" had returned from Havre and is in the house. "Do you want to see her?" he challenges (p. 165). His imagination, once engaged, allows him to create a story of his own, one which at the end of the novel, he seems determined to turn from lie to fact when he says, "Next time I'd do it right. Buy her a couple of cremes dementhe, maybe offer to marry her on the spot" (p. 175). The projection is somewhat tentative, but the intent is to close the literal and emotional distance between himself and the girl and to make his story true.

The other event which dramatizes the effect of his new knowledge is the cow-in-the-mud scene. Despite the fact that he wants to ignore the stupid animal, he does not. He enters into a frantic struggle to save the cow, committing all his strength and energy to the task. In the process the pent up anger that has cut him off from his family and the land is spent. "What did I do to deserve this?" he asks (p. 169), meaning not just the job of saving the cow but all the suffering he has been through. He goes on, "Ah, Teresa, you made a terrible mistake. Your husband, your friends, your son, all worthless, none of them worth a shit . . . Your mother dead, your father—you don't even know, what do you think of that? A joke, can't you see? Lame Bull! The biggest joke—can't you see that he's a joke, a joker playing a joke on you? Were you taken for a ride! Just like the rest of us, this country, all of us taken for a ride" (p. 169). The narrator's anger is directed at himself, at everyone around him, at society, at the country. It is a bitter anger, but it is anger tempered by a sympathy and passion he had not demonstrated before. Earlier, he could say dryly that he never expected or got much from Teresa, but now he feels something for her, a mixture of anger and sympathy. He sees that she is a victim too. He sees beyond himself. His fury purged, he begins to move again saying, "I crouched and spent the next few minutes planning my new life" (p. 169). Having discovered the distant past in Yellow Calf's and his grandmother's story, having resolved the crucial event in his own past by reliving Mose's story, and now intently engaged in the physical present, he projects into the future. He verbalizes no projections and the dilemma of the moment re-engages him, but the very ability to consider the future is encouraging; coupled with his deter-mination to find the girl who had left him, it signals a coming to terms with life that he has not been capable of before.

On another level the cow-in-the-mud scene reintegrates the narrator with the natural environment in a dramatic way. He has walked and ridden the land but has not been a part of it. Now he is literally sucked into it. As the earth has sucked First Raise and Mose into it, it now draws the narrator, so that symbol-ically he is linked with those who are now past, those for whom he feels the strongest emotional ties. In triumphing over the earth, he had become one with it. As the rain begins to wash the mud from his face, he wonders "if Mose and First Raise were comfortable. They were the only ones I really loved, I thought, the only ones who were good to be with. At least the rain wouldn't bother them. But they would probably like it; they were that way, good to be with, even on a rainy day" (p. 172). Though again he is alone, he is also at one with the earth and at peace with himself and his place on it.

James Welch's use of oral tradition in *Winter in the Blood* is a subtle one. He has adapted the traditional form to suit the needs and style of modern fiction. He has transformed it from an essentially narrative mode to one that carries the theme of reintegration of the alienated contemporary Indian. It is not, however, a simply thematic device to facilitate a positive ending in an essen-tially ironic, even cynical novel. The function of storytelling in Indian commu-nities is to keep life going, to provide a continuum of the past into the present, to allow for the predication of a future. The narratives in *Winter in the Blood* are broken. Those which do come together are painful for teller and reader alike, and they do not promise a happy future. What they do provide for the narrator is knowledge and insight into the past, a painful acceptance of the present, and maybe, just maybe, the strength and understanding to build a future.

ELAINE JAHNER

An Act of Attention: Event Structure in Ceremony

After reading Leslie Silko's novel *Ceremony*, many readers know the novel possesses an energy that engages their sense of themselves as persons. That energy seems to elude discussion because the labeling required in any kind of analysis appears more than usually inadequate for describing the act of attention that is an essential part of the reader's experience. But then there are those like myself who sense that trying again and again to talk about the quality of attention evoked by the book can be an important part of developing more sensitive understanding not only of Leslie Silko's own work but of other Native American writers who might also require of readers a particular attention directed toward matters that their previous experience of novels may not have demanded. Perhaps one way of describing the magnetic field of attention is to say that the lodestone in this field is the experience of event rather than sequentially motivated action as the determinant of plot coherence; but that is too cryptic a statement to have much meaning without explanation.

In this context the word "event" has a specific meaning that is best described through looking at Silko's novel. Once event has been defined, we can contrast the nature of its structuring force with that of other, more commonly experienced ways of developing coherence within any novel. Since giving event structure priority over temporal structure seems to be a characteristic of art that is intimately related to an ongoing oral tradition progress made toward understanding event may be progress toward understanding relationships between oral and written literatures.

Reprinted from the *American Indian Quarterly* by permission of the University of Nebraska Press. © 1979 University of Nebraska Press.

One of the pivotal events in *Ceremony* is that which describes the protagonist Tayo singing the sunrise song after his first encounter with the mysterious woman. If we examine that passage, we can identify the essential features of Silko's sense of event:

> He stood on the steps and looked at the morning stars in the west. He breathed deeply, and each breath had a distinct smell of snow from the north, of ponderosa pine on the rimrock above; finally he smelled horses from the direction of the corral, and he smiled. Being alive was all right then: he had not breathed like that for a long time . . .
>
> Coming closer to the river, faintly at first, faint as the pale yellow light emerging across the southeast horizon, the sounds gathered intensity from the swelling colors of dawn. And at the moment the sun came over the edge of the horizon, they suddenly appeared on the riverbank, the Ka't'sina approaching the river crossing. He stood up. He knew the people had a song for the sunrise . . .
>
> He repeated the words as he remembered them, not sure if they were the right ones, but feeling they were right, feeling the instant of the dawn was an event which in a single moment gathered all things together—the last stars, the mountaintops, the clouds, and the winds— celebrating this coming. (pp. 181–82).

Almost every aspect of the long quotation is significant. Tayo's experience of event is precisely realized in language replete with the most exact sensuous detail. There are distinct smells, sounds and colors, all qualities of definite and real places. Each detail shapes the way Tayo experiences this particular intersection of life and story. Ostensibly alone, Tayo does not experience the moment as isolation. He senses the presence of the Ka't'sina and knows he is in touch with very fundamental life forces. In this place, at this time, he gives them full recognition. His own act of attention is complete. We know from earlier developments in the novel that the place where he finds himself able to sing the sunrise song is a specific place, marked by the stars themselves. It is Tayo's center of the world, using that phrase in the sense in which it is used in American Indian ceremony. It is also an emergence place for him because he moves into a new level of experiencing his role in an all-encompassing story.

Tayo's participating in the sunrise event is both convergence and emergence. Past understandings of the meaning of experiences converge and permit emergence to new levels of comprehension, new parts of the story and new aspects of ceremonies. Events are boundary experiences marking stages of life for the protagonist. They also mark stages of the story for the reader who can experience their impact by relating to their significance as primary human experiences that are at one and the same time, acts of recognition and experiences of renewal of energies. As recognition, event implies pattern, form that is enduring yet specific as to time and place. As experience, it implies conscious participation in the dynamic energies that generate and perpetuate life and form. Both the pattern and the experience are, by their very nature, culturally specific; and it is at this level that a reader must bring his or her own cultural experiences into relation with those of the protagonist.

There is nothing of chance or absurdity in the meaning and experience of event which can only be experienced by one who knows how to recognize its signs. Such knowledge is by no means universal and the novel *Ceremony* has as its theme, the gaining of that knowledge. Furthermore, the novel itself is shaped by the processes that lead to the capacity to experience event in life or in art. The ebb and flow of narrative rhythm in the novel creates an event in the process of telling about event. The entire process is ceremonial, and one learns how to experience it ceremonially by achieving various kinds of knowledge attained not through logical analysis but through narrative processes that have their own epistemological basis.

Although many types of narrative function in *Ceremony*, jokes, personal experience stories, rumor, gossip, two major types of narrative shape the events of the novel and affect the way the other types interweave as they lead to different kinds of perception. These two types are the contemporary and the mythic tellings, the timeless and the time-bound narratives. The two are not independent of each other in that they constantly shape each other, but finding out how they interact is complicated by the fact that all which occurs in the time-bound framework is confused because the ways of knowing, the various kinds of narrative are all entangled. Reader and protagonist alike must learn to untangle, and the reader can follow Tayo from event to event by moving from poetry to prose and back again to poetry. Silko juxtaposes the mythic portions of the novel and the story of Tayo's efforts by stating the myth in poetic form to contrast with the prose that carries forward contemporary realizations of the meaning stated in poetic sections.

The first event of the novel occurs while Tayo is a soldier. The dense jungle rain, so different from rain in the desert, appears malevolent and Tayo curses it. When he returns home, there is drought and Tayo assumes responsibility for it, believing that his curse caused it. His belief derives from the

fact that he knows or intuits the power of words in relation to myth but he
follows the results of his powerful words to the wrong mythic prototypes.
His experiences at this stage are like those of the character Auntie whose
feelings are "twisted, tangled roots, and all the names for the source of this
growth were buried under English words; out of reach. And there would be
no peace and the people would have no rest until the entanglement had been
unwound to the source" (p. 69). As the first poetic portion tells us, the mythic
story is the source and it gives rise to ritual and ceremony, situations in which
words bring things into being:

> See, it is moving.
> Thee is life here
> for the people.
> And in the belly of this story
> the rituals and the ceremony
> are still growing. (p. 2)

At the beginning of the novel, Tayo is sufficiently in touch with the
nature of mythic life to recognize the potential significance of the first event
of the novel—his cursing the rain. What he can not understand is the event's
actual significance. Silko's description of the event clearly indicates both the
convergence and the emergence aspects of its meaning. When Tayo acts out
of a firm sense of event, he knows that his actions can not be insignificant;
there is the experience of gathering together and moving onward:

> He started repeating 'Goddamn, goddamn!'; it flooded out of the last
> warm core in his chest and echoed inside his head. He damned the rain
> until the words were a chant, and he sang it while he crawled through
> the mud to find the corporal and get him up before the Japanese saw
> them. He wanted the words to make a cloudless blue sky, pale with a
> summer sun pressing across wide and empty horizons. The words gath-
> ered inside him and gave him strength. (p. 12)

What Tayo can not understand is the literal effect his words will have
so he can not emerge from this first event into new levels of understanding
without help from medicine men—help he receives later in the novel. Alien
ways of looking at the world prevent a full understanding of the event experience. Entanglement is Silko's main metaphor for describing obstacles to the
event experience, and its use in early sections of the novel helps readers sense
the feeling and meaning of Tayo's need to truly understand the connections

among acts that will lead him to full event experience. "He could feel it inside his skull—the tension of little threads being pulled and how it was with tangled things, things tied together, and as he tried to pull them apart and rewind them into their places, they snagged and tangled even more" (p. 7).

Reader and protagonist alike go from event to event trying to learn the connection between contemporary action and the mythic prototype. To perceive the wrong bonds is to be caught up in the wrong boundaries of experience and to misunderstand the nature of cause and effect. After the first event, the main patterns of imagery in the novel have to do with vaguely understood or false boundaries and relationships. Tayo knows he is caught between different ways of seeing relationships, and he senses that the real boundaries have to do with mythic prototypes: "Years and months had become weak, and people could push against them and wander back and forth in time. Maybe it had always been this way and he was only seeing it for the first time" (p. 18). False boundaries lead to death and while he is in a state of confusion about the meaning of relationships, Tayo lives a kind of death in life: "He inhabited a gray winter fog on a distant elk mountain where hunters are lost indefinitely and their own bones mark the boundaries" (p. 15).

As he struggles with various conflicts and watches the drought-stricken land, Tayo remembers the actions narrated in the second poem of the novel which tells of the argument between Reed Woman and her sister Corn Woman, an argument that results in Reed Woman abandoning the present world and going to an earlier one so that the rain disappears. Because he knows that his actions have something to do with myth, Tayo blames himself for the drought. The relationship between cause and effect, though, is more complex than Tayo realizes; and the second section of the novel emphasizes what it means not to know the connections. In this section, the medicine man Ku'oosh helps Tayo understand both the fragility and the complexity of the connections and relationships. Both the imagery and the plot elements having to do with boundaries come together in the event that is the medicine man's ceremony. As always, Silko's description of time and place are specific. It is a windy afternoon: Tayo is at home but he must remember and mentally enter a cave near Laguna that he knows well. After the medicine man has led Tayo to an understanding of the meaning of his ceremony by making him remember the meaning of a particular place, he brings Tayo to a profound experience of not knowing. He explains the fragility of the world, the need for the telling of the story behind each word and he asks Tayo for his own story of the war—a story that Tayo can not convey to him. According to the medicine man, telling the entire story is the human responsibility; Tayo realizes the difficulties of the responsibility and becomes ill once again.

The imagery and action that cluster in the third section of the novel have to do with trying to evade responsibilities seemingly too big to be understood. Tayo has learned that the medicine man does not know the right bonds anymore. Tayo himself must search for them because, as the medicine man says, "It is important to all of us. Not only for your sake, but for this fragile world" (p. 36). With the theme of responsibility for searching for new links between prototype and contemporary action, there is also concentration on the meaning of the process of transmission of stories. Silko shows us that the transmission of such knowledge is a far more complicated process than scholars usually describe. Transmission involves not only the sharing of knowledge but the sharing of how the knowledge has been shaped through one's living with it. Any event by event analysis of the entire novel is impossible in a short paper but since all the specific events have to do with the learning process that is part of the transmission of knowledge about stories, I will simply sketch the learning process for subsequent events.

Some characters, like Harley, evade the responsibility that goes with the entire learning process. They accept quick solutions, quick magic, but they can not perceive the right relationships and boundaries. As one of the poems says,

> They thought they didn't have to worry
> about anything
> They thought this magic
> could give life to plants
> and animals.
> They didn't know it was all just a trick. (p. 48)

Unlike Harley, Tayo has known and loved people who knew how to make the right stories relate to the right points in the ongoing movement of life. One important teacher was his uncle Josiah. The phrase, "Josiah said," introduces the many sections of the novel that narrate Tayo's childhood learning about the meaning that event can have: " 'You see,' Josiah had said, '. . . there are some things worth more than money.' He pointed his chin at the springs and around at the narrow canyon. 'This is where we come from, see. This sand, this stone, these trees, the vines, all the wildflowers. This earth keeps us going' " (p. 45). Josiah understood the importance of the conjunction between the right place and the right time. Such respect for place and its relation to time is an important element in learning how to experience mythic knowledge which, in turn, leads to the event experience.

There was also a woman called the Night Swan who understood the need to seek for real boundaries in the life process. She understood too the need to relate one's understanding of real boundaries to one's capacity to feel. Her experiences with her first lovers had taught her only that some paths can not lead to emergence from anything: "She kept him there for as long as she could, searching out the boundary, the end to the power of the feeling. She wanted to prowl those warm close places until she discovered the end because at that time she had not yet seen that the horizon was an illusion and the plains extended infinitely; and up until that final evening she had found no limit" (p. 85). The Night Swan taught Tayo that the experience I am calling event is the key to maintaining every form of life because it relates change and continuity. Some people, like Tayo and herself, are different. These people are part of change and the way in which these "different ones" experience event is a fundamental part of the way the prototypical myths remain a vital part of human life. She says to Tayo, " 'You don't have to understand what is happening. But remember this day. You will recognize it later. You are part of it now' " (p. 100).

Tayo does recognize it later when the teacher Betonie finally prepares him for the full experience of event and brings home to him the fact that learning the transmission process of myth involves learning to bring the meaning of all the changes he has experienced in life to the way he feels the stories. If he can bring the meaning of his actions to the way he feels the stories, then he will be attentive enough to sense the subtle shifts and movements that define the way the story takes shape through the people who allow it to come into their lives. When the story comes into lives, it sets the important boundaries because it shapes events that relate past to present, prototype to immediate experience. Through the ceremonies that Betonie performs for him, Tayo realizes a little more about how to allow story to shape his experience as event so that both he and the story remain alive. Through ceremony he begins to learn to feel the gathering of meaning that occurs in story: "He remembered the black of the sand paintings on the floor of the hogan; the hills and mountains were the mountains and the hills they had painted in sand. He took a deep breath of cold mountain air; there were no boundaries; the world below and the sand paintings inside became the same that night. The mountains from all the directions had been gathered there that night" (p. 145). In any event, space and time, inner and outer come together. The significant boundaries are between what and who are or are not part of the event; between what is gathered together and what is scattered.

Betonie also teaches Tayo that an important part of the experience of events is the experience of transitions: " 'There are balances and harmonies always shifting, always necessary to maintain' . . . It is a matter of transitions, you see; the changing, the becoming must be cared for closely. You would do as much for seedlings as they become plants in the fields'" (p. 130). Transitions are a part of the emergence phase. During the transitional times, Tayo must nourish the feelings that enable him to respond fully to events when their time and place has come. That there is a right time and right place and that these are specific, real places is something that Silko carefully establishes. One could document references to the right time and the right place for all the event experiences of the book, but the major ones are set with special care.

Betonie explains to Tayo that he must watch for the right mountain, the right stars and the right woman before he will be able to finish the Ceremony. When he finds the right conjunction of all, he is able to sing the sunrise song, the event quoted at the beginning of this paper. Once he comes to this inter-section of time, place and story, Betonie's teachings become "a story he could feel happening—from the stars and the woman, the mountain and the cattle would come" (p. 186). Once Tayo has come to this realization, he is a conscious participant in the development of the story. He can shape the story because he understands something about the real boundaries that relate and separate actions and persons. He has many kinds of new strength when he can untangle the twisted roots of his thoughts and he knows that some things outdistance death and destruction:

> The mountain outdistanced their destruction, just as love had outdis-tanced death. The mountain could not be lost to them, because it was in their bones; Josiah and Rocky were not far away. They were close; they had always been close. And he loved them then as he had always loved them, the feeling pulsing over him as strong as it had ever been. They loved him that way; he could still feel the love they had for him. . . . This feeling was their life, vitality locked deep in blood memory, and the people were strong, and the fifth world endured, and nothing was ever lost as long as the love remained" (pp. 219–20)

Understanding and participating in event is knowing that vitality and love endure. This is Tayo's healing experience. He re-creates himself in creating the new boundaries in his life, not those of logic, but the traditional ones of story. Even witchery can be handled within the boundaries of story. It is only those events that do not seem part of any pattern at all which are utterly destructive. They intrude upon lives without preparation and rearrange them so that there can be no transitions among events and all pattern seems irrelevant; even ceremony appears irrelevant. But once the true pattern is perceived by those participating in it, the story goes on and the right ceremonies are in the belly of the story. The story perpetuates life and love; and people experience the story as event.

Through the narrative events of the novel, protagonist and reader gradually learn to relate myth to immediate action, cause to effect; and both reader and protagonist learn more about the power of story itself. The reader seeks to learn not only what happens to Tayo but how and why it happens. The whole pattern of cause and effect is different from most novels written from a perspective outside the mythic mode of knowledge. To employ myth as a conscious literary device is a quite different thing from employing the mythic way of knowing as the basic structural element in a novel as Silko does. But as they read the story, readers are not likely to analyze what kind of energy is at work; they continue reading because Silko is a skilled story-teller. Then, in direct proportion to the degree of their belief in mythic reality, critical readers are likely to distance themselves from the novel's world and begin to consider the nature of its impact. It is at this stage of inquiry that the concept of event structure can have meaning. Perhaps the experience of event is something all people have but the novel poses interesting questions. What constitutes the experience for different people in different cultures and how is it shaped by different kinds of narrative? More specifically, how does the novel as a particular kind of narrative function in shaping and describing event experience?

The critic Irving Buchen says that "the novel is not a defined but a discovered form." In the context of Silko's writing we can carry this statement further and say that a certain type of novel is becoming a form (and forum) for re-discovering narrative potential in a contemporary context. For the traditional tribal artist, narrative forms have always had to do with particular ways of knowing and learning; they have not been mere objects of knowledge. The novel is a narrative genre well-suited for examining how the traditional ways of knowing function in a multi-cultural world where the meanings of narrative are often twisted and tangled. The novel can accommodate enough detail and can juxtapose enough different kinds of narrative to show how it is possible to untangle our responses to different ways of knowing and follow them to their experiential roots. For that is what event is, a primary experience of sources of knowledge shaped not by logical concepts but by the action of story. Such an experience requires of readers a special act of attention that combines the oldest mode of attentiveness—the mythic mode—with a contemporary one shaped by our successive experience with novels. If we accept Dan Ben-Amos' characterization of any genre as a cluster of thematic and behavioral attributes, then we can easily focus on the concept of event as a cluster of both thematic and behavioral attributes that are shaping an emerging type of American Indian novel, one that has interesting differences from other types of American novels because its emphasis is less on what is known than on how one comes to know certain things and because it demands an attentiveness from the reader that has less to do with grasping what the action is than it does with feeling how actions have meanings that live and grow according to the many different ways human beings have of knowing about them.

LOUIS OWENS

"He Had Never Danced With His People": Cultural Survival in John Joseph Mathews's Sundown

With the publication of *Sundown* in 1934, the mixedblood Osage writer John Joseph Mathews introduced the modern American Indian novel, laying out a pattern for novels by Indian writers that would be confirmed two years later when D'Arcy McNickle published *The Surrounded* (1936) and again and again during succeeding decades. Like *The Surrounded*, *Sundown* is the story of a mixedblood living both in and out of his tribal culture, and it is a nearly fatalistic tale that at a superficial glance seems to mesh neatly with the popular naturalism of the twenties and thirties. While Hemingway had chosen to emphasize at least an earthly continuum in his title for *The Sun Also Rises*, another novel of deracination and despair, at first glance Mathews would seem to focus starkly upon the other end of daylight, showing us the tragic results of the oil boom in Osage County—what had until only recently been the Osage Reservation.

Mathews himself served as an unlikely model for his protagonist, Challenge Windzer. Like Chal, Mathews was born on the Osage Agency of mixedblood parents, and like Chal the author studied at the University of Oklahoma and went on to become a pilot during World War I. Like Chal, Mathews came of age amidst the oil boom that brought wealth and disaster to many Osage people, but unlike his character, Mathews graduated from the University of Oklahoma, served in France during the war, and later received degrees from both Oxford and the University of Geneva. Mathews, described by his publisher, Savoie Lottinville, as possessing "many of the qualities of

From *Native American Literatures*, Forum 2–3. © 1992 by SEU.

the English gentleman blended with those of the gentleman Osage," may be in fact the most acculturated of all Indian novelists. After completing his degree in International Relations at Geneva, where the League of Nations was in session, he toured France by motor bike and bummed around Europe. It was while on a big-game hunting trip in North Africa that, after encountering a wild group of Arab horsemen, he decided to return to his home and learn about his Osage relations.

Mathews received 560 acres and a headright when Osage land was allotted in 1906 and broken into individual holdings, and he came to take a deep interest in his tribe, writing about his people in *Wah'Kon-Tah: The Osage and the White Man's Road* (1932), in his autobiographical *Talking to the Moon* (1945), a kind of Osage *Walden*, and in *The Osages: Children of the Middle Waters* (1961). From 1934 through 1942 Mathews also served on the Osage Tribal Council.

Sundown seems to offer a quintessential post-colonial scenario as described by the authors of *The Empire Writes Back:* "A valid and active sense of self may have been eroded by dislocation, resulting from migration, the experience of enslavement. . . . Or it may have been destroyed by cultural denigration, the conscious and unconscious oppression of the indigenous personality and culture by a supposedly superior racial or cultural model." Like others in such a post-colonial drama, including nearly all Native Americans, Mathews's characters are beset by "a pervasive concern with . . . identity and authenticity." Prior to the opening of *Sundown*, the Osage, like Ridge's Cherokees, and many other tribes, had been forcibly relocated by the federal government. Their culture had been exposed to the denigrating pressures of missionaries, including schools, and disruptive Euramerican values. And, with the discovery of rich oilfields on tribal lands, this process had been accelerated enormously. The Osage in Mathews's novel are finally overwhelmed by outsiders who (with their extreme sense of racial and cultural superiority) consciously and unconsciously destroy traditional values and attempt to displace the Indians yet further—through miscegenation, marriage, and simple murder in order to gain control of headrights and, thus, oil money.

Sundown begins with Chal Windzer's birth at a critical point of transition for the Osage Nation between old and new worlds. "The god of the great Osages was still dominant over the wild prairie and the blackjack hills when Challenge was born," writes Mathews in the novel's opening line. "He showed his anger in fantastic play of lightning and thunder that crashed and rolled among the hills; in the wind that came from the great tumbling clouds which appeared in the northwest and brought twilight and ominous milk-warm silence." The ecosystemic world of the Osage is intact in this scene and can be comprehended mythically. From these first sentences to the final lines of the novel, associations with the natural world—the sacred geography of the Osage people—will serve as an index to Chal Windzer's character and well-being. During those moments when, for a brief time, he is immersed in nature he will feel nearly whole and close to something instinctual and sustaining; when he is removed from intimate contact with the natural world, he will become ever more displaced and confused.

"On this birthright," Mathews continues as the novel begins, "the red, dim light which shone from the narrow window of the room where his mother labored, seemed faint and half-hearted in the moonlight; faint as though it were a symbol of the new order, yet diffident in the vivid, full-blooded paganism of the old; afraid, yet steady and persistent, and the only light in the Agency on this tranquil, silver night of silence" (1–2). Associated with the sun, for the Osage the most powerful manifestation of the creator, the color red figures as a crucial link to the traditional Osage world in which the sun was honored in virtually every aspect of life. In this birth scene, however, the color seems to emanate from Chal's fullblood mother—the "only light in the Agency"—whose Indianness remains steadfast throughout the novel as a touchstone to unchanging and essential values. However, in its half-heartedness in the face of the sacred moonlight—symbolic of the older, immutable Indian world—the red light underscores the tenuousness of even the mother's hold on traditional identity. Cast into this uncertain light at birth, Chal Windzer is born into the easily recognizable post-colonial and modernist position of deracination, alienation, and confusion.

Mathews's opening scene introduces the dialectic that will inform the novel's plot: the struggle between old and new—Indian and Euramerican—"orders." In keeping with this dialectic, the color red becomes sacred to Chal almost from birth, when he reaches out for the red dress of the Euramerican "har'd" girl. Red, Chal learns later, is the color of the Sun "who was Grandfather, and of Fire, who was Father, and of the Dawn, sacred to Wah'Kon-Tah" (13).

John Windzer, Chal's father, declares at his son's birth, "He shall be a challenge to the disinheritors of his people. We'll call him Challenge" (4). Ironically, however, Chal never overtly challenges the new order, attempting instead to mold himself according to the new, non-Indian values which he accepts but never comprehends. This attitude he inherits from his mixed-blood father, who sits at home reading "Childe Harold"—a canonized artifact of the privileged culture, and a romantic narrative that reinforces the Euramerican's epic, and thus entropic, view of the vanishing, historic past.

This "*Triste tropiques*" myth of cultural ruin and decay dovetails neatly, and ironically, with the Euramericans' desire to brush the Osage aside while appropriating Osage oil. Chal's father, one of the rapidly growing population of politically influential mixedbloods amongst the Osage, is proud to be a descendant of British nobility in the form of Sir John Windzer, an artist who lived among the Osage, and he boasts that "If it hadn't been for the progressives on the council, there never would have been any allotment, if it was left up to the fullblood party" (45). He is referring to the Osage's belated acceptance of allotment, which required tribes to terminate collective ownership of tribal lands and to allot the reservations to members on the tribal rolls, effectively ending millenia-old patterns of land use among the tribes. With this declaration, Mathews is also illuminating the bitter division between fullbloods and mixedbloods within the tribe, with the former generally struggling to retain traditional ways of life while the latter pushed increasingly for adoption of "civilized" values.

Serving as a pawn in the whites' maneuvers to control and rob the Osages, John Windzer actually facilitates the disenfranchisement of the son he named Challenge. In the end, it is Mathews's depiction of Chal Windzer's descent toward ruin which challenges "the disinheritors of his people," a descent culminating when Chal swears to himself, "I wish I didn't have a drop of God damn' Indian blood in my veins" (160).

In a recurring pattern throughout the novel, Chal identifies with animals and the natural world. As a child he imagines himself consistently as animal: "a panther lying lazily in his den" or "a redtail hawk circling high in the blue of the sky" or "an indefinite animal in a snug den," or a coyote stalking the prairie. On an almost unconscious level, he remains aware of the older Indian world outside of his parents' comfortable house and the increasingly civilized town:

> And then sometimes, when he waked early in the morning, he could hear some mourner on the hill which bordered the creek, chanting the song of death, and always some inscrutable sorrow welled and flooded him; something that was not understandable and was mysterious, and seemed especially fitting for the dense dark hours just before dawn; the hours most fitted for that questing, that feeble attempt to understand. (44)

Chal's own unstated quest in this passage is for the impossible: an understanding of a world that has been made remote from him at birth. The song of death and the "inscrutable sorrow" are for the Osage world disappearing at astonishing speed in the course of Chal's life as oil money pours into what had been the reservation. This is the romantic posture toward American Indian existence adopted and celebrated by the non-Indian world. Writers from Freneau and Cooper to Faulkner and LaFarge would stop here, with a crocodile tear for the dying noble savage. Writing from within the supposedly "dying" culture rather than from the outside, however, Mathews goes beyond such a stock response, making of Chal's story a more complex narrative of cultural survival. The "dark hours just before dawn" are Mathews's subject; a "feeble questioning" of the dilemmas of Indian existence and identity in the twentieth century is his method; and an awakening to a renewed sense of self—authenticity—for Native Americans would appear to be his goal.

Central to Chal's childhood is the nearby creek where he swims and about which his life seems to revolve. And it is the creek which serves as an index to how far the destruction has progressed in the name of progress. Even as the oil boom is just beginning, Chal notices a change: "It had been several years since he had heard the wild turkeys flying up to roost along the creek, and he could scarcely remember what the howl of the wolf was like" (64). As the "civilized" values of the town grow too intense for Chal, he invariably returns to the creek, still searching for that "something that was not understandable and was mysterious." One night he rolls up in his blankets to sleep beside the creek only to be awakened by the abrupt howling of coyotes: "There was the moon, large and white, hanging in a gleaming sycamore. The coyotes stopped as suddenly as they had begun. A great unhappiness filled him, and for the briefest moment he envied the coyotes, but he didn't know why" (71). He rises and studies the moon and then "he crossed the creek and climbed a little hill in the full flood of the ghostly light. He stood there, then spread his arms toward the moon. He tried to think of all the beautiful words he had ever heard, both in Osage and English, and as he remembered them he spoke them aloud to the moon, but they would not suffice it seemed; they were not sufficient to relieve that choking feeling" (71).

Chal envies the coyotes because they know, instinctively, how to celebrate the sacral significance of the moon—nature—something he cannot do. In his desire to utter a polyphony of "beautiful words," Chal is attempting to create a prayer that would comprehend the potentially rich heteroglossia of his world, to fuse the "internally persuasive" language of his Osage heritage with the "authoritative" discourse of English in a syncretic utterance, and by speaking this hybridized utterance to the Osage moon, to put the parts of himself together in an identity that can comprehend both worlds. Could Chal conflate the "beautiful" in both discourses, he might solve the painful dilemma of his inauthenticity and achieve a "temporal unification of the past and future with the present" that leads to a coherent sense of self. He is, with his desire to "think of all the beautiful words he had ever heard" and to speak them, attempting to emulate the coyotes. But Chal's dissociated sensibility cannot speak in one voice; he is choked into silence by his inability to artic-ulate—to put the pieces of the self together into a coherent utterance. "But this mysterious unhappiness came to him only at times," Mathews writes, "and never except when he was alone on the prairie" (72). At other times, Chal achieves a kind of transcendent awareness of his place in the natural order of the traditional, sacred Osage world: "The sun was setting and the west looked like leaping flames that had been suddenly solidified. . . . Then, very suddenly, that mysterious feeling came over him. A mild fire seemed to be coursing through his veins and he felt that he wanted to sing and dance; sing and dance with deep reverence. He felt that some kind of glory had descended upon him, accompanied by a sort of sweetness and a thrilling appreciation of himself." (73)

As the oil boom draws more of the "civilized" world to the Osage country, Chal grows more distant from the natural world. When he leaves for the state university with his friends, Sun-on-His-Wings and Running Elk, his disinheritance from his Osage identity becomes almost complete. From the beginning, he is annoyed with his childhood friends "for acting like Indians" (94). When he flees the university to walk along the river, he daydreams about his future: "He couldn't dream fast enough to visualize all the honors that came to him. He even visualized a great feast and dance held in his honor by the Osages when he arrived back home for Christmas. They had made a song and invented a dance especially for him, and they gave him a name, but he couldn't decide what the name should be." In Indian cultures a name is earned—as Chal's father has told him earlier in the novel—and it comes from the community to both confer an identity and confirm one's place within the community. Indian identity is communal, and Chal has lost his place within his Osage community; thus he cannot conceive of an Osage name. At this point the daydream evaporates, and in place of a rich heteroglossia Chal is left with only the authoritative discourse represented by the American dream of being "self-made": "As pleasant as the dream was, he decided to leave the Osage part of it out. He didn't want to call attention to the fact that most of his blood was of an uncivilized race like the Osages. He believed that they didn't have any backbone, and he certainly wanted to make something of himself" (153). Chal's reflection mimics the observation of one J. E. Jenkins, an inspector for the Indian Office, who reported approvingly in 1906 that the Osage mixedbloods—who by the turn of the century outnum-bered fullbloods—"act like white people, well educated and intelligent." A year earlier, however, Frank Frantz, the Osage agent from 1904 to 1905, had reported that if the fullbloods were an improvident lot, the mixedblood was "a worse proposition" and did not "deserve any efforts in his behalf."

As Chal prepares to go to a college dance, he remembers his reflection: "At the last impression of his face in the mirror that evening, he had seen a bronze face in the black-and-white; the white making the bronze stand out, and he had wondered if he wasn't too dark" (124). By the (white) values of the privileged culture, Chal finds himself unacceptable. However, Mathews does not allow Chal to completely repress his Osage way of viewing the world. As Chal dances with Blo, his beautiful (white) date, Mathews writes: "But this was a new experience, merging with someone in such fervency; someone like the Moon Woman, who, like many things beautiful, lived briefly. Like the Moon Woman of his childhood who reigned over the forgetfulness of the night; over the tranquil world of dreams; the world of Wah'Kon" (124). Mathews adds later: "He wondered why he had a feeling that was something like a religious emotion when he thought of Blo. Of course it never occurred to him that it might be the tribal heritage of religion associated with beauty and dreams" (155). For a moment, Chal's Osage self has achieved the upper hand in this political struggle, reversing the pattern that denigrates an Indian world-view, removing his date from the referential context that had made him feel "too dark" and displacing her into an Indian system of reference. She is made beautiful and given significance within the mythic paradigms of his tribal heritage.

Chal leaves the university to enlist in the Army Air Corps, and upon graduation from ground school "He thought of himself as being separated by a great abyss from Sun-on-His-Wings and Running Elk, and from the villages and the people moving among the lodges" (208). So separated is he that he tells a female admirer that he's Spanish rather than have her guess his real identity. Nonetheless, Chal is still profoundly Indian, and his ambivalence is underscored when he looks down from his airplane: "He had a feeling of superiority, and he kept thinking of the millions of people below him as white men" (218). In the air, radically displaced, alone and controlling the most sophisticated example of American machinery, Chal fuses his resentment of the white man with a sense of having beaten the whites at their own game of individualism and machinery. Still, when he begins to gain self-assurance brought on by the admiration of women, "he felt that he had begun to be gilded by that desirable thing which he called civilization. He was becoming a man among civilized men" (230).

When his father is murdered, Chal returns home and becomes another of the directionless Osages drinking and driving fast cars. In this aspect of

Chal's malaise, Mathews reflects an accurate picture of the cultural disintegration besetting the Osage. In fact, while the bootleg liquor Chal drinks was
a major problem among the Osage as among other portions of the American
population, even drugs had become a scourge of the newly wealthy Indians,
with morphine, cocaine and marijuana provided by an influx of "pushers." A
seizure of $50,000 worth of drugs in a single cache in Osage County in 1929
was reportedly the largest single drug seizure in Oklahoma prior to World
War II. On a drinking spree, Chal goes in search of the old special place by
the creek only to find that "Several black wells stood about on the prairie
above the trees and from each a path of sterile brown earth led down to the
creek, where oil and salt water had killed every blade of grass and exposed the
glaring limestone. Some of the elms had been cut down, and the surface of
the water had an iridescent scum on it" (250). Again, nature mirrors the
condition of the Osage. Later, after an all-night drunk, Chal returns to the
creek to try fishing, but "The water was lifeless" (285).

   While Chal was away, his friend Running Elk has also been murdered
by whites trying to gain control of allotments. Before his murder, however,
while drying out in a detoxification ward, Running Elk provides a vivid
nightmare image of what has befallen his people. When Chal visits him,
Running Elk describes a terrifying dream in which a "fat white man,
completely naked and glistening, would stand at the door of his room with a
spear in his hand" (273). This nightmare vision illuminates the displacement
of the Indian by the avaricious (fat) white man who has, as the spear and
blocked doorway suggest, both looted Indian culture and trapped the Indian.
The particularly deadly displacement of Indian males—which will be a
concern of future generations of Native American novelists—is suggested in
the sexually aggressive posture of the naked white man with the phallic,
appropriated, spear. There would appear to be no place left for the Indian
male except escape through alcohol and unconsciousness.

   As foils for Chal, Running Elk and Sun-on-His-Wings stand at opposite ends of the spectrum of possibilities for the Osage. While Running Elk
has sought oblivion through alcohol, Sun-on-His-Wings has turned toward
Osage tradition and the new peyote church. Visiting his childhood friend,
Chal takes part in a Sweat Lodge ceremony and is moved by the experience.
After the ceremony, "they went back into the lodge, picked up their blankets,
and dispersed. Chal drew his blanket closely around him . . ." (277). To Chal,
as for others, the blanket has always been a sign of traditional, "primitive"
Indians, and as such something to be scorned. Here, following the sweat and
the prayers of the ceremony, Chal becomes, briefly, one of those scorned
"blanket Indians." With this brief touch, Mathews hints at a potential return

to traditional, immutable values through the new, syncretic peyote ceremonies.

The promise seems short-lived, however. During the Sweat Lodge ceremony, Watching Eagle, the Road Man, has told a man named White Deer: "Your son and those People who have been killed by these white men, followed that road which they thought was white man's road. Your son married white woman. You have children of your son, but they are not your children. They can never have a name among their people. They have no people . . ." (273–74). On a literal level, Watching Eagle is refering to the fact that according to tribal laws the offspring of Osage men and white women could not receive allotments or headrights, though children of Osage women married to white men could. Even though his mother is Osage, Chal, too, has no name among his people. As a mixedblood, he seems, in fact, to very nearly have no people. When he takes a group of drunken whites to see an Osage dance, Chal feels a strong urge "to go down on the floor and dance." He does not dance, however, because, as Mathews writes, "he had never danced with his people. . ." (260). Chal's alienation is further emphasized when shortly after the Sweat Lodge ceremony he thinks that "He wanted to be identified with that vague something which everybody else seemed to have, and which he believed to be civilization" (285).

Near the end of the novel, after drinking all night, Chal dances alone as he had in childhood:

> He stopped the car suddenly and climbed out and started talking to himself; talking nonsense. He kept repeating to himself, "Extravaganza," without reason, as the word was not associated with his frothy thoughts. . . . He arose with difficulty, with an intense urge for action. Suddenly he began to dance. He bent low over the grass and danced, and as he danced he sang, and as he sang one of the tribal songs of his people, he was fascinated by his own voice, which seemed clear and sonorous on the still air. He danced wildly and his blood became hotter, and yet that terrific emotion which was dammed up in his body would not come out; that emotion which was dammed up and could not be exposed. As he danced he wondered why that emotion which had begun to choke him did not come out through his throat. He was an Indian now and he believed that the exit of all spirit and emotion was the throat, just as the soul came out through the throat after death. (296–97).

Chal's dance is an extravaganza, a frenzied celebration of nothingness rather than a ceremonial act expressive of one's place within the tribal community and natural world. In its frenzy his dance contradicts the traditional poise and dignity of Osage dances, which never embraced the wilder "fancy dancing" of Plains tribes. Mathews's irony is heavy when he writes, "He was an Indian now," for in his extravagance (i.e., *extra*—outside, and *vagant*, *vagari*—to wander about) Chal is far from his Osage people. He still cannot fathom that mystery he sensed as a child: "He wanted by some action or some expression, to express the whole meaning of life; to declare to the silent world about him that he was a glorious male; to express to the silent forms of the blackjacks that he was a brother to the wind, the lightning and the forces that came out of the earth" (297). Drunk and without the teachings of his people, Chal has no language for such expression. He is inarticulate. His performance is, from the white perspective he has learned to value, simply another "extravaganza."

Sundown does not end on a fatalistic note. In the final scene, Chal boasts foolishly to his mother (while correctly associating linguistic facility with political power), "I'm goin' to Harvard law school, and take law—I'm gonna be a great orator." (311) He then falls asleep with his head on his arms. Around him, in the novel's final lines, nature comes alive:

> The nestlings in the nest above settled down to digest their food. A flamewinged grasshopper rose in front of Chal's still form, and suspended there, made cracking sounds like electric sparks, then dropped to the grass and became silent. The flapping and splashing of the mother robin, as she bathed in the pan under the hydrant, was the only sound of activity. (312)

The natural imagery of this conclusion, enveloping the sleeping Chal, strikes a positive note. Thus far, Chal has failed as a challenge to the disinheritors of his people. He has been disenfranchised culturally and is adrift in a wasted land. However, the novel, within which natural imagery has served consistently as an index to whatever is positive in Chal's world, ends with the purifying image of the bathing robin. A few lines earlier, a sparrow has pushed from the nest and killed one of the robin's young, but the mother goes on; she has other young and proceeds to cleanse herself. It is a small story of loss followed by renewal and hope. The flamewinged grasshopper sounds a more portentous note, rising like a warning before the sleeping Chal. In the grasshopper may also be seen a sign of hope, however, for in this image Mathews merges the natural world of the Osage—the sacred red, or flamecolor—and the "civilized" world of electricity. As the novel ends, unlike Running Elk, Chal is alive and sleeping peacefully near his mother in whom Osage values still live. The natural world, represented by bird and insect, remains intact.

Sundown ends on a somewhat ambivalent note, leaving the future of its mixedblood protagonist and of the Osage people unresolved. Just as the strong identity and self-assurance of the more traditional Sun-on-His-Wings balances the despair of Running Elk's disintegration and death, the novel depicts starkly the consequences of oil and acculturation for the Osage while simultaneously refusing to accept the familiar pattern of simple doom for the Indian, the "vanishing American" pattern so familiar to American literature and thought. In *Sundown*, Mathews leaves open the possibility of "another destiny, another plot" for the American Indian, refusing any romantic closure that would deny the immense difficulties confronting the displaced Native American, but simultaneously rejecting the cliché of the vanishing American as epic, tragic hero. In this repudiation of the simple, entropic plot assigned to the Native American Indian by Euramerican myth-making, Mathews anticipates the major direction of Indian fiction into the 1990s. Perhaps the author saw other possibilities for Chal in the model that he, John Joseph Mathews, had to offer as a sophisticated, worldly, educated mixedblood and member of the Tribal Council. Perhaps Mathews is anticipating the possibility articulated by a member of a succeeding generation of Osages, Kenneth Jump, who wrote in 1979: "Could it be that Indian blood mixing with other bloods will create a new type of Indian? If this be true then the Osages will not be engulfed by present society but a new type of Osage Indian will emerge from this propagation." Chal may indeed represent the "new type of Indian" who figures so prominently in contemporary American Indian fiction.

KENNETH M. ROEMER

Ancient Children at Play—Lyric, Petroglyphic, and Ceremonial

"Nintendo," "golf," "playing ball," "Six Flags Amusement Park," "Disney World." If sociologists administered word association lists to suburban Americans and the word "play" were included, I imagine that the responses would tend toward games, amusements, recreations—words that connote fun and relaxation at the peripheries of their lives. One of the most significant contributions Native American literatures (both oral and written) can make to modern readers is to teach them old and new concepts of play that transform narrow and peripheral notions of recreation into delightful, complex, and profound ideas of re-creation.

As the quotations above illustrate, throughout his writing career, N. Scott Momaday has been fascinated with notions of play. Evidence of this is especially strong in his new novel *The Ancient Child* (1989). Even before readers reach page one, they should be aware of this. There's word play in a tide that's an ironic oxymoron. There is title-page visual play in the water-color(less) black and gray horizontal bands/streams and vertical title blankets—images that are repeated in condensed and excerpted form at the beginnings of each of the four books of the novel (planes, lines, shapes, shadows). The actual point at which the streams converge is an optical tease. It is either obscured by the blankets (title page) or just beyond the edges of the right margins (book openings). The way the top stream crosses over the others transforms three shades into four. On each of the two blankets there is a thin horizontal band that crosses the letter "l." In a novel in which the

From *Critical Perspectives on Native American Fiction.* © 1993, 1997 by Passeggiata Press.

"complete" healing does not occur in the text and in which transformations, layering, and intense autobiographical overtones are central, these visual plays are certainly relevant foreshadowings. There are also verbal-visual plays: for instance, the listing of the "Characters" as if the novel were a "play" (e.g., the last entry is "OTHERS, as they appear"). This layout—the stark listing of names bereft of complete sentence and paragraph contexts—immediately calls attention to the many puns suggested by names such as Grey, Bent Sandridge, Lola Bourne, and Locke Setman (which is a bilingual pun; "set" is "bear" in Kiowa). Considering all this verbal and visual play even before page one, it is not surprising that when Charles L. Woodard asked Momaday for "some examples" of his interest in "play," he "immediately" thought of *Ancient Child* (31–32).

In one essay, I certainly can't pretend to offer a comprehensive analyses of the many Kiowa, Navajo, Jicarilla Apache, Modernist, satiric, and other senses of play in *Ancient Child*. Instead I will focus on illustrations of three types of play: lyric, petroglyphic, and ceremonial. All celebrate the use of imagination; all involve transformations and ancient children; all imply Momaday's self image as poet and painter; and all suggest the joy and profundity the best contemporary Native American authors express in their best acts of delightful and sacred play. *Ancient Child* also expresses the danger of play. Once the game has begun, the player may be "uncertain of the / passion's end" (lines from Yvor Winter's "Quod Tegit Omnia," the epigraph for Book 2, 127). And ceremonies improperly done can turn healing into suffering. Then too there is risk for an author whose imaginative play centers on playing, replaying, and re-re-playing certain tribal and autobiographical stories and on fragmenting, layering, and reassembling them with many other Indian and non-Indian stories. The results can be wonderful fulfillments of Momaday's belief that at least "once" we should all "give [ourselves] up to a particular landscape in [our] experience, to look at it from as many angles as [we] can . . ." (*Rainy Mountain* 83). Or the play could turn narcissistic, obscure, and pretentious; the images of Ahab as a great grisly bear "burying himself in the hollow a tree . . . sucking his own paws" or of Ishmael accusing the old "prophet," a giver of fragmented hints, of pretending to have "a great secret in him" come to mind (Melville 153, 93). *Ancient Child* is a delightful and healing play. It is also a dangerous game, a risk-taking adventure that Momaday obviously felt was necessary for the health of author and reader.

II

"Lyric" is an apt descriptive term for many of the best passages in *Ancient Child* because of their intense emphasis on imagination, emotion, and beauty. Momaday's lyric play can be sensed in three passages from different works that define various shades of emotional intensity expressed in words. In "The Man Made of Words," he celebrates storytelling as "an act by which man strives to realize his capacity for wonder, meaning and delight" (104). This striving is especially evident when humans encounter some object or experience so full of beauty and awe that they must transform their strong feelings into intense word images and stories. In *The Way to Rainy Mountain*, for instance, Momaday imagines that the Kiowa felt such urgency when they first saw Tsoai (Devil's Tower): "because they could not do otherwise," they "made a legend," the story of the boy-turned-bear who chased his seven sisters up an amazing rock-tree that lifted them to safety in the sky (8). The third passage also involves chasing girls, but this lyric play is more comic. Near the end of *Ancient Child*, we find some verbal jousting between Grey and Perfecto Atole, a Jicarilla Apache horse and bear man she has enlisted in her attempt to heal Set. (He must "play [his] part" [281].) As Perfecto talks to and looks at Grey, he recalls—first vaguely and then with intensive (macho) lyric detail—a powerful image of Grey at "a time—a moment, an *instant*" just after he had taken her virginity. "He nodded, savoring the image . . ." (282–83). Throughout *Ancient Child*, Momaday singles out intense moments for savoring; that is part of his lyric play. But here as elsewhere, he places these intense images within the play of other ongoing stories. In this case, Perfecto's savoring is truncated by Grey's blunt announcement that she had "'cut the tops off'" of the beautiful red boots he had given her, boots that were a key element in his savored image. Grey's announcement is full of male deflowering word play, especially since earlier in the novel she had punished a crude Anglo (Dwight Dicks, who raped her) by circumcising him with cutting pliers (100–01).

Taken together, the three passages from "Man Made of Words," *Rainy Mountain*, and *Ancient Child* suggest the delight and urgency behind transforming wonderful objects and experiences into intensely felt images akin to Keat's urn image or the tableau in Faulkner's "The Bear." Despite their intensity, Momaday will not, however, allow these instants to become "set" and isolated pieces. As in the Perfecto instant, they take on meaning through associations with previous events and images and continue to gather meanings as they are immersed in the play of images and stories that follow.

In *Ancient Child* many of these lyric plays grow from images of faces, bodies, and landscapes. In at least two cases, face, body, and landscape come together. In one, a child-woman takes on overtones of primortality; in the other an old and dying man is possessed by a wonderful sense of childlike delight and then infantlike serenity. Together they suggest the age-range of Momaday's spectrum of play with (for) ancient children.

Grey is the child-woman. A powerful instant occurs during an afternoon after she has made a glorious and frightening turtle skull mask topped with "scissortail and red-tailed hawk feathers" (198). (In *Rainy Mountain*, Momaday recalled the tortoises that crawled the "red earth" of Kiowa country [5].) To "show [the mask] off," she "took off all her clothes," mounted her horse (using only bridle and blanket), and rode off across the Southern Oklahoma plain carrying a brightly painted willow lance and emitting "terrible sounds" and "war whoops" (198–99). By itself, this image certainly has delight, urgency, and meaning, but it takes on more meaning because of an earlier episode of face painting (Set paints Grey's face in preparation for dancing with other women before the Kiowa black leggings men's society dance (112–14; see Schien 13), because of our knowledge of her incredible horse(wo)man-ship, and because of her intense artistic engagements with dramatic horse rides. Earlier we've seen Grey savoring personal and written images of Pueblo and Navajo riders and seen her attempts to write out and act out these passages (164–69). (There are playful acts of self-celebration and self-satire in this section. The unidentified written passage that Grey reads is from Momaday's *The Names* [130–31], and Grey outdoes Momaday's passage after reading it.) The image of the turtle-mask ride continues to take on meaning as it plays against the responses of the men who witness the event. Her Kiowa uncle, the Rev. Milo Mottledmare, "ejected" himself from his chair to see her ride by. Her great uncle Worchester Meat, at work in a melon patch, laughs and begins to dance in his "cleated work shoes." Dwight Dicks is struck dumb and then monosyllabically polite. Even when she asks how his "injured member" is, he can only reply, "'Oh, it's fine, Miz Grey, thank you'" (199–200). His response adds a comic surrealism to the entire episode.

The dancing Worchester Meat is at the center of the other lyric play mentioned previously. We have been prepared for his "moment" by previous descriptions of the Oklahoma landscape and of Worchester, who up to this point has been presented as kindly but also as one of the least distinguished of the Kiowa side of Grey's family (33); even when dressed like a warrior, "He was the comic caricature of a warrior" (113). Near the end of Book 3, he is approaching death. The Rev. Milo and his wife Jessie respect Worchester's wish to go off to his little house alone to die, but he is not isolated during his lyric moment. The plants and insects of the Oklahoma prairie help him to change from a dying, undistinguished old man into a wonderfully vital and then serene celebrant. His (Emily) Dickensonian perceptions and his ritual dance might have even achieved what Set claimed was his highest artistic "goal—to astonish God" (39):

> There were bluebonnets, yellow violets, and strawberries in patches in the grass. He stopped and stood among the wildflowers. Tears came to his eyes, blurring and magnifying his field of vision. And through his tears he perceived the brilliance of the meadow. The wildflowers were innumerable and more beautiful than anything he had ever seen or imagined. And when he thought his heart could bear no more, a dragonfly rose up, glancing and slipping just above him. In his brimming eyes it divided again and again to effect an iridescent swarm upon the sky. And he took a step, laughing, and another—dance steps. Then he declined slowly to the ground, and he was serene and refreshed in his soul. (301)

Momaday signals his great delight in, savoring of, and respect for this lyric moment by letting it conclude section 4. But, as in the case of Grey's masked ride, Worchester's dance gains new meanings as it is placed within the flow of other images. When we turn the page to section 5, the first two lines that greet us are the subtitle—"They are the shapes of immortality"— and the opening sentence—"Through the summer, life flourished at Lukachukai" (302). The location has changed from Kiowa to Navajo country (the Lukachukai Mountains are even mentioned in the Navajo Mountainway stories [Wyman 157]), but the two lines are apt benedictions for an ancient Kiowa child's final rite of passage.

III

Once we have grasped the nature of lyric play in *Ancient Child*, especially the type of petroglyphs characterized by repeated layerings of image upon image and by striking effects caused by juxtapositions of different types of images, it is not difficult to understand the petroglyphic and ceremonial play. The associative layering and the juxtaposing that build up to and flow away from the lyric moments are the bases for the petroglyphic play; and, as Grey's ride and Worchester's dance indicate, the lyric instances often involve ritual performances.

The petroglyph is an appropriate analogy for the structural play in *Ancient Child*. Momaday is interested in petroglyphs; he even associates the "origin of American literature" with Utah's Barrier Canyon rock art ("Native Voice" 5). Scholars, notably Susan Scarberry-Garcia, have argued convincingly that the structure of and responses to *House Made of Dawn* can be compared to petroglyphic layering: the overlapping, the super-impositions, the accretion of images all suggest stories "peeking through" each other. Associated images from different time periods invite viewers to connect and create reinforcing meanings (Scarberry-Garcia 120–21; see also Ballard's comments on strata levels, and planes 10). There are, of course, other appropriate analogies: the modernist novel, especially Faulkner's (see Schubnell 68–70); Kiowa family storytelling sessions (see Roemer, "Interview" 48–49). But considering Momaday's and his protagonist's interest in painting and the discontinuous narrative of *Ancient Child* (it is much more fragmented than *House Made of Dawn*), the petroglyph is an especially apt analogy for the structural play among the planes, lines, shapes, and shadows of *Ancient Child*.

With what does Momaday play? How does he play? What are the "effects" of the play? Momaday plays with four major stories through which many other stories peek. There is the story of the unsettling of Set who is going through a mid-life crisis. He is a successful artist (set for life) torn between what he is inspired to paint and the styles set by his agent and public. Set is also unsettled by a growing awareness that he is an ancient "set" (Kiowa-bear). By the end of the novel, with the help of an Anglo, Lola Bourne, and Grey and other Kiowa and Navajo friends and relatives, the placeless and orphaned Set has found settings (Kiowa and Navajo land) and is moving toward vital artistic and spiritual (human/bear) identities, though Set's identity is not yet set, and probably never will be. Then there is the story of Grey, the book's most colorful character. She is mostly Navajo and Kiowa, but she is also Mexican, French Canadian, and Scotch-Irish-English. Her Kiowa name, Koi-ehm-toya is also the name of Set's great-great-[great?] grandmother and the name of an ancient woman who Momaday imagines as seeing the original bear-boy. She is the youngest major character (19–20 years old); and she is also the oldest. She is ancient, not only because her Kiowa grandmother, Kope' mah, trained her in old curing traditions, but also because ancient Kiowa and Navajo stories peek through her story: for example, the story of the Tai-me who helped the Kiowa in a time of need (*Rainy Mountain* 36; Ballard 11); and stories from the Navajo Mountain way about Elder Sister, the Bear Maiden, who is associated with both destructive and healing bear powers. (See below. Also one of the epigraphs before Book 1 is taken from a description of equipment used in the Mountain way. Grey gives Set a bear medicine bundle.) Grey is a chameleon; Grey is several Koi-ehm-toyas; Grey is destructive and kind; Grey is a child and an ancient personage of many transformations, a changing woman, a changing being, a holy being.

If the two stories of Set and Grey represent the (bear) male/female balance in this ceremonial play of four stories, then the two other major ancient child stories—Billy the Kid and the Kiowa bear-boy story—represent an AngloAmerican / Native American balance of stories of the West. Billy's story may seem to be the odd-man-out tale in this novel of bear-people stories. But Momaday's Billy is bearlike in the senses that he embodies a wild-ness/wilderness associated in the novel with bears as early as the list of char-acters and because the quality that fascinates Momaday most about Billy, his relentless and expressionless drive towards self-preservation, can also be associated with the force of the bear. (I will admit, however, that Momaday compares Billy to a shark [*Ancestral Voice* 24–27].) Of course, Billy's story is also linked to the other stories because his story is Grey's story, is Set's story, is Momaday's story. Before she could be a proper healer for Set, Grey had to imagine and re-imagine (and write down) Billy in many ways; she had to live out her adolescent fantasy and creatively "exorcise" him from her identity (Momaday, "Discussion"). Momaday's own writings about Billy and his own childhood fantasies about Billy recall a similar process (*Ancestral Voice* 22). The Kiowa bear-boy story is also Set's, Grey's, and Momaday's story (*Ancestral Voice* 13), and it too is told from a variety of viewpoints. It first appears briefly on page one as it had appeared in Momaday's earlier works with a few minor changes (centered type, one word deleted [just], one word changed ["tree" to "trunk"]). Then it reappears in various manifestations and in significant numbers and places: four times in Book 1 (sections 2, 4, 8, 24 [lost boy-bear story]) and then once at the beginnings of the three other books and again as part of the epilogue.

The overlapping relationships among the four major stories again suggests the petroglyph analogy. It also recalls the way traditional oral narra-tion works—the interlinked story cycles, the many repetitions with variations. Momaday plays on and with the four major stories and their subsidiary narra-tives on several planes. In terms of overall structure, he divides his four books into subsections, each section having approximately half the number of sections as the previous one (1 [25], 2 [12], 3 [5], 4 [2]). This regular pattern of reduction gives a sense of design to Set's often chaotic journey toward healing and, in combination with the accumulative overlapping of lyric moments and stories, gives a sense of dramatic movement from fragmentation toward unity and balance (a key development in Navajo curing ceremonies).

On the plane of smaller textual units, (the 44 subsections—note 44 doubles the sacred 4), Momaday's play exhibits many ingenious combinations of tribal storytelling, Classical rhetorical, and modernist techniques—especially juxtaposition, condensation, and expansion (the latter two are also forms of repetition with variation).

In my discussion of lyric play, I have already offered examples of how juxtapositions can generate meaning (e.g., the lines following Worchester's death/life dance). Momaday's multiple presentations of the Kiowa bear-boy story suggests his approaches to condensation and expansion. In *The Way To Rainy Mountain*, Momaday has identified the compact form of the story (labeled Prologue in *Ancient Child*) with a version told by his grandmother Aho. He has heard other versions and is no doubt familiar with the much longer version published in 1983 in the second volume of Maurice Boyd's *Kiowa Voices* (87–93). But, for many of the same reasons Faulkner began his multi-layered *Go Down, Moses* with a highly condensed version of Uncle Ike's story, Momaday chose to begin with his (grandmother's) condensed version. It initiates—for both Set and the reader—a dramatic movement (a play) that opens with a remembered, though dimly understood, whole story and proceeds through a series of unwindings and fragmentations that through processes of association lead toward a reunification of the whole illuminated by the experience of traveling through all the unwindings. (Again there are strong parallels to Navajo ceremonialism.) This cyclical process is also a fulfillment of the novel's epigraph ("For myth is at the beginning of literature, and also at its end. Borges"), as the concise Prologue and Epilogue demonstrate. The unwindings between the two compact wholes display Momaday's ability to expand stories. He expands by opening up possibilities of narrative viewpoint: for instance, in Book 1, different versions of the bear-boy story appear from a limited omniscient voice focusing on the boy's sensations (Sec. 2); a tribal voice recounting the birth of a boy-child (Sec. 4); the old-woman Koi-ehm-toya's worried perspective as she watches the playing children move from meadow to forest (Sec. 8); and Set's father's voice telling his son a long Kiowa story of the lost bear-boy (Sec. 24). Of course, the entire Set story can be viewed as a long contemporary unwinding of the bear-boy narrative, as Grey's story could be perceived as an expansion of several episodes of the Navajo Elder Sister narrative (see below).

Even Billy the Kid is expanded, not only because Grey imagines numerous episodes in his life from different angles, but also because she imagines him after his death meeting with another legendary Western figure, Set-angya (Sitting Bear), the leader of the Kiowa Crazy Dogs warrior society. This is one of the most playful scenes in the novel. Billy pays his respects with a Victorianic Hollywooden speech ("'. . . Hear me, old man brave to madness, O my warrior!'" [256]). It turns out his "girlfriend" (i.e., Grey) wrote the speech. Billy's not good with words. He's no speech writer, and unlike Set-angya, he had no time to sing (a death song) when he dies. As a matter of fact, he "'can't sing'" (260). This expansion of Billy's story is also a sign of his exorcism from Grey's imagination. Her Billy imaginings have been "a memorial to her own childhood" (175); she will always respect this memorial, but it's time to move on. Thus, it is appropriate that the paragraph that follows the Billy-Set-angya meeting emphasizes her awakening, her "arranging her thoughts," and her drawing "lines on the red earth" that point toward her future directions with Set. These acts and the word "Lines" end Book 2, which is entitled Lines, and point toward a fuller, more three-dimensional expansion (Book 3 is entitled Shapes).

What are the "effects" of Momaday's petroglyphic play. First, as in the case of the lyric play, there is the sheer delight of play. The layering, the peeking through, the juxtapositions, the associations, condensations, and expansions are all reflections of an author's delight and invitations to readers to share that delight. Petroglyphic play is also an appropriate and powerful way to express the multicultural nature of modern Indian, indeed The Modern, experience. Set's story alone attracts, repels, represents, and masks many non-Indian stories (for instance, the stories of "success," the Romantic artist, the male mid-life crisis, the alienated individual) and Indian stories. I've emphasized traditional Kiowa and Navajo stories. There is also a Sioux bear transformation story at the outset of Book 4. There are, moreover, dramatizations of many contemporary Indian stories. Set acts out the quest for a native identity; Grey's early teenage years in fact and in imagination hint at the Indian cowboy/cowgirl story; Rev. Milo suggests the Christian Indian story. As different as many of the healers in contemporary Indian fiction are (and Vizenor's Proude Cedarfair, the ceremonial bear, Silko's Betonie, Welch's Yellowcalf, and Erdrich's Fleur and Nanapush are very different), they all know that understanding 20th-century Indian experiences requires an awareness of the rich, confusing, and agonizing layers of many Indian and many non-Indian experiences. Momaday's petroglyphic play invites readers to delight in and agonize through some of these layers.

IV

As I've already indicated, in *Ancient Child* lyric plays are often ritual acts and the whole process of petroglyphic play can be viewed as a ceremonial process. There are also views of specific ceremonies in *Ancient Child* (though, out of respect for sacred rituals, Momaday rarely offers detailed descriptions of traditional ceremonies). For instance, Section 5 of Book 3 concludes with the "marriage" of Set and Grey—a ceremony that combines elements of a Navajo Blessingway and a Pan-Indian peyote ceremony and is expressed in a language that mixes Navajo chant and Faulknerian written cadences with a touch of the Romantic: "In ceremony, in tradition out of time, in a sacred manner, in beauty they were married forever" (299).

More important than any specific ceremony is the entire course of Set's illness and movement toward healing, which shares much with traditional Navajo concepts of ceremonial diagnosis and healing. (Scarberry-Garcia has convincingly demonstrated Momaday's familiarity with Navajo ceremonialism.) The role of the Navajo diagnostician is played by a white woman, Lola Bourne, in this multicultural ceremony. She is obviously not a traditional Navajo hand trembler or star gazer, but she does know that Set's possession by Bear Power and other elements of his life have made him "sick in [his] mind" (237). (Mountainway deals with, among other illnesses, mental imbalances caused by contacts with mountain animals, especially bears [Wyman xi, 17].) Like a good Navajo diagnostician, she does point Set toward an appropriate healer. In fact she even delivers Set to Grey (with a bit of word play: after she leaves Set, Bourne feels "unburdened" [255]).

By Book 3, Grey has exorcised her adolescent Kid fantasy and is ready to be a healer. Book 3 is full of ceremonial plays that over-and under-tone Set's journey. The movement toward a reenactment of the Kiowa bear-boy myth (at the end through fasting, running, and vision) is obvious. Perhaps less obvious are the parallels to the Navajo Mountainway. Even small acts have parallels, such as the use of emetics to induce cleansing in the ceremony and Set's vomiting (276). More important are general similarities between Grey's life and Mountainway stories of the bear Maiden, Elder Sister Bispáli. She and Grey have been taught knowledge and power by ancient holy beings (in Elder's case, the Yei bichai; in Grey's, Kope' mah), and both have been seduced by bear men (in Elder's case, the old Bear Man from the mountain; in Grey's, Perfecto Atole, the Jicarilla "keeper of a bear paw" [284]). (For Momaday's version [as told by Ben Benally, the Night Chanter] of the Bear Maiden story from the Mountainway, see *House Made of Dawn* [188–89].) In "real" life, Grey is actually a younger sister, and she does share some affinities with the Younger Sister Glispah who was seduced by Snake-man, lived on "the plain," and eventually became a powerful medicine woman associated with the Navajo Beautyway (O'Bryan 134–35; Scarberry-Garcia 66). (If Dwight Dicks is the seducer, she certainly took care of his snake.)

Besides the parallels to mythic figures associated with Mountainway, we also find dramatic ritual acts. The "part" that the Jicarilla Apache Perfecto plays is to terrify Set by riding after him and clawing him on the throat with his bear paw (286–88). In the Navajo Mountainway and Red Antway and in the Jicarilla Apache Holiness Rite, one possible ritual is a Shock Rite (Wyman, *Mountainway* 23, Wyman 56–58, *Red Antway*). The parallels between Set's experience and the Shock Rite are, to say the least, not exact. In the Red Antway rite described by Wyman, the Bear impersonator comes at the patient four times on all fours, and the patient is supposed to faint. [*Red Antway* 56–58]. But, as Gladys Reichard's comments indicate, the general parallels are striking: the Shock Rite "purports to induce and correct symptoms due to the contemplation of supernatural things too strong for the patient" (717), for Set, things like Bear Power. Reichard also observes that an "impersonator of an animal or god frightens a patient." After he or she revives, the patient "is not only immune to all danger from the deity impersonated—Bear, for example—but may even count upon him for protection" (92). Set is not yet immune to the tremendous powers of the Bear, but after his experience with Perfecto, his will power is "restored" (through humiliation and anger), he feels "purged by his own distemper," and he is able to pray (288).

Less dramatic, but of equal importance are daily rituals. Set moves with Grey into Grey's mother's hogan. (Navajo are matrilineal.) Daily life becomes a repeated pattern of running, painting, bathing (in water and in a traditional sweat lodge—both Mountainway rites), riding, talking, loving. As the time for his reenactment of the Kiowa bear-boy's run in the shadow of Tsoai approaches, Set has regained spiritual and physical health and created new life. Grey is pregnant.

Nonetheless, Momaday does not hide the dark side of sacred play. (The final book is named shadows not lights.) Especially in Kiowa culture, but also among the Navajo bear power can destroy as well as heal. Several times in San Francisco, Set's growing awareness of his bear identity almost destroys him (e.g., 242). Even at the end of Book 4 when everything seems to be coming together, there is terror. Set is in the right place, near Tsoai camped where Grey (and indirectly Kope' mah) had told him to go (311). He has his medicine bundle; he has fasted four days. On The Night, the full moon rises; so does the Big Dipper (the seven sisters in Momaday's version of the Kiowa myth). Set has the vision he sought: "the image of a great bear, rearing against Tsoai" (312). (See Al Momaday's illustration in *Rainy Mountain* [9].) Even the language of the novel is coming together. In the last description of Tsoai, all the words used as book titles appear—planes, line[s], shapes, shadows (312). And, as anticipated, as Set runs, he relives the bear-boy's experience presented in the Prologue. But Set's run (as far as we are allowed to see it) does not end in the wondrous delight and serenity of Worchester's dance. It leads instead to isolation and ambiguity: "a loneliness like death. He moved on, a shadow receding into shadows. Shadows" (314). This darkness is balanced in the Epilogue by an optimistic look toward a future generation, an heir of Set and Grey (Koi-ehm-toya) who "never saw Tsoai" but knew it so well that he could paint powerful shield images and imagine the "whole" history of this people "played out in myriad points of light." Still, this heir's final dream is of children entering "into the darkness" (315).

V

Considering the rich network of reinforced (reenacted) meanings outlined by the ceremonial play of *Ancient Child*, it is clear that Ishmael would not accuse Momaday of playing a pretentious game of empty "secrets." And yet, as a reader familiar with Momaday's other works, I do have some questions about the risks taken in the plays of *Ancient Child*. These questions might best be expressed through comparisons to the ceremonial play in *House Made of Dawn*.

Does Set have enough of a foundation for the ceremonial play to "take"? In *House Made of Dawn*, Abel certainly has shaky foundations. But his childhood, though very troubled, was filled with a strong sense of place, and the grandfather who raised him had strong senses of place and story. Set is initially much more of a placeless and storyless character. After his mother's death during his birth and his Kiowa father's death in 1941 (Set was seven), Set lived at the Peter and Paul Orphanage from which he was adopted by the kind and wealthy philosopher Bent Sandridge of San Francisco. His memory of his father is vague: "There was only something like a photograph, old and faded, a shadow within a shadow" (64). He does, however, recall the Kiowa lost boy-bear story that his father told him, and we are privileged to hear it as if Cate Setman were telling it to his young son. It is a story about a lost boy who wanders into camp; by story's end he seems to have never existed because he has no name and his tracks have turned into bear tracks (119–22). This story certainly has great relevance to Set's childhood and adulthood. Nonetheless, is it enough upon which to build the type of Native American cure that depends so heavily on internalized senses of place and story? Or maybe the point of Set's terrible loneliness at the end of Book 4 is that the foundation was not deep enough and he is still a lost child, though the

Epilogue argues against that conclusion. (Abel's Prologue run also ends with him "alone," but the preceding sentences make this a much more hopeful state of isolation [2].)

Other striking differences between the stories of Abel and Set are that Set's narrative concentrates much more tightly on one period of his life during his mid-forties and his healing process seems shorter. Abel's story focuses on two crucial periods in his young adulthood (just after his return from World War II in 1945 and just after his release from prison in 1952), and there are powerful (some sustained) flashbacks to his childhood (e.g., with his brother Vidal) and to his war years (e.g., the encounter with the tank). Furthermore, the alternating possibilities for healing and frightening setbacks are distributed throughout the novel, from the opening pages describing his run and the beautiful Jemez landscape to his performance of final rites for his grandfather and the book's closing run. This is relevant to the ceremonial play of the novel because in traditional healing ceremonies (especially Navajo ceremonies like the Nightway from which Momaday derived the title *House Made of Dawn*) the mythological models for the healing depict a long accumulation of specific setbacks and steps toward recovered balance. Even if we were not aware of this tradition and even if we conceded that some healing begins before Book 3, we might ask if the relatively short Books 3 and 4 are too short a "time" for the ritual play to create a believable transformation.

The nature of the illness and the degree to which it engages readers' sympathy also raise questions. Despite his outbreaks of violence and his acts of insensitivity to Francisco, Milly, and Ben, Abel is certainly worthy of our sympathy. The many sufferings of his childhood, the nightmare war experiences, the tragedies of his encounter with the albino, his trial, his prison sentence, his poverty, the physical beatings he receives in L.A.—all help us to understand why Abel needs (deserves) strong healing ceremonies. Set too has suffered. But the comfort and security in childhood and adulthood offered by his stepfather, the tremendous artistic and financial successes that come at an early age (he was already recognized at 30), and the ready availability of beautiful women to help him all may make it more difficult for readers to sympathize with him. As Kathleen M. Donovan has argued forcefully and well, the roles of the women help(mat)ers—Lola, Alais Sancerre, and Grey—suggest a type of female devaluation that is especially problematic. By the end of *Ancient Child*, even the strong and independent Grey is centered around Set and her voice has been, in effect, silenced by the centering on his story. As Donovan points out (29), this is particularly ironic because the narrator has informed us that when Grey and Set establish their daily rituals at her mother's home, her language undergoes a wondrous change. It "was made of rhythms and silences that [Set] had not heard before" (290). We never get to hear these new rhythms. Grey no longer speaks directly (in dialogue); we only hear about her. This is a serious problem within the context of this particular text; within the context of Momaday's canon (in *House Made of Dawn*, one sign of the depths of Abel's separation from his culture and of his psychological seizure is his voicelessness), and within the broad contexts of Native American ceremonialism (in the Navajo Nightway, for example, the restoration of voice [siné] is a crucial element in the healing process).

Of course male writers as great and as different as Shakespeare and Fitzgerald have demonstrated convincingly that rich, famous, and women-aided men can sincerely need healing. Still, there were times when I wanted to swat Set and to allow Grey to go off either to Jemez Pueblo to further the healing of Abel or just to go off on her own.

Two other relevant contrasts relate to the explicitness and the autobiographical immediacy of the ceremonial play. Some critics, have complained of the "obscurity," of *House Made of Dawn* (Larson 78–79). Others, like Scarberry-Garcia, have discovered the power of the gradual and oblique references to the traditional stories and ceremonies "behind" Abel's painful movement toward healing. *Ancient Child* is not as obscure. At one point, Billy the Kid announces that "You got to point" (170). (See also 186.) Momaday does more pointing in his second novel. Some of his narrator's and characters' comments and a few of the subtitles (e.g., "The bear is coming," "The bear comes forth") make it quite clear that Set is a reincarnation of the Kiowa bear-boy, that Grey is the fated healer, and that Set will undergo a healing ceremony. At times, it almost seems as if *Ancient Child* parodies parts of *House Made of Dawn*, Silko's *Ceremony*, and other ceremonial healing novels by contemporary Native American writers. I say "almost" because the intensity of the lyric plays, the complexity of the petroglyphic play and of many of the mythic reverberations, and the unresolved nature of Set's vision run all mitigate against reducing the novel to a parody or a formulaic fiction.

Although there are autobiographical elements in *House Made of Dawn* (e.g., Momaday spent most of his adolescent years at Jemez Pueblo), there are enormous distances between Abel and Momaday. The distances are much smaller in *Ancient Child*. Set is *not* Momaday. Nevertheless, their birth dates, their paternal tribal ancestries, their early successes, their love of painting, their names (one of their names is Tsoai-talee, Rock Tree Boy), their belief that they can be possessed by bear power, and numerous other linking details (Set lives on Scott Street) establish strong autobiographical connections.

There's nothing wrong with autobiographical fiction. Why not allow the author to be master of ceremonies? But in this case, the autobiographical overtones could make the text vulnerable to interpretation as a narrow and idiosyncratic ceremonial play, or to association with the circular and introspective image, noted earlier, of the Ahab-bear isolated in his tree feeding upon his own paws, or to the projective Ahab image—wherever Ahab looks, he sees Ahab. *Ancient Child* is not impervious to such criticism, but it does have some imposing defenses. Although Grey has affinities with Momaday (e.g., a childhood fascination with Billy the Kid), there are great distances between Grey and Momaday, and, in my opinion, Grey is the most fascinating character in the novel. There are also encouraging doses of self-satire. The mere fact that Momaday's narrator could portray Set behaving at times like a spoiled, self-centered child suggests a healthy perspective on character and self. (See, for instance, the word play on "spoiled" and "self-centered" on 237). If, indeed, part of Momaday's play was self-satire, then *Ancient Child* also functions as a healing game of personal therapy.

The entire network of lyric, petroglyphic, and ceremonial play can, moreover, have powerful heuristic and therapeutic effects on modern readers. The network can invite us to question what readers can, should, and shouldn't expect from texts that combine intense mixtures of oral tribal, Euro-American written, and personal literatures, especially if these texts are associated with famous writers who are perceived as leading speakers, if not for their people, at least for their people's contemporary literary expressions. *Ancient Child's* playful layering of literatures suggests the complexities and brilliance that contemporary Indian fiction can bring to mainstream American literature. But what if that gift doesn't seem to play according to a preconceived notion of how leading texts on the margin should speak. (In very different ways, recent works by Leslie Marmon Silko, *Almanac of the Dead*, and Louise Erdrich-Michael Dorris, *The Crown of Columbus*, also raise this question.) I hope we can face these occurrences by examining each text carefully and by placing its characteristics within relevant cultural and literary contexts. And I hope we can avoid two extreme responses: trying to cover up the characteristics of the text that don't seem to fit the desired image of a Native American text or focusing so intently on these elements that we distort them and lose sight of other characteristics of the text.

The potential for therapeutic effects of *Ancient Child's* network of play grows. As we discover moments of lyric intensity, see how old and new stories overlap and peep through each other, and begin to grasp the design that may cure Set. We can also begin to see how in experiential and imaginative ways we can become sensitive to the play(s)—both delightful and dangerous—in our own landscapes and stories. Like the effects of the Navajo concept of hózhó (beauty, harmony), the effects of many of the plays in *Ancient Child* can radiate outward helping to cure observers as well as patient.

JAMES RUPPERT

Textual Perspectives and the Reader in
The Surrounded

When D'Arcy McNickle wrote and rewrote *The Surrounded*, he was
clearly working with a set of conventions he knew his audience would understand. As he revised and edited to satisfy each potential editor, he made a
virtue of necessity and richly layered his narrative closer to what he perceived
to be a publishable novel.

McNickle's experience and the published text of *The Surrounded* is used
here to illustrate Wolfgang Iser's insight that fiction differs from ordinary
discourse because it provides several channels of communication governed
by different intentions, which create different perspectives. Ultimately, the
convergence of these intentions, these perspectives, is in the reader. While
the perspectives construct a text that encourages the reader to respond in
prestructured ways, the reader must participate in the changes of perspectives bringing about the convergence. Thus, when Iser looks at a text he
concludes that meaning comes into existence only in the act of reading.
Criticism of McNickle's work has lacked insight into the dynamic relationship between the four textual perspectives (implied author, plot, characters
and implied reader) and the meaning of the text which the reader takes away
from the novel. A close exploration of this dynamic relationship illuminates
the quality of McNickle's art and the fullness of his meaning.

Iser has theorized that since the act of reading is sequential, the careful
reader must view one perspective at a time, letting the new material modify
his view of the text's meaning. As the reader does so, each character

From *Narrative Chance: Postmodern Discourse on Native American Indian Literatures.* © 1993 by the
University of Oklahoma Press.

constructs a specific viewpoint which becomes a momentary, central theme, to be viewed against the horizon of what has gone before. The reader must readjust his understanding of past action and form new expectations concerning the future. However, since the perspective on the meaning shifts from one viewpoint to another and modifies what has come before, the reader is constantly being set up only to have the ground of his perceptions pulled out from under him. This process whereby the reader sets up new conventions and expectations encouraged by the writer and then continually modifies them has been referred to as "misreading." As the reader progresses through the text, he eliminates partial and inadequate understandings of meaning, leaving a series of possible viewpoints. The impetus is always present for the reader to discard attitudes inadequate to the understanding of the text, and he may shed some of those very conventions with which he began to read the text. By following the four textual perspectives (implied author, plot, characters and implied reader), then, the reader changes, grows, transforms. Thus, the reader is always a potential being in a dynamic relation to the text, a being that the act of reading has created.

In *The Act of Reading* Iser explains the first perspective, that of the implied reader, by clarifying the tension created between "the role offered by the text and the real reader's disposition." It is clear to Iser that the role offered to the reader by the text is not simply one of receiving a definitive message. The reader starts with a set of conventions about society, fiction and the text. McNickle works against these assumed values by manipulating the four perspectives on meaning. Iser refers to the role given to the reader by the text as the "implied reader."

For McNickle, the implied reader was the conventional reader who held the values of the white, literate public of the early 1930s, a public with limited preconceptions of Indian life and values. But the text manipulates the implied reader's role, working it against the other perspectives. The reader is placed in a variety of roles such as a storyteller's audience, confidante, synthesizer of the "clash of values" and interpreter of allegory. McNickle's task is to transform that typical reader of 1936 into one aware of Indian cultural values and the fallacies of white attitudes toward Indians.

The plot offers a second perspective on the meaning of a text since the series of events may undercut, transform or reinforce the conventions understood by the reader. In *The Surrounded* the events which portray hope, conciliation, entanglement and despair create an accelerating, tragic vortex where event undercuts emotion.

A third and easily accessible perspective on the meaning of the text is offered by the main character or characters. As characters think, speak and act, each of them presents a view on meaning, a view the reader can accept or reject. The thoughts and words of Archilde, the young half-breed protagonist; Max, his Spanish, rancher father; Catherine, his Salish, religious mother; Grepilloux, the benevolent, paternal missionary; and Modeste, the old Salish medicineman, embody distinct viewpoints on meaning expressed in the text.

The fourth and final perspective on the text is that of the implied author. Readers form a conception of the author based on style, manner of telling and selection of material. These may or may not have relevance to the person described on the dust jacket. Many critics follow Wayne Booth's suggestion that we refer to this persona as the implied author. As McNickle offers the reader a role, so he creates a persona for himself. While writing of the boy Archilde who grows up much as he did but who dies tragically in Montana, McNickle is not writing of the young man living the literary life of Depression New York. Critics must not fuse the narrator of *The Surrounded* and McNickle the man too quickly. For the tragedy of the novel to work for the reader, the implied author must believe in Archilde's inevitable destruction, a belief that McNickle need not necessarily hold.

The implied author believes that Archilde is enmeshed from the beginning, but he reveals this attitude to the reader slowly. He does not believe that Archilde is the hope of the future as do some characters and as Archilde later in the novel starts to believe. As Archilde struggles to accept his Indian past, the implied author embeds his own wideranging, discouraging insights into the text. Even while Archilde feels free and strong, the implied author structurally counteracts Archilde's hopeful outlook by presenting the perspectives of the powers-that-be (such as the Indian Agent and the Sheriff) that will eventually destroy Archilde. The implied author strives to destroy any hope; his perspective is that human action and volition are ineffectual. Yet this obstacle allows the reader to create a synthesis and ultimately see that Archilde's actions and newly found wisdom are valuable human efforts. For the same reasons, the actions of protagonists of American Naturalism, such as those in the novels of Dreiser, Crane and Norris, embody the human spirit and create value.

In the book's first chapter, Archilde returns home from the white world (Portland, Oregon) after a year's absence. He plans to do the pleasurable things of his youth one more time and maybe settle some old antagonisms before he goes out into the world forever. He intends to reach back and touch the good things of his youth, unifying memory and reality to form a solid base of past experience and family relationships to remember as he travels off. Here the distance between the perspectives of the implied author and the implied reader is very slight. The reader's preconceived mores are reinforced and exploited. It is only right that a young boy leave his family and find his fortune in the big world. He is a dutiful son because he returns and wants to make peace before he goes off. He tries to remain neutral, yet becomes concerned when faced with family distrust and "warfare." When Archilde refers to an endless round of fighting and stealing, the reader agrees with his perspective that he should get away and "make something of himself."

In this chapter the implied author, implied reader, and plot only vaguely credit the comments of the old woman, Katherine, whose knowledge of the world is severely limited and who seems locked in her own routine and archaic ritual relationships. Neither the implied author nor the implied reader seem to understand or appreciate these. Max, her husband, is more accessible but unsympathetic. He seems cantankerous and unloving, yet he offers to save Louis' neck. It is clear that the young boy should be off on his own with people of his own age, people who hold values similar to the reader's. Archilde's good motives are presented with great sympathy and his perspective merges with that of the reader. Consequently, the plot seems to be a straightforward return-of-the-native, and the implied reader settles into a comfortable return-of-the-native pattern of response (though that pattern is one that writers since Hamlin Garland had been deconstructing). The plot also suggests a subplot through Louis: where is he and what will become of him?

The average white, literate reader of the 1930s is encouraged to adapt a conventional viewpoint on textual meaning, one which reinforces the white patterns of cultural expectations. The unity of viewpoints in this chapter creates a clear foreground to which one small disturbing fact is backgrounded. True, Archilde seems to be coming home for a vacation: he wants to relax, to go fishing and riding and to climb a mountainside. But it seems that no one wants to fish anymore; the pieces of Archilde's neat construct do not easily fall into place. Much of Archilde's memory world remains the same; yet Archilde's young nephews want him to buy hooks. When Archilde offers to help them fish in an older, more Indian way, they decline his pastoral vision. It seems as if the rosy sense of memory and the joyous sense of the experience of nature do not motivate anyone except Archilde. The naive pastoral romanticism with which the implied reader has been encouraged to identify is already under revision. Also, the cultur- ally correct ideas of revering one's mother and father begin to dissolve when one is faced with their reality, and Archilde's desire to flee takes on a deeper epistemological questioning in which the reader participates.

The next few chapters begin to assail the perspective asserted in the first chapter. The desirability of material progress is questioned by Max, then the paternalism and self-centered superiority of the priests becomes evident. Archilde also begins to question assumed white values, and because the reader has identified with him, the reader begins to question also. The plot continues to create situations which force Archilde to confront the contradictory perspectives of Max and Catherine, and later Modeste and Grepilloux. Since the main characters express motivations which do not find easy support in the conventional morality or cultural code, the plot entangles Archilde in what appear to be insoluble problems and encourages his disaffiliation.

Conventional morality is again questioned through the introduction of Grepilloux's diary and Modeste's story. The private motivations of both the whites and the Salish clearly express misunderstanding of each other. Grepilloux reads his diary to Max and the reader, but the protagonist, Archilde, is not allowed to see it. The implied reader is offered privileged insider information and sees more completely than any character, including Archilde. The plot and character interaction stop completely at these two points, while the implied author interjects material which creates non-personal, historical and mythic background and ironically comments on the plot and characters in order to create an allegorical parallel. As a result, the implied reader is presented with historical and mythic stories as if he were an audience at the foot of a story-teller. The total effect is that of fore-grounding the questioning of the conventional morality: since the reader can not assume the perspective of either story (they are so obviously in contrast, and each admits many erroneous assumptions) he must create a perspective that is a synthesis.

While the reader revises his understanding of "what is right" in Indian/white relations, Archilde becomes more relaxed with his people, his past, and their strivings and limitations. As the first half of the book concludes, the characters reveal the bankruptcy of the white idea of progress for the Indian as well as the ruinous effect of white religion and education on the social and personal structure of Salish life.

When the double murder takes place, the reader is ready to revise his understandings or cultural code. The plot makes it clear that Archilde is not responsible for the murder though he appears to be in the conventional world of white morality, and he is supposed to report the killings though his family and cultural ties keep him from doing so. Love of family, a value that is foregrounded at the beginning, is now in conflict with observance of the law. Archilde and his mother have begun placing Salish code over white cultural code, yet neither can see what the future will bring. Archilde sees her and the old people as "shells and husks of life forms that had once possessed elastic strength." The implied author is skeptical of either code's efficacy and certain of the misunderstanding that the conflict creates, but the implied reader is torn. The plot pushes toward entanglement and tragedy as a consequence of misunderstanding good motives.

Futhermore, the perspective of the plot is drastically separated from that of Archilde; it predominates. While the plot's complications become foregrounded, the implied reader must revise his perspective as Archilde revises his understanding and actions. It is clear that he must believe in the value of reconstructing the Indian identity, yet that requires giving up the values of white society and its laws. Because Archilde continues to feel like an outsider, ineffectual to change the despair he sees, the reader must supply suggestions for actions and values. Iser explains this movement to a position of insight when he writes:

> We call this meeting place the meaning of the text, which can only be brought into focus if it is visualized from a standpoint. Thus, standpoint and convergence of textual perspectives are closely related, although neither of them is actually represented in the text, let alone set out in words. Rather they emerge during the reading process, in the course of which the reader's role is to occupy shifting vantage points that are geared to a prestructured activity and to fit the diverse perspective into a gradually evolving pattern.

In the episode of the Indian dance, the value that the dances had and may have again for the Salish is expressed in the way the old people are shown turning away from the white world. While their action creates meaning, it is a reactionary, stop-gap measure, one which the reader recognizes as a dead-end. The reader must place his hope in the young like Archilde. But the white dance section which follows the Indian dance introduces Elsie, a desperate young Indian and product of a boarding school. The view of whites and Indians at the dance effectively discourages any easy conclusion by the reader about the beneficial influences of white culture on young Indians. Presented with two opposing, parallel views of white/Indian interaction, the reader must synthesize a perspective that is separated from Archilde's confusion, the plot's increasing entanglement, or the implied author's belief in inevitable tragedy.

Iser explains how the reader's changing perspective is created by new information from the wandering perspective: "Thus the reader's communication with the text is a dynamic process of self-correction, as he formulates signifieds which he must then continually modify." The reader's expectations and revised understanding of previous events in the text, or misreading, are a necessary part of endowing a text with meaning.

In chapter twenty-six, Archilde contemplates the misery and poverty around him and the implied reader again is tempted to follow Archilde's perspective, but the reader's perspective has been permanently separated from that of any character. In the story of the mare, Archilde's good motives are attacked by the implied author, but the conventional, white reformist attitudes that Archilde expresses are also denied the reader. In this episode the implied author cuts out the characters' perspectives and talks directly to the reader. By challenging the perspective of the reader, a perspective that has been so carefully encouraged, he foregrounds again the conventional mores that had formed the foreground of the first chapter and the background of the intervening chapters, but now they are assailed critically.

Archilde's perspective is not that of his people who want to return to the past or to hide from the present. Neither is it that of the implied reader. Archilde's perspective, which has functioned as the theme, is questioned at this point and the reader must reassess Archilde's good motives (fortunately Archilde will learn from this encounter as he does from all the encounters in the book). The reader is encouraged to find a new viewpoint from which he can reconstruct meaning and good action. To do this he must reassess and reject prior viewpoints that encouraged white cultural superiority or espoused reformist attitudes. As a consequence he adopts one which values Indian autonomy yet recognizes that the present system is not working and something new must be created. Here the reader's viewpoint is decidedly different from Archilde's who is not ready to give up white reformist values, from the plot's which will entangle him if he does or does not, and from the implied author's who is telling the implied reader a tale—the allegory of the mare with its despairing prediction of disaster. After this story it is clear that Archilde wants something better, but he is not sure what it is or how it will come about.

His answer seems to come at his mother's death bed when he becomes stronger, almost a leader. Since Archilde is not sure what he must do to make things better, the implied reader must figure out how to do that. Archilde acts because the emotions feel right, but the reader is encouraged to develop an independent understanding. Because the reader can't completely accept any perspective presented, he must begin to question social values that determine federal Indian policy, questions that are deeper and more practical than anyone in the book is asking. Archilde punctuates the implied reader's position by continuing to question him and compel him to answer, such as, "How could he really help Mike and Narcisse. . . . there ought to be something better." The reader must create meaning for the novel out of the confluence of the perspectives. As Iser explains:

> . . . the observer finds himself directed toward a particular view which more or less obliges him to search for the one and only one standpoint that will correspond to that view." By virtue of that standpoint, the reader is situated in such a position that he can assemble the meaning toward which the perspectives of the text have guided him.

Near the end of *The Surrounded*, when the narrative voice moves to the Indian Agent, the forces that precipitate the tragedy are developed. By shifting to a previously unused narrative voice the implied author helps the reader believe in the inevitable tragedy, but the reader is further pushed to question social forces and values. He sees the flaws in the white social machinery, flaws which will ensure tragedy. His position of superior knowledge reveals the petty, uninformed and unimaginative perspective of the agent and even of the best of white society. He is pushed even more strongly to a synthesis outside of the text, one which will make sense of the tragedy and eliminate the inevitability of the tragedy by creating cross-cultural understanding.

In the final chapter the reader's perspective is further separated from Archilde's. If he is to create a progressive synthesis from the various perspectives, the reader clearly must reject Archilde's lethargy and the vague flirtation with "paganism" that motivates Archilde's trip into the mountains with Elsie. It is Archilde's questioning that makes him a worthy protagonist and thus tragic, and it is his questions that encourage the reader to find answers and his own perspective. After the idyllic moment with Elsie, Archilde starts to question again. He becomes active and exercises his volition. However, at this point the plot and the implied author's perspectives diminish his centrality to the action. Both perspectives imply that Archilde's volition is ineffectual and will lead to ruin.

The final chapter is often reduced by critics to a single perspective— that of the plot which entangles or of the implied author who weaves this tale of lost chances (perhaps to suggest that Archilde should have gone away and retained white values as the nagging voice of conventional morality might suggest to the reader). For critics today, perhaps the desire to emphasize the tragic ending is a function of a heightened liberal conscience. In 1987 many readers express a belief in Indian self-determination that white audiences of 1936 did not generally share. Some readers tend to identify with such perspectives as Modeste's or even Archilde's. However, these perspectives are clearly incomplete and it is unlikely that McNickle intended the reader to unconditionally adopt them. While pessimistic, absurdist tragedy is a common artistic stance today, more can be gained in understanding the ending from the perspective of naturalism. Here human value is created by the protagonist's struggle, not his victory.

To create the meaning of the text, all perspectives must be merged and each redefined by the others. If the reader follows the shifting perspectives he is exalted by Archilde's quest and illuminated by what Archilde learns. The reader realizes that conventional white mores will not serve the Indians. The Indian agent voices conventional wisdom with which the reader would have agreed at the beginning of the book, but by the end of the book the reader is transformed and that transformation is positive. His standpoint is outside the text and the meaning of the text is created by him. The textual structures direct the reader to the only standpoint that will correspond to the confluence of the various perspectives; at this viewpoint he can assemble the meaning toward which the perspectives of the text have led. He has seen the history of misunderstanding on both sides; he knows that while the return to tradition and the past which Modeste and Katherine represent sustains Indian identity, it will not serve to avoid the tragedies of the present. While the character Archilde is doomed, the lasting transformation of *The Surrounded* is in the reader as he adopts new attitudes and adds them to his store of experience. Or as Iser concludes: "The text must therefore bring about a standpoint from which the reader will be able to view things that would never have come into focus as long as his own habitual dispositions were determining his orientation."

In *The Surrounded* McNickle has richly structured his text. The struggle and tragedy of the text have led the reader to new understandings through a process similar to the way that Archilde begins to understand Max only after the tragic killings, and Archilde perceives his strength and relation to his people only as his mother dies. Through the use of questioning the reader moves background concerns with social values into the foreground. Likewise McNickle uses doubling to encourage the implied reader not to identify with any one character's perspective. Ultimately his use of allegory and storytelling sets the implied reader into the position of a synthesizing audience through which the reader connects with the external world.

ARNOLD KRUPAT

The Dialogic of Silko's Storyteller

Autobiography as commonly understood in western European and Euro-American culture did not exist as a traditional type of literary expression among the aboriginal peoples of North America. Indeed, none of the conditions of production for autobiography—here I would isolate post-Napoleonic historicism, egocentric individualism and writing as foremost—was typical of Native American cultures. To the extent that the life stories, personal histories, memoirs or recollections of Indians did finally come into textual form (traditional Indian literatures were not written but oral), it was as a result of contact with and pressure from Euro-Americans. Until the twentieth century the most common form of Native American autobiography was the Indian autobiography, a genre of American writing constituted by the principle of original, bicultural, composite composition, in which there is a distinct if not always clear division of labor between the subject of the autobiography (the Indian to whom the first-person pronoun ostensibly makes reference) and the Euro-American editor responsible for fixing the text in writing, yet whose presence the first-person pronoun ostensibly masks. Indian autobiography may thus be distinguished from autobiography by Indians, the life stories of those christianized and/or "civilized" natives who, having internalized Western culture and scription, committed their lives to writing on their own without the mediation of the Euro-American. In autobiographies by Indians, although there is inevitably an element of biculturalism, there is not the element of compositeness that precisely marks Indian autobiographies.

From *Narrative Chance: Postmodern Discourse on Native American Indian Literatures.* © 1993 by the University of Oklahoma Press.

The earliest examples of Native American autobiography are two by Indians dating from the decades surrounding the American Revolution. These did not attract much attention; indeed, the more extensive of the two by Hendrick Aupaumut was not even published until 1827 and then in a journal of rather limited circulation. It was only six years later, however that the first Indian autobiography, J. B. Patterson's *Life of Black Hawk*, appeared. This book did gain widespread notice, coming as it did at a time of increased American interest in Indians (the book was occasioned by the last Indian war to be fought east of the Mississippi) and in the type of writing then only recently named autobiography (in 1809 by the poet Southey). Both of these interests are developed in this earliest type of Indian autobiography, which presents the acts of the world-historical chief or (of particular concern in the first half of the nineteenth century) the Indian hero. The historical orientation of Indian autobiography persisted in some form into the 1930s and 1940s after which none of the warriors was left alive to tell his tale. By that time there had already occurred a shift of interest on the part of Euro-American editors from history to science. In the twentieth century professional anthropologists rather than amateur historians would most commonly edit Indian autobiographies.

In our time Indian autobiographies continue to be co-produced by historians and social scientists working with traditional native people, but their labors have very nearly been overshadowed by the autobiographical writing of a new generation of Indians, educated in Western literate forms yet by no means acculturated to the point of abandoning respect for the old ways. These autobiographies are not only contributions to historical and scientific record, but also works of art (particularly the autobiographies of N. Scott Momaday and Leslie Marmon Silko, whose claim to national attention came not from their relation to American religion, history or anthropology, but from their relation to American literature as previously established in their fiction and poetry).

The history of Native American autobiography could be charted thematically as a movement from history and science to art on a line parallel to the history of European and Euro-American autobiography. To chart it thus would demonstrate that Native Americans have had to make a variety of accommodations to the dominant culture's forms, capitulating to them, assimilating them, sometimes dramatically transforming them, but never able to proceed independent of them. However, Native American autobiography differs materially from western European and Euro-American (though not strictly western American) autobiography through its existence in specifically individual and composite forms, or, both monologic and dialogic forms.

To introduce the terms monologue and dialogue is to invoke an important recent development in literary theory: recent interest in the Russian theorist, Mikhail Bakhtin.

So much has been written on Bakhtin of late that any attempt to summarize his thought is bound to be incomplete. In this country, at least, what is generally understood by reference to "Bakhtin," is very far from settled. To be sure "Freud" and "Marx" mean different things to different people as well; but there seems to be for Bakhtin, more than for these other major thinkers (and it is by no means generally agreed that comparison of Bakhtin to major thinkers is justified), a pronounced ambiguity. This openness may be functional, a practical illustration of what has been theoretically proposed. Perhaps it is not so much "openness," that Bakhtin's writing exhibits, but such inconsistency and ambiguity that it is difficult or pointless to specify the particulars of his thought. Hence, any attempt at an approximately neutral summary automatically becomes partial, a choice not between nuances but real differences. Nevertheless, the following briefly outlines what is at issue in Bakhtin and therefore at issue in any Bakhtinian reading of Native American autobiography.

Bakhtin calls human language "heteroglossic, polyvocal," the speech of each individual enabled and circumscribed not so much by language as a system as by the actual speech of other individuals. (In this he differs from Saussurian structural linguistics and its fascination with *langue*.) Speech is social and meaning is open and in flux, inevitably a dialogue among speakers, not the property or in the power of any single speaker. ". . . [A]ll there is to know about the world is not exhausted by a particular discourse about it . . . ," Bakhtin notes in a typical statement. Still some forms of written discourse and social practice seek to impose a single authoritative voice as the norm, thus subordinating or entirely suppressing other voices. It is the genre Bakhtin calls the "epic" that provides models of this monologic tendency in literature, while the totalitarianism of Stalinism under which Bakhtin lived provides the socio-political model of monologism. In opposition to the totalizing thrust of the epic, the novel testifies to its own (inevitable) incompleteness, its ongoing indebtedness to the discourse of others. The novel is the prime literary instance of dialogized speech.

Bakhtin seems to be committed to dialogue on empirical grounds, inasmuch as the term claims to name human communication correctly, pointing to the way speech and social life "really" are. But Bakhtin seems also to be committed to dialogue on moral and esthetic grounds; he approves of and is pleased by that which he finds di-, hetero-, poly-, and so on. For him, truth and beauty are one, but what this equivalence is to mean ultimately in a dialogic theory of language and of social life remains to be determined.

Does Bakhtinian dialogic envision a strong form of pluralism in which all have legitimate voice: truth having its particular authority, beauty having its, and both having equal (cognitive) force over other voices, which, although worthy of being heard, can be judged decidably less forceful? Or does Bakhtinian dialogic envision a kind of postmodernist free play of voices with no normative means for deciding their relative worth or authority? We do not know whether Bakhtin's dislike of what he calls monologue permits some forms of relatively stable assertion, in particular truth and beauty. Such statements as "the last word is never said,"—and there are innumerable such statements in Bakhtin's writing—may intend a radically ironic, a schizophrenic refusal (in Jameson's very particular sense) of any form, however relativized, of grounded meaning. Or they may insist only that no single language act has the capacity to encompass the entire range of humanly possible meaning, as no single mode of political organization can give full latitude to human potential.

In this latter regard the issue is particularly complicated because, while we do know from Bakhtin that the novel is supposed to provide the fullest literary illustration of relativized, dialogic discourse, we do not know whether the nearest thing he gives us to a socio-political equivalent of the novel, rabelaisian "carnival," represents an actual model for social organization or an escape from too rigid social organization. In either case, we do not know what Bakhtinian carnival might actually entail for current or future social formations. To examine Native American autobiography from a Bakhtinian perspective, then, is not only to consider it as a discursive type— a kind of literature, generically closer to the epic or the novel as Bakhtin understands these Western forms—but as a social model which allows for the projection of a particular image of human community.

Let me now offer a reading of Leslie Marmon Silko's *Storyteller* in relation to these issues.

Merely to consider *Storyteller* among Native American autobiographies might require some explanation, since the book is a collection of stories, poems and photographs as much as it is a narrative of its author's life. Of course a variety of claims have been made in the recent past for the fictionality of autobiographies in general, the autobiography being recognized as the West's most obviously dialogic genre in which a conversation between *historia* and *poesis*, documentation and creation, is always in progress. And some of these claims might easily be used to justify classifying *Storyteller* as an autobiography.

Indeed, to justify the book's classification as an autobiography in this way, would not be mistaken; it would, however, be to treat it exclusively from a Western perspective, failing to acknowledge that traditional Native American literary forms were not—and, in their contemporary manifestations usually are not—as concerned about keeping fiction and fact or poetry and prose distinct from one another. It is the distinction between truth and error rather than that between fact and fiction that seems more interesting to native expression; and indeed, this distinction was also central to Western thought prior to the seventeenth century. Thus the present "blurring of genres," in Clifford Geertz's phrase, in both the social sciences and in the arts, is actually only a return to that time when the line between history and myth was not very clearly marked. But that is the way things have always been for Native American literatures.

From the Western point of view, Silko's book would seem to announce by its title, *Storyteller*, the familiar pattern of discovering who one is by discovering what one does, the pattern of identity in vocation. This is useful enough as a way to view Silko's text. In the West it has been a very long time since the vocational storyteller has had a clear and conventional social role. In Pueblo culture, however, to be known as a storyteller is to be known as one who participates, in a communally sanctioned manner, in sustaining the group; for a Native American writer to identify herself as a storyteller today is to express a desire to perform such a function. In the classic terms of Marcel Mauss, person, self and role are here joined.

Silko dedicates her book "to the storytellers as far back as memory goes and to the telling which continues and through which they all live and we with them." Having called herself a storyteller, she thus places herself in a tradition of tellings, suggesting that her stories cannot strictly be her own nor will we find in them what one typically looks for in post-Rousseauan, Western autobiography or (as Bakhtin would add, in poetry) a uniquely personal voice. There is no single, distinctive or authoritative voice in Silko's book nor any striving for such a voice; to the contrary, Silko will take pains to indicate how even her own individual speech is the product of many voices. *Storyteller* is presented as a strongly polyphonic text in which the author defines herself—finds her voice, tells her life, illustrates the capacities of her vocation—in relation to the voices of other native and nonnative storytellers, tale tellers and book writers, and even to the voices of those who serve as the (by-no-means silent) audience for these stories.

It is Silko's biographical voice that commences the book, but not by speaking of her birth or the earliest recollections of childhood as Western autobiography usually dictates. Rather, she begins by establishing the relation of "hundreds of photographs taken since the 1890s around Laguna" that she finds in "a tall Hopi basket" to "the stories as [she] remembers them." Visual stories, speaking pictures, here as in the familiar Western understanding will also provide a voice; and Silko's developing relation to every kind of story becomes the story of her life.

Dennis Tedlock has made the important point that Zuni stories are fashioned in such a way as to include in their telling not just the story itself but a critique of or commentary on those stories, and Silko's autobiographical story will also permit a critical dimension, voices that comment on stories and storytellers—storytellers like her Aunt Susie, who, when she told stories had "certain phrases, certain distinctive words/she used in her telling" (7). Both Aunt Susie and Aunt Alice "would tell me stories they had told me before but with changes in details or descriptions. . . . There were even stories about the different versions of stories and how they imagined these differing versions came to be" (227). Silko's own versions of stories she has heard from Simon Ortiz, the Acoma writer whom Silko acknowledges as the source of her prose tale, "Uncle Tony's Goat," and her verse tale, "Skeleton Fixer," also introduce certain phrases and distinctive words that make them identifiably her own. Yet these and all the other stories are never presented as the final or definitive version; although they are intensely associated with their different tellers, they remain available for other tellings. "What is realized in the novel," Bakhtin has written, "is the process of coming to know one's own language as it is perceived in someone else's language . . ." (365) and so, too, to know one's own language as bound up with "someone else's language." Any story Silko herself tells, then, is always bound up with someone else's language; it is always a version and the story as version stands in relation to the story as officially sanctioned myth, as the novel stands to the national epic. Silko's stories are always consistent with—to return to Bakhtin—attempts to liberate ". . . cultural-semantic and emotional intentions from the hegemony of a single and unitary language," consistent with a ". . . loss of feeling for language as myth, that is, as an absolute form of thought" (367).

Stories are transmitted by other storytellers, as Silko wrote early in her book:

> by word of mouth
> an entire history
> an entire vision of the world
> which depended upon memory
> and retelling by subsequent generations.

. . . .
. . . the oral tradition depends upon each person
listening and remembering a portion. . . . (6-7)

But the awareness of and respect for the oral tradition, here, is not a kind of
sentimental privileging of the old ways. Indeed, this first reference to the
importance of cultural transmission by oral means comes in a lovely memorial to Aunt Susie who, Silko writes:

> From the time that I can remember her
> . . . worked on her kitchen table
> with her books and papers spread over the oil cloth.
> She wrote beautiful long hand script
> but her eyesight was not good
> and so she wrote very slowly.
> . . . .
> She had come to believe very much in books

It is Aunt Susie, the believer in books and in writing, who was of "the last
generation here at Laguna, / that passed an entire culture by word of
mouth. . . ." Silko's own writing is compared to oral telling by a neighbor,
who, finding her "Laguna Coyote" poem in a library book, remarks:

> "We all enjoyed it so much,
> but I was telling the children
> the way my grandpa used to tell it
> is longer."

To this critical voice, Silko responds:

> "Yes, that's the trouble with writing . . .
> You can't go on and on the way we do
> when we tell stories around here.
> People who aren't used to it get tired" (110).

This awareness of the audience is entirely typical for a native storyteller who
cannot go forward with a tale without the audience's response. As Silko writes:

> *The Laguna people*
> *always begin their stories*

with "humma-hah":
that means "long ago."
And the ones who are listening
say "aaaa-eh" (38)

These are the stories, of course, of the oral tradition. Silko invokes the feel of "long ago" both in the verse format she frequently uses and in the prose pieces, although perhaps only those sections of the book set in verse attempt to evoke something of the actual feel of an oral telling.

It is interesting to note that there are two pieces in the book that echo the title, one in prose and the other set in loose verse. The first, "Storyteller," is an intense and powerful short story which takes place in Alaska. The story-teller of the title is the protagonist's grandfather, a rather less benign figure than the old storytellers of Silko's biographical experience; nonetheless, the stories he tells are of the traditional, mythic type. The second, "Storytelling," is a kind of mini-anthology of several short tales of women and their (quite historical, if fictional!) sexual adventures. The "humma-hah" (in effect) of the first section goes:

> You should understand
> the way it was
> back then,
> because it is the same
> even now (94).
>   [aaaa-eh]

The final section has its unnamed speaker conclude:

> My husband
> left
> after he heard the story
> and moved back in with his mother.
> It was my fault and
> I don't blame him either.
> I could have told
> the story
> better than I did (98).

In both these pieces ("Storyteller" and "Storytelling") we find a very different sense of verbal art from that expressed in the West in something like Auden's lines (in the poem on the death of Yeats), where he writes that "poetry makes nothing happen. . . ." In deadly serious prose and in witty verse, Silko dramatizes her belief that stories—both the mythic-traditional tales passed down among the people and the day-to-day narrations of events—do make things happen. The two pieces refer to very different kinds of stories which, in their capacity to produce material effects, are nonetheless the same.

Among other identifiable voices in Silko's texts are her own epistolary voice in letters she has written to Lawson F. Inada and James A. Wright, the voices of Coyote and Buffalo, and those of traditional figures like Kochininako, Whirlwind Man, Arrowboy, Spider Woman and Yellow Woman—some of whom appear in modern day incarnations. In stories or letters or poems, in monologues or dialogues, the diction may vary—now more colloquial and/or regional, now more formal—or the tone—lyrical, humorous, meditative. Yet always, the effort is to make us hear the various languages that constitute Silko's world and so herself. If we agree with Bakhtin that, "The primary stylistic project of the novel as a genre is to create images of languages" (366), *Storyteller* is a clear instance of novelized discourse, Native American autobiography of the dialogic type. It remains to say what the implications of this particular dialogic discourse may be.

I have tried to read *Storyteller* as an example of Native American autobiography in the dialogic mode, that is, against the backdrop of Bakhtin's meditations on language and society. By way of conclusion, it seems useful to see what Silko's book has to say about these important subjects, or more accurately, what projections about language and society might be made from the book. To interrogate the text in this way is not to treat it foremost as ethnic or hyphenated literature (although it cannot be understood in ignorance of its informing context) but as a candidate for inclusion in the canon of American literature conceived of as a selection of the most important work from among national texts (*American* literature) and texts (for all the blurring of genres) of a certain kind (American *literature*).

Let me review the possibilities. In regard to its understanding of language and the nature of communication, on one hand a commitment to dialogism may be seen as a recognition of the necessity of an infinite semantic openness. Here the inescapable possibility of yet some further voice is crucial inasmuch as that voice may decisively alter or ambiguate any relatively stable meaning one might claim to understand. On the other hand, a commitment to dialogism may be seen as a type of radical pluralism, a more relativized openness, concerned with stating meanings provisionally in recognition of the legitimate claims of otherness and difference. In regard to its implied model of the social, a commitment to dialogism may be seen as envisioning, "a carnivalesque arena of diversity," as James Clifford has described it, "a utopian . . . space," where the utopian exists as a category of pure abstraction, an image out of time and oblivious to the conditions of historical possibility: diversity as limitless freeplay. Or a commitment to dialogism may envision—but here one encounters difficulties, for it is hard to name or describe the sort of democratic and egalitarian community that would be the political equivalent of a radical pluralism as distinct from an infinite openness. No doubt, traditional Native American models of communal organization need further study in this regard, although it is not at all clear how the present-day Pueblo or the nineteenth-century Plains camp circle might be incorporated into models of some harmonious world-community to come.

Let me, then, name the alternative to dialogism as carnival and polymorphous diversity, what Paul Rabinow has called cosmopolitanism. "Let us define cosmopolitanism," Rabinow writes, "as an ethos of macro-interdependencies, with an acute consciousness (often forced upon people) of the inescapabilities and particularities of places, characters, historical trajectories, and fates." The trick is to avoid "reify[ing] local identities or construct[ing] universal ones," a trick, as Rabinow notes, that requires a rather delicate balancing act, one that the West has had a difficult time managing. For all the seeming irony of proposing that the highly place-oriented and more or less homogenous cultures of indigenous Americans might best teach us how to be cosmopolitans, that is exactly what I mean to say. But here let me return to *Storyteller*.

Storyteller is open to a plurality of voices. What keeps it from entering the poststructuralist, postmodernist or schizophrenic heteroglossic domain is its commitment to the equivalent of a normative voice. For all the polyvocal openness of Silko's work, there is always the unabashed commitment to Pueblo ways as a reference point. This may be modified, updated, playfully construed: but its authority is always to be reckoned with. Whatever one understands from any speaker is to be understood in reference to that. Here we find dialogic as dialectic (not, it seems, the case in Bakhtin!), meaning as the interaction of any voiced value whatever and the centered voice of the Pueblo.

If this account of *Storyteller*'s semantics, or theory of meaning, is at all accurate, it would follow that its political unconscious is more easily conformable to Rabinow's cosmopolitanism than to a utopianized carnival. The social implications of *Storyteller*'s dialogism might be a vision of an American cosmopolitanism to come that permits racial and cultural voices at home (in both "residual" and "emerging" forms) to speak fully and that opens its ears to other voices abroad. This is an image, to be sure, not a political program; and to imagine the "polyvocal polity" in this way is also utopian, but perhaps only in the sense that it is not yet imminent.

Silko's book says nothing of this, offering neither a theory of communication nor of politics. To take it seriously, however, is to see it as more than merely evocative, amusing, expressive or informative (to the mainstream reader curious about the exotic ways of marginalized communities). It is to see its art as a matter of values that are most certainly not only aesthetic.

GREG SARRIS

Reading Narrated American Indian Lives:

Elizabeth Colson's *Autobiographies of Three Pomo Women*

One cold winter night some twenty-five years ago I listened to Great-Grandma Nettie tell the following story about her life:

"Come that man what his name. That one, that old man come. Come there that time. Put hands on table, like that [gesturing with her hands turned down]. Give meat, first thing. That way know if poison man. Come to poison or what. Don't know. Watch. Listen.

"Just girl that time. Ten, maybe twelve. But that man stranger man. Come looking for mother. Says that, come looking for mother. Saying that. Where mother? Says that. Not here. No mother here. Come in anyway, that man. Come in like that.

"Me just girl that time. Ten years. Ten. Sitting alone. No mother. But start looking for meat. Only thing dry meat—*bishe*. Need live meat old rule way. Need live meat for poison people. But put dry meat out. Put there. Put like that.

"Don't talk Indian, that man. Talk only Spanish. Look like Spanish, too. Light skin, that man. Still, half-Indian know something. Like old man Sensi. Done like that. Done old lady Mary other side creek like that. Done basket putting like that. He done like that, they say.

"Don't touch meat, that man. Nothing. Talking Spanish. Talking,

From *Keeping Slug Women Alive: A Holistic Approach to American Indian Texts*. © 1993 by The Regents of the University of California.

talking, talking . . . Ten that time,' bout that age. Only girl. Only know
sí. Mean yes. Yes. I say sí [laughing]. Say that, that's all. Say sí. Say like
that. Say sí.

"Then happen man eat meat. Then happen never go again. Sitting
there all day, that man. Sitting there hands on table, like that [gesturing
with her hands turned down]. Hands like that, same. Maybe rape, do me
like that. I start working roots. Start working basket roots, watching that
man. Work, watching that man. Put food out sometime, acorn.

"Nighttime mother come up. Come up road there. Later time
mother say good thing keeping busy. Good watching that man. Fool
that man. Fool that way. Trust no stranger people. No stranger people.
Old man Sensi. Done old lady like that, they say.

"Don't know what. Not poison me. What. Don't know. Don't know.
Mother don't say. Just talking to that man. Just talking. Talking like that.
Talking, talking, talking, talking . . ."

At the time Great-Grandma Nettie, as she was known to half our neighborhood, must have been ninety years old. She was small and wizened, with a
shock of straight white hair. Yet Nettie was formidable. She commanded attention. You saw when she flicked her wrist, pointed with her extended chin and
great downturned mouth. She sat leaning forward in an overstuffed chair
opposite the television, her gnarled hands clutching the ends of the armrests,
as if at any moment she would spring to her feet and set things straight.

That particular night Old Auntie Eleanor was visiting Great-Grandma
Nettie. Eleanor was a big, boisterous woman who lived down the road. She was
younger than Nettie, but not by much. She walked over a mile to visit and
reminisce with Nettie. Sometimes they argued about this or that. They
gossiped. They always conversed with one another in Indian, in their central
Pomo language, and talked, whether or not anyone was listening, no matter
how loud the television was. And that's what caught my attention: Great-
Grandma Nettie switched to English. And when she saw that I was listening,
she cast a suspicious glance. I felt self-conscious, confused. Was she saying
something for me or about me? Was I an *insider* or an *outsider*?

Unlike most of the children in the room just then, I was not a direct
descendant of Nettie's, not one of her grandchildren or great-grandchildren.
And I was a mixed blood. I was living back and forth in Indian and white families. Nettie was telling a story from her life, but with her suspicious glances
and all that talk in English about strangers, she called to mind my own life, that
uncomfortable borderlands existence that I was reminded of at times like this.

I became Indian. I ignored her. Silence, the Indian's best weapon, an aunt of mine once said. Be an Indian, cut yourself off with silence any way you can. Don't talk. Don't give yourself away. I knew certain Kashaya words, phrases. The Kashaya Pomo, or southwestern Pomo, language is different from but similar to the central Pomo language Great-Grandma Nettie and Old Auntie Eleanor spoke. When Nettie finished her story, or at a given point in the story, she switched back to her Indian language. I was still listening, even with my eyes fixed on the televisor. She repeated the word *bishun*, or a word that sounded like *bishun*, which means "stranger" in Kashaya. Then she said something like *chu 'um qat 'to mul*, "Don't forget this!" And now, looking back, I imagine she said something that meant the same as this: *mi qe bake 'eh mau ama diche mu*, "This story is for you."

Great-Grandma Nettie's story haunts me. Throw it out the back door and find it looking through the front room window. I see it in a glance, the way someone is looking at me. I hear it in people's voices, in the words they use to talk to me. They don't say the exact words, but I hear the words all the same. Insider. Outsider. Indian. White.

I found this story again as I read and thought about Elizabeth Colson's *Autobiographies of Three Pomo Women*. Though Colson changed the three Pomo narrators' names as well as the place-names of the area in which they lived, it is clear that the narrators, called Sophie Martinez, Ellen Wood, and Jane Adams, were central Pomo. And, like Nettie and Eleanor, who were central Pomo, the narrators were born during the latter part of the nineteenth century. They probably spoke a central Pomo language identical or similar to Nettie and Eleanor's. Each of the three Pomo women came from a different central Pomo group and spoke a different central Pomo dialect (Colson 1). Nettie and Eleanor probably spoke one of these dialects. They probably would have been able to understand to some extent whatever language any one of these three Pomo narrators spoke. They shared the same history as the three Pomo narrators. They talked about some of the same things: people's names and how Indians name people; the poisoners and the medicine men and women and their stupendous deeds; the slave raids and the "raping time," first with the Spanish and then with the Mexicans and the American squatters who followed the Spanish as invaders of Pomo territory.

> My mother called me *tidai*. She would say that to me. She called me *mata* too. *Tidal* is just language. *Mata* means "woman," but not that way. In some different way, I think.
>
>   Sophie Martinez (Colson 40)

I was sick. I had lain in bed about five months. . . . Everybody doctored

me that time. . . . That's why we have no beads. We paid those five
people. They were all singing doctors.

Sophie Martinez (Colson 78)

Those days when first Mexicans came up here, they just grab the girls
and take them in bushes. Have the pistol in one hand and do what they
want and then let them go. My old aunt say they take her once. They
put them in a house. One night she pried a board away and got away.

Ellen Wood (Colson 112–113)

Once I was sick for a long time. Something was wrong with my legs—
somebody had poisoned me. They had taken my shoes and put them in
a poison place.

Ellen Wood (Colson 169)

When I was a little girl, I used to go around with my mother digging
basket roots. It wasn't so hard that time. We sneak around the river. But
now [white landowners] won't let you. They make you get out of their
place.

Jane Adams (Colson 202)

So I thought of Great-Grandma Nettie and Old Auntie Eleanor as I read.
But when I gave the text a chance, when I looked at what I was reading, I found
much that was different from what I remember hearing, especially in terms of
language and narrative format and what was said or not said about certain
things. I remember Nettie's English as different from that of the three Pomo
narrators. Nettie repeated herself often. She seldom used pronouns and
frequently began sentences with a verb which she repeated in successive
sentences. Nettie rarely talked to strangers, especially about strangers. "Don't
talk much with outside people," Nettie and Eleanor admonished. "Careful what
you tell." When the professors visited each summer, Nettie became silent.
Eleanor gave short, flat answers and told stories no one in the house had ever
heard. My memory of Nettie's silence and Eleanor's short answers reminded me
that the three Pomo narrators were talking to Colson. Isn't it likely that the
three Pomo narrators edited their stories in certain ways for Colson? The
anthropologist Elizabeth Colson not only went into the central Pomo community and collected the autobiographies, which has something to do with what
was said, but she also edited and wrote them, which has something to do with
their language and narrative format.

As I thought about the three Pomo narrators and Colson, I remembered hearing the old ones talking that winter night. I thought of Great-Grandma Nettie's story and her suspicious glances. I felt uncomfortable again. My impulse as a critic was to say what was truly Pomo, so that I could show what Colson missed, how ignorant she was as an outsider to Pomo culture. But who am I to speak for and define the central Pomo or any Pomo? To what extent would I be creating an Indian just as Colson had, albeit an Indian different from Colson's? Who am I as a spokesperson for either the Pomo or Colson? Who am I as a Pomo Indian ? Who am I as a critic? I am caught in the borderlands again. Nettie's story once more. *Autobiographies of Three Pomo Women* is also a story for me. The text says to me: *mi qe bake 'eh mau ama diche mu.*

In this chapter I want to read *Autobiographies of Three Pomo Women* (hereafter referred to as *Autobiographies*) so that I may begin to understand it as a cross-cultural project. But, at the same time, I must begin to understand it as a story for me, not only as a story that positions me in certain ways but also as a story that can inform me about that position. In light of the constitutive characteristics of narrated American Indian autobiography and of critical work surrounding the genre, I will etch out a way to read the text so that I can see the text as well as myself as reader, so that I might inform the text and allow the text to inform me. Then I will come back to and further the discussion of myself and the text that I have started here. Of course even in my discussion of the genre and an approach to it, I will be talking about myself and the text, specifically in terms of the questions this relationship provokes. While much of this discussion is narrow in focus, principally because it concerns one reader and one text, I hope that it raises questions and offers suggestions about reading narrated American Indian autobiography in general, and so might contribute to larger discussions of reading cross-cultural texts in various cultural contexts.

READING STORIES, READING STRANGERS: READING AUTOBIOGRAPHIES OF THREE POMO WOMEN

Naturally not all American Indian autobiographies are narrated. Here I am discussing narrated autobiographies, and distinguishing them from those that are written. With narrated autobiographies, a recorder-editor records and transcribes what was given orally by the Indian subject. Written autobiographies, on the other hand, are written by the Indian subjects themselves with or without the assistance of editors. Arnold Krupat, who refers to narrated Indian autobiographies as Indian autobiographies, as opposed to autobiographies (written) by Indians, notes: "The principle constituting the [narrated] Indian autobiography as a genre [is] that of *original bicultural composition*" (31). This principle not only provides the key to the narrated autobiography's discursive type but "provides as well the key to its discursive function, its purposive dimension as an act of power and will. [It is the] ground on which two cultures meet . . . the textual equivalent of the frontier" (Krupat 31). Yet seldom is the story of that meeting apparent or revealed in the text. While there is a wide spectrum of editorial strategies for dealing with point of view in narrated Indian autobiography, the oldest and most common is what David Brumble calls the *Absent Editor* strategy, where the editor edits and presents the Indian's narrative "in such a way as to create the fiction that the narrative is all the Indian's own . . . that the Indians speak to us without mediation (Brumble 1988, 75–76).

The notion of autobiography as fiction, or interpretation, is nothing new. The autobiography, whether narrated or written, is not the life but an account or story of the life. A narrated American Indian autobiography then is in actuality an account of an account, a story of a story; the name of the self is hardly the Indian's own (Eakin 214). As Vincent Crapanzano (1977) observes, "[the life history] is, as it were, doubly edited, during the encounter itself [between recorder-editor and narrator] and during the literary reencounter" (4). In the encounter between non-Indian recorder-editor and Indian narrator, it is important to remember that given the specific social contingencies of the exchange, the Indian may be editing and shaping his or her oral narrative in certain ways, just as Old Auntie Eleanor gave the professors short, flat answers and told stories no one in the household had ever heard. Then, after the Indian has presented an oral narrative, the recorder-editor translates and shapes it in certain ways. The language and format of the original narrative are often altered significantly as they are translated into English or into a more "standard" English and shaped to meet the requirements of linear chronology, human motivation, and so forth imposed by the autobiographical genre. Yet, as mentioned, the extent to which the Indian's narrative is altered in these ways by the recorder-editor is often unclear and is not discussed at length, or at all, by the recorder-editor. In addition, it is difficult for the recorder-editor to know the ways the Indian narrator may have edited the narrative for the recorder-editor.

In *Autobiographies* Elizabeth Colson provides introductory material about her collecting and editing the Pomo womens' autobiographies. She also offers "a considered sketch" (2), or brief ethnography, of Pomo culture as well as her analysis of the autobiographies. She notes in her introductory material that for each of the three Pomo narrators she provides a long autobiographical account and a brief autobiographical account. She says that her method was first to collect this latter brief account from the women and then to ask questions to get them to enlarge on certain points, to identify persons mentioned, and to present material in chronological order (Colson 4). She then combined each one's brief initial account with the responses to these questions to produce the longer autobiography. She says the verbatim record of the brief autobiography can be found in an appendix after each long autobiography "since for some purposes it is essential to know just what was regarded as important by the narrator, or at least what she was willing to tell of her life given the time and circumstances" (2). Colson talks not only about the questions she asked and about how she combined them with the brief autobiographical narratives but also about the changes she made in the narrators' English (the interviews were conducted in English). But everything Colson says in her introductory material about her collecting and editing the narratives is from her point of view. What of her biases that she may not have been fully aware of? What of the ways her presuppositions about language and narrative format influenced her decisions regarding her editing of the narratives? How much could she have known about each Pomo woman's community and her position in it? What of the Pomo women's point of view about what Colson says? Or their point of view about the collaboration in general? Or about the written text? All that can be known from Colson's introductory material regarding these last three questions is that the Pomo women did not take part in the literary reencounter, that is, in the editing of what they had already said for Colson. They were not consulted in any way. Colson made the decisions about editing the spoken text on her own.

It is not enough then just to study Colson's introductory material if I want to understand how *Autobiographies* was made, how both Colson and the three Pomo women participated in its production. Except for including in the longer autobiographical accounts the questions she asked the narrators, Colson does not place herself in the texts of the narrators and functions as Absent Editor. She does not say in her introductory material how the questions she asked may have influenced the women's responses. Granted, her introductory material regarding her collecting and editing of the narratives is abundant, more extensive than that of many other recorder-editors. But fundamental questions about what each collaborator contributed to or omitted from the text remain. How do I deal with those fundamental questions, specifically those I raised about Colson and her biases? About the Indian women's biases and how the Indian women may have edited their spoken narratives for Colson? I have come back to my original questions then. How do I begin to understand *Autobiographies* as a collaborative endeavor? And what of my own biases, my position as a reader? If I can inform the text in given ways, how might the text in turn inform me?

It is clear at this point that my approach to *Autobiographies* must consider the cultural and historical background of both Colson and the Pomo narrators. Then I might be able to gain a sense not only of what each collaborator contributed to the text and of the nature of the relationship between the collaborators but also of myself as a reader. If I overlook or do not consider seriously one of the collaborator's roles in the production of the text, I am blinded to what that collaborator may have contributed to the composite text and hence to what makes for a fuller understanding of the relationship between collaborators. But, just as important, I may be blinded to the ways I am reading, to my presence and the nature of my relationship with culturally diverse perspectives. When I consider both Colson and the Pomo women, I am reminded of my often uncomfortable position in the cultures of both Colson and the Pomo women and of the ways those cultures intersect in time and place. Those cultures intersect in *Autobiographies*. By using what I know from research and experience, I can speculate on what each collaborator brought to their meeting that resulted in the text at hand. Thus I can gain a broader picture of the relationship between Colson and the narrators and of what constituted the relationship and the making of the text. What constituted the relationship, say patterns of avoidance or projection in the case of one or both parties, illuminates and is located in the history of Pomo and white interrelations. Since I am located in this same history and am positioned as a cultural subject by it, I can now begin to see more clearly how these particular interrelations affect me and in turn how I might affect them. Reciprocity characterizes the approach; I inform a text which informs me.

I emphasized the word *speculate* for definite reasons. The objective here is not to frame *Autobiographies*, not to tell the story of the text's making or of Colson or the Pomo women. Since in the text there are at least two parties present, in addition to a reader, there is no one story, nor can there ever be. And, again, as a reader I cannot assume knowledge and authority to speak for others and their relationships. Rather, the objective is to open a dialogue with the text such that I can continue to inform and be informed by the text. Then my dialogue, my representation of my relationship with the text, can inform and be informed by other readers with different stories who read the text. In this way, the history, and what constitutes the history, of interrelations between the Pomo and white communities is continually opened and explored. The text can be opened and explored in terms of other histories or a larger history of which the text may be a part. So much depends on the readers and what they bring to the text and to my reading of the text and on what the text and my reading can suggest to them.

The danger, and likely consequence, of assuming knowledge and power in my encounter with *Autobiographies*, specifically in the ways I might define Colson or the Pomo narrators, is that in losing sight of my presence as a reader I will not see how my critical work is tied historically and politically to a real world. Scholars of narrated American Indian autobiography sometimes position themselves in their encounters with the texts in such a way that they do not seem to see the limits of their work or its consequences in a historical and political realm. They may define the autobiographical works as bicultural and composite, but they do not consider each of the collaborator's histories and cultures on the respective collaborator's terms, at least not in a way that might enable the scholars to think about the nature of their work as scholars and its consequences.

Arnold Krupat, for example, argues for a historic approach in his principal study of the genre, *For Those Who Come After*. He examines the relation of various narrated autobiographies to a historical period, to the discursive categories of history, science, and art (literature), and to Western modes of emplotment (xii) in order to answer questions regarding the text's production. But the historical period Krupat discusses in detail is, in point of view, distinctly EuroAmerican. He observes that recorder-editor S. M. Barrett, influenced by the objectivism of turn-of-the-century American social science and salvage anthropology, presents Geronimo, in *Geronimo's Story of His Life*, in a way that Geronimo is "denied the context of heroism [and] of individuality as well; for he is no different from 'any captive,' any 'prisoner of war,' no world-historical figure, but just another 'vanishing type'" (63). But what about Geronimo and Apache history, culture, and language? What about the ways Geronimo may have accommodated or resisted such a presentation of his life? Krupat does not see or discuss how he also has denied Geronimo context, in this case as a collaborator in the making of a composite text.

David H. Brumble in *American Indian Autobiography* may account for the Indian's part in the production of a particular narrated autobiography, but he invents "an Indian" as a way to make sense of this individual. He identifies anything nonrecognizable or unfamiliar in a narrated American Indian autobiography, such as the presentation of seemingly disconnected deeds or actions, as authentic, as Indian as opposed to Euro-American. From this identification he deduces a tribal (Indian, nonliterate, unacculturated, ahistorical) sense of self distinguishable from an individual (Euro-American, literate, cultured, historical) sense of self. Brumble concludes that Gregorio's sense of self in *Gregorio, The Hand Trembler* "was essentially tribal": "[For Red Crow, like Gregorio] we search in vain for any examination of his self,

any self-definition, any sense that he might have been other than he was. . . .
We are allowed to see clearly just how a preliterate, unacculturated, tribal
man conceives of his life and what it means to tell the story of a life"
(101–11). The reality of the situation is that the self which is identifiable as
Indian, and has come to signify Indian in the text, is Indian in contact with
non-Indian. As Brumble points out, Gregorio listened while Alexander and
Dorothea Leighton interviewed other Navajos in his neighborhood before
he told them his story in 1940 (111). Gregorio probably ordered and
presented an account of his life in a way he thought appropriate given the
circumstances; he probably talked about things he figured the Leightons
wanted to hear and that he had heard other Indians discussing with the
Leightons. Seemingly disconnected deeds or actions are likely to indicate
Gregorio's unease with the genre and circumstances rather than his inability
to examine and define his self. Of course Brumble was looking for the ways
Gregorio, as he is presented textually, fit Brumble's definition of "Indian,"
and he did not consider the ways Gregorio and the situation of the text's
making may have qualified that definition.

In *American Indian Women: Telling Their Lives*, Gretchen Bataille and
Kathleen Sands examine "several autobiographies in terms of what they tell
us about the reality of American Indian women's lives" (viii). They propose a
"close examination of individual texts . . . to discern the thematic patterns [of
tradition and culture contact, acculturation, and return to tradition]" (24).
But Bataille and Sands seem to forget that these themes or thematic patterns
not only may have been invented by them for the texts and understood in
terms of their particular interests (and their lives as non-Indian women), but
also may emerge in the written documents as a result of the particular interests of the recorder-editors. Bataille and Sands never question how their
themes may or may not be relevant from the point of view of the Indian
women narrators.

Just as Brumble invents an "Indian self," so Bataille and Sands use
themes and interests to frame or make sense of the Indian. The Indian has
no voice of his or her own; the Indian is not considered in terms of his or her
history, culture, and language. Krupat, Brumble, Bataille and Sands have all
thus essentially positioned themselves so that questions of Indian history,
culture, and language cannot inform their work. If Krupat, for example, in
his encounter with *Geronimo's Story of His Life*, had in fact considered Apache
history, culture, and language, particularly as presented by Apache Indians
orally or otherwise, he might have seen himself as present and gained a
broader understanding of the text. He would have had to ask, or at least he
would have had the opportunity to ask, questions that might have reminded

him of his presence and bias. Can Apache stories, songs, and so forth be read or heard and thus understood in terms of Euro-American-specific expectations of language and narrative? If not, why not? What is gained or lost when they are? What from Krupat's perspective or an Apache perspective hinders Krupat's understanding of Geronimo? What might help Krupat understand? How might answers to these questions promote a better understanding of Barrett, or of that history, culture, and language in *Geronimo's Story of His Life* which may have seemed more familiar to Krupat? If Krupat knew more about himself as a reader and more about Geronimo, he might have been able to ask more questions about his reading of Barrett and so to see Barrett in new ways. Likewise, the Indian narrator's background might have helped Brumble and Bataille and Sands open a broader understanding of themselves and the texts they read. They might have seen the limits and consequences of their inventions and themes in their attempts to understand the Indian narrators. In any event, what all these scholars do not seem to see is that while purportedly defending Indians and enlightening others about them, they replicate in practice that which characterizes not only certain non-Indian editors' manner of dealing with Indians but also that of an entire European and Euro-American populace of which these editors and scholars are a part. The Indians are absent or they are strategically removed from the territory, made safe, intelligible on the colonizer's terms.

The questions and issues raised in terms of these scholars' work should not be thought of as simply insider/outsider problems. It is important to note that, regardless of the reader's cultural and historical affiliations, he or she is not a perfect lens into the life and circumstances of either the non-Indian recorder-editor or the Indian narrator. A non-Indian scholar using a historical approach, for example, to understand a non-Indian recorder-editor's historical and cultural influences, may be unfamiliar with or unaware of the recorder-editor's community, place, and time and of how these affect what has been recorded and how the recorded material has been edited. S. M. Barrett worked at a time before Krupat was born. Differing subjectivities are at play within any tradition. An Indian, either as a scholar working in the university or as a nonuniversity tribal scholar working as a consultant for a non-Indian's scholarly enterprise, is not an objective purveyor of the so-called truths of his or her culture. This is certainly the case among the Pomo, where what constitutes, among other things, authentic cultural and religious practices can vary in definition from group to group and even from family to family within a group. And what an Indian knows from his or her tribe may not apply to other tribes. In terms of their histories, cultures, and languages Indian people are different, sometimes radically different, from tribe to tribe.

In any narrated American Indian autobiography there are at least two parties present. And, just as in my own reading of *Autobiographies,* readers cannot assume knowledge and power to know and represent others and their relationship to a text. If a reader is knowledgeable about a given historical period or a particular collaborator's culture, questions still remain regarding what constitutes the reader's knowing. Specifically, how does the reader understand and use his or her own knowledge to frame or make sense of elements in a text? For the presence of both a non-Indian and a Pomo Indian in the single text provokes those questions. Who am I as a reader? Indian? Non-Indian? Scholar? How do I position myself and what are the consequences of that positioning? For many non-Indian readers questions might arise as a result of their encounters with the Indian narrator's culture and language. Whatever it is, wherever the tensions are felt, is a place to start, a place for readers to open dialogue with both the non-Indian recorder-editor and the Indian narrator in a text. It is a place to see the questions that arise from the tension, and ultimately a place where the reader can begin to explore the questions and possible answers. The dialogue that starts in one place opens the text and the readers' stories of their relationships with the text, stories that, in turn, inform other readers' stories, continually opening and exploring the *original bicultural composition* at hand.

So much of what we do as readers of texts is unconscious. We aren't aware of all the cultural and personal influences that determine how we read; we aren't aware of our self-boundaries and how we work to tighten or widen them in our encounters with texts. In the approach I have described the reader can begin to unravel what may be unspoken and unconscious in the making of a bicultural text as well as what may be unspoken and unconscious in the reader's reading, in this case of a text put together by two culturally diverse individuals. Readers can understand their encounter with the text as an instance of culture contact, where, as Gabriele Schwab notes, "[the reading] would not only consider our individual acts of reading as a form of culture contact, but also the processes by which we are socialized into our own reading habits. It could stress the social powers that control our reading inducing us to reduce the text's otherness as much as it could stress the subversive powers of the text that reside in its otherness" (112). As Schwab suggests, the task is not to assimilate the text or any element of it to ourselves nor to assimilate ourselves to the text. It is not to reduce difference to sameness nor to exoticize or fetishize it. Rather, the task is to become aware of our tendencies to do any of these things. Maintaining a dialogue that works to validate and respect the subjectivities of text and reader is a way to accomplish the task (Schwab 107–36). In terms of narrated American Indian autobiography, beginning and maintaining that kind of dialogue makes for a way to begin to understand the interrelations between cultures within a text and, hence, between the reader and those interrelations within a text of which the reader has become a part.

It seems that I have been in the middle of Pomo and white interrelations for as long as I can remember. As I have said, my life is made visible in a glance, the way someone is looking at me, and in the sound of a voice. It is made visible with stories, too.

Insider. Outsider. Indian. White.

Of course in many cases I am self-conscious, projecting my own insecurity. Great-Grandma Nettie's story about the stranger who came to her home may not have had anything to do with me. My insecurity and fear might have shaped the way I heard her voice and understood her glances that night. Certainly Colson and the three Pomo women did not have me in mind in their meeting together during the summers of 1939, 1940, and 1941. But *Autobiographies*, like Great-Grandma Nettie's story, provokes the same insecurities, the same tension. It is the glance, the sound of a voice again. It is the face looking through the front room window. I want to fit in. I want to belong. I don't want to be told I am a stranger.

When I was fourteen, a mixed-blood Indian named Robert taught me to box. Actually, it was Robert and another guy named Manuel, who was Portuguese. Robert was part Portuguese. People whispered that both of them were really black. They were a few years older than me and the roughest guys in town. They said I had what it took to be a good fighter. "Hate in your eyes, brother," they said. "You got hate in your eyes." By the time I was sixteen I beat the hell out of people every chance I could, mostly white people. In the city park I beat the hell out of a white boy just because I didn't like the way he was looking at me. Not many Indians I knew liked and trusted whites. I was a good Indian then. Any Indian could see I was.

Rejection. Distrust. Anger. Hatred.

These things seem to characterize so much of the history of Pomo and white interrelations. Again, think of the Spanish invasion, the missions. Think of the slave raiding. Think of the land theft. On and on. Think of the Indian resistance, the Bole Maru. The infanticide of mixed-blood children by certain Pomo tribes continued even as the same tribes attended Christian churches and listened to the sermons of Catholic and Protestant clergy who provided the Indians food and shelter. The Indians feigned Christianity, and the clergy and surrounding white community thought they finally had converted and civilized the Indians. The Indians attended separate "Indian" churches; they remained Indians, separate from and not equal to the whites, but understandable, or seemingly understandable, on the whites' terms.

Old patterns of domination, subjugation, and exclusion by whites continue, albeit in different and sometimes more subtle configurations. And the Indians continue to react. My father was heralded by his high school as one of its most valuable and cherished athletes. Yet when he went to date the town fathers' daughters, the wealthy white girls, he was told at the door, "Sorry chief, we aren't hiring any gardeners. Get lost." My father got five of those white girls pregnant. My mother was one of them.

My father became a professional boxer. In the Navy, where he started boxing, he was undefeated. His friends say he knocked down Floyd Patterson. When my father fought, he went crazy, his friends say. You could see it coming in his eyes. The same as when he drank.

My father married three times. Three white women. Two of them told me he beat them. He died of a massive heart attack at fifty-two, after years of chronic alcoholism.

A cousin told me that my father's mother, my grandmother, used to tell my father to "stay away from those white girls. You'll get in trouble and they'll have your ass strung up on a pole. They're like that."

My mother died ten days after she had me. She was sixteen. My father was twenty-one at the time and married to his first wife. My mother and father had been seeing one another for three years, since she was thirteen and he was eighteen. She never breathed a word, never said who the father of her baby was. She could have had his ass strung up on a pole.

"Don't marry no white woman," my cousin says to me. "Look, it was your father's downfall." Every time my cousin sees me she admonishes, "Them whites are no good. White women are whores."

Rejection. Distrust. Anger. Hatred.

This history is not just mine. It is not just my story. It informs *Autobiographies*. It informs the world in which Elizabeth Colson found herself the moment she stepped out of her car, or off the train, on that summer day in 1939. It was there, in Mendocino County, and she became a part of it. *Autobiographies* can say something about this history. It can tell a story.

From the three Pomo women and from other sources, Colson learned that "the Pomo had a generalized hatred of whites and that they resent Pomo treatment at the hands of whites and feel them the source of much of their discomfort" (222). But what Colson could have known about this history, and how well she could have understood what she learned, depended on who she was at the time of her meeting with the three Pomo narrators. Here Colson's abundant commentary—her introductory material, overview of Pomo culture and history, analysis of the autobiographies—is useful, for in it she reveals, often inadvertently, much about herself at the time she stepped into that world of the three Pomo women. Yet, as mentioned a while back, as I begin to consider the text here, specifically in terms of what Colson reveals about herself and her background and her editing of the narratives, I must at the same time consider the narrators as Pomo speakers and thinkers. And, again, only in that way can a broader picture of the relationship between Colson and the Pomo narrators and of the making of their collaborative text be discerned. Only in that way can *Autobiographies* illuminate its history, my history, and tell a story.

It is important to remember that Colson was an anthropologist in a given time and place, which of course had much to do with how she thought and positioned herself in the Pomo community and, subsequently, with what she did or did not see about herself and the Pomo women. As Colson notes in her introductory material, the autobiographies "were gathered during the summers of 1939, 1940, and 1941, when [Colson] was a member of the Social Science Field Laboratory under the direction of B. W. and E. G. Aginsky" (2). Specifically, she was interested in issues of acculturation and wanted to gain "insight into the life of Pomo women of a particular generation" (1). She worked at a time when the field of anthropology had become increasingly enmeshed with neighboring sciences, particularly psychology. Still, this newer anthropology, like its Boasian forerunner, maintained the split between fact and interpretation. When Colson writes that "this paper is the presentation and analysis of the life histories of the three Pomo women" (1), she is apparently assuming that what is presented as actual life history, whether in a given narrator's long or brief account (remember, Colson provides a long as well as a brief autobiographical account for each narrator), is different from the analysis of the life history, in that the accounts are presented to the reader as artifacts independent of Colson's interpretation, that is, of her editing of the narratives. She is likely assuming that her editing of the presentations has not affected them as "pure products" (Clifford 1988), as mirrors that reflect the Pomo women's lived lives.

What Colson notes about her transcriptions of the Pomo women's narratives makes questionable the extent she presents facts or pure products. She says: "An attempt has been made to make the English more grammatical and at the same time to preserve some of the terms of speech which give the flavor of the original. Connectives have been placed where no connectives existed; identities have been made a little more secure by such devices as substituting the appropriate gender of pronouns; and occasionally whole sentences have been inverted and knocked into a more 'English' shape" (9). As Colson observes, the three Pomo women "speak habitually and think in this language" (1), and while the interviews were conducted in English, the Pomo English that Colson edited undoubtedly has features typical of, or associated with, the mother language. To see what Colson might have edited here, or to see what was at stake in terms of a "pure product," it is important to explore, if only briefly, features of the mother language that may have influenced the shape of the narrators' English.

In *Kashaya Texts* Robert Oswalt notes that Kashaya Pomo, which, again, is grammatically similar to the women narrators' central Pomo, "has no articles and, although it does have a pronoun for 'he,' 'she,' and 'they,' such reference is customarily accomplished by verbal suffixes indicating the relative timing of the actions of the two verbs and whether there is a switch or combination of agent between the verbs. [ba], for example, signifies that the verb to which it is attached is subordinated in an adverbial way to the main verb in time, and that both have the same agent" (18). It is no wonder then that English speakers who "speak Pomo habitually and think in this language" would have trouble with connectives and articles, and Colson's adding connectives or appropriate genders of pronouns would not necessarily affect the meaning or sense of the text as the narrators presented it.

But what might have happened when Colson "inverted and knocked whole sentences into a more 'English' shape"? Again Oswalt notes "a common feature of Kashaya Pomo narrative style . . . is the verb repeated in successive sentences with only one small new piece of information: He ran off. Having run off, he ran along. He ran like that. He arrived running" (19). In his translation Oswalt presents the pronoun "he" not only as the subject of the sentences but also as the salient feature of the sentences and indeed of the entire passage. Yet Oswalt infers—and is correct—in his study of Kashaya grammar that the salient feature of the language is the verb. *Action*, and not *subject*, is thematized in Kashaya Pomo. The subject of a Kashaya sentence, whether a pronoun or not, is characteristically suffixed to, and subordinate to, the verb. The verb |*mensi*| ("to do so") often begins the second sentence (i.e., of a narrative) and serves only as a carrier for the suffix (Oswalt 19), thus further stressing the action. Note the same passage Oswalt refers to in a more literal translation:

mobe	*mensiba*	*mobe*	*menmobe*	
run off	having run off he	run off	like that run off	

| *mensiba* | *bele* | *mo* |
| having run off he | come | here |

While Pomo English speakers of the generation Colson interviewed—those Pomo born during the latter part of the nineteenth century—cannot replicate Pomo syntax in English, they often attempt, intentionally or otherwise, to thematize action when speaking English. You might hear something like: Run off, way off, he did. Running like that. Running till he come here. Kathy O'Connor, a linguist who studied central and north central Pomo languages, notes that here too the verb is the salient feature of the language as it is in Kashaya Pomo. Again, the languages are similar grammatically and sound somewhat alike. (The Kashaya are the southwestern tribe of Pomo located approximately sixty miles west and south of the central Pomo tribes.) O'Connor suggests, however, that the central and north central Pomo speakers do not seem to use the verb |*mensi*| ("to do so") as often as the Kashaya Pomo. Still, we can look back at Great-Grandma Nettie's central Pomo English as I remember it and see again how she repeated verbs in successive sentences and worked to thematize action, at least in terms of the topical features of her English. This must have had much to do with her dominant central Pomo language. Now examine the following passage from an autobiography of one of the central Pomo narrators Colson talked with. The narrator, Sophie Martinez, was from the same generation and general locale as Nettie.

> Those boys made that thing. They were singing, singing, singing; and they were making some kind of feather basket with red feathers. They put it on the top of their heads and they put a fish tail on it. Just like a fish they made it. Then they put marks on something on it, and they put it in the water. It was finished. They sang as they put in the water. It floated around there, and they called it back again. (51)

The copious use of verbs is apparent. But imagine a text where the verb, or action, is thematized:

> Singing, singing, singing, making thing, them boys. Singing and same time putting red feathers on. Singing and putting red feathers. Making thing with fish tail on, them boys. They putting mark on later time. Putting mark, like that. Then singing more and putting in water. Putting fish tail thing in water. Putting so floating around there. Then calling back, them boys. Calling back later time. Calling back like that.

Of course the passage quoted from *Autobiographies* may be quite close
to the way it was presented by Sophie Martinez. Perhaps Martinez and the
other Pomo narrators spoke a more "standard" English than Great-
Grandma Nettie. Perhaps they altered their English for Colson in a way they
thought suitable for her, more in line with Colson's English. Unfortunately,
there is no way of knowing. For, as Colson claims, she "no longer [has] any
of the field notes used in preparing the accounts" (i). Yet Colson does say that
"occasionally whole sentences have been inverted and knocked into a more
'English' shape." It is clear here that she edited the narrators' English, but it
is not clear how often or to what extent. What does Colson mean by "occasionally"? Again, there is no way of knowing since there is no record of the
narratives as they were presented by the narrators. But in light of my cursory
study of Pomo linguistics and my experience with Pomo elders from the
same generation as these Pomo narrators, it seems that when Colson
"inverted" and "knocked" she is likely to have masked the narrators' efforts
to stress action in a subjectoriented language. Or, if the narrators were not
stressing action but adjusting their Pomo English for Colson, then what
Colson was likely to have edited was the narrators' slips, or lapses, into their
Pomo English. Even if the narrators regularly used an English close to what
we find in Colson's transcription, Colson probably edited slips, or lapses, that
revealed a Pomo English. Undoubtedly, there is more here to talk about than
the thematization of action or subject; undoubtedly, I have ignored many
other factors regarding the narrators' grammar and Colson's transcription of
it that may have affected the presentations as we see them. Suffice it to say
that Colson's editing altered, perhaps in significant ways, the text's purity as
a product of "Pomo women of a particular generation."

It is important to note here that linguistic features thematized in a
language do not necessarily represent how the speaker thinks, or conceives,
of his or her world. As Chester C. Christian, Jr. observes, "It is futile to
create a science either of culture or of language through the use of language
characteristics of any given culture" (149). Further, he cites in a footnote M.
Edgarton, Jr. whose work he suggests "implies not only the limitations of
language as an instrument of science, but also the persistence of culture and
the relation of language to culture" (155). Violet Chappell, a fluent speaker
of Kashaya Pomo, says: "Yeah, us people of the [Kashaya] language think
different, like our language is different [from English]. But it's more to it
than just that." To suggest that linguistic features alone reveal how the narrators truly conceive of their world is to ignore the complex relation of
language to culture and history and, consequently, important cultural issues
related to the collaborative endeavor in question. To begin to understand the

complex relation of language to culture and history, it is imperative that scholars and other readers have an accurate sense of the speaker's language. If Colson or her readers take the Pomo narrators' textualized narratives as virtually pure presentations, or representations of those presentations, unaffected by Colson's editing, an understanding of that relation of language to culture and history is lacking. It seems ironic, given Colson's interest in issues of acculturation, that she doesn't consider seriously the relation of the women's Pomo English to their Pomo language and culture and history. If she had, might her readers have found a different text, a different English used by the Pomo women?

Colson has not just edited the narrators' grammar, but also certain features of their narrative formats, which again raises questions regarding the "factual" state of the presentations. Colson mentions in her introductory material that "in presenting the data, [she] has attempted to arrange them in chronological order, which has meant in general the sacrifice of the sequence of thought of the informant. The accounts given in the interviews have been cut and chopped to fit into the procrustean bed of chronological sequence. Also where several accounts of the same event are available, these have been combined and worked into one running description" (9). Older Pomo narrators, like speakers from many other traditionally oral cultures, move back and forth in time and place to use the past to comment on the present and vice versa. When Mabel McKay tells me stories she moves in and out of given time frames. She might be talking about a man she knows and then in the next moment begin talking about her greatgrandmother and then shift back to the man. For Mabel there is probably a clear connection between these time frames and the players in them, a connection I often do not readily discern and that only becomes intelligible to me in subsequent conversations and personal reflections or not at all. Speakers from traditionally oral cultures are not the only ones who repeat stories and details or disrupt "the procrustean bed of chronological sequence." Imagine editing Faulkner's *Go Down, Moses, The Sound and the Fury,* or *Absalom, Absalom!* to fit into this bed and how such editing would affect meaning as Faulkner understood and intended it.

A Pomo narrator's mere mention of a place or name can work to set the scene or to thematize action in a story. The narrator might, for example, mention a taboo mountain which will color events in a narrative in given ways for a Pomo listener familiar with the lore associated with the particular mountain. The narrator will often repeat things—the name of a place or person, certain anecdotes—to underscore a theme or idea. The name of the taboo mountain, or an anecdote associated with it, might be repeated over and over again by the narrator to achieve a certain effect or response from the listener. Or the narrator may repeat the name or anecdote simply because it is integral in some way to the story as the narrator understands and remembers it for himself or herself. I remember that Great-Grandma Nettie kept repeating her age when she told the story that winter night in Santa Rosa. She might have been reminding herself and Old Auntie Eleanor of how young she was at the time and how she nonetheless knew to behave in given ways around strangers. Or she may have had other reasons for repeating her age. She may have had many reasons. I don't know. But to edit out, or to "combine and work into one running description," Nettie's repetitions of her age or anything else is to overlook and make unavailable for readers these possibilities in Nettie's narrative.

In rereading my version of Sophie Martinez's passage, I note that I mention "red feathers" twice. In Colson's edited presentation of this narration, Martinez, as I also note, mentions "red feathers" only once. For many Pomo the color red is associated with human blood, with evil, and is, hence, taboo. Red feathers—the red feathers of a woodpecker's topknot—are used in "sun baskets," baskets made for the purpose of poisoning people. Perhaps as a Pomo scholar I inadvertently repeated "red feathers" because of my own associations with them and the color red. Interestingly enough this passage was excerpted from a story about how a lake became taboo. Might Martinez also have repeated "red feathers" more than once? Again, there is no way of knowing.

Colson says, "since condensing many accounts into one leaves the reader with no indication as to the common motives or particular interests of the informant, the recurrence of themes or an eagerness to repeat a given event will be indicated in a footnote or dealt with in the final analysis" (9). Naturally, it is impossible for Colson, who spent only three summers in the central Pomo community, to fully comprehend the significance for the narrators of certain places, names, or anecdotes that are repeated, unless perhaps Colson asked about the repetitions. But the reader cannot tell from anything Colson says in her introductory material and analysis or from the questions she poses (and inserts) in the narratives whether she asked about the repetitions. All that can be known is that Colson made the decisions as to what constituted a "common theme" or a "recurrence of theme," and, as with the issues of grammar, Colson's biases are likely to have influenced her decisions.

Colson does mention that she is "fully aware of the disadvantage involved in thus extensively editing life history materials, especially in the drastic revisions necessary to humor the historical bias of our own culture"

(9). And she concludes that she has "attempted to compromise somewhere halfway between the popularized life history and the truly scientific account" (10). If this is an admission regarding the extent the presentations are in fact interpretations and that she is present in the autobiographical accounts as an editor, then it is eclipsed by her additional material, particularly her brief ethnography of Pomo culture "both past and present" (2), without which, in Colson's words, "the life histories lose much of their point" (2). This overview frames the narratives in given ways and works to maintain that split between fact and interpretation, as if the ethnography were a key that unlocks the raw presentations. Readers are provided an ethnography written by Colson that describes pre-contact and post-contact Pomo against which her readers can measure or place the women's "unedited" lives and see the extent to which the women are acculturated. The underlying assumption is that the ethnography is objective, a clear record of Pomo lifeways, just as the women's narratives are clear records of their lived lives. Both are presented as if Colson is fundamentally absent.

Colson's mention of her editing of the narratives' format may refer to her work on the longer autobiographical accounts, since she notes that the brief autobiographical accounts she provides for each narrator are "verbatim" (2), as opposed to the longer ones where she asked the narrator questions to have them enlarge on certain points and where she presented the material in chronological order. But given the issues of grammar discussed above, one wonders how verbatim even the brief autobiographical accounts are. Sophie Martinez, for whom "speaking in English was probably an effort" (Colson 6), uses the same English in both her long and brief narratives. Despite David H. Brumble's observation that "no interpreters were used" (*An Annotated Bibliography* 11), Colson notes that "on one occasion [Sophie Martinez] asked [her granddaughter] to act as an interpreter" (Colson 6). Colson continues: "The greatest amount of editing has been done on the account of Mrs. Martinez. That of Mrs. Wood and that of Mrs. Adams stand substantially in the language in which they were given" (9). Interestingly enough, the English of Wood and Adams, in both their long and their brief accounts, is largely indistinguishable from that of Martinez. Is this mere coincidence? Did Colson shape Martinez's English to look like that of Wood and Adams?

It is important to note that Colson influenced the direction of the "spontaneous" (5), brief autobiographical accounts, even if it was merely to suggest that Sophie Martinez "start when she could first remember and tell as much as she could remember about her life" (4). With Ellen Wood, Colson asked specific questions (i.e., "What did children about that age do when you were young?") in several interviews before asking for a life history (4). Colson says, "The spontaneous, unquestioned, life history had already been obtained [by another fieldworker] from Mrs. Adams" (5). It is not clear then how spontaneous or unquestioned Mrs. Adams's account is since Colson either did not know or does not mention whether the fieldworker asked any questions of Mrs. Adams or gave her any suggestions regarding what to talk about. But given the suggestion Colson gave Martinez and the questions Colson asked Wood, how can the autobiographical accounts of Martinez and Wood be considered "spontaneous, unquestioned"?

Thus far I have talked only about language and narrative format, specifically about the ways Colson's editing may have affected the texts as mirrors in which Colson and her readers can see reflected the Pomo women's lives. It might be assumed that if Colson had left the women's narratives alone, if she had transcribed them exactly as they were spoken (if that were even possible), we might in fact have "pure products." But, as Vincent Crapanzano pointed out, the spoken text is not only edited by the recorder-editor in the literary reencounter with the recorded text, but it is also edited by the narrator as she is speaking for the recorder-editor. Just as Colson edited what she recorded, so the three Pomo women are likely to have edited *what* they told Colson. Perhaps Sophie Martinez did not repeat "red feathers" on purpose because she was talking to Colson. The point is that Colson's presence in the Pomo community surely positioned the narrators as speakers (and Colson as a recorder-editor) in certain ways. Even though an autobiographical account seemed spontaneous to Colson, it was nevertheless most probably being edited by the Pomo narrator in telling it to Colson.

Although Colson learned from the three Pomo women and from other sources that "the Pomo had a generalized hatred of whites and that they resent Pomo treatment at the hands of whites and feel them the source of much of their discomfort" (222), she claims her relationship with these women was good because she and other members of the Field Laboratory treated them "as equals" (8) and because she was "someone who was fairly neutral and who made no attempt to judge them" (8). The question remains whether these Pomo women treated Colson as an equal, or as one of them, that is, a nonwhite insider. Given Colson's appearance and her education, her obvious membership in the dominant white culture, and given the Pomo Indians' "generalized hatred of whites," it is unlikely that the three narrators saw Colson as one of them. And it must be remembered that these particular narrators grew up at a time when the revivalistic Bole Maru movement which preached Indian nationalism and isolationism was at its peak among the Pomo. Speaking or interacting unnecessarily with non-Indians was viewed by the Bole Maru advocates as sinful, as compromising the movement's resistance to white cultural and religious domination. To speak with a white person was to speak with the devil. As an Indian, you exercised extreme caution. You never said any more to a white person than you had to.

The Pomo I know are generally very private, not given to open exchange with outsiders, particularly about personal and religious matters. From what I have been told by my Pomo elders, this reserve was characteristic even before contact with the European invaders. People from one village were cautious and respectful of those from another village, even a village just across the creek or at the other end of the same valley. Furthermore, telling stories and long tales during the summer months—when Colson did all her interviewing—was considered taboo. Many elders still follow this ancient rule, insisting that they will speak of stories and such things only in winter. "[The ground] got to be clear of snakes, crawling lizards," Old Auntie Eleanor used to say. Mabel McKay said: "If you think about them things [tales and stories] during summer, you going to step on lizard, snake, or something. Not watching where you are going. Don't talk about to nobody then." So by approaching these women during the summer months, Colson may have invaded their privacy and asked them to break taboo. Colson notes how Sophie Martinez "would suddenly switch [topics of conversation] to a description of basket types or of food before [Colson] had realized that someone was approaching" (6). She received "some material regarding the women by other informants" (9), largely about topics the women did not discuss, such as one woman's involvement in a religious cult (99). In changing the topic of conversation and in omitting information about their lives, it is clear the narrators edited their material for Colson.

The fact still remains that the Pomo women were willing to talk to Colson and to tell her stories. Certainly money had much to do with the women's willingness to speak. Colson relates that "almost every informant at some point argued that [twenty-five cents an hour] was insufficient and that they had been advised by other Pomo not to work unless they were paid more" (7). These Pomo women interacted with Colson at a time when virtually every Pomo community had had over thirty years of experience with ethnographers and others who were interested in various aspects of Pomo culture and willing to pay for information and material goods. Ethnographer S. A. Barrett had worked with the northern, central, and eastern groups of Pomo as early as 1906. Pomo women had been selling and trading their baskets to whites since the 1870s. Clearly, the Pomo saw in these interested whites the opportunity to make money, which they usually desperately needed. From what Colson notes about the narrators' mention of money, it seems these three Pomo women too saw the opportunity to make money, in this case by working with Colson.

Of course money does not guarantee unedited information. I have watched Pomo informants, as they have been called, make an art of editing what they tell "them scientists." One Pomo woman calls it "giving-them-a-piece work." She says: "I give them pieces of this and that. I tell them a few things. Even things we shouldn't talk about [to non-Indians]. They never get the whole picture, not with just pieces of this and that. Besides, they make up what they want anyway. They tell their own stories about whatever I tell them." Another Pomo elder refers to her experience with anthropologists as "money-storytelling-time." Speakers will often compare notes about their stories for anthropologists, and these discussions are full of raucous laughter. The so-called informants I know come from a long tradition of "giving-them-a-piece work" and "money-storytelling-time." At the time the three Pomo narrators worked with Colson, this tradition was probably already over thirty years old and had been in existence for as long as Pomo speakers had been talking to anthropologists and other whites interested in learning about Pomo culture.

This is not to suggest that the three Pomo women were lying to Colson or that they were editing their accounts in the manner of these Pomo speakers just described. Sophie Martinez, Ellen Wood, and Jane Adams talked to Colson about some of the same things I remember hearing Great-Grandma Nettie and Old Auntie Eleanor talk about, but Nettie and Eleanor were more guarded about some of these same things. When the professors visited each summer and asked about "charms" and "poisoning," Old Auntie Eleanor told stories no one in the house had ever heard. She certainly did not talk to the professors about these things in terms of people she knew or in reference to members of her own family, whereas the three Pomo narrators did talk about these things and often in terms of people they knew or in reference to their own families. Sophie Martinez, for example, related the following about a snake charm:

> My father's wife tried to get a baby that time. Some of them who want a baby would catch a bull snake. They catch it alive and put it around the woman's waist. I couldn't stand that bull snake around my body, but I saw them do that. She was crying and afraid of the bull snake. My grandfather did that [to her father's wife]. (Colson 43)

Colson notes Martinez also mentions "ten deaths in her immediate family which she ascribes to poisoning" (223).

Given what these narrators did say, the question arises again regarding what motivated these women to work with Colson. Surely there may have been factors besides monetary payment. Perhaps the Pomo women saw in a recorded and written record of their lives the opportunity to clear up community rumors about them, to set the record straight about their lives and their families. Maybe in talking about the deaths of her family members Martinez saw the opportunity to convey her grief or view of what happened to others. In talking about her Dreams Ellen Wood might have been using her conversation with Colson to convey to others her power as a Pomo Dreamer. Perhaps these narrators wanted to show other Indians in their community that in talking to Colson and earning money they could talk about certain "private" matters without giving away valuable tribal information. Perhaps they had their individual versions of "giving-them-a-piece work." Any combination of these possibilities and others I have not thought of or mentioned may have motivated the narrators to work with Colson.

Today a number of Pomo elders want to record life histories, songs, and tribal stories. Often they want a written record for the younger generations. They take pride in working with anthropologists, since in many ways the anthropologists' presence in their homes signals to others the elders' knowledge of tribal history and culture. I doubt, however, that the three Pomo narrators worked with Colson to pass down tribal information or to demonstrate to others how knowledgeable they were about their history or culture. They grew up at a time when talking about these things to outsiders was taboo, and apparently these narrators were still guarded about many subjects they discussed with Colson, particularly in front of other Indians. I have heard a rumor more than once about Colson having been forced by the narrators to change names and place-names because the narrators did not like what Colson had written. A Pomo elder told me: "One of them ladies [narrators] said to that white lady she was going to have her done in. Killed. Poison Indian way. Fix her for writing them things. She say to that white lady 'you better change my name, not say where this place is.'" Did one of the narrators talk about certain things and then change her mind about having them printed? Was she bending under community pressure? Was it a way for her to get paid and still be safe or unaccountable for anything she should not have talked about?

We can only conjecture at this point about what motivated the Pomo women to work with Colson, about how the women edited their life stories for Colson, and about the kind of English they spoke. More should be said, particularly from a Pomo perspective, about the intersecting cultures and histories of Colson and the Pomo women and the contingencies of exchange as they have affected the production of the autobiographical narratives. More stories should be told, not to figure out the story or truth of the collaborators' relationship and the making of their composite text but to further explore linguistic and cultural factors as they may have affected the collaborators' work. More should be said from a Pomo woman's perspective about the relations between white women and Indian women in the central Pomo region. White women in one town in the central Pomo region passed an ordinance near the turn of the century forbidding the hiring of Indian women as domestics. This ordinance came after the Pomo women had been working in the same white households for nearly two decades and it expressed the white women's concern about the half-breed children of the domestic help. This story is told among Indian women today, and from what my cousin said to me about white women and my father, it seems that some Pomo women still do not particularly care for white women. However, the ways in which I can understand my cousin's remark and her anger are limited, since what I can know and understand culturally and historically about the relations between Indian women and white women is shaped in gender-specific ways. Pomo women and white women and women who are both Pomo and white and women who are neither Pomo nor white can tell stories and open the text in ways I cannot, in ways that are relevant to them and that inform my own story of and relationship with the text.

My discussion of Colson and the Pomo women serves only to suggest possible factors and scenarios that may have been at work as Colson and the Pomo women made *Autobiographies*. It shows what may have constituted fundamental differences in language and culture between Colson and the Pomo narrators that may have affected how they understood their own and each other's lives and how they were able to communicate. Of course the history of interrelations between these cultures that is associated with these differences also affects interaction between members of the respective cultures. In short, it is clear that Colson's presence as a recorder in the Pomo women's community and her work as an editor of the women's spoken texts have affected the content, language, and shape of the women's texts that are presented in *Autobiographies* and consequently the pictures readers get of the Pomo women's lives. These pictures do not simply mirror the women's lives as the narrators see and understand them. They are not pictures the women might have drawn in other situations and for other listeners. Rather the pictures here are composite ones, which again is the case for any narrated American Indian autobiography.

Anthropology, like other social sciences at Colson's time, stipulated that the social scientist could and should be objective, that the social scientist's presence, including culture-specific biases, could and should be put aside, transcended during the "scientific" undertaking. It becomes understandable, then, why Colson positioned herself as absent from her work, and why, as a result, she did not see how her presence affected the presentation. If she did not see herself as present in the Pomo women's community, as someone sharing a history and associated with the Pomo women, how could she have seriously considered the ways the women might have been editing their accounts for her? If she did not see herself as present in her literary reencounter with the women's recorded texts, as someone influenced by certain linguistic and narrative biases, how could she have seen the ways her editing may have been significantly altering the spoken texts? How could she have begun to understand the Pomo women (and herself) other than she did?

In her "Analysis of the Life Histories" she treats the autobiographical accounts as raw data. Her tone is detached, authoritative, conclusive. She writes, for example, "When one turns to in-group relationships the picture is entirely changed [from the Pomo's relationship with outsiders]. There is evidence from the life histories that aggressive feelings find an outlet in three forms: physical violence, poisoning, and gossip" (223). Another example: "This last fact [of Catholics underwriting Pomo subsistence] may account for the relatively little concern evinced in the life histories for subsistence" (225). This last observation appears ironic, given Colson's earlier testimony that "almost every informant at some point argued that [twenty-five cents an hour] was insufficient and that they had been advised by other Pomo not to work unless they were paid more." It seems that even while the narrators in their accounts may show little concern for subsistence, they certainly did in fact care about issues of money and subsistence. Colson seems to be forgetting throughout her "Analysis" that she is looking only at the accounts that she received from the narrators and then edited. She overlooks much of what she actually experienced with the women narrators, such as their concern for money.

In any event, had Colson been more aware of her role and influence in the collaboration, she might have seen the Indians differently. She might have come to different conclusions about the Pomo women and their lives. Despite the fact that these three Indian women lived in the midst of cultural flux and that they had many marriages, raised and lost several children, and moved from place to place, Colson concludes: "Pomo life, as portrayed in these three life histories, emerges as a fairly simple one from the point of view of its participants, for they live through much of the same events with little variation in happenings to distinguish their lives" (233). Colson's interest in the lives of these three Pomo women was in large part scientific.

For, and to some extent with, the Pomo women she created a language that was flat and simple, a language which might lead one to think that "Pomo life, as portrayed in these life histories, emerges as a fairly simple one from the point of view of its participants." Here, it seems, the text begs its interpretation.

The story I have drawn of Colson and the making of *Autobiographies* is not unusual or surprising. Krupat pointed out that earlier in the century the objectivism of American social science influenced S. M. Barrett in the making of *Geronimo's Story of His Life*. This objectivism not only influenced a host of recorder-editors working on Indian life histories, but also many others, most of whom were social scientists working with American Indians and other indigenous peoples. The detached observer mode was standard. Lately, some social scientists and various social critics have seen objectivism as a myth and pointed to its limits and dangers (Clifford 1983, 1988; Marcus and Fischer 1986; Rosaldo 1989). They have pointed to the limits of what "objective" observers can see and know about themselves and those they observe, and they have pointed out that under the guise of objectivism these observers often assume authority to make sense of and represent others (i.e., Clifford 1983), an attitude often affiliated with hegemony and empire, particularly in members of a dominant group in their interactions with subordinate groups (i.e., Rosaldo 1989). These scholars are not suggesting that critical activity is impossible, but they seem to be saying that critical activity is tied always to the subjectivity of observers and the relationships they establish with what they are observing or reading.

By positioning herself as an objective observer in relation to the women, Colson does not appear to notice the history she shared with them nor the ways her scholarly endeavors may have replicated and reinforced historical patterns of Pomo and white interrelations. It appears that to some degree Colson made the narratives sensible or intelligible to herself so that she could analyze them in her own terms; and, in making the decisions about editing the accounts without consulting the narrators, Colson's encounter with the women repeats historical patterns of Pomo and white interrelations. Pomo country is again cleaned up, made intelligible on white people's terms. Open, proactive intercultural communication collapses. Colson, like the nineteenth-century Catholic and Protestant clergy who provided the Pomo people "Indian" churches, could not see or imagine how the Indians were anything but what they seemed to her as an "impartial" observer. Just as the clergy did not see the Pomo in terms of their participation in the revivalistic Bole Maru cult, so Colson did not see what various aspects of Pomo language, culture, and history may have revealed about them (and her), nor could she appreciate how her behavior reinforced certain Pomo attitudes about whites, especially those interested in learning about Indians. The Pomo elder who told me one of the narrators threatened to kill Colson said: "See, that's how them whites are. No respect. Do things, write anything they want. So don't tell them about us in the school. Don't trust them. They're like that white lady [Colson]. I tell all [Indian] young people about that."

I believe Colson was sincere when she said she was "someone who was fairly neutral and who made no attempt to judge [the women]" (8). I believe she treated the women "as equals" to the best of her ability and did not regard the Pomo Indians in the racist manner of the general local white community at the time. The discussion thus far is not meant simply to criticize Colson and place responsibility for problems regarding Pomo and white interrelations on her shoulders. Colson could not have fully understood the nature and consequences of her work, and indeed no one can see all of the ways he or she is not "fairly neutral." The story of Colson and the Pomo women and their making of *Autobiographies* teaches not only about the possible limits and dangers of objectivism, but also about the necessity for collaborators in any cross-cultural project to see themselves as present, as persons working in a given place at a given time, if they are to begin to understand the nature and consequences of their work.

Social scientists who discuss the limits and dangers of objectivism stress the necessity for participants in a cross-cultural endeavor to see themselves as present, often speaking of subjective knowledge and self-reflexivity and of polyvocality, both in one's encounter with others and in one's representation of the encounter. But all of this must also hold for the practice of reading texts, especially those where readers must negotiate differing cultural perspectives. Again, in narrated American Indian autobiographies readers must negotiate not only what in the texts may be different or upsetting in terms of their own lives but also what in the texts may create differences or tension between the parties that made the texts. Of course I am not the first to suggest readers think about, or historicize, their positions as readers and critics. David Bleich (1986) and Edward W. Said (1989) have certainly sounded the trumpet. But these critics, like others in various fields of study, present their arguments in conventional argumentative narratives, the forms of which usually hide not only a record of the critic's interaction with the text but also the critic's autobiography, a necessary component of the reading practice the critics are calling for. Hence the politics of reading (Boyarin 1991) are not seen.

In this chapter I hope to have documented in some degree my interaction with *Autobiographies*. Any story or lesson, any reading, if you will, that I gather from the text has to do with that interaction. Other readers can see,

at least in terms of what I have revealed, what constitutes my reading; they
have in hand both my reading of the text, which opens and extends its story
in certain ways, and my encounter with it, which shows my influences and
biases as a reader. They can see, to some extent, how my reading of
Autobiographies is my own. Other readers can engage with what this document contains and point out my limits and possibilities, failures and
successes, and replications and inventions in terms of this text and its history
as well as other texts and other histories. The making of *Autobiographies*
cannot be described by just one story based on one reader's interaction with
the text since the text itself provides the opportunity for many stories, readings, and a great deal of critical exchange; however, one story can start the
talk, touch other stories, teach the reader. My one story is brief and, as I
noted, not so unusual in certain ways, but from it I see much of my history
and understand, finally, how *Autobiographies* is a story for me.

HEARING THE OLD ONES TALK

For a long time I wanted to dismiss Colson. I wanted to show her as
ignorant, arrogant, typically "white." I wanted to run her out of the territory.

I wanted my anger.

As an Indian that's what I know best. But that isn't exactly my case. My
anger is also that of a mixed blood caught in the middle.

Early on I learned to take sides. I chose the Indian side. Or I was quiet,
never letting anyone know my predicament. I passed as white. Always, I
denied. I took a stand within myself. I took a stand against myself.

In the academy we are trained to take a stand and defend it, and
perhaps I have done well and become a professor because of all that early
training. In the academy scholars now want "an Indian point of view." And
Indians want and need to talk, to tell their stories. But what constitutes "an
Indian point of view"? By what and whose definition is a point of view
"Indian"? How might an Indian's story in turn define "Indian" ? What of an
Indian's story that is not "Indian" ?

I felt I had to take sides. As a scholar I had to be "Indian," a Pomo
Indian who knows and discusses what is "Pomo," which in turn can help
make sense of *Autobiographies* from a "Pomo point of view." I could say what
was "Pomo" and what was "Colson." I kept looking at *Autobiographies* from
an "Indian point of view." I kept thinking of how "Indians" really are. I
wanted to utilize a so-called Indian perspective, one that is, say, anti-white,
and that shows outside scholars always to be the enemy, who is always wrong

about us. I didn't want to be reminded of my situation in two worlds. I didn't want personal experience to get in the way of my "Indian analysis and discussion" of the text. It would cloud a pure, authoritative reading from an "Indian" perspective. It would cloud a distanced academic stance that was now Indian. Indian and objective.

More denial. Rejection. Frustration and anger.

So I wanted to take my anger out on Colson. I could do it objectively, truthfully.

Objectivity, or that which inheres in any supposed practice of it, namely the user's separation from his or her self and from whatever it is that is being viewed or studied, kept my anger alive. It also kept me blinded. By taking an "Indian stance," by keeping myself separate from both my larger personal experience and the text, I continued old patterns. My "Indian" objective truth based on my so-called Indian perspective versus Colson's objective truth as a non-Indian scientist. Either truth precludes our seeing the larger picture of the forces which position us as knowers of ourselves and others. Either truth precludes our seeing the limits and consequences of the truth we paint. In the case of Colson and the three Pomo women and myself, we become a part of an old and vicious cycle. One says what the other is. The other gets defensive and says what the one is. No one sees what we do to ourselves and one another. No one sees beyond themselves. Personal and cultural boundaries are rigidified. We don't see how our worlds are interrelated. We don't see our very real situations in both worlds. There is nowhere to see, no way to talk to one another. Oppressive situations are internalized by individuals in given ways and played out again by the same individuals in given ways. It is the operation of a vicious cycle, a mean history.

Denial. Rejection. Frustration and anger.

Luckily, I kept hearing Great-Grandma Nettie. She wouldn't stay down. She and Old Auntie Eleanor were, after all, the only central Pomo I knew from the same generation as the three Pomo women. When I looked to Nettie and Eleanor for answers about what was "Pomo," they shot back those suspicious glances. Who was I? Was I Indian? Was I a stranger? They didn't allow me to represent or define them for others. They reminded me of my story. And if I am reminded by them of my story, then I am taught by what I discerned in *Autobiographies* why I should not forget my story. And that's how *Autobiographies* is a story for me. It shows me the dangers of being absent, of attempting to separate myself from what I do, from my own life situation as a scholar, an Indian, and a human being in time and place. It shows me not only the importance of my stories but also the importance of talking about them openly and honestly, so that I might, in whatever I do or read, see them anew. It brought me back to the old ones, to their stories, and to hearing the old ones talking, so I can see how something they say might be for me.

I am that man, that one at the table. With light skin. I am a quarter-breed man. But like half-breed man, I know something too. I know Indian poison. White poison, too. I know many ways to poison.

The old medicine people say a good medicine person must know about the poisons. Only that way can the medicine doctor know what to do to counteract them. What herbs to use. What songs to sing. The doctor has to know those poisons so well that the doctor could use them against other people. But a good doctor doesn't do that. That's not the purpose of learning about the poisons. Good medicine people know better.

What I have to say can work like good doctoring songs, good medicine. Listen to my story.

So when I sit before you talking, talking, talking, talking, you know who I am. Listen because I carry our history, yours and mine, ours. Some of it, anyway. Whoever you are.

Talk back. Tell stories. Put food out, meat. I will eat it. I'm not here to harm. I'm talking, telling stories. Watch. Listen.

Then you'll know I'm no stranger.

CECILIA SIMS

The Rebirth of Indian and Chinese Mythology in Gerald Vizenor's Griever: An American Monkey King in China

Vizenor's novel is the trickiest of all the trickster tales. Vizenor introduces Griever de Hocus, a trickster figure of cross cultural influence, doubling as both the Monkey King of China and a mixed-blood Native American tribal trickster. Griever exists as a contemporary, postmodern trickster.

Arthur Kroker describes, in the video *Panic Sex*, the postmodern condition as the "implosion of grand narrative" and the "implosion of dualism in the animal mind" (Kroker). The trickster figure lives as an animal of exploded dualisms; he acts upon no distinctions between moral and amoral, between sacred and nonsacred. The inward destruction of "grand narrative" correlates to Jean Francois Lyotard's phrase describing the postmodern world as one of "incredulity toward metanarrative" (Mielke). Vizenor's novel pinpoints more than mere doubt of grand explanatory narratives, such as liberal myths of progress or Marxian historical didactics; Vizenor inspires doubt of Western narratives.

The union of the classical motif of the trickster in myth—an ancient yet perennial narrative—with the chaos and panic dispersed within postmodern literature results in a poetic collision. An analysis of such collision, *Griever*, necessitates the simultaneous study of both classic Native American and Chinese trickster elements converging on the postmodern scene and resulting in a paradoxical creation—the postmodern beast fable. Vizenor's

From *Critical Perspectives on Native American Fiction.* © 1993, 1997 by Passeggiata Press.

fable displays various connections to the Chinese folktale *Monkey* and to the Native American mythic stories, and reflects such common traits of postmodern expression as "experiential transcendence," panic sex, and criticism of Western metanarrative. (Lifton 65)

Griever follows a journey pattern common in myths. Griever de Hocus, a mixed-blood tribal teacher from a reservation in North America, travels to Tianjin, China to teach Chinese students. During his sojourn in Tianjin, Griever works his trickster trade by freeing nightingales, chickens, and political prisoners. Everyday, the trickster fills his world with games: he bombards a People's Republic of China anniversary dinner with paper airplanes until officials discard him for improper attire (Griever never wears a tie): he breaks into the campus radio room and exchanges the morning wake up music of "The East is Red" with "Stars and Stripes Forever"; he amuses the housemaids as he accidentally locks himself from his guestroom, naked. (Vizenor 135)

Though he reasons as a man, Griever's mannerisms, actions, and habits are overwhelmingly bestial. A short, little creature, Griever possesses an "outsized nose" and hands that "lurch like an arboreal animal" (Vizenor 38, 29). Wild with gestures, Griever attracts attention, tumbling as he walks and snorting as he talks.

Vizenor unites the Indian trickster motif with the Chinese Monkey King persona, as best displayed in a humorous chapter title "Griever-Mediation." In an act of "experiential transcendence," Griever escapes the crowded bus system of Tianjin and returns to grade school. Robert Lifton defines "experiential transcendence" as "a state so intense that time and death disappear," a state of "the mystics, involving principles of ecstasy or 'losing oneself'" (65). The scene emphasizes temporal elasticity and transmigration of the soul, both Native American mythic elements. The Choctaw, for instance, believe dreams signify the spirit's escape from the body to meet with aspects of life known to the sleeper only after waking (Coffer 9–10). Though the Choctaw believe meeting a large animal spirit migration issues ill omen, Griever, fortunately, not only meets, but mimics and liberates a small animal in his dream memory. The following is an excerpt from "Griever Mediation":

> "Remember children," said the teacher . . . the [frogs] we are about to dissect this morning, you see, will not matter in the over-all world of frogs."
>
> "Do frogs have science teachers?" Griever pressed his nose and one cheek hard against the glass case and watched the teacher move between

the frogs inside.

The teacher ignored the question . . .

"Do frogs know who they are?" Griever threw his question from a distance, over the case of live frogs . . .

"Griever has an unusual imaginative mind," [a] teacher [once] wrote, "and he could change the world if he is not first taken to be a total fool."

"Do you know who you are?" retorted the science teacher.

"Yes, a frog," he said from behind the case . . .

"But frogs, my little man . . . are not humans . . . Here, we are humans."

Griever croaked like a tree frog . . .

"Griever de Hocus," the science teacher summoned in a firm tone of voice.

"Little man, where have you hidden our frogs?"

"No place," he promised.

"We must have the frogs to finish our experiment," she demanded . . .

"The frogs are alive," he pleaded . . .

"Mark my words, little man, you will be punished for this . . ."

"Not by the frogs."

"This is a scientific experiment."

"Not by the frogs."

Griever packed the frogs on top of his lunch in a brown paper sack and liberated them one by one on the shaded cool side of the school building. There, in the gentle fiddlehead fern, he imagined that he became the king of the common green frogs (Vizenor, 48–51).

The escape from wordly time and the liberation of imprisoned animals appear in both Indian and Chinese trickster cycles. Griever escapes temporal bounds by shooting docks with a pistol and by the use of his imagination. The combination forms Griever's nature, as Vizenor describes:

> Griever resolves his brother and concern in the world with three curious gestures; he leans back on his heels and taps the toes of his shoes together; he pinches and folds one ear; and he turns a finger in search of a wild strand of hair on his right temple. The third habit . . . was his search for one 'metahair, the hair that transforms impotencies, starved moments, even dead-ends' (Vizenor, 31).

Griever's compulsive habits and much of the tribal trickster's antics and dreams originate in the folk novel of China by Wu Che'eng-en (translated by Arthur Waley), *Monkey*. *Monkey* relates the well known origin of the monkey figure of Chinese pantheon in its recount of a "journey to the Western Paradise in order to obtain the Buddhist scriptures for the emperor of China" (Christie 123). The historical introduction of Buddhism into China appears in the story given the fact a pilgrim, Thang Seng (historically Hsuan Tsang) searched India, with the aid of the "Monkey Fairy," Sun hou-tzu, for Buddha's true scriptures (Christie 123). A figure transformed into the trickster Monkey King, the "Monkey Fairy" fell victim to the "same hardships and failures as human beings," and "represented human nature and its propensity to evil" (Christie 123).

The story of *Monkey* entertainingly recounts the trickster's adventures. Monkey, the trickster's proper name, is born of stone and learns at a young age both magic and transformation abilities; Monkey enjoys any shape or size, plus the ability to fly. Monkey becomes Monkey King after he slays sinister monsters and dragons. As a trickster feeds a large ego, Monkey's self-title, "Great Sage, Equal of Heaven," causes authority problems with the Chinese Gods (Waley 49). Though Monkey thinks himself capable of ruling heaven and earth, the Lord of Heaven assigns him to oversee the Heavenly Peach Garden. Holding rebellion in the palm of his hand, Monkey eats the sacred peaches in revenge for not receiving an invitation to the Peach Festival, and he becomes immortal.

Because the gods fail to tolerate or to change Monkey's behavior, Buddha creates a magic stone mountain and imprisons Monkey. Obliged to accompany pilgrim Tripitaka on the journey for Buddha's scriptures as recompense for release, Monkey obeys. Monkey battles monsters and evil spirits, and he receives aid from Pigsy, an obese, gruesome pig, and Sandy, a rapid, friendly horse. The pilgrims succeed, after eighty dangerous and humorous trials, and secure the scriptures. Buddha then titles Monkey "Buddha in Victorious Strife" (Waley 303).

Vizenor's fable recounts similar legendary activities. Like Monkey, Griever takes a journey in search of scriptures. Rather than securing Buddha's sacred writings, however, Griever quests for a secret recipe for "blue chicken made with mountain blue corn" (Vizenor 230). Instead of fighting monsters and dragons, Griever battles political authorities, teachers, soldiers, and foreign affairs officials; instead of using a sword, Griever employs the humor of words.

A longing for biological immortality controls Griever's thoughts as it possesses Monkey's. Griever reads of Monkey's theft of the immortal peaches, and he dreams of himself in the role. Griever's thirst for immortality connects with longevity through metanarratival questings of closure as Vizenor describes:

[Griever was] driven to be immortal because nothing bored him more than the idea of an end; narrative conclusions were unnatural, he would never utter the last word, breathe the last breath, the end was never his end. (Vizenor, 128)

In a chapter entitled "Peach Emperor," Griever achieves his immortality by impregnating Hester Hua Dan, the Chinese daughter of Egas Zhang, Foreign Affairs Director.

Unlike Monkey, Griever loses that which he cannot recover—before the shameful birth occurs, Egas kills both his daughter and Griever's child. Afterward, Griever proves himself "victorious over strife," through his escape from Tianjin on an ultralight airplane with Hester's mixed-blood sister and his cock companion. This final act of the flight of two culturally mixed characters from a prejudiced land concludes the story in archetypal symbolism. The flight itself relates to the Native American belief of wings as immortal keys. Lifton identifies mechanical flight as a means to achieve experiential trancendence.

Many of Vizenor's characters, too, parallel the characters of *MONKEY*. Griever, as Monkey, journeys through China and meets the white cock and trickster companion, Matteo Ricci. Because Matteo entices and enables Griever to free seventeen hens from a Chinese Market, and then accompanies the Monkey King throughout the novel, one links the cock to the pilgrim, Tripitaka. Matteo keeps Monkey in check and acts as an anti-trickster, cooling Monkey's hot temper and his mischievous conduct.

Other characters in *An American Monkey King in China* incorporate simultaneous cultural myths. Sandie, the horse in Monkey, appears as a "government rat hunter" and befriends Griever, taking him to Obo Island ["Obo," Griever explains, is a tribal word that means 'cairn,' a tribal place where shamans gather and dream" (164)]. On Obo Island Griever meets Pigsie, no longer the obese nuisance for Monkey but now a "bourgeois nuisance" because of his "bestialities" (Vizenor 165). Pigsie and Sandie herd swine and catch rats for the government, along with Shitou, the stone shaman.

Of the three characters, Shitou's existence seems the most ambiguous and the most fascinating. Shitou functions as a character of converging cultural myths implicated in his medium of stone. His character brings together Monkey's stone birth and stone prison, with a Native American motif of stone's immortal powers. The Tlingit illuminate, in their Raven trickster myth, the Native American connection of stone with immortality:

[Raven] tried to make human beings out of a rock and out of a leaf at the same time, but the rock was slow while the leaf was very quick. Therefore human beings came from the leaf . . . That is why there is death in the world. If men had come from the rock there would be no death. (Radin 159)

Shitou, who "breaks stones with one hand," encourages the mental and spiritual liberation of Griever; the trickster identifies his own role as Shitou chants, "this old hand breaks stones into laughter" (Vizenor 72). Though the soldiers call Shitou a "broken monkey" to demoralize his action of releasing humor, Griever insists, "Shitou is a stone," an immortal representative of both trickery and creation, like the trickster himself. (Vizenor 74, 75) "Deep inside the stone," Shitou says to Griever, "is a bird and humor," pointing again to the immortality of life in stone, in flight, and, with the trickster's help, in laughter. (Vizenor 172)

As Griever creates life in China, he creates, in equal doses, chaos. Paul Radin delineates the trickster's dichotic nature and helps explain Griever's transgressive acts:

Trickster is at one and the same time creator and destroyer, giver and negator, he who dupes others and who is always duped himself. He wills nothing consciously. At all times he is constrained to behave as he does from impulses over which he has no control. He possesses no values, moral or social, is at the mercy of his passions and appetites, yet through his actions all values come into being. (ix)

Vizenor's trickster is thus appropriately over-sexed. Many of Griever's acts of transgression take a sexual nature, linking him with a common Native American trickster figure, Mink, "whose appetite is mainly sexual" (Bierhorst 37). Griever's sex acts are acts of panic sex, to use Arthur Kroker's term for "the flawed, anti-Laurentian, post-AIDS, spastic sexuality of the postmodern era" (Mielke). Vizenor toys with Kroker's idea of panic sex by presenting it in bestial form, congruous with Kroker's claim of sex as cynical and fascinating only "above reckless discharge and upheaval" (Kroker). Panic sex involves, according to Kroker, an act of sheer barrier breakdown, an act of transgressive means but without satisfactory ends; it relates to the body's inability to satisfy human desire because of physical frailty and limitation.

The relatively new concept of panic sex, when linked to the old motif of the trickster's primary instinctual characteristic of lust produces fascinating results. Following the release of the chickens from the free market, Griever illustrates the destroyed dualism within the animal mind as he nurtures a fantasy of sex with Sugar Dee, another teacher. In the imagined act, Vizenor assigns no boundaries, either physical or mental. The scene links Griever to Coyote, the Winnebago trickster figure who also has "no true sense of sex differentiation" (Radin 137):

> Griever turned a strand of hair between his fingers . . . He spreads
> his fingers beneath the poppies [on Sugar Dee's dress] Sugar Dee tossed
> her hair back . . . [Griever] became a woman there beneath her hair . . .
> (Vizenor 55)

Radin describes the sex transformation as the trickster's ultimate trick, "played on an oversexed individual in order to show to what lengths such a person will go, what sacred things he will give up and sacrifice to satisfy his desires" (Radin 137). Wu Ch'eng-en's *MONKEY* provides the best example of the blasphemy associated with the trickster's phallic fetish. While pretending to be the Three Sacred Immortals of the Taoist temple, Monkey, Pigsie, and Sandy feast on the holy offerings to the true Immortals, then urinate in the altar vases. Three Taoists drink the urine, thinking it divine elixir, before realizing the "rare game" of the tricksters (Wu Ch'eng-en 225).

Carl Jung associates the phallic emphasis and the fluency of trickster's sex to the unconscious:

> Because of . . . [the trickster's unconscious] . . . [the trickster] is
> deserted by his (evidently human) companions, which seems to indicate
> that he has fallen below their level of consciousness. He is so uncon-
> scious of himself that his body is not a unity . . . (Jung 202)

The Winnebago trickster cycle contains a humorous anecdote of the trickster's lack of bodily unity. The coyote's left arm grabs a buffalo, and the right arm screams, "Give that back to me, it is mine! Stop that or I will use my knife on you!" (Radin 8). Though Griever's arms never wrestle one another, his sexual identity does wrestle itself. "The trickster," Jung attests with a similar metaphorical note, "is a primitive 'cosmic' being of divine-animal nature, on the one hand superior to man because of his superhuman qualities, and on the other hand inferior to him because of his unreason and unconsciousness" (Jung 204).

Like a true trickster, Griever twists Jung's 'divine-animal' classification because Griever's imagination embodies his "unreason and uncon-sciousness." He becomes a monkey who appears bestial and territorial in urinating but because he imagines the act as much as he performs the act, his unconscious surrenders to reason. Vizenor creates a "close relative to the old mind monkeys," a trickster who "holds cold reason on a lunge line while he imagines the world," then acts with reason and hilarity. (Vizenor, *Liberty* x)

Griever's use of imagination releases the importance of the unconscious from that of mere transcendence to that of evolution and cultural change. As Griever's science teacher explains, his "imaginative mind" could change the world if we see beyond the foolishness of his actions. Vizenor explains how Griever's imagination changes discourse and propels narrative beyond normal narrative, beyond metanarrative. In Griever's imagination, words live independent of bounds they impose. Where the words end, the trickster's language begins:

> When the trickster emerges in imagination, the author dies in a comic discourse . . .Words, then are metaphors and the trickster is a comic 'holotrope,' an interior landscape behind what discourse says . . . (Vizenor, *Liberty* x-xi)

Though the landscape seems far and elusive, Griever insures us of its proximity—within each of us. "This is a marvelous world of tricksters," Griever concludes in a summation which, in resisting closure, echoes a fable's moral lesson. Griever's conclusion hints of an expansion of the postmodern scene, an expansion of world view tending toward the optimistic rather than the previous limited and pessimistic Western view. As the world inhabitants therein we become the humans, the animals, the words, the metaphors—the tricksters.

A. LAVONNE RUOFF

Alienation and the Female Principle in
Winter in the Blood

> But the distance I felt came not from country or people; it came from within
> me. I was as distant from myself as a hawk from the moon. And that was why
> I had no particular feelings toward my mother and grandmother. Or the girl
> who had come to live with me (p. 2)

In the words quoted above, the nameless narrator of *Winter in the Blood*
summarizes the sense of alienation which plagues him and which must be
exorcised before he can become whole within himself and can close the
distance he feels between himself and the external world. To do so, he undertakes a spiritual and physical journey into experience and memory to find the
truth about his own feelings and about his family and girlfriend. Through
most of the novel, the only people he really loves are his brother Mose and
his father First Raise. After Mose was killed by an automobile on the highway
while the two boys were herding cattle back to the ranch, the narrator
became a "servant to a memory of death" (p. 38). Though the loss of the
brother was immediate, the loss of his father was gradual. Following the accident, First Raise was home less and less often until he finally froze to death
on a drunken binge. In the ten years since his father's death, the narrator
has been able to do nothing of consequence. The closeness he feels to them
contrasts with the distance he feels from the females in the novel—human
and animal. The purpose of this paper will be to examine the causes and

From *Critical Perspectives on Native American Fiction.* © 1993, 1997 by Passeggiata Press.

resolution of the narrator's sense of alienation through an analysis of the cultural context—traditional as well as contemporary—of his relationships with and characterizations of these females.

The chain of circumstances which ultimately leads to the narrator's feeling of separateness begins with his grandmother, who is at once the unwitting cause of the family's isolation from the Blackfeet tribe and the means by which the narrator can partially learn about them and his family. Despite the many stories about her early life which the grandmother told her young grandson, she revealed only part of the truth about her life with Standing Bear's band of Blackfeet. In order for the narrator to determine the truth about her life and about the identity of his own grandfather, he must obtain the other parts of the story from blind, old Yellow Calf after his grandmother's death.

A beautiful girl thirty years younger than her husband, she slept with Chief Standing Bear only to keep him warm and to sing softly in his ear. The "bad medicine," which isolated not only the grandmother but also her descendants, began with the migration of her husband's band of Blackfeet from their traditional hunting grounds. After moving into Gros Ventre territory, they endured one of the hardest winters in memory. The details of the starvation winter of 1883–84 come from Yellow Calf, who lost all of his family to starvation or pneumonia.

After Standing Bear's death in a raid on the Gros Ventres, the young widow of not yet twenty was made an outcast by the band. The grandmother attributed their action to the women's envy for her dark beauty and to the men's fear of the women's anger if they helped her as well as to their own reticence because of her position as Standing Bear's widow. However, Yellow Calf attributes the mistreatment to a combination of physical, psychological, and religious causes: "She had not been with us more than a month or two, maybe three. You must understand the thinking. In that time the soldiers came, the people had to leave their home up near the mountains, then the starvation and death of their leaders. She had brought them bad medicine" (p. 154). Her beauty, which had been a source of pride, now mocked them and their situation. Thus, in the case of the grandmother, the source of alienation was external, resulting from circumstances beyond her control. Her isolation from the band became permanent when they were driven like cows by the soldiers to the new Blackfeet Reservation, established in 1888 at the same time as that for the Gros Ventres and Assiniboins at Fort Belknap. Because the band did not mention her to the soldiers and because she had moved a distance from the band in the spring, the soldiers thought she was Gros Ventre.

In addition to attempting to determine the facts about the band's treatment of his grandmother, the narrator also tries to find out who hunted for her. Frustrated by Yellow Calf's refusal to answer his questions, the narrator suddenly realizes—at the moment his horse Bird farts—that Yellow Calf was that hunter. Solving his puzzle also solves those of the identity of his grandfather and of his own tribal heritage. At the beginning of the novel, the narrator explains that his grandmother "remained a widow for twenty-five years before she met a half-white drifter named Doagie, who had probably built this house where now the old lady snored and I lay awake thinking that I couldn't remember this fact" (p. 37). However, he does remember the rumors that Doagie was not his real grandfather.

Between the time she was abandoned by the Blackfeet band and the time she took in Doagie, the grandmother continued to live in isolation, separated by three miles from Yellow Calf, her secret visitor. Despite his realization of his grandfather's identity, the narrator cannot explain the distance between Yellow Calf and his grandmother: why the two waited twenty-five years after Standing Bear's death to procreate a child or why they continued to live separately afterward. Certainly the respect both had for Standing Bear is a very important part of the explanation. Their separation prior to the conception of Teresa may also be partially explained as an allusion to one of the myths about the origin of the Blackfeet. Although men and women lived separately at one time, Old Man (Na'pi), a creator-trickster figure in Blackfeet mythology, brought them together so that they could continue and so that the men would abandon their lazy dissolute ways and learn from the women's example of orderly self-government and mastery of agriculture and domestic arts. The theme of the separation of males and females is repeated in the relationships between Teresa and First Raise and between the narrator and Agnes.

A third part of the explanation may be found in the traditional Blackfeet taboo against intermarriage within the band. Because the male members of the band were considered relatives, there was an old law against such intermarriage. By the time the bands were settled on the reservation, intermarriage was no longer considered a crime but was still bad form. Consequently, when the grandmother (then about forty-five) and Yellow Calf conceived a child almost at the last opportunity before the onset of her menopause, they were violating a taboo in order to recreate a new race of Blackfeet in an alien land. Having done this, however, they chose to remain apart and the grandmother chose to obscure the fatherhood of the child through living with Doagie. Nevertheless, this violation of custom was one more portion of the bad medicine passed on to the daughter Teresa.

The unwitting cause of the family's isolation from other Blackfeet, the grandmother still serves as its link to the tribe's culture and history. The power of the oral tradition she transmits is retained in the memory of the narrator. Advancing age has not diminished the strength of her contempt for those who made her an outcast or her hatred for such old enemies as the Crees. Too weak and feeble now even to chew regular food or to go the toilet by herself, she is still fierce enough to wear a paring knife in her legging and plot ways to slit the throat of Agnes, her grandson's Cree girlfriend. Almost a hundred years old when the novel opens, the grandmother now communicates with her family with an occasional "ai" or squeak of her rocker.

In her silent old age, she must endure the vulgar teasing of Lame Bull, in violation of the old Blackfeet taboo that a man should not speak to his mother-in-law or even look at her, which was equally binding on her. Also violated is the taboo that although a mother-in-law might be supported by her son-in-law, she must live not in the same tepee with him but rather in a smaller one set up some distance away. She must also endure the disinterest of her grandson, who usually regards her as a subject for bad jokes or detached curiosity. His treatment of her is a deviation from the traditional respect children were expected to show elders.

Though she clung to the old ways in life, she is denied them in death by Teresa, who insists that she be properly prepared for burial by the undertaker in near-by Harlem. Ironically, she is sealed up in her shiny coffin so that no one gets to see his handiwork. Her funeral is neither Catholic nor traditional Blackfeet. Only her grandson observes a bit of the old burial customs by throwing onto her grave her one surviving possession from the old life— the tobacco pouch with its arrowhead. Having reached the end of his odyssey to find the truth about himself and his background, the narrator casts away the bundle containing the bad medicine which has plagued the family.

Teresa combines her mother's solemn dignity and fierce determination to survive with her own alienation from Blackfeet traditions. Because she rejected these in favor of acculturation, she is alienated both from the beliefs of her mother and from the dreams and desires of her first husband and sons. The most valuable material possessions passed on to Teresa by her mother are the land acquired through mistaken identity and a house built by a man she wrongly believed to be her father. Although the ranch supports the family, it has destroyed what has been traditional Blackfeet role structure by making the male financially independent on the female and by forcing the male to give up hunting for ranching to provide for his family. For solace and understanding, she turns to Catholicism and to friendship with the Harlem priest, who makes Indians come to "his church, his saints and holy water, his feuding eyes" (p. 5).

The differences between Teresa and the men in her family are revealed in her son's description of her as having always had "a clear bitter look, not without humor, that made others of us seem excessive, too eager to talk too much, drink too much, breathe too fast" (pp. 134–35). She approves hard work on the ranch and disapproves foolishness and fighting. Whatever natural intolerance she possessed has been sharpened by her experiences with First Raise and her son. As a result, she has developed the ability to interpret things as she wishes to see them and to ignore what she does not, as her memories of First Raise demonstrate. At the same time that she tells her son that his father was not around enough, she insists that he accomplished what he set out to do. When her son points out her inconsistency, she merely says that he has mixed his father up with himself. Her only explanation of why First Raise stayed away so much is that he was a "foolish man" who "could never settle down"—a wanderer just like her son and "just like all these damned Indians" (pp. 19, 20).

Because Teresa is primarily concerned with doing what has to be done in order to provide for her family and to keep the ranch going, she marries Lame Bull shortly after her son arrives home from his latest spree in town. Clearly, she has no illusions about Lame Bull, whose advances she has previously resisted. When he jokes that her son has said she is ready to marry him, she replies in her clear, bitter voice that "my son tells lies that would make a weasel think twice. He was cut from the same mold as you" (p. 9). Although after their marriage she complains about Lame Bull's sloppy habits and his teasing of her mother, she is obviously sexually attracted to him. Lame Bull responds to her complaints only by grinning a silent challenge, and "the summer nights came alive in the bedroom off the kitchen. Teresa must have liked his music" (p. 23).

Her relationship with her son is complicated both by her own personality and by his inner turmoil. Like his father, whom he describes as "always in transit" (p. 21) before his death, the narrator can neither live with Teresa nor leave her permanency. The conflict between mother and son is clear from Teresa's first words after he arrives home. Immediately accosting him with the news that his "wife" Agnes took off with his gun and electric razor shortly after he left for town, she simultaneously urges him to get his property back and defends herself for not stopping the girl: "What did you expect me to do? I have your grandmother to look after, I have no strength, and she is young—Cree!" (p. 3). Her tactic of squeezing into one breath as much advice, criticism, and self-defense as possible only antagonizes and further alienates her son. Because she feels that her son's only real problems are that he is a wanderer like all Indians and that he is too sensitive, she cannot understand why he did not stay on at the Tacoma hospital, where he was offered a job after having an operation on his leg. His explanation that he was hired only as a token Indian male to help the hospital qualify for grant money does not penetrate her consciousness. His bitterness at her lack of understanding is summed up in his comment that "I never expected much from Teresa and never got it. But neither did anybody else. Maybe that's why First Raise stayed away so much" (p. 21).

The narrator's discussion with Teresa about his pet duck, Amos, which precedes their discussion of First Raise and of the narrator himself, dramatically reveals the nature and possible consequences of their conflict. It is Teresa who reminds her son about Amos, and her habitually negative recollections become a springboard for her running commentary about her first husband, sons, and Indians in general. She recalls that First Raise won Amos pitching pennies at the fair when "he was so drunk that he couldn't even see the plates" and that the other ducklings drowned because her sons did not keep the tub full of water for them—"You boys were like that" (p. 15). When the narrator tries to explain that Amos, who had remained perched on the edge of the tub while his siblings plunged to the bottom, survived because he was smarter than the other ducklings, she dismisses his theory with the remark that "He was lucky. One duck can't be smarter than another. They're like Indians" (p. 15). As far as she was concerned, the other ducks were crazy.

Like the narrator, Amos inexplicably survived a disastrous accident which killed his siblings. While the narrator is just as unable to solve this puzzle as he is that of his own survival when Mose died, he does, in the course of this conversation with Teresa, learn that she killed Amos—a truth so horrifying that he desperately tries to avoid comprehending it. When he realizes that the answer to the question of who killed Amos, one he did not want to ask, is going to be either his mother or First Raise, the implications so traumatize him that he tries to suggest, instead, that one or the other of them killed the hated turkey which used to attack him, not Amos, who must have been killed by the bobcat. Matter-of-factly leading her son to a truth he does not want to face, Teresa quietly confesses that she did indeed kill Amos. In her own eyes, she has done what her husband and sons could not do—sacrifice sentiment for practicality by killing the pet duck for Christmas dinner. Her act symbolizes the reversal of traditional male and female roles: because the hunter now can only dream of bringing elk meat home from Glacier Park, the mother is forced to provide food by whatever means available. Although the narrator is reacting to what he feels is the deliberate murder of Amos by his mother and to becoming an accomplice when he unknowingly eats his pet, he does not yet really perceive that the power of life and death Teresa held over Amos is held over him as well. This realization is revealed symbolically as he recalls his dream after the sexual encounter with the barmaid from Malta.

The conflict between mother and son is intensified by the intrusion of the opposite sex. Although Teresa treats Agnes with cold politeness because she thinks the girl is her son's wife, she does not hesitate to point out that the girl is not happy and belongs in town, which the narrator realizes means Agnes belongs in bars. Consequently, she disapproves of her son's wanting to bring Agnes back. Teresa's marriage to Lame Bull and her friendship with the Harlem priest increase the narrator's hostility toward his mother. He cannot bear to see his father replaced by Lame Bull, whom he detests as a crafty, vulgar clown and whom he thinks married his mother for her ranch. Realizing that marriage to Lame Bull means that her son must leave, Teresa tells her son to start looking around because there is not enough for him on the ranch. The narrator also cannot bear his mother's drinking partnership with the priest. When the latter sent Teresa a letter, the narrator wants to read it, "to see what a priest would have to say to a woman who was his friend. I had heard of priests having drinking partners, fishing partners, but never a woman partner" (p. 58). Instead, because he cannot even bring himself to see her name inside the envelope, he tears the letter up between his legs.

The Oedipal jealousy he feels is part of his inability to separate himself from her and to see himself and his mother as they really are rather than as his distorted perception makes them seem. Welch provides evidence that the narrator's view is not held by everybody. When the bartender in Malta comments that Teresa is "a good one—one of the liveliest little gals I know of," the narrator wryly comments that "She is bigger than you are, bigger than both of us put together" (p. 56). The best example of the tender side of her nature is her care and love for her mother. The narrator is so distanced from himself and her that he has no perception of how hard the physical and psychological drain of running the ranch, raising her family, and caring for an aged mother, have been on Teresa. Now fifty-six years old, she is worn down by the endless demands on her by a mother almost a hundred years old and son of thirty-two whose chief occupation seems to be getting drunk, laid, and beaten up. Her acts of genuine caring and her grief at the death of her mother contrast with the behavior of both the narrator and Lame Bull. Rather than join her new husband and her son in drinking "Vin Rose" after the grandmother's grave is dug, she walks into her bedroom to be alone. During the bizarre funeral, she falls to her knees in grief. The narrator's slowly increasing perception of the hard lives of both his grandmother and mother is reflected in his growing awareness of the fact that Teresa has come to resemble her mother. How much she differs from his one-night stands is revealed in his comment, made while digging the grandmother's grave, that "from this distance she looked big and handsome, clean-featured, unlike the woman I had seen the night before" (p. 137).

Deprived of the affection he needs from Teresa, the narrator seeks it in a misplaced attachment to Agnes and in casual sexual encounters. Because Agnes is a Cree from Havre, scorned by the reservation people, a permanent union with her would continue the bad medicine passed down from the narrator's grandmother. The narrator vividly recalls the stories she has told him about the Crees, who were good only for the whites who had slaughtered Indians, had served as scouts for the soldiers, and "had learned to live like them, drink with them, and the girls had opened their thighs to the Long Knives. The children of these unions were doubly cursed in the eyes of the old woman" (p. 33).

The contempt of the Blackfeet for the Crees was based not only on their longstanding warfare and on the Crees' close interaction with the whites but also on their strikingly opposed attitudes toward female sexual morality. Among the Crees, chastity was desirable but not essential, and illegitimacy was not a cause of great concern. An adulterous wife might be given to the lover in exchange for a gift, and wife exchange operated similarly. Among the Blackfeet, chastity was of supreme importance. Because illegitimate pregnancy was regarded as a severe family disgrace, young girls were closely watched by their mothers and married off as soon as possible after puberty. Women's prayers uniformly began with the declaration of their purity; and the most important ceremonial, the Sun Dance, began with the vow of a virtuous woman for the recovery of the sick. On the other hand, the Blackfeet male's efforts at seduction were actively encouraged by his family. Perhaps because of this double standard, the Blackfeet traded with the Crees for love medicine, which the former called Ito-wa-mami-wa-natsi (Cree medicine.)

Agnes' conduct, as well as her tribal background, reinforces the conclusion that the narrator has made a disastrous choice. Agnes is interested only in exchanging sex for a good time and whatever she can get or steal. As the narrator puts it, she is "a fish for dinner, nothing more" (p. 22). When she grew bored reading movie magazines and imagining she looked like Raquel Welch, she took the narrator's gun and electric razor and headed for Malta, where she quickly found a new man. Despite his recognition that she is "Cree and not worth a damn" (p. 33), the narrator is haunted by the image of her body by moonlight, a memory stronger than the experience itself. Because he cannot get her out of his blood, he hesitatingly decides to go after her. Like the medicine man Fish, whose interpretation of the signs after Standing Bear's death was partially responsible for making the grandmother an outcast from her band, Agnes possesses a power which cannot be withstood: her "fish medicine" is strong enough to separate the narrator from his grandmother and mother. He longs to recapture what he has convinced himself that he and Agnes had together before she left. But when the narrator finally finds her in Havre, he ducks so that she cannot see him: "I wanted to be with her, but I didn't move. I didn't know how to go to her. There were people counting on me to make her suffer, and I too felt that she should suffer a little. Afterwards, I could buy her a drink" (p. 102).

This same ambivalence is demonstrated in his physical descriptions of her. He is attracted by her combination of open sexuality and childlike innocence. When he meets her in a bar, she is wearing a dress cut almost to the waist in back and pulled up over her thighs. Nevertheless, her eyes "held the promise of warm things, of a spirit that went beyond her miserable life of drinking and screwing men like me" (p. 113). Because of his growing desire to reform himself and to believe that she really is capable of warmth and affection, he tries to persuade her to settle down by learning a trade like shorthand. Although she curtly rejects his advice in disbelief, his attempt to reform her is an essential step toward achieving his own regeneration because he had expressed concern for the welfare of someone with whom he wants a close relationship; "I was calm, but I didn't feel good. Maybe it was a kind of love" (p. 113). Unfortunately, Agnes' reaction to his plaintive confession that he is not happy leaves no doubt that he will get even less sympathy from her than he has from Teresa: "That's a good one. Who is?" (p. 113).

Neither her rejection of his suggestion for a new life nor the beating administered by her brother breaks the bond which ties him to her. Although he lies to his inquisitive neighbor Mrs. Frederick Horn when he tells her that Agnes came back with him, he obviously intends to try to fulfill this wish. By the end of the novel, he has healed enough internally to think about going to a doctor about his injured knee but not enough to risk losing Agnes by taking the time necessary to recover from surgery. His need to end the spiritual and emotional pain of his longing for her is stronger than his need to end the physical pain in his knee: "Next time I'd do it right. Buy her a couple of cremes de menthe, maybe offer to marry her on the spot" (p. 175). Given the evidence about Agnes' attitudes and behavior, his wish for stability and closeness through marriage is not likely to be fulfilled. He may catch his "fish" again, but he probably will not be able to hang onto her. However, his wanting a close relationship with a woman, even if he has to commit himself to marriage, demonstrates how far he has progressed from the distance he felt within himself and from the women in his life which he expressed at the beginning of the novel.

While tracking down his missing girlfriend, the narrator meets Malvina, who represents what Agnes will probably be like at forty. However, Malvina, unlike Agnes, has tried to make something of herself by training at Haskell Institute to become a secretary, only to have her skills rejected. When the narrator meets her in a Harlem bar, she is tough and aggressive in her disgust at the older men's conversation, her demand that they buy her a drink, and her successful attempt to pick up the narrator. She offers him neither affection nor unlimited sex. Her cocoon-like bedroom is carefully furnished to give the illusion of sensuality. The many pictures of her smiling in earlier days contrast with her present toughness. The globes of bubble-bath remind the narrator of the unused ones in Teresa's bedroom given her by First Raise. Although the sensuality of Malvina's bedroom and volup-tuousness of her body arouse renewed desire in the narrator, she verbally castrates him for wanting more than she is willing to give. Her sharp commands to "beat it" (p. 84) freeze first his hand reaching between her thighs and then his groin. Like Teresa and Agnes, Malvina has cut him off.

The characterization of the female as castrator is graphically drama-tized by Belva Long Knife, who owns her ranch and is perhaps the best cowboy in her family, including her son Raymond, who won a silver belt buckle for "All-around Cowboy. Wolf Point Stampede, 1954" (p. 26). After wrestling calves to the ground and castrating them, she would throw the testicles into the fire: "She made a point of eating the roasted balls while glaring at one man, then another—even her sons, who, like the rest of us, stared at the brown hills until she was done" (p. 24). The economic power of women over men is seen as a less dramatic form of castration. Emily Short, for example, has the best fields on the reservation because she serves on the tribal council. The combined image of sexual and economic power of the woman is demonstrated in the complaint of the gas station attendant to the narrator that he cannot fire his helper who is more intent on masturbation than work because "his old lady'd cut my nuts off," (p. 75). The power of wives over their husbands is shown both in the example of the regular bartender in Malta who is not working because he has wife troubles and in that of the airplane man who was reported to the FBI by his wife for embezzlement.

The anonymous barmaid from Malta represents another experience in sexual frustration. Her namelessness emphasizes how insignificant she is to the men in the bar attracted by her hips and breasts. To them she is a "nice little twitch" (p. 50), an object to devour with their eyes and to compare with their wives. Even the nameless and mysterious embezzler, the airplane man, for whom she used to dance, cannot place or identify her. For the narrator, she becomes more than an object of lust because she involved him in additional searches for truth to determine her past relationship with the airplane man and to find out what happened between her and the narrator in the hotel.

As he gradually awakens with a hangover the morning after meeting the barmaid, he recalls his dream filled with images of sexual abuse of the barmaid and his mother. In this dream, which serves as a kind of vision, the elements of his past experience form a montage of destruction and regeneration foreshadowing experiences to come. He first describes the image of a girl slit and gutted like a rainbow trout, begging men to turn her loose. She then becomes the barmaid, screaming under the hands of leering men. The final image is as a gutted fish being fallen upon by men. Despite the specific allusion to the barmaid, the implied allusion to Agnes, his particular "fish," is clear.

The images of Teresa present her as a sexual victim and a person with both verbal and procreative power. She is described as hanging upside down from a wanted man's belt, which becomes the narrator's, in a helpless sexual position with strong Oedipal overtones. Next she is described as being fondled by the men who comment on her body as they spread her legs wider and wider until Amos waddles out and soars up into the dull sun, which is the most sacred deity (Natos) of the Blackfeet. By linking Amos, the survivor, to the sun, Welch may be alluding to the myth of the morning star in which A-pi-su'-ahs or Early Riser is the only one of all the many children of the sun and the moon (Ko-Ko-mik'-e-is or Night Light) who is not killed by pelicans. In Blackfeet traditional terms, Amos, the animal which has appeared to the narrator in his dream, has become his medicine or secret helper. Ironically, the instrument of Amos' death has become the means of his rebirth in the dream; symbolically, the instrument of the narrator's physical birth and spiritual death has become the means of his rebirth. By releasing her son, Teresa frees him to soar out of her grasp. The act foreshadows the rebirth of the narrator later in the novel. However, Teresa is not described as being so helpless as the barmaid. In addition to having the power to give birth, she also has the vocal power to warn the airplane man and rage at the narrator. Further, her voice, which the narrator does not escape in the dream, becomes the medium to carry him from this episode to the next, which involved the boys' driving the cattle back to the ranch. The emphasis on the power of her voice indicates both his acceptance of her verbal domination and his need for her assistance in recalling images from his own memory. It also contrasts with his inability to communicate in the dream because his guts are spilling out of his monstrous mouth. The image foreshadows his verbally spilling out his anguish when trying to pull the cow out of the slough.

After awakening from the dream, the narrator cannot remember whether or not he had intercourse with the Malta barmaid. However, he gradually remembers being in bed with her and seeing her body, especially the image of the button strained between her breasts. Despite his inability to remember the details of the episode, its significance in terms of the development of his ability to care about someone else is shown in his feeling almost ashamed that he might have intruded on her relationship with the airplane man.

His recollection of their coming to his room at the hotel returns when the sight of her hips from the rear rouses his sexual desire and the memory of popping the button between her breasts. His reactions to the barmaid in terms of parts of her anatomy indicate the fragmented state of his mind, which makes him as incapable of effectively reestablishing contact with the barmaid as he was with Agnes. Because he does not know her name and realizes the clerk of the hotel she has entered will not help him, he is overcome with helpless frustration in a "world of stalking white men" and violent Indians: "I was a stranger to both and both had beaten me" (p. 120). After waiting two hours for the barmaid to come down from her room, he gives up in despair and picks up Marlene, who becomes the victim of his frustrated lust.

Ironically, Marlene is the woman who shows him the most sympathy. Bulky, with teeth blacked around the edges, Marlene makes up in compassion what she lacks in beauty. When she first sees him on the sidewalk after he has been beaten, she both expresses concern and offers to get him something to drink. Later, when he has taken her to a dingy hotel, her eyes water every time she looks at his swollen eyes. Although she allows him to hide in the softness of her body, he feels no similar compassion for her. In his state of frustration and alienation, he perceives her merely as his "great brown hump" (p. 121) and as an object to be examined like a scientific specimen.

When he covers her with his own body, she becomes to him the symbol of the three women who have frustrated him sexually—Agnes, Malvina, and the barmaid. Her repeated requests for him to "kiss my pussy" (pp. 121, 123) cause him to explode into violence, slapping her hard and then holding her down so that she cannot move. He feels no emotion as he watches her sob. Nevertheless, the act of violence has brought him a kind of peace because he does not feel the need for anything, even sex. No longer the receiver of violence at the hands of the white rancher at the beginning of the novel or of Agnes' brother, he has transmitted the violence from within his spirit onto the body of someone weaker than he. Unable to communicate his anger and frustration verbally, he resorts to communicating through blows. This act of violence frees him from being so driven by frustrated lust that he cannot cope with the other problems in his life. Although she struggles against him, Marlene harbors no strong resentment. Because his treatment of her seems only to remind her of how sick he is and because her loneliness causes her to seek companionship, whatever the cost, she offers to forgo any money he might give her to persuade him to stay and talk with her.

The effect of the release of his pent-up frustration is shown in the sympathy he feels for the small, sickly daughter of the Michigan professor with whom he gets a ride home after leaving Marlene. Noticing that the child is frail and white, with eyes as dull as a calf's, he gradually becomes aware that she suffers some kind of discomfort, which causes her parents to stop the car so that she can vomit. After the girl comes out from behind the bushes, he returns her smile, forgetful of the pain the act of smiling will cause his swollen nose. He performs a final act of graciousness when he allows her father to take his picture before leaving the family. His compassion for her continues after their separation, as exemplified by his eating, out of loyalty rather than hunger, the peach she gave him. His odyssey now over, he has come full circle back to his home, and having been able to feel some measure of sympathy for someone other than himself, he is ready to take the final steps to close the distance within himself. That these final steps will necessitate death and the threat of death in order to bring back the full memory of the accident which killed Mose and the exorcism of the bad medicine in his family's blood is evident from his recollection on his way home of killing the hawk as a boy out hunting with Mose. The allusion to the hawk, to which he compared himself at the beginning of the novel, emphasizes the circular nature of his odyssey. The description of the dying hawk's futile efforts to communicate parallel those of the narrator.

Although the women and the young girl figure in the causes and resolution of the narrator's alienation, they are not the only females whose actions affect him. Two crucial incidents in the novel involve cows. The death of his brother Mose in a car accident, a major cause of his alienation, resulted from the actions of a wild-eyed spinster cow. Sent by First Raise to round up the cattle for the winter, the twelve-year-old narrator and his fourteen-year-old brother rush to head back all the cattle in one day. The physical appearance of the wild-eyed cow and her spinsterhood in a herd consisting primarily of mothers with calves set her apart from the others, just as the grandmother in her youth was set apart from her band because of her appearance and childlessness. Avoiding the calves with outraged dignity, the wild-eyed cow ran across the valley and raced headlong down the incline across the highway. Inexplicably, she refused to go through the gate on the other side, which caused the cattle behind her to bunch up along the highway. When a speeding car killed Mose, the narrator did not even see the accident because his horse Bird had bolted after a stray calf. The narrator was thrown to the ground, injuring his knee, after Bird jolted down the shoulder of the highway.

Despite the fact that the narrator always associates the wild-eyed cow with the accident, he realizes that, as an instrument of an uncontrollable fate, she is no more to blame than the boys themselves. His acceptance of this signals his growing awareness that perhaps Teresa was no more to blame for the destruction of the family unit and his own sense of disorientation than is he himself. Nevertheless, the accident was ultimately responsible for the loss of the only two people he really loved—his brother and his father.

Twenty years after the accident, a wild-eyed cow becomes the means of the narrator's regeneration. The mother cow and her calf serve as a focus for his readaptation to ranch life after the violence of the town. The chores he performs for them provide an opportunity to feel concern and commitment for something other than himself and thus provide a transitional stage to the development of these feelings for humans. Further, the mother cow's stubborn refusal to be separated from her calf and its dependence on her can be compared with the relationship the narrator has with his mother and the one that many of the children in the novel have with theirs. Although Teresa, unlike the cow, recognizes that she must wean her son, she still continues to be concerned about him. In contrast, Malvina seems to show little concern for the destructive impact her lovers will have on her son. Similar parental indifference is evident toward the two small children left alone in the car. Parental abandonment through death is described in the magazine story— about the pregnant woman killed in Africa whose child is born alive—which the narrator reads at the beginning of the novel. Animals, such as the mare and her colt which the narrator sees as the novel opens, seem to care more for their young than do humans.

The attempts of the mother cow and her calf to get together recur throughout the novel and their cries to one another provide transitions into various episodes. When the narrator is attempting to convince Lame Bull that he was an adult of twenty when the flood occurred, among the sounds he hears are the mother cow's answering from the slough the cries of her calf. One of his first chores in the novel is to shoo the sucking calf away from its mother. When the calf erupts under the narrator's arm as he pins it against the fence, the touch of his thigh triggers his first memory of childhood—that of riding calves with his brother. Although he chases the cow back to the slough, he knows she will be back because her udder is full. Later, the tender sight of the cow's licking the head of her calf in the corral precedes his conversation with Teresa about Amos, First Raise, and himself. The sudden bawling of the calf interrupts his memory of how the ducks drowned. When the narrator tries to saddle Old Bird and ride out to visit Yellow Calf for the first time, the calf follows the bucking horse and rider out of the corral, not sure whether to go with them or return to its mother. Its confusion parallels that of the narrator.

The sound of the calf's bawling at feeding time catches the narrator's attempts to get her out become his epic battle for the possession of truth and of his own soul, for which he has been purified by a ritual bath shortly before the episode and by his visit to the trickster-holy man, Yellow Calf. Temporarily overcome with hatred for what the other wild-eyed, equally stupid and hateful cow did to his life, he nonetheless realizes that he must risk re-injuring his knee and possible death by wading out into the mud to save this cow. Out of his intense physical effort, prolonged by Bird's initial disinclination to help, comes the ability to verbalize his anger and self pity and then to perceive that his mother—like everybody—has been taken for a ride: "Your husband, your friends, your son, all worthless, none of them worth a shit. Slack up, you sonofabitch! Your mother dead, your father—you don't even know, what do you think of that? A joke, can't you see? Lame Bull! the biggest joke—can't you see that he's a joke, a joker playing a joke on you? Were you taken for a ride! Just like the rest of us, this country, all of us taken for a ride. Slack up, slack up! This greedy stupid country—" (p. 169).

Renewed through his verbalization and revelation, he finds the strength first to plan a new life and then try to finish the job of hauling the cow out of the mud with the help of Old Bird, who dies in the attempt. The narrator's sacrifice for the cow, though apparently unsuccessful, makes him feel closer to Mose and First Raise, although he has rejected the temptation of joining them in death by allowing himself to sink into a grave in the mud. He also feels closer to nature, enjoying the sensation of the cleansing, summer rain. Both cow and calf are now silent, the mother presumably dead and the calf weaned. The narrator is now ready to make his final peace with his grandmother's bad medicine, his mother, and himself and to propose one with Agnes. The winter in his blood has thawed.

JANET ST. CLAIR

Fighting for Her Life: The Mixed-Blood Woman's Insistence Upon Selfhood

The task of the mixed-blood woman in the contemporary Native American novel is self-creation. Being and becoming, it is commonly conceded, are derived from relationships: a meaningful sense of self evolves from connections to family, place, community, and language. Yet the mixed-blood woman is typically defined not by the cultural constructs to which she is connected, but by the multiple categories from which she is excluded. Initially alienated even from herself by a linguistic label that nullifies wholeness and implies genetic taint, she is denied the right to think, speak, and act fully within the social forum of either of her heritages. The mixed-blood woman, successively more displaced by gender subjugation, class hegemonies, and physical appearance is inevitably Other. Silenced, stereotyped, rejected, and obscured, she is denied a birthright of voice, story, history, and place.

Her triumph lies in her refusal to acquiesce to cancellation. Every such woman in the contemporary Native American novel sets out either to reconstruct or to create a context of interrelationships through which she can throw off impotence and invisibility. Although access to every channel of personal and communal power is systematically and deliberately pinched off, she resists the inexorable opposition and struggles in isolation toward kinships and connections. Transcending both divided allegiances and a fractured or unfinished sense of self, each one, to varying degrees, repudiates the artificial binaries of her mixed blood and recognizes the healing and mediating potential of that rejection.

From *Critical Perspectives on Native American Fiction.* © 1993, 1997 by Passeggiata Press.

For the mixed-blood woman, obliteration of self begins at birth. Parents are typically absent, abusive, or emotionally incapable of support. Pauline Puyat (*Tracks*, Louise Erdrich, 1988) leaves home as a child, hoping —in a significant choice of words—to "fade out" until she loses all traces of the Indian blood she despises (14). She rejects and denies her own daughter, so that Marie Lazarre (*Love Medicine*, Erdrich, 1984) never learns the identity of either of her parents. Albertine Johnson, a character in the same novel, never knows her Swedish father but must listen constantly to her mother's denigration of Albertine's white blood. Between herself and her mother "the abuse was slow and tedious . . . living in the blood like hepatitis," driving Albertine from home to the streets of Fargo at the age of fifteen (*Love Medicine* 7). Rayona Taylor (*A Yellow Raft in Blue Water*, Michael Dorris, 1987), the only character in contemporary Native American fiction who is half Indian and half Negro, also runs away, although she has no real home from which to escape. Her mother, ignorant of the circumstances of her own birth and incapable of assuming the responsibilities of parenthood, has already deserted Rayona. The girl's father is seldom present and never supportive. So desperate is Rayona for the identity endowed by parents that she picks up a scrap of letter thrown away by some more fortunate child and constructs for herself an elaborate scenario of domestic security.

Some of the women's mothers are inadequate or damaging parents because of the internal antagonisms resulting from their own mixed blood. Mary Theresa, mother of Cecelia Capture (*The jailing of Cecelia Capture*, Janet Campbell Hale, 1985) detests her Indian husband, hates herself for the Indian stain that corrupts her Irish lineage, and viciously shames and abuses Cecelia for being one of the "damned dumb Indians" who "think you're something" (83). Cecelia attempts to win her father's approval by becoming the son he always wanted, but the alcoholic Will Capture grows increasingly distant as Cecelia is thrust reluctantly toward womanhood. Ephanie Atencio (*The Woman Who Owned the Shadows*, Paula Gunn Allen, 1983) is the half-breed daughter of a halfbreed daughter, both of them products of unrelenting social exclusion. Ephanie's mother—bitter, hostile, and perhaps paranoid—offers her daughter little protection or affection as a child, and becomes for the adult Ephanie a half-mad, knife-wielding apparition whom she must fear, just as Ephanie's mother feared her own defiant mother.

The unraveling of self becomes yet more acute when the children enter school. Singled out and ostracized as a result of their mixed blood, they find it difficult to form and sustain friendships. Rayona's inability to make friends results both from her mother's frequent moves and her own conspicuous combination of Indian and Negroid features. She strives toward invisibility by remaining silent, reclusive, and studious, but she nevertheless generates hostility from her peers, and suspicion and annoyance from teachers who expect her to be stupid. Cecelia, subjected to abuse and humiliation in a white school, is daily made to feel that "She didn't belong there. They didn't like her being there. She wasn't their kind" (76). Later, having changed to a school populated almost exclusively by blacks and whites, she feels as if she is being held in a foreign prison (76). The convent school is for Ephanie "an alien place" filled with terror, guilt, and grief, where the existence of other children is scarcely even acknowledged (153). Ephanie's only childhood friend is Elena, "A Chicana girl her age, almost, who was also an outsider, a stranger" (151). The friendship with Elena allows Ephanie to forget that she is ostracized by everyone else, until Elena's mother, worried about the girls' closeness, forbids her daughter to see Ephanie again.

As the mixed-blood girls grow older, they discover that the ostracism they experience in school reflects the attitudes of their entire community, whether white or Indian. In Watona, Oklahoma, setting for Linda Hogan's *Mean Spirit* (1990), "Indian" identity is apparently largely a matter of choice. Belle Graycloud, the protagonist, is "a light-skinned Indian" with a blonde daughter and granddaughter and a mixed grandson, yet the Grayclouds distinguish themselves from the "mixed-blood people," an amorphous, faceless, nameless group that is expected to keep to themselves (70). Paula Gunn Allen speaks of this community ostracism most eloquently. Since Ephanie's grandmother married a "squawman" (41) and gave birth to halfbreed children, each generation has been banished from tribal participation and social involvement. Although the family lived at the edge of the village, "they might as well have lived in Timbuktu, as her mother used to say" (150). Even relatives refused to visit. Living on both literal and figurative peripheries, Ephanie knew little of the Indians' business beyond the fact that "that business included her exclusion" (72).

The women are no less isolated when they abandon their natal communities for others. Rayona Taylor leaves Seattle to live on the reservation where her mother grew up, but her feelings of ostracism only intensify because of the impossibility of remaining inconspicuous. A cousin enlists his friends in ridiculing Rayona's mixed blood, and the local priest further alienates her by singling her out for special attention because of her "dual heritage." After sexually assaulting her, Father Tom buys her a train ticket out of town to protect his own reputation, rationalizing that she "won't feel so alone, so out of place" in the anonymity of the city (63). When Rayona gets a job at a resort, she is the only girl that the boys are incapable of regarding as a sexual partner. Teen-aged Cecelia Capture runs away to San

Francisco, where she initially feels comfortable in the ostensibly nonjudgmental hippie community of Haight-Ashbury. But soon they too all seem to be "involved in some kind of conspiracy against her," so Cecelia begins hanging out in Indian bars. Although she identifies more closely with these "hopeless, displaced people. No longer Indian, yet not white either," she finds no community beyond some loose bond of despair (112). Ephanie Atencio, too, seeks out the Indian community in San Francisco, but finds it both counterfeit and clannish. Liberal whites who court her seem only to be assuaging their own senses of guilt by assigning her an identity that they can pity. Even Vivian Twostar (*The Crown of Columbus*, Dorris and Erdrich, 1991)—surely the most buoyant and self-assured of the mixed-breed protagonists—is constricted by the exclusionary artifices of her community. She knows that she has been hired to the faculty of Dartmouth College because of her "heritage, a mixed bag of new and Old Worlds," so she conforms to her "role" by dressing with ethnic eccentricity and assuming the prescribed expression that she interprets as "stern," yet "wistful for a lost past, distant and harmless" (9, 14).

Because of the women's uncreated, damaged, or schizophrenic senses of self, their relationships with men and the marriages that frequently result are typically destructive. Pauline, conceiving of sexuality as a sinister monster to be vanquished, cleaves body from mind in order to preserve psychological inviolability. She attempts to destroy both Eli and her sexual fascination for him through the innocent body of Sophie, loathes with insane intensity the embryonic "bastard girl" within her own womb (*Tracks*, 198), and praises God in murderous exultation after she strangles the father of her child with her rosary. Sustaining the violent splintering of mind and body leaves her obsessed until death with mad, ascetic aberrations. Cecelia marries Nathan, a privileged white graduate assistant at her college, hoping "that by marrying him she could take on his upbringing, his happy childhood, his confidence, as easily as she had taken on his name" (199). The connection does not, of course, endow her with identity; rather, her husband's pompous condescension devours the feeble sense of self-esteem that she had so courageously nurtured. She learns that she is for Nathan merely a fashionable badge of political rectitude and a nostalgic reminder of a Mexican prostitute with whom he had once been sexually obsessed. He dismisses his wife as dull-witted, undisciplined, and recalcitrant, and expects her silently to defer to his judgments about her own best interests. After leaving him, Cecelia seeks validation and approval in a random pastiche of meaningless sexual encounters, but the squalor of the associations leaves her feeling even more "empty and lonely and stupid" (19).

Ephanie Atencio, numbed by despair after being abandoned by an insensitive and brutal husband, depends upon her friend and "hermano" Stephen for compassion and protection. Instead, he takes advantage of her trust to seduce her, then leaves in disappointment. Later, having run away to San Francisco, Ephanie marries Thomas, a second-generation Japanese-American, in hopes that he will understand her. "Nisei. Halfbreed," she reasons. "At least he knew what she knew, as she knew it. . . . He knew about confusion. Identity. . . . Not [being] this or that" (92). But Thomas is too involved in his own misery and impotent fury to respond to her. He even makes love to her as if she were not there. Ephanie is driven to the edge of madness—and to divorce—by her sense of invisibility in his presence.

At least two of the women are empowered by their relationships with men, but that strength is engendered by their fierce and tenacious resistance to cancellation rather than by the relationships themselves. Marie Lazarre, ignorant of her parents' identities, grows up thinking of herself as "the youngest daughter of a family of horse-thieving drunks" (Love Medicine 58). Unwittingly possessed of her birthmother's monomaniacal obsession to be revered, though, she enters the convent determined to become so saintly that everyone who ever looked down on her would love to kiss her toenails. Turning even violent rape into triumph, she makes Nector Kashpaw relinquish his beloved Lulu and marry her. Having gained respectability by acquiring the Kashpaw name, Marie determines to win her own glory by moulding him to her purposes. Through sheer force of defiant will, Marie painstakingly constructs identities for herself and her husband from the raw materials of their legal connection.

Vivian Twostar repeatedly vows to terminate her relationship with the arrogant, self-absorbed, and condescending Roger Williams, but mutual irresistible sexual attraction continually wrenches them both from stolid resolution to vexed reconciliation. Roger incessantly denigrates Vivian's intellect, character, and judgment, and pouts in ostentatious injury when she fails to be grateful for his sagacious guidance. When she unexpectedly becomes pregnant with his child, the uncomfortable connection becomes harder for Vivian to dissolve. After the birth of their "tan-colored baby, light-haired, mixed by God," the ever-ebullient and irrepressible Vivian determines to shape a family out of the fragmented collection of clashing personalities represented by Roger, herself, their difficult daughter, her rebellious teen-aged son from a previous failed marriage, and her stubborn and judgmental Indian grandmother (369). Vivian's way, however—inevitably smoothed by her indulgent creators, Erdrich and Dorris—is made considerably (and, it might be argued, artificially) easier by Roger's epiphanous near-death experience and their serendipitous discovery of the crown of Columbus that vaults Vivian into the heady spheres of academic acclaim.

Marie's and Vivian's inflexible insistence upon personal validation reflect the mixed-blood woman's characteristic refusal to accede to inefficacy and invisibility. The processes of self-invention/self-authentication are agonizingly protracted because the women have little or no support against overwhelming and unrelenting opposition. Their triumphs, moreover, may seem limited. Nevertheless, it is significant that all of them ultimately reject despair and defeat, struggle to reconstruct or make a context of interrelationships within which they can formulate wholistic self-definitions, and weave for themselves an integral and inalienable place in the social and spiritual web.

Reclamation of voice and language is the first prerequisite to the women's affirmations of self. But before they say Yes, they must say No: to negation, to silence, to coercion, victimization, restriction, and trivialization. The apathy that signals acquiescence to erasure must be turned outward into anger. Outrage must be transformed into deliberate action. The insistent but tentative No that has allowed each woman to survive with sufficient strength to continue her battle for authenticity is replaced by a firm and final articulation of resistance that redirects the course of the women's lives.

Of all the women considered, Ephanie and Cecelia come closest to defeat before their ultimate affirmations: both decide to kill themselves. When Cecelia faces distorted charges of welfare fraud and realizes that conviction would mean the end of her dream to practice law, she finds herself utterly depleted of strength and will. Her entire life has been resistance: against her mother's hatred, her father's disappointment, her peers' humiliations. She has raised her son alone and gotten a college degree despite her social worker's suggestions that she is presumptuous, unrealistic, and immoral. She has sacrificed the certain security of marriage to Jim out of unwillingness to accommodate his imaginative constructs of her. She has withstood for years the bullying and self-righteous disdain of Nathan, and insisted on studying law—on defining herself in her own terms and by her own merit—despite his insistence that he is incapable of serious and sustained effort. She passionately misses the children she left behind for law school, but knows she has nothing to give them until she has a self of which to give. Finally, seeing her last dream being stolen by indifferent forces that cannot even profit from the theft, Cecelia admits defeat. Having arranged for her children's care, she carries a loaded gun to the grave site of her son's father and prepares to take her life.

Ephanie, too, gives up: she cannot reconcile the apparently antithetical halves of her identity. *"Her Name was Stranger,"* first chapter of *The Woman Who Owned the Shadows*, explains Ephanie's alienation from her own name. "Like her it was a split name," she thinks, "a name half of this and half of that . . . An almost name . . . Proper at that for her, a halfblood. A halfbreed. Which was the source of her derangement. Ranging despair. Disarrangement" (3). She, too, leaves her two children behind, recognizing that she must either find or make a self upon which they can depend. But every desperate, innervated attempt she makes at self-definition is thwarted; every relationship she forms leaves her more uncertain of who she is. In despair, she cries, "I don't live here in me . . . I have nowhere to go" (134). Tormented by the mixed blood that signifies kinships built on enmity, self-directed animosities persuade her finally that she is locked in mortal combat with "a monstrous other" bent in its "terrifying, alien rage" upon her destruction. Her horror is exacerbated by her inability to know "which is me and which is the other" (133, 136). Convinced that she is the corrupted agent of corruption, and that further resistance is futile because "all the ways of fighting played into the destruction" (186), she carefully ties a rope to a strong ceiling pipe, tightens the slipknot around her neck, and steps off her high stool.

Neither woman dies. Instead, the ghastly recognition of their complicity in society's indifferent obliterations inspires both toward unyielding affirmations of self-worth and strength. Even more significantly, each comes to appreciate her potential to act as mediator or interpreter between the conflicting cultures represented in her mixed blood. Cecelia determines first of all to "find a place" for herself and her mixed-blood children. She vows to complete her Doctor of Jurisprudence degree, symbolically resolving the conflicts of her mixed-blood by casting herself as mediator between white law and Indian exploitation. Having claimed voice, place, kinships, and direction, Cecelia is empowered by an unfamiliar sense of liberty that makes her feel "more like herself' than she has ever felt before (201).

When the despondent Ephanie feels the rope choking off her life, she is suddenly jolted into rage against "Those who wanted her dead. Herself for listening to them" and curses, "I won't die, damn you. I won't die" (164). Having survived both her suicide attempt and "the grief, the unbearable anguish, the loneliness" that had driven her to it, she goes into retreat to read, write, and remember, seeking to mend the rupture of her halfbreed "Half mind half knowing" (164, 177). Finally, with the help of spiritual mentors, she comes to recognize not only the alliance of all creation, but her own role as prophet of unity. Claiming personal integrity, communal franchisement, and spiritual authority, she assumes her place as one of "the women who created, the women who directed people upon their true paths. The women who healed. The women who sang" (211).

Although Hogan's Belle Graycloud never specifically identifies herself as a mixed-blood woman—despite physical appearances—she, too, assumes an interpretive role. The novel itself is oddly schizophrenic: while it remains implacably polemic in its condemnation of "white" cultural characteristics, it nevertheless concerns itself deeply, although more implicitly, with convergences. Belle Graycloud's very name suggests prophetic mediation: her voice, like a bell, is a herald; gray is the color of comingled opposites; clouds, the suspended mixture of water and air. She goes to jail to protest the slaughter of eagles, creatures that live on the earth and in the heavens.

In her despair over injurious divisions she looks for healing power in "bat medicine," which acknowledges the power of creatures who traverse the borderlines of night and day, bird and beast, cave and sky. She intercedes to allow the Indian girl Lola to marry the white son of Lola's court-appointed guardian, and she is present when their mixed-blood baby girl is given the prophetically suggestive name of Moses. The novel ends with the whites' total destruction of the Grayclouds' home, but with the family—including its white and mixed-blood members—intact and celebrating the wonder that, despite their displacement, "they carried generations along with them" (371).

Vivian Twostar's mediation begins with the ecumenical premise that division is fundamentally artificial. She explains.

> I belong to the lost tribe of mixed bloods, that hodgepodge amalgam of hue and cry that defies easy placement. . . . We're called marginal, as if we exist anywhere but on the center of the page. Our territory is the place for asides, for explanatory notes, for editorial notation. . . . "Caught between two worlds," is the way it's often characterized, but I'd put it differently. We are the catch (121–22).

She mediates not only between white and Indian cultures—forging a united family out of an unlikely miscellany of culturally and generationally antagonistic personalities—but between things, places, and times as well. Everything reminds Vivian of something else; every place is like someplace else. She sees even Christopher Columbus, pillager and enslaver of Indian lives and lands, as himself a man separated from place, kinships, community, and voice; a man of blurred outlines, ultimately somebody else's invention.

Vivian's is the most unmixed triumph among those of the mixed-blood women. But each such central character in the contemporary Native American novel succeeds in resisting social abrogation and accepting the liability of isolated self-creation. Defined in terms of negations—not Indian, not white, not male, and not part of a recognized cultural continuum—she must find or make her own connections concurrently with the erosion or repudiation of her claims to kinships, place, community, and voice. The inevitable despair and apathy resulting from gratuitous abuse must be turned outward; resources must be found to discredit those who denigrate and reject her. In each case—although in different ways and to different degrees—the mixed-breed woman claims both worth and integrity; and in most cases, she acknowledges and develops the culturally remedial potential of her own process of recovery. In a postmodern age where doubt is the only certainty and cynicism the acknowledged sanity, the self-engendered power of the Native American mixed-breed woman repudiates the inevitability of isolation and reiterates the imperative of solidarity.

KIMBERLY M. BLAESER

The New "Frontier" of Native American Literature: Dis-Arming History with Tribal Humor

I
Whose History is This Anyway?

In his 1987 introduction to *Harper's Anthology of 20th Century Native American Poetry*, Brian Swann characterizes Native American poetry as "poetry of historic witness" which "grows out of a past that is very much a present" (xvii). In his 1985 forward to the anthology *New and Old Voices of Wah'kon-tah: Contemporary Native American Poetry*, Vine Deloria, Jr. claims native poetry will "tell you more about the Indian's travels in historical experience than all the books written and lectures given" (ix–x). These statements of Swann and Deloria point to an essential strand in the web of all contemporary Native American literature: the weight of history. I don't mean to claim simply that history *informs* native literature, but rather that in a very real way history *forms* native writing. It provides, of course, much of the subject and the impetus, but beyond that the consciousness of historical continuum is sounded in the voice of native writers, and traced in the form and methods of their literary expression. Much of contemporary Indian literature in style alone writes itself against the events of Indian/White contact and, perhaps more importantly, against the past accounting of those events.

Deloria characterizes the work of the native writers as presenting a "reflective statement of what it means and has meant to live in a present which is continually overwhelmed by the fantasies of others of the meanings

From *Native American Perspectives on Literature and History*. © 1994 by the University of Oklahoma Press.

of past events" (x). Indeed, any discussion of the literary representation of history in the Americas finds it center in the notion of possession, not merely physical possession of the land and its resources, but ideological possession, because to a large degree the two have gone hand in hand: those who control the land, have controlled the story (the his-story) of the land and its people. This possession of history has compelled not merely the "facts," but the perspective of the accounts and the methods of representation as well. In his introduction to the collection *American Indians and the Problem of History*, Calvin Martin, for example, discusses the standard imposition of an anthropological perspective onto the history of Native American people who themselves proceed from a biological metaphysic and he characterizes such a move as "ideological colonization" (9). The situation is further complicated because, of course, the creation and interpretations of histories have also functioned directly as the justifications for possession or dispossession, and the forums for supposed historical accounts have always included the various literary genres. Among the many contemporary scholars who have recognized these connections between history, literature and colonization are Richard Drinnon (*Facing West: The Metaphysics of Indian-Hating and Empire Building*), Richard Slotkin (*Regeneration Through Violence: The Mythology of the American Frontier, 1600–1860*), and Ward Churchill, whose recent study *Fantasies of the Master Race: Literature, Cinema and the Colonization of American Indians* includes subsections entitled "History as Propaganda of the Victors" and "Literature as a Weapon in the Colonization of the American Indian."

In the trenches of the Native American literary movement, the responses to the representations and misrepresentations of history have appeared in many forms ranging from Neihardt's rendering of Black Elk's account of Little Big Horn and Wounded Knee in the "autobiography" *Black Elk Speaks*, to Linda Hogan's dramatization of the Oklahoma oil boom in her novel *Mean Spirit*, to Simon Ortiz's exploration of the history and implications of mining in the Grants Uranium Belt in the poetry and narrative of *Fight Back. For the Sake of the People—For the Sake of the Land*, to Vine Deloria, Jr.'s challenge of the bases and tenets of Western history in essays like those from *God is Red*. Within these various literary forms, the tacks Native authors have taken also run the gamut of possibility and have included revisionist accounts, pre-emptive interpretations of contemporary historical events, "eye-for-an-eye" propagandistic distortions, attempts at completely autonomous representations, and multiple combinations of all of the above. However, the literary representations of history by Native American writers I find the most compelling and ultimately the most rewarding are those which, by their humor, work to unmask and disarm history, to expose the hidden agendas of historiography and, thereby, remove it from the grasp of the political panderers and return it to the realm of story. Among those who have approached the deadly serious business of history with trickster humor are Carter Revard, Gerald Vizenor, and Gordon Henry. Through their play and intellectual bantering they force a reconsideration of the processes and powers of historical reckoning and thus, essentially, liberate the reader from preconceived notions and incite an imaginative reevaluation of history.

Key to the ability of these writers to undertake such a liberation, is their keen awareness of the contested visions of history and their imaginative rendering of the places (both physical and intellectual) of cultural historical contact. In discussing American Literature, American Indian author and scholar Louis Owens makes an important distinction between, notions of territory (unoccupied space) and frontier (place of contact) ("Mixedblood Metaphors: Identity in Contemporary Native American Fiction"). Revard, Vizenor and Henry write works about the frontier; that is they do not proceed from the illusion of any pristine historical territory, untouched by the accounts of the opposition. Instead they draw their humor and power from an awareness of the reality of the place where the diverse accounts of history come into contact with one another. They take for granted and force recognition of the already embattled visions all readers bring to the text. Is American virgin land or widowed land? Did native peoples migrate to this continent or emerge here? Are the stories of native peoples to be classified as myth or history? Was America discovered or invaded? These authors expend little of their wit and energy to advance either of the opposing sides of these arguments; instead, they flesh out the frontier in all its immense complexity. They shift and reshift their story's perspectives, turn the tables of historical events, unmask stereotypes and racial poses, challenge the status of history's heroes and emerge somewhere in a new frontier of Indian literature, somewhere between fact and fiction, somewhere between the probable and the possible, in some border area of narrative which seems more true than previous accounts of history.

II
"what if a much of a which of a wind"

One of the more easily analyzed moves of these writers involves perspective. By a deft twist of the popular vision of history, they submerge their readers in the "what ifs" of historical interpretation: What if the actions of history were reversed? Would this affect the moral interpretations of events? What if history's heroes were not what textbooks make them out to be? What if *white* society were envisioned as the demonic "other"? How would their actual cultural practices measure up to their professed standards of evaluation? Perhaps most fundamentally, what if things did not happen exactly as they have always been portrayed, the issues, the sides, were not as neatly drawn as they have been made out to be? And, finally, what happens to our understanding of events if we recognize the subjective quality of history?

Vizenor begins this game of reversals with the most basic assumptions about tribal origins. In the film *Harold of Orange*, when one of his characters is asked about his opinion of the Bering Strait migration theory, the character responds with his own question: "Which way?" At the confused response of his interrogator, he clarifies his question: "Which way across the Bering Strait?" The moment of humor and imbalance such a scene creates for the audience is Vizenor's wedge in, his ploy to soften their resistance to other "betrayals" of historical dogma, and a move to incite the audience's own re-reading of history.

Another of Vizenor's moves to dis-arm history reverses the perspective on the possession of remains. In a scene in *Harold of Orange*, Harold implies that the bones in a museum case may actually be, not those of an Indian, but those of a white anthropologist lost in a snow storm and later mistaken for a dead Indian. In his novel *The Heirs of Columbus*, the characters struggle for possession of the remains of both Pocahontas and Columbus. Vizenor's playful reversals in these stories challenge readers to reconsider the readily accepted treatment of the remains of "primitive" cultures as museum objects and the implied hierarchy that allows or endorses such practice. Thus Vizenor employs the Pocahontas scenes to raise issues not only about physical remains but about tribal identity as well for, as Will Roscoe notes in his review of *Heirs*, "Whoever controls the artifacts of history controls history" (11). The Pocahontas myth of American popular literature has made her into a perfect stereotype of the primitive "other," an Indian princess, emblem of the romantic past and of the primitive's adoring devotion and humble gratitude for the salvation of civilization. Vizenor moves to expose the stereotype and the motivations behind its creation and to recover the story and identity of Pocahontas, an identity and a story representative, of course, of the larger tribal culture.

Henry offers his own commentary on the museumization of culture and the appropriation of cultural identity and story in a wonderful tale of a leg which is woven throughout his novel *The Light People*. Through a series of bizarre circumstances, the ceremonially dressed and amputated leg of an Anishinaabe man, Four Bears from Fineday Reservation, becomes the discovery of a young graduate student in anthropology and the pride of a metropolitan museum. Years later, when it is discovered there by Osahwa, another young man from the reservation, a legal battle for the leg ensues. In the untangling of the story of the leg, the musings of characters, and the courtroom drama, Henry tracks the passionate arguments of each side and illuminates the subtle philosophical, moral and religious implications of the actions of each of the involved parties. In a section called "Requiem for a Leg," for example, he offers this insightful lament of the museumized leg, describing it as:

> catalogued in curio stasis, as if the vanished were never meant to exist in a moment beyond "the fictional situation, but were instead left to struggle with another simulated reconstruction, as invisible victims of the interpretation of artifact. (136)

In other places Henry's analysis is humorously cast as when the anthropologist of the story recounts the debate of the museum board over the significance of the leg. The various theories of the board members, those Henry later labels "Eurocentric intellectual culture-mongers and mythmakers" (179), serve to suggest the sometimes ludicrous methods of science and to raise questions about the accuracy of what is enshrined as scholarship. The odd series of interpretations they offer alternately claim the leg was "an emblem of warfare" cut off in torture and floated down the river "as a reminder to enemies"; "part of a ritual to test the manhood of warrior initiates"; "a ritual for getting rid of diseases in the community, a dream ritual in which the leg takes the diseases into the purifying waters of the river"; or part of a ritual in which "the leg is given to the rivers to insure good fishing" (173–4). Ultimately, the official museum plaque claims "Though it is not known why the leg was left like this, some scholars believe burying a leg like this in full ceremonial legging was a common practice in the reservation period" (137). The predisposition of anthropology and the relegation of Indians to a romantic past are further exposed in Henry's story when the scholar who discovered the leg admits that "he never considered the possibility of the leg belonging to a living twentieth-century Ojibway" but had "as soon as he saw the leg" thought of "an Indian of the past" (175). Finally, the authority of the scientific community is again undermined and the scholar's motivations questioned in the story when the tribal attorney belittles the rationalizations the anthropologist offers for his actions:

"Gee, I don't know. A leg floats to you out of nowhere, and your first thought is that no one around the village will know anything. . . I bet you saw an opportunity in the leg, a chance to capture something unique, a one of a kind find that would forever connect your name with an authentic artifact." (177)

Here and elsewhere both Henry's storyline and the rich suggestiveness of his prose compel the reader to a succession of reexaminations and reevaluations of the issues of cultural appropriation.

In this trickster vein, the work of Revard, Vizenor and Henry also derive much play from the doctrine of discovery, from the record of Columbus' declarations and the ethnocentric evaluations of native peoples in his diary, from the rhetoric of manifest destiny, and from the plethora of popular Indian stereotypes. In "Report to the Nation: Claiming Europe," for example, Revard turns the tables on discovery. From aboard a Thames excursion boat, his protagonist claims England. Stopping at gas stations throughout France to issue proclamations, he lays claim to multiple areas of that country. "Whether they understood that France now belongs to us," Revard writes, "was not clear" (167). The author thus succeeds in altering the reader's perspective of the historical rights of discovery and conquest and he incites a challenge of the validity of the European claims. In the story, he also recalls the absurd and unfounded judgments made about Native American intelligence, religious practices, commerce, etc. through the equally rash evaluations made by his own protagonist (many of which echo—with a cultural twist—the descriptions recorded by Columbus). Revard writes, for example, that the Europeans "do not know how to use the land" and that their religious shrines "certainly have a lot of torture scenes in them, and these are the models for spiritual life they say" (169). His text also offers commentary on the many actions which result from the presumption of cultural superiority and exposes the double standard inherent in the colonial definition of civilized behavior. His "explorer," for example, reports, "It may be impossible to civilize the Europeans"; and then offers as evidence this accounting of their actions: "The Europeans kill each other pretty casually, as if by natural instinct, not caring whether they blow up women, kids or horses, and next day display the mutilated corpses on front pages or television screens" (166–67). He then proceeds to outline his own (equally violent) plan for dealing with the savage Europeans: "Possibly we could even teach the poor souls our Osage language, although if our faith and goodness can't be pounded into them we may just have to kill them all" (169), and finally predicts and justifies the outcome of the encounter: "We will, however, as the superior race, prevail in the end" (170). Thus Revard challenges one of the most basic tenets of the theory of manifest destiny—inherent moral superiority. These are but a small sampling of the passages in the satiric text which cast the discovery and its fallout in new light.

The targets of each of the authors are numerous and include general policies as well as specific military encounters and particular historic figures. But in each case, in Vizenor's satiric play in *Heirs* and *Harold of Orange*, Revard's in "Report to the Nation," and Henry's in *Light People*, their works garner their force from their reader's knowledge of historical events, documents, accounts and interpretations. By overturning the enshrined accounts of history with trickster reversals, they arouse in a reader an awareness of the way that history can and has been possessed. The intentions of the authors, however, are not to re-possess history nor to replace one historical account with another, but to incite the reader to an imaginative re-evaluation of both the accounts and the processes of history. Vizenor, for example, tells a tale in *Heirs* too fantastic to be mistaken for substitute doctrine. He claims Columbus himself descends from Mayan ancestry, claims also that "The Maya brought civilization to the savages of the Old World," and that Columbus' misdirected adventure to the Americas was a "return to his homeland" (9). He recounts the sexual union of Columbus with a tribal woman named Samana from which issues the mixedblood heirs of the novel, and generally embellishes history's staid accounts of Columbus with a wild irreverent tale of sex, gambling, intrigue over the remains of the explorer, murder and general mayhem. He caps the novel off with a new story of discovery, the discovery by the heirs of the Columbus' genetic signature of "survivance." In a final reversal, Vizenor's novel credits the explorer, whose appearance in the Americas signaled the beginning of an era of destruction of Native American cultures, with becoming the source of their survival through the healing genes of his remains. This zany trickster tale seeks to relieve the reader of the burden of historical truth. As Barbara Babcock has noted, the "excitement" of the trickster story "lies in the suggestion that any particular ordering of experience may be arbitrary and subjective" (181). Vizenor's aim is to liberate the reader from the so-called facts of history and to allow them to imagine for themselves the what-ifs of story.

III

Righting History

But the satiric intentions and effects of Vizenor, Henry and Revard's works extend beyond the events of history to the very documents which record and fix its interpretation, and to the philosophy and politics which empower such documents. For example, the reported declarations of Christopher Columbus and his diary account are recalled to the minds of readers by Revard and Vizenor when they employ language in their fiction which simultaneously mimics and ridicules the historical documents. The account of Columbus' claiming of the West Indies reads this way:

> The Admiral called to the two captains and to the others who jumped ashore and to Rodrigo de Escobedo, secretary of the whole fleet, and to Rodrigo Sanchez of Segovia, and said that they should bear faith and witness how he before them all was taking, as in fact he took, possession of the said island for the King and Queen, their Lord and Lady, making the declarations that are required, as is set forth in the testimonies which were taken down in writing. (33)

Revard, of course, plays off this passage in "Report to the Nation." And in *Heirs*, Vizenor's recounting of the claiming of Point Assinika by the heirs of Columbus' is filled with mocking echoes:

> The Heirs of Columbus bear faith and witness that we have taken possession of this point in the name of our genes and the wild tricksters of liberties, and we made all the necessary declarations and had these testimonies recorded by a blond anthropologist. (119)

In addition to undercutting Columbus' declarations of ownership, the Vizenor passage also derides the implied authority of this and other written testimony (particularly authority claimed principally or solely on the basis of something having been recorded in writing). By specifically identifying a blond anthropologist as recorder of the testimonies, Vizenor unleashes his satiric force on two of his favorite targets—the social sciences and anthropologists. His humor works to unmask the colonialism and ethnocentric assumptions which he believes underlie the practice of Indian anthropology, particularly the practice of raising to the level of ultimate explicator recorders of culture on the single basis of their being themselves from an-"other," dominant and supposedly superior culture. Vizenor's playful challenge of such arbitrary status finds voice elsewhere in the novel when, in another deft turnabout, he essentially removes Columbus' "otherness" (and therefore, his inherent cultural status) by making Columbus himself a mixedblood and American Indian (Mayan). Of course, another of

Vizenor's implied targets here is the false notion of cultural or racial purity.

Historical documents and the philosophy which empowers them also become the targets of Henry's satire in *The Light People*. A chapter entitled "The Prisoner of Haiku," through the haiku poetry of the character Elijah Cold Crow, recalls the practice in many historical documents (treaties, deeds of allotment, etc.) of representing tribal consent by an "x":

> Signatures, names,
> the undersigned, with marks and lines
> anglicized in print
>
> Clan leaders, head men
> scripted identities so
> many with an x.
>
> Andayk, Flatmouth, Sweet,
> Minogeshig, Broken Tooth,
> an x by the name. (82)
>
> Abetung he who
> inhabits his X mark
> in the presence of——. (85)

In other haiku of Cold Crow's, Henry writes of "name energy" and identifies the "tracks of birds in dirt" as "hieroglyphs." Read together with the previous haiku, these seem to suggest the possibility of meaning in languages and signs other than those "anglicized in print" and to imply the loss or theft of "name energy" through the enforced use of English. Henry's novel contains an essay by another character, Bombarto Rose, which also analyzes—in a language imitative of the often convoluted legal documents and philosophical treatises—various implications of the representation of X: "the artificial parameters of a metaphysical residence" (89), the document as "abstract, a function of language" (90), and the collision in the document between a "static historical reference point" and an "ahistorical reference to . . . natural time" (86). Thus, through the interplay of the haiku themselves and their connections with the larger story including Rose's essay and the punishment Cold Crow suffered in boarding school for the speaking of his native language, Henry succeeds in suggesting much about the definitions of literacy and their political expediency: the dominance of the written over the oral, the privileging of English over tribal languages, and the devaluation of culture and identity which results from labels of "illiteracy." The story also suggests the questionable nature of the historic documents themselves and attests to the way the historic contest has come to be at least partially symbolized in language. Henry writes of Cold Crow, for example, that something was "deeply embedded in the prisoner's history. A partial loss of language, new forms, old forms were part of his existence" (71).

For Native American authors, too, the contest has come to be symbolized in language, and has in its literary manifestation involved both old and new forms. Native peoples have recorded oral histories and created native language publications in addition to writing history and literature in English in both western and "non-standard" forms. Publications like N. Scott Momaday's *The Way to Rainy Mountain* and Leslie Silko's *Storyteller*, for example, illustrate the mixed-genre creations which refuse to honor scholarly distinctions between myth and history, history and story, autobiography and history, prose and poetry, etc. because they recognize and value the relationships among and inevitable overlapping of these categories.

The literary works of Vizenor, Revard and Henry likewise challenge in various ways the forms and methods of history, sometimes in the mock-rendering of standardized historical forms (as noted in Henry's *The Light People*), sometimes in a style deliberately anti-historical, anti-literary, or perhaps even anti-form. The work of Vizenor, for example, often replaces the honored cause and effect structure with the disarray of chance just as Henry's novel creates a cacophony of forms and a tangle of storied layers. Revard's work, too, is amass with layers and, in "Never Quite A Hollywood Star,' it becomes a quagmire of shifting narrative grounds. This story, written in a metafictive mode, whips the reader back and forth between story, reality, and the self-conscious framing of narrative. What these various reformings of historical accounts achieve is reader awareness. Revard's meta-fictive approach, for example, succeeds in exposing the multi-directional fields of influence between such factors as history, art, politics, news, life, and story. Among his subjects in "Never Quite a Hollywood Star" is Wounded Knee, the selective and slanted news coverage that surrounded the event, and how that reportage created the historical "truth" of the event:

> The feature will explain that these are not real Indians. The surrounding Airborne Division soldiers, the machine guns on the APC's . . . their tracer bullets that come into the church at night so brilliantly shining and kill an Indian lying next to its wall, are not real either. They are, the reporter explains, a public relations exercise. . . . The crows tell a different story. It is kept in a blue cage made of western skies and cannot

reach *The New York Times*. Here come the press trailers and vans full of
equipment pulling out of Wounded Knee. Behind them shots break out
but do not exist. (220)

As another part of his move to expose the multiple range of influences
on our thinking, Revard positions his fictive personae within the mind of the
imaginary reader and in philosophical opposition to the reader, identifying
his action as "an Indian attack." Naturally, the actual reader is then motivated
to respond, most likely to disassociate from the thinking Revard's personae
exposes as somehow faulty. Revard gives his reader a stake in the story and in
history and causes the reader to discover how implicated each individual is in
the telling of history. As Henry writes, "We apprehend the truth as we
become part of the story" (145).

Vizenor's book *The People Named the Chippewa* (whose very title recalls
the renaming of the Anishinaabeg) also has as its purpose the re-forming of
history into personal story. The subtitle of the book identifies the pieces as
"Narrative Histories" which Vizenor places in opposition to linear historical
accounts:

> The Anishinaabeg did not have written histories; their world views were
> not linear narratives that started and stopped in manifest binaries. The
> tribal past lived as an event in visual memories and oratorical gestures:
> woodland identities turned on dreams and visions. (24)

So in his accounts, Vizenor chooses a narrative form, he allows the historical
significance of oral tradition, dreams and visions, and perhaps most significantly, he makes a place in historical telling for imagination. E. M. Forster
claimed in *Aspects of the Novel* that "fiction is truer than history, because it
goes beyond the evidence, and each of us knows from his own experience
that there is something beyond the evidence" (63). Through the power of
imagination (what Momaday called "speculation"), Vizenor attempts to
"relume" the past, to bring it to life by imbuing the evidence with suggestion, implication and possibility.

"Shadows at La Pointe," as one of Vizenor's "narrative histories,"
displays the multiple dimensions and multiple perspectives he strives for. In
this narrative, he clearly intends to expose the invisible seams that lie behind
the apparent gloss of history, to reveal the inevitable effects of personality on
historiography and the effects of historical accounts on culture. To illustrate
these interconnections, Vizenor, like Revard, employs a meta-literary technique, here a meta-historical strategy which mimics the realistic complexity

of any accurate account. He creates a kind of house-that-jack-built effect. "Shadows at La Pointe" tells a story through the eyes of two young mixed-blood women from Madeline Island who play hooky from school, romp in the spring weather, recall the fine stories they have heard at the trading post, dream of their place in history, and hatch a plot to stow away on a steamer. It at once encompasses: the events of an era, the historical story about the events of an era, the tales that were told about the inventors who wrote the historical story of an era, the life stories of those who told the tales about those who wrote the historical story of an era, and finally, the thoughts and dreams of those who ultimately have their identities formed by all the previous stories. We can extend the range of the piece, the range of histor-ical influence, yet further if, as Linda Ainsworth suggests, the probable target audience for Vizenor's narrative histories includes the contemporary "people named the Chippewa" whose survival Vizenor hopes will be the next story. The survival though, Vizenor contends, depends upon the recognition of the lie of history and the truth of imagination. For only if the Anishinaabeg refuse to accept and be determined by the romantic linear history which ends with the tragic death or museumization of Indian people, can they continue to imagine their place in the story of ongoing life. Therefore, the very literary style of Vizenor, Revard and Henry writes itself against the events of history and the forms of history's recounting to contest their dominance and to claim and enact liberation and healing from the past tyranny of history.

This re-forming of history into healing story is part of the repertoire and purpose of all three authors. Vizenor writes in *Heirs* about "story energy" and those "paramount healers" whose "stories and humor" become "in some way, the energy that heals" (164). Through Vizenor's new Columbus story, his other trickster tales and his narrative histories, readers in general and perhaps tribal people in particular are, like the deformed children of the *Heirs* novel, "mended in one way or another" (164). Because historical stories, imaginative stories, cultural stories work to form our identity, the disarming of history through satiric humor liberates and empowers us in the imagination of our destinies. Henry's character Rose Meskwaa talks about stereotypic images of Indian people—"the cowboy killings, the product faces"—and how "knowing the images inside can kill you and put faces on you that you can't get off" (26). But Rose used art, painting, to "turn images inside out from the mind to the hand" and, more importantly, discovered "the [new artistic] images could replay healing images inside someone" (26). Henry, Vizenor and Revard all turn old images and old forms inside out with trickster humor because they, too, know the powers of story and humor: "Humor," writes Vizenor, "has political significance" (*Heirs* 166), and

"Comedy," writes Revard, "is worth more than tragedy any time where survival is at stake" ("Report" 180). So it is with survival humor that many contemporary Native Americans attempt to right history in their literary creations and "replay healing images inside" their reader's minds.

ROBERT DALE PARKER

To Be There, No Authority to Anything: Ontological Desire and Cultural and Poetic Authority in the Poetry of Ray A. Young Bear

The Wordsworthian preoccupation with identity, targeted by writers as diverse as Robert Pinsky, Jacques Derrida, Kathy Acker, and Charles Bernstein, takes another kind of hit in the poetry of Ray A. Young Bear, deep-image surrealist, Mesquakie, cultural isolato, and—at the same time—communal cultural nationalist. Young Bear's first two books, *Winter of the Salamander: The Keeper of Importance* and *The Invisible Musician*, have a contemplative intensity that often risks the indecipherable. His third and latest book, *Black Eagle Child: The Facepaint Narratives*, explains itself more patiently, integrating cultural exposition with poetic narrative, at times almost like a novel. The blend might recall the way some of Leslie Marmon Silko's poems displace anthropological annotation by having an elder explain things to a child (Mattina 146–47), except that Young Bear's irreverence keeps the sensibility more ironic and slippery.

In all three books Young Bear pursues something like a Euro-American surrealism while also writing more thoroughly from within a native culture than any other Native American writer I know of. Readers often feel lost amid the esoteric reference points; and the abrupt, often dream-inspired zigs and zags do little to accommodate our bewilderment. (A typical title, for example, is "in dream: the privacy of sequence.") The tight, crowded cultural frame is possible, perhaps even likely, for a

From *Arizona Quarterly* Vol. 50, No. 4. © 1994 by the Arizona Board of Regents.

Mesquakie, because the Mesquakie, compared to most other American Indian peoples, have a history of tenacious cultural and linguistic independence. With the mix of the Mesquakie and the surreal, it is difficult for non-Mesquakie readers versed in European and American poetic tradition, and I should think for those Mesquakie readers not so versed, to pick out what in Young Bear's poems we can usefully call surrealist, Mesquakie, or somehow his own.

Young Bear also writes against some thorny cultural resistances. The Mesquakie prefer to keep their culture to themselves. When Fred McTaggart went to the Mesquakie settlement expecting to find people happy to tell stories for him to record and write about, he should not have been surprised to find them courteously uncooperative. Young Bear himself insists that there is much he cannot say. Moreover, he writes in a larger culture that is mostly too ignorant, impatient, or hostile for the immensely detailed ontological routine of Mesquakie life and thought. Even compliments, of course, can betray. A favorable review of *The Invisible Musician* dwells on the beautiful cover, praising Stella Young Bear for the photo of a beaded bag without realizing that the cover credits her for beading the bag, not for photographing it (Kallet). Mesquakie culture is a self-reinventing flow of the present, not a relic of the past.

Meanwhile, as Robert F. Gish writes, "Young Bear is generally acknowledged by poets, critics, and students of American Indian literature as the nation's foremost contemporary Native American poet," and is "destined for even wider and more fulsome recognition." Still, this is a curious claim for a writer who remains almost unwritten about, daunting to read and teach, and much of whose work is out of print. For now, Young Bear's readers are confined to the small if growing audience committed to reading Indian poetry, rather than the still small but much larger audience for American poetry in general.

That sorry limit need not be so big a problem; many Indian writers are quick to say that they write mostly for other Indians. Young Bear doesn't discuss other Indian poets, but two of his poems address non-Indian poets' and editors' readings of Indians in general and, in one case, of the Mesquakie in particular. The same two poems, "in disgust and in response to indian-type poetry written by whites published in a mag which keeps rejecting me" and "for the rain in march: the blackened hearts of herons" (Young Bear has a particular genius for titles), also address Mesquakie identity and the Mesquakie world with the suggestive obscurity of so many of his other poems, but their address to the non-Mesquakie literary world helps make the obscurity more penetrable to outsiders. For Young Bear's cultural worlds and imaginative universes, like any other writer's, are hybrid, including his sense of what it means to be Mesquakie.

"in disgust and in response" puts the question of being Mesquakie in its first line, "you know we'd like to be there," and then takes up the many things that line struggles to enunciate. "You know" has a casual talkiness, yet also the oracular tone of a culture formally elaborated and reproduced, from generation to generation, through oral tradition. It also sneers sarcastically at those who only presume they know, those who see Indians as a vanishing remnant (the last of the Mohicans) mired in the past. Yet at the same time, Young Bear's "you know" suggests that the Mesquakie *would* like to be there. This is a poem, and in many ways Young Bear's is a body of poetry, about trying to be wherever there is, there where Mesquakie culture is, or in this case where it once was, since even Mesquakie can get drawn into the cultural fantasy that displaces a people's identity and essence to a vanished past. Being there promises to mean being in some kind of "balance," to pick out words from later in the poem, "whole and complete." Or maybe not so whole and complete, if that turns out to be impossible, but still in a dream of wholeness and completeness, a vision that—in the poem's final line—"is no authority to anything."

Indeed, Young Bear puts so much weight on how "we" "would" like to be there, repeating the expression in a separate line, that he sets up an expectation that such desire will be trailed by a "but we can't" that the poem never fills out, as if to rely on our sense of the ever-receding *différance* between the wish and its object, between the present and the ever-receding past that pulls at the present so strongly:

> you know we'd like to be there
> standing beside our grandfathers
> being ourselves
> without the frailty
> and insignificance of the worlds
> we suffer and balance
> on top of now
> unable to detect which to learn
> or which to keep from
> wearing the faces
> of our seasonal excuses
> constantly lying each other
> and ourselves about just how much
> of the daylight
> we understand

we would be there:
with the position of our minds
bent towards the autumn fox
feasts
feeling the strength and prayer
of the endured sacred human tests
we would set aside the year's
smallpox dead
whole and complete
with resignation
like the signs from the four legs
of our direction
standing still
sixty years back in time
breathing into the frosted lungs
of our horses the winter blessings
of our clan gods (*Winter* 118)

This is not typical of Young Bear's poetry, for mostly he writes without nostalgia about contemporary life, not about the past that is all that most popular myths can see for Native Americans. Here, however, he opposes "beside our grandfathers" to a "now" of "frailty / and insignificance," of "constantly lying to each other / and ourselves." Then, when he specifies the past he refers to as sixty years ago, the notion of grandfathers hardens into the literal. Rather than referring to ancestors at large, it zeroes in on the specific past of two or three generations ago, repeated in the reference to smallpox, which ravaged the Mesquakie in 1902 (Joffe 298). The specificity allows us to suspect that such grandfathers may sometimes have felt as frail to themselves as they now appear strong to their grandchildren, who may in turn gain strength in the nostalgia of their descendants. The mythical past shatters before the immediate Mesquakie specificity that, more in Young Bear's usual mode, magnifies through the rest of the poem. Only against the backdrop of that Mesquakie world, in so many ways unintelligible to outsiders, does Young Bear at the end of the poem finally address the disgust and response that his title promises.

On the way, he specifies "grandfathers" even more. It is a masculine term (as the "we" of this poem turns out to be masculine), and here it refers to the men of a group that is "separate and apart," for—as *Black Eagle Child* explains—in those days "the tribe broke into family groups during winter" (166). The horses, Young Bear writes,

                    would carry our belongings
and families to the woodlands
of eastern iowa to hunt our food
separate and apart
from the tribe
following and sometimes using
the river to cleanse the blood
from our daughters and wives
not knowing that far into
our lives we'd be the skulls
of their miscarriages
as a result:
the salamander would paralyze
our voice and hearing
under instruction
our sons the mutes would darken
their bodies with ash and we'd assist
them erect sweatlodges with canvas
water plants fire and poles
from the river
the scent of deer and geese
the hiss of medicine
against the heated rocks
belief would breathe into their bodies
camouflage and invisibility (*Winter* 119)

The masculine focalization may seem automatic, but in other poems Young Bear writes more of grandmothers than grandfathers, especially his own grandmother. He opens his first collection with his best known and most accessibly eloquent poem, "grandmother." Here, in "in disgust and in response," it is not easy to read the consequences of gender distinctions. Like so much of Young Bear's poetry, these are difficult lines to follow through their cultural assumptions and suggestive enjambments, and sometimes they seem to ask us to rest in uncertainties, in "not knowing," and in the paralysis of "voice and hearing / under instruction." Not that the uncertainties can never he diminished so much as that uncertainty itself is part of the intercultural and interpersonal being that these poems labor to represent and to suspend in continuous performance.

Indeed, Young Bear often suspends his lines in opposite notes, as in the haunting "one chip of human bone," which reads, in its entirety:

> one chip of human bone
>
> it is almost fitting
> to die on the railroad tracks
>
> i can easily understand
> how they felt on their long staggered walks back
>
> grinning to the stars.
>
> there is something about
> trains, drinking, and
> being an indian with nothing to lose. (*Winter* 19)

One chip isn't much, but this chip marks a death. It is almost fitting, but it doesn't fit. Young Bear can easily understand the many suicides on the railroad tracks that bisect the Mesquakie settlement, suicides that multiply through his poems, because he knows the world that produces them. Yet in another, uncapitulating sense he can never understand such tragedies. He is "no authority to anything." As in "in disgust and in response," it boils down to "being an indian." Or as *Black Eagle Child* puts it, "All this internalized agony led us to hurt / or seriously injure one another for no reason / other than sheer disgust in being Indians," and "All else has been a long uncomfortable adjustment to being an Indian, *E ne no te wi ya ni*, in the world of the white man" (5, 167). In "one chip of human bone," that being provokes Young Bear to wonder whether Indians can know themselves and their cultures when it is so hard to see through the veil of all they have lost. If they decide they have nothing left to lose, then that can make them lose everything.

"in disgust and in response" sets out to define the ontological anguish of that wondering. It describes the ceremonial production and reproduction, in sweatlodges with "the hiss of medicine / against the heated rocks" of "belief" that "would breathe into their bodies / camouflage and invisibility." But invisible belief will not translate easily into a world of schooling disputes and mass-marketed, tv-induced urges to conform. The modesty that even the strongest belief assumes, if its form seems invisible, makes it a hard sell in a world that wants things to buy and that refuses to see or hear such opposite notes.

Part of the difficulty is that at some level of existential challenge, "in disgust and in response" suggests that it is no easier for Young Bear—the "invisible musician"—or for any other Mesquakie to say in a "whole and complete" way what is Mesquakie than it is for outsiders. In some ways, none of us knows who we are. The Mesquakie people would "like to be there . . . / being ourselves." But like anyone else, they can always feel as if they are only "wearing the faces" of themselves, can always feel the gap between being one's self and the expression of such being without which, in a vicious cycle, we can't conceptualize our being in the first place. Thus being is never convincingly being, and expressing can never reach the signified it would express. Identity, as a social narrative shaped by traditions in disequilibrium, is always evolving, versus the cultural myth that Native Americans shape native identity only by looking to the past. "We would set aside the year's / smallpox dead / whole and complete," as if the only way to be whole and complete were to be dead.

Beyond that grim hint, this may all sound ordinarily poststructuralist, but I am not suggesting that this poem submits to the poststructuralist formulas that spin my discussion of it, any more than it submits to the formulas of cultural fantasy about Native Americans. For in Young Bear's spin on Mesquakie ontology, identities can be appropriated. That is not what poets do: it is what witches do.

> somewhere an image of a woman's hand
> would lunge out from the window
> of a longhouse
> and it would grab from our fingers
> the secret writings of a book
> describing to the appointee
> the method of entering
> the spirit and body
> of a turkey
> to walk at night in suspension
> above the boundaries of cedar incense
> to begin this line of witchcraft
> traveling in various
> animal forms
> unaware of the discrepancy
> that this too is an act of balance
> a recurring dream of you
> being whole and complete
> sending the glint of your horns
> into the great distances
> of the gods
> acquainting yourself with ritual

and abandonment of self-justification
to realize there is a point
when you stop being a people
sitting somewhere and reading
the poetry of others come out easily
at random
unlike yours which is hard to write
to feel yourself stretch
beyond limitation
to come here and write this poem
about something no one
knows about
no authority to anything (*Winter* 119–20)

There, without a period's closing authority, the poem ends. The words "this too" signal an analogy. Young Bear likens the secret writing of witchcraft, which tells how to take animal forms, to the transformations of poetic imagination, for each is a "suspension / above . . . boundaries," "an act of balance / a recurring dream of you"—addressing himself in the second person, as if to make his readers hear their own poetic transformations— "being whole and complete." A romanticizing essentialist might stop at "whole and complete," asserting the organic unity so iconized by New Critical tradition and still in many ways dominant, even more in the world of *belles lettres* and poetry "mags" than in literary and cultural criticism.

But that would entail a "self-justification" at odds with the personal humility of Mesquakie culture and ritual. And beyond the personal, it would provide a romantic cultural chauvinism hardly better than that of the white writers of "indian-type" poetry and the editors who favor them. Instead of offering an image of the Mesquakie as whole and complete, Young Bear— whose poems neither shy away from nor obsess over differences between Mesquakie—musters a Mesquakie resentment to help him take being Mesquakie to more than being Mesquakie: "to realize there is a point / when you stop being a people / . . . / to feel yourself stretch beyond limitation."

Thus he projects a post-Wordsworthian transcendence of identity, yet at the same time describes himself escaping such limits so as to reimmerse himself in them. For if he would stretch beyond the limits of identity, it is still his self that he professes to stretch. His insistence that this poem "stretch / beyond limitation" clashes with his insisting nevertheless that this poem is "about something." He aspires to "write this poem / about something no one / knows about," which is also to be someone who knows about it. The two uses of "about" invert each other. The first one affirms, while the second denies yet remains embedded in the affirmation. That ontological corkscrew permits Young Bear to open his claim both to be "no authority to anything" and to have an authority that other poets assume only by fraud.

Whirling out of such an extra-logical stance, the cultural consequences of Young Bear's position evade any neat formula. At the frankest common denominator, it means that he can write about it and non-Indian poets can't. The tougher part comes in the why. The writing of such poems is not the province of just any Mesquakie—far from it. Nor can he write such poems simply because he knows what he's talking about while the white dabblers and impostors do not. The difficulty lies, again, in the always receding object of "about," the about *what* (what is a Mesquakie, what is an "I," a self, a "we," an identity, a subject position). And it lies in Young Bear's sense not only that he can never catch, mount, and display that object, but also that the quest to catch it and the recognition that it will always flutter over the horizon are not the same for him and for someone outside the Mesquakie world, anymore than they would be for him and for another Mesquakie.

"We'd like to be there," then, but we can't be there. We'd like to be our truest selves, but the limit of "self," "our," and "truth" always disappears over memory's horizon. Still, if it is not always easy for Young Bear or other Mesquakie or anyone else to say who they are, that hardly means they are not anything. Wearing a face is not the same as being a self, but masks can perform self, dramatizing and producing the subjectivity and displacement that they figure. That includes the mask of self-contradiction, the extra-logical cultural stance that allows Young Bear to claim an impossible knowledge about what no one knows about, and to say that his position as a Mesquakie gives him an authority to write about Mesquakie being, even though a Mesquakie—like anyone else—is "no authority to anything." A Mesquakie is not even an authority on "being whole and complete" as a Mesquakie, except in the performative sense that such wholeness and completion are what this poem calls "a recurring dream." Thus in an interview, Young Bear can say "I am extremely fortunate to come from a tribe that is known for its conservative practices. As such, our language, beliefs, history and ideology is unaffected by cultural deterioration." Even his verb, "is" rather than "are," underlines his sense that Mesquakie language, belief, history, and ideology are one and the same. He explains that "self-prescribed, self-imposed geographic isolation has vastly contributed to our stability," yet in the same interview he discusses how Mesquakie music has recently adapted to the "southern style of drumming" and "the latest Northern Plains style of high-pitched singing." He adds: "There is a high probability that

Mesquakie song, dance, and drum styles have changed because of cultural change and adaptation. . . . My feeling is, as long as the people who are responding to these subtle idiosyncrasies are Mesquakie—Mesquakie improvising at being Mesquakie—then it is of little concern. Should there ever be a time when the influence of Puccini, Verdi, Beethoven can be heard in our music, then I'd be worried."

As long, he says, as the people are Mesquakie. What then is a Mesquakie? There is no doubt that, compared to most Native American peoples, the Mesquakie have steadfastly kept up their cultural independence. Still, any notion that they have hovered in place flies in the face of everything we know about post-contact Mesquakie history. The French, for example, aimed an explicit policy of genocide directly at the Mesquakie and came so close to accomplishing it that the Mesquakie could recover only through large-scale adoption from other native peoples, who brought much from their own cultures, as well as large-scale return of captured Mesquakie, who brought much from the cultures that had held them captive. And like other Indian peoples, the Mesquakie have absorbed a great deal from widening intertribal contacts and an intensifying, pan-Indian sense of common cultural position. They have stuck it out so successfully (by comparison) not only because of their conservatism but also because of their resourceful mix of conservatism and adaptability, or, in Young Bear's term, improvisation. In *Black Eagle Child*, he describes the resistance to change while concluding, nevertheless, that "Change was unavoidable" (60). For Young Bear, conservatism and isolation are not sufficient to explain Mesquakie cultural survival. As his remarks about music indicate, a Mesquakie is not anything we can capture in static definition; a Mesquakie is, circularly and performatively, a "Mesquakie improvising at being Mesquakie." Hence, although a Mesquakie has a special authority about such "being," still, since such being is always recreating itself, a Mesquakie is at the same time "no authority to anything."

Indeed, the anthropological literature singles out the Mesquakie for their indifference to authority. Walter B. Miller argues persuasively that European concepts of authority, hierarchy, and leadership were deeply foreign to the Mesquakie social system when astonished Europeans first described it in the seventeenth century. Even after almost three hundred years of change, Miller finds that twentieth-century practices pervasively reiterate what he finds for the seventeenth century. Things may get done, but the institutions of social power that accomplish them are so informal as to seem almost invisible. In a similar vein, Frederick O. Gearing describes modern Mesquakie independence and resentment of authority as well as the factional political strife that such a perspective leads to now that the

Mesquakie must articulate their social system to non-Mesquakie institutions and expectations. Thus when Young Bear, having already asserted his position as a Mesquakie and Native American authority, beginning with the comic, resentful title of his poem, then arcs to an anguished conclusion in denial of that authority, his very denial enacts the ontology of authority as it appears—almost invisibly—in Mesquakie performance.

≈≈≈≈≈≈

As "in disgust and in response" decries "indian-type poetry written by whites," so "for the rain in march: the blackened hearts of herons" denounces two particular poems: W. D. Snodgrass' "Powwow" and James Wright's "I Am a Sioux Brave, He Said in Minneapolis." Like "in disgust," "for the rain in march" goes most of its length without even mentioning the offending poems; Young Bear may occasionally respond to white poets, but he has plenty to say on his own without needing them to prompt him. He may be their "other," but they are not his.

On the contrary, "for the rain in march" begins with modesty and inferiority, begins as "no authority to anything":

> i see myself sleeping
> and i see other ignorant people
> locked securely in their houses
> sleeping
> unaware of the soft dawn-lit
> furbearing animals
> wrapping themselves with the bark
> and cone from pinetrees
> within each of their thoughts
> there is the vision
> of the small muskrat's
> clasped hands
> the struggling
> black and yellow
> spotted body of a salamander
> freeing itself from a young
> girl's womb (*Winter* 163)

This has nothing to do with Snodgrass' poem (which I will focus on) or with Wright's. This poem is "for" the rain in March, not for the white poets, not even deigning, until it is mostly over, to respond with disgust.

But even while the bulk of this poem has nothing to do with Snodgrass' poem, it also has everything to do with it. For the disconnection shows how ludicrously far afield Snodgrass is when he takes it for granted that he knows the Mesquakie mind. He assumes he has been to the Mesquakie interior, weighed it, and found it wanting, found nothing there but a false consciousness that reflects the ideologies of Snodgrass' own world in degraded derivation. Where, to Snodgrass, do the Mesquakie get their culture? "They all see the same movies," he begins, as if that will explain everything, not only for the Mesquakie but also the Sioux, the Chippewa, and (in a lump) all the rest, which tells more about what Snodgrass himself does not see when he looks at the Mesquakie (such meager looking as he pauses for). "The Indians," Snodgrass explains elsewhere, "seemed dreadfully beaten down, poverty-stricken, sodden or didn't seem to know any more than I did about Indians. I really had the feeling that they also had picked up all their Indian lore from Grade B movies. Yet, that was our fault, too, so it just seemed like one more guilt" (qtd. in Gildner and Gildner 133). He sees no Indian subjectivity. To Snodgrass, Indian culture—represented solely by what ignorant eyes can see at a powwow—is a passive product of "our" culture, as if only readers who are part of his "our" were allowed. He does not see the Mesquakie being, the visionary but modest (Young Bear even says "ignorant") being that lives with animals, the furbearing animals wrapping themselves with bark, the muskrat like a fetus, the spotted salamander slithering from a girl's womb. Such things, such being, invisible to Snodgrass, not only do not come from movies, they also antedate movies by millennia and remain utterly invisible within them. They are unparaphraseable in the cultural and linguistic vocabulary of Snodgrass' dominating world, which, to say the least, includes (more or less) the world of written and English-language literary criticism, as opposed, for example, to Mesquakie oral tradition.

In that vein, Young Bear then continues the poem by telling about a certain badger:

> in my dark blue pickup
> i came upon a cigar-smoking
> badger
> who invited himself and
> later came to my home
> gathering chips and splinters
> of my firewood and starting
> a fire

for an hour we sat
and then he suddenly stood
on his hindlegs and walked
over to the stove
and opened it
he took out two narrow pieces
of burning wood and rammed them
into his eyes
he fell on all fours
and then he made rumbling sounds
mocking my pickup with its two
dull headlights
disappearing into
the forest (*Winter* 164)

Like the opening lines, the story of this trickster badger has nothing directly
to do with Snodgrass, but it has the effect of satirizing him by reversal. He
reads the Mesquakie through the lens of his own cultural being, whereas
Young Bear reads an ill-mannered animal rather like Snodgrass through the
lens of Mesquakie being. Like the badger, Snodgrass comes to Young Bear's
home uninvited, or if he is invited in the sense that everyone is invited to the
annual powwow (a major source of income for the settlement), then he
exceeds that invitation in the invasive presumptions of his poem. Before this
badgering trickster with his rumbling mockery, the securely locked homes of
the opening lines seem exposed and threatened. But the badger's mockery,
like the mockery from tricksters through much of Native American oral
literature, soon turns back on him, driving him from the home he invades
and the hospitality he abuses.

  Though not always unsubtle, the rampant abuses in Snodgrass' poem
make it an inviting target. In language imported from racism against African
Americans, he sneers at the dancers' "shuffling," recalling that sorry epithet,
"prairie niggers." If Indians are all the same to him (he excepts "Only the
Iroquois," apparently unaware that there are hundreds of American Indian
peoples, most of whom couldn't be represented at even a well-attended
powwow), it almost seems as if non-whites are all the same to him too. Their
ceremonial clothing amounts to "braveries" (he might almost as well say
squaw-eries, if that were a word) they are "tricked out" in. If he "others"
them as shuffling blacks, then he others both blacks and Indians, en masse,
by feminizing them: "They all dance with their eyes turned / Inward—like a
woman nursing." If we stop there, at the end of an enjambed line, the femi-

nization might almost appear laudatory, suggesting contemplation and gentleness. But the false pause turns out to be an abuse of late-forties and fifties high-formalist play, for nothing else in the poem corroborates such softness. On the contrary, when we cross the enjambment to find that the dancers are "like a woman nursing / A sick child she already knows / Will die," it turns out that we have been set up for another patronizing, infantilizing, and misogynist cliché about the femininely impractical and childish red man, vanishing ward of the state, the sort of counter-factual dirge that would help make possible the Eisenhower administration's disastrous effort to do away with ("terminate") reservations.

Young Bear, writing from a conservative culture with its own language, cosmology, and social system, with a body of ceremonial ritual large enough to beggar the Vatican, a culture so private that it finally succeeded in repelling a sixty-year onslaught of anthropologists, skims through most of these insults and focuses with incredulity on the thinness of his culture in the eyes of Snodgrass and Wright:

> coming back I read the poem pow-wow
> written by w. d. snodgrass after
> visiting my people's annual tribal
> celebration
> you can't get away from people
> who think what they see
> is in actuality all they will
> ever see
> as if all in one moment they can sense
> automatically what makes a people
> what capabilities they have of
> knowledge and intellect
> he was only shown what was allowed
> to be shown
> what the hell did he expect
> out of his admission fee?
> and as far as he thinking that he knew
> more about indians than they themselves did
> he should have thought twice
> it's the same way with the poem
> i am a sioux brave, he said in minneapolis
> by james wright and countless others
> he will never know the meanings

of the songs he heard
nor will he ever know that these
songs were being sung long before
his grandfathers had notions
of riding across the ocean
long before translators
and imitators came
some claiming to be at least a good 64th
grabbing and printing anything
in scrapbook form
dedicating poems to the indian's loss
writing words and placing themselves
within various animals they knew nothing of
snodgrass will never know what spirit
was contained in that day he sat above
the feathered indians
eating his hot dog

he saw my people in one afternoon
performing and enjoying themselves
i have lived here 26 years and although
i realize within my life i am incomplete
i know for a fact that my people's
ways aren't based on grade-b movies (*Winter* 171–72)

Young Bear, a composer, singer, and drummer with a huge repertoire of songs, like many other Mesquakie spoke only Mesquakie until he went to school. For years he wrote his poems in Mesquakie and then translated them into English ("Connected" 340–41). From that perspective, Snodgrass and Wright's ignorance of Indian song and ritual, if it were not so stultifyingly familiar, would be as unimaginable as Indian song and ritual are to Snodgrass and Wright. Snodgrass even supposes that the old drummer cannot remember what the song's words mean, just because Snodgrass presumes the song is too ancient and the culture too disconnected from its traditions. Yet Snodgrass thinks that he knows it is the "tribe's song for the restless young," as if any Indian song the man sings would have to be a Mesquakie song and belong to the people as a whole. Nor does it occur to him that the song could be contemporary or that it could be rehearsed, with its words part of a patterned genre regularly repeated through diverse variations in ritual or daily life.

And yet Young Bear says that despite the thickness of ordinary Mesquakie life that he knows so closely and that Wright and Snodgrass do not even suspect, Young Bear himself does not know. Knowing that he does not know, however, allows him to "think twice" as he complains that Snodgrass will not. Ironically, soon after Snodgrass wrote "Powwow," he won fame as a poet of self-examination, but here he speaks from a position of self-presumed authority, by contrast with Young Bear, who calls his own position "incomplete." A smaller-minded poet would take the argument to the level of children in a sandbox: I know this stuff and you don't. But Young Bear continues to offer his knowledge as "no authority to anything," or, as he puts it in more personal and familial terms in "for the rain in march":

> i will never know who i actually am
> nor will the woman who lives with me
> know me or herself or the children
> we want
> i am always surprised at how many
> different minds drift across each other
> some resenting everyone
> some imitating what they will
> never be
> others make room for others
> and then there are us
> afraid of everyone because they
> are afraid of us
> unable to fit anywhere (*Winter* 169)

At a level more interpersonal than intercultural, this draws a more delicate taxonomy than any drawn by the anthropologists that Steven Polgar describes who, sometimes with considerable interpretive resourcefulness, graph ascending and descending degrees of acculturation, more delicate even than those Polgar himself draws when he speculates helpfully about Mesquakie "biculturalism," as if such doubleness had not long before been described in W.E.B. Du Bois' notion of "double-consciousness" (16–18). At Snodgrass' crude level, biculturalism or double-consciousness is unimaginable: Mesquakie culture, in a proto-Baudrillardian parody, comes straight out of Hollywood. Thus when the Mesquakie don World War II combat issues, to Snodgrass their khaki must he castoff. He seems unaware that these Mesquakie would be veterans like himself, and that military service is a point of extraordinary pride for the Mesquakie and for most Native

American peoples. Young Bear, for example, has published poems in honor of veterans and takes particular pride in singing songs in their honor. Serving in the armed forces is not simply a way for Indians to move into the dominant culture; it is also itself a proud feature of contemporary Indian culture.

Matching the ethnic stalemate between Snodgrass' irritation and Young Bear's mixture of disgust and incredulous indifference lies a conflict pitched along class lines. In this sense, the first two words of "Powwow" are key: "They all," soon repeated in the line "They are all the same." Snodgrass' superior tone implicitly pits elite culture and the caressed distinctions of high formalist verse against a patronized mass culture of dungarees, trailers, and "jobs in truck stops and all-night filling stations," a culture that, he supposes, foregoes fine distinctions to wallow in the undifferentiated morass of "they" and "all" and the "same." The Indians depend on a powwow with hot dogs and bleachers for their income, versus the erudite poet who can afford to go slumming. He'll even step down for a moment to eat a hot dog, a detail that Young Bear's canny ear picks out, as if to suggest Snodgrass' patronizing humor. Snodgrass can look, but beyond eating his hot dog, he erects an intellectual quarantine to seal himself off from the Indian world and from the broader culture of poverty and the working class that he consigns it to. He specularizes the powwow, enjoying the cheap frisson of looking at it while sustaining the fiction that he and his family share none of the desires it represents. It is for "they" and them. The real beauty of it, if you can find the way out that those unaccommodating Indians won't explain to you, comes in the relief of escape, the driving away.

Young Bear plays on the class anxieties by having the Snodgrassian badger mock Young Bear's pickup, exactly the kind of vehicle that threatens Snodgrass. Eventually, staggered by Snodgrass' presumptions and fears, Young Bear extends the badger parody into an astonishing ad hominem, as if to bring out how such responses are beneath arguing with. It remains only to show Snodgrass how it feels to be Snodgrassed, and perhaps even to out-Snodgrass him:

> and i also know that the only thing
> he will ever experience in life as being phenomenal
> will be his lust
> stirring and feebly coming alive
> at the thought of women
> crumbs from the bread
> of his hot dog

> being carried away
> by images of crushed
> insects (*Winter* 172)

Young Bear mocks Snodgrass by extrapolating from one poem to Snodgrass' whole life, just as Snodgrass extrapolates from an afternoon at the powwow to all of Mesquakie culture. Young Bear even has the insect images from the end of Snodgrass' poem carry away his poor hot dog, figuratively castrating him for the wish to make entomological profundity compensate for Indian superficiality. Ironically, Young Bear's response concludes in the kind of "deep image" associated with Wright. The Wrights and Snodgrasses of the world, he suggests, sacrifice their lust to their images. Aesthetically colonizing their denied selves and the cultures they look at and barely see—a repressed analogy between self and other that only colonizes the more—they convert their evasions into poetic capital.

Of course, any poem transmutes experience into poetic capital. Young Bear is not free of that. In "The Dream of Purple Birds in Marshall, Washington," he recounts (to quote his prose summary) that he "realized through dream or reincarnation that I had once witnessed the brutal homicide of two white women by two white men" (Invisible 96–97). Two birds, the souls or "once-life of [the] two women / whose body parts lie scattered / and hidden safely under the blue rocks," come "beckoning" him "from dream, from Iowa, from yourself," but he insists:

> *I refuse to be*
> *their spiritual conduit and release*
> . . .
> *in a valley where a large, red fluorescent*
> *cross is physically so much stronger*
> *than I . . .*
> (*Invisible* 88, closing ellipses are Young Bear's)

How should we compare Young Bear's transmutation of experience to Snodgrass'? Readers might wonder what provokes Young Bear's dream, and if imagined or projected violence against women provides the raw material of his poetic capital as disturbingly as patronizing racism does for Snodgrass' "Powwow." Indeed, for a poet more readily assimilable to the dominant culture, it might seem grandiose to compare one's powers, even unfavorably, to those attributed to the Christian deity. But such a reading would entail a colonizing misconception of the routines of Mesquakie ontology, in which there is nothing so extraordinary about dream power. And it would miss the fact that, unlike Snodgrass' Olympian sneer, Young Bear's dream pretends no superior vantage point over the spirits he describes. Distrustful of authority, he only backs away from the presumption that he can assume any authority or do anything to resolve their suffering. Contrary to pop-critical vulgarizations, Freud describes dreams not as wish-fulfillments per se, but as compromises of the dream-work that makes competing wishes clash, as congealings of a dialectic between defenses and drives. Hence Young Bear dreams of more than violence against white women. He also dreams of resisting that violence. And since such violence, terrifyingly commonplace, is regularly dealt out to the Mesquakie by whites, directly and indirectly, the condensation of dream-work suggests a still broader resistance to violence, both in the reversal of races and in the urge to rescue the victims. Yet Young Bear, still stirring the stew of competing urges, pleads no thank you to the rescue fantasy (as Freud called it), in his typical, un-pin-downable way of making melody from cacophonous notes: the invisible musician.

Hence Young Bear's universe of poetic authority, instead of converting others' labor to his own poetic capital, seeks a place in a communal arena where there is room for his imagination and room for others. Not that anything others might do is okay. As we have seen, Young Bear is ready to oppose what some poets write. His politics of poetic and cultural authority is rather more like politics on the Mesquakie settlement, where factional strife proliferates, but the factions hold together in their disdain of pressures to distribute land for private ownership (allotment) and in favor of communal ownership.

Mostly, Young Bear writes about the Mesquakie, not about whites. Occasionally, as with "in disgust" or "for the rain in march," he criticizes white poets' presumptions about Indians, and in "in viewpoint: poem for 14 catfish and the town of tama, iowa," he seethes in a blistering critique of local white racism. In another mode, Young Bear can also write of how the modest refusal of authority can make common ground across cultures. In "Quail and His Role in Agriculture," Young Bear goes to the Tastee Freez, drumming on the dashboard while he waits his turn. The beat attracts the attention of several farmers who also wait in line, but they do not chuckle or sneer like Snodgrass. Young Bear imagines that,

> With the constant drone of harvesting
> machinery in their ears, they probably
> thought the tapping was yet another
> mechanical trouble to contend with. (*Invisible* 77)

They allow him to imagine that they imagine his doings as part of their own, even while, when they look, they can surely see the difference as well as hear the rhythmic likeness. Then he completes the poem with these lines:

> It was a hot September day, and we
> had all stopped to have strawberry
> sundaes; I, to celebrate my song;
> and they, to soothe the grain and dust
> in their throats. Midwesterners, all,
> standing in the monolithic shadow
> of a hydraulic platform, which lifted
> the semi-truck's cab to the sky
> to violently shake and dislodge
> its cargo of yellow corn—
> the historic sustenance
> which was now to some
> a symbol of abject poverty.
> For others, like myself and all
> my grandfathers before me, it continues
> to be a transmitter of prayer.
> Beautiful yellow corn . . .
> (*Invisible* 78, ellipsis is Young Bear's)

Their differences and their likenesses need not always undermine each other, even if they sometimes do. Perhaps, especially for a poem with a national audience, a giddy hint of comedy creeps into the pride in the corn harvest and heartland solidarity, and yet that pride also sounds a note of anti-coastal defiance. "Midwesterners, all," in their differing ways, differing senses of being, they are not "all the same." But Young Bear and these "horticultural-ists" (77), as he calls them half-reverently and half-teasingly, all produce their evolving, competing, and overlapping cultures in ways he can envision as analogues to all the grandfathers of his past and to each other.

ALAN VELIE

The Indian Historical Novel

A growing number of historians—most prominent among them in this country, Hayden White—is reevaluating the conception that written histories are more or less objective accounts of "what actually happened" in a given time and place. Instead they are considering them more in the way that literary critics have evaluated imaginative works, examining the way histories reflect the authors political and philosophical biases, and the way their authors shape events to conform to literary patterns. This new way of examining history is helpful in analyzing historical fiction, which always is consciously or unconsciously based on an underlying philosophy of history.

White borrows concepts from a range of thinkers from Vico to Northrop Frye in describing the way historians write history. His ideas provide a very useful schema for examining the artistic, historical and philosophical concepts underlying historical novels. Classic studies of historical fiction, works like Georg Lukács' *The Historical Novel*, are still useful as studies of writers like Scott and Manzoni, but they are naive in their conceptions of historical objectivity. Lukács was the first critic to explore in depth the different conceptions of history underlying works of fiction. He begins with Walter Scott's Waverley novels, which he contrasts with works like Flaubert's *Salammbô*, and Thackery's *Henry Esmond*. Lukács insists that Scott is *"objective"* (the italics are his) in his depiction of historical events, as opposed to Thackery, who Lukács says "dispels historical objectivity" (203). I would argue that no work of literature is objective about history, and furthermore, that no work of history is objective either. In this article I will

From *Native American Perspectives on Literature and History.* © 1994 by the University of Oklahoma Press.

use White's ideas to examine two recent historical novels, James Welch's *Fools Crow* and Gerald Vizenor's *The Heirs of Columbus* in terms of form, politics, and conception of history.

According to White, historical narratives are verbal models—he also uses the word "icons"—of historical events (30). The historian begins with an essentially poetic act in which he "both creates his object of analysis and predetermines the modality of the conceptual strategies he will use to explain it" (31). White describes three "levels" or "modes" the historian uses in organizing his material: emplotment, argument, and ideological implication.

Before describing these terms in any detail, I should say that I am aware that they may strike the reader as arbitrary, perhaps procrustean. Too rigidly applied they would be reductive at best, and distortive at worst. However, White does not use his categories simplistically, and I will apply them less rigorously than he does. I use them chiefly to provide a vocabulary, a set of categories that is necessary in discussing any set of items. To proceed eclectically, using a variety of terms but no system, seems more confusing: e.g., referring to one historian as "Hegelian," another as "progressive," a third as "belle lettristic."

By "emplotment" White means the shape of the narrative segment. White borrows categories from Northrop Frye: romance, tragedy, comedy and satire. In a romance good triumphs over evil; in satire it is the opposite: the leader fails, his country falls. Comic histories end with reconciliations between antagonists. Tragic histories end with the death of the protagonist, but not the destruction of his world.

White's categories of emplotment apply to segments of histories, series of events, as well as complete historical works. Motifs that indicate patterns of emplotment are seen in all historical narratives. Inaugural motifs include things like "Louis's troubles began when . . ." Terminating motifs include: "And so the battle of Hastings ended Saxon control of England, and brought the end of an era." Obviously the end of one era is the beginning of another, (or the middle of one conceived differently) and so an event can serve as the basis of an inaugural or terminating motif, or a transitional motif, which links the other two.

White also identifies four modes of argument: formist, organicist, mechanist, and contextualist (13ff). Formists emphasize events in their uniqueness, often focusing on the lives of national leaders. To them history is often primarily a matter of biography. Contextualists think in terms of historical trends, which imply that events are related, and periods have general tendencies. They focus on the things that make the "Gilded Age," "Progressive Era," or "Roaring Twenties" distinct from the periods that precede or follow them.

Organicists believe in patterns in history; events reflect the working of a great force, such as Hegel's World Spirit, or the inevitable progress of a nation to freedom and democracy. Mechanists are somewhat less mystical; they believe in patterns of events, but attribute them to the working out of historical laws rather than an organic force. Examples of laws would be oft repeated dicta like "the more oppressive the tyranny, the more violent the revolution," or, "people tend to revolt not when they are most downtrodden, but when their condition has begun to improve."

White chose political categories to describe Europe in the 19th Century—anarchist, radical, liberal, and conservative (22ff). These are not really suitable to Indian novels. Most Indian novels deal with the interaction of whites and Indians, and the political questions revolve around whether to be confrontational or accommodating—that is, whether to make war or peace—and whether to live separately to preserve the tribal culture, or whether to integrate into American society.

Adapting White's terms to suit the world of 19th Century Plains Indians, *Fools Crow* is a romance in terms of form, is organicist in its conception of history, and is informed by the politics of compromise.

To begin with form, readers may have trouble recognizing *Fools Crow* as a romance if they assume a novel by a plains Indian about clashes between whites and Indians in the late 19th Century would necessarily be tragic or ironic. Plains Indians did lose most of their land and much of their culture as a result of defeats at the hands of the white soldiers, but Indian writers have had a range of responses to the events.

Certainly historical works reflect the politics of their writers. For instance, most American historians, as well as popular adapters of history for Westerns, have looked on the period covered in *Fools Crow* as the "Winning of the West." Their historical and fictive accounts are generally romances, showing the settling of the West by whites and their conquest of the Indians as a good thing, a triumph of civilization.

Accounts written from an Indian point of view, like John Neihardt's *Black Elk Speaks*, have, not surprisingly, often taken the ironic perspective: the subjugation of the Indians and their forced assimilation into American life is a great loss to the Indians, a form of spiritual extinction as a people. It is interesting to note, however, the fact that Neihardt had a bleaker view of Indian history than Black Elk himself did. Neihardt neglects to point out that Black Elk became a Christian, and evidently viewed his life in more comic terms than his biographer—comic not in the sense of humorous, but in the sense of warring cultures coming to an accommodation and blending. Neihardt ends his narrative with the massacre at Wounded Knee, and Black

Elk's horrified reaction to it Neihardt makes Black Elk's last words:

> A people's dream died there. . . . There is no center any longer, and the
> sacred tree is dead. (276)

Lame Deer, who also wrote a memoir of Sioux life, tells of Black Elk
riding a horse with his daughter behind him reading him the Bible (216).
Neihardt chooses not to include Black Elk's conversion; he chooses to make
the narrative a satire in White's terms, a tale of the death of a culture.

Stanley Vestal's biography of Sitting Bull is tragic in that it ends with
the death of an individual, but the survival of his people. Furthermore, the
individual, Sitting Bull, is transcendent in death. Vestal ends the book:

> Sitting Bull, leader of the largest Indian nation on the continent, the
> strongest, boldest, most stubborn opponent of European influence,
> was the very heart and soul of [the] Frontier. When the true history of
> the New World is written, he will receive his chapter. For Sitting Bull
> was one of the Makers of America. (315)

Isabel Kelsay's biography of the great Mohawk leader Joseph Brant is a
comedy in the sense that it ends with the merging of two cultures. Since the
time of Menander, literary comedies have ended in marriage. Histories that
use the comic form of emplotment end with the marriage of peoples. This
does not imply an equal partnership. In a paternalistic society the female
partner loses a large measure of her identity in the marriage, and that is the
fate of the Indians in their absorption into the American family.

Joseph Brant died in exile from his tribal lands. Kelsay ends her book
with a description of his reburial years later:

> After a while the people of the Grand River (many of whom were
> becoming excellent plowmen and who, with a good income from their
> investments, would soon be able to do without presents, and whom
> almost nobody looked upon as "savage") took prideful thought of their
> great man who lay so many miles away. By the side of the little, old
> Mohawk church they set about to prepare a proper resting place for
> him.... And on the shoulders of strong, young grandsons of men he had
> known, Joseph Thayendanegea was carried, by relays, back home. (658)

White Americans, whether sympathetic or not to Indian concerns,
tend to view Indian history in tragic or ironic terms, thinking primarily in

terms of Indian failures and disasters. Virtually all Oklahomans know about the Trail of Tears; few are aware that Tulsa was founded by the Creeks, many of whom became successful ranchers and businessmen. That negative orientation leads readers to assume literary works like *Fools Crow* are tragic or ironic.

In fact, the description of *Fools Crow* that appears on the book jacket describes the novel as a tragedy. Like many Americans who believe themselves sympathetic to Indians, the blurb writer is so predisposed to see Indians as a "people with a plight" that he or she imagines a tragic ending even though Welch didn't write one. Although the book skirts tragedy, it ends on a positive, indeed triumphant and defiant note, the hallmark of romance:

> For even though he [Fools Crow] was, like Feather Woman burdened
> with the knowledge of his people, their lives and the lives of their chil-
> dren, he knew they would survive, for they were the chosen ones. (390)

Welch is of course aware of the hardships—indeed, disasters—endured by the Blackfeet after they were forced to abandon their traditional way of life. However, he chooses to depict Blackfeet history in a positive rather than negative manner, as a romance rather than satire. To anyone with a developed sense of literary form, it ought to be apparent from the beginning that *Fools Crow* will end with the hero triumphant. The book is a *Bildungsroman* of sorts. At the beginning the hero is a bit older than the traditional youth; White Man's Dog, as he's called at the time, is eighteen, but he clearly is callow and unaccomplished. Welch starts with the "poor luckless lad" language that traditionally introduces the rags to riches motif:

> Not so lucky was White Man's Dog. He had little to show for his eigh-
> teen winters. His father, Rides-at-the-door, had many horses and three
> wives. He himself had three horses and no wives. His animals were
> puny, not a blackhorn runner among them. He owned a musket and no
> powder and his animal helper was weak. Many times he had prayed to
> the Above Ones for stronger medicine but he knew that wasn't the
> way. It was up to him, perhaps with the help of a many-faces man, to
> find his own power. (3, 4)

In depicting White Man's Dog in these terms, Welch is drawing upon two traditions. One is the Blackfeet myth of Scarface, an unpromising hero who begins poor and disfigured, but becomes a hero and teaches the Blackfeet the ritual of the Sundance. The other tradition is the Horatio Alger tradition of the lad who pulls himself up by his bootstraps. In understanding that Welch thinks of himself as Blackfeet and draws on Blackfeet myths and traditions, we should not forget that he grew up in America soaking in the same myths from the books, comics, films, and television shows as other Americans, black, white or Asian.

Knowledge of either the Indian or Anglo tradition should tip off the reader that White Man's Dog is destined for great things—and sure enough, he is. He distinguishes himself in a raid against the Crows, gaining many horses. His wealth and reputation allow him to acquire a beautiful wife. He becomes a many-faces man himself, a man of great power. At the climax of the novel he undertakes a quest which teaches him why the Blackfeet are having such a difficult time. They are the people of Feather Woman, the wife of Morning Star, daughter-in-law of Sun and Moon, who transgressed a taboo and was punished by banishment. Her punishment extends to her people the Blackfeet, whose afflictions come at the hands of the Napikwans, the whites. Feather Woman tells Fools Crow that

> "One day I will rejoin my husband and son. I will return with them to their lodge and there we will be happy again and your people will suffer no more." (352)

Until that happy day Fools Crow is to prepare the Blackfeet for the times to come, and to pass down the stories of their greatness, so that their descendants know what a great people the Blackfeet were.

This is a muted sort of romance compared to more melodramatic works like *The Odyssey* or Hollywood westerns, where the good guys destroy the bad guys, but it is a romance nonetheless. Welch has a choice to end his novel with the Blackfeet being massacred by the Cavalry, an event he describes (378), or with the decimation of the Blackfeet by smallpox, which he also describes (371). He could have concluded the novel with the total demoralization of his people, or with their pride in surviving. He chooses to end it on a note of pride:

> That night there was much feasting in all the Pikuni camps. Winter was over and the men talked of hunting, of moving the camps out of the valleys, of moving on. The women prepared their meager feast and fed their men, their children, their relatives and friends. They knew that soon the meat pots would be full and the hides would be drying in the sun. Outside, the children played in the rain, chasing each other, slipping and skidding in the mud. They were Pikunis and they played hard. (390)

This is not the language of tragedy or satire; it is the language of romance.

Welch's depiction of history in *Fools Crow* as the result of the action of the gods is organicist in conception. That is, historical events are related as what White terms "components of synthetic processes" (15). Hegel, who saw history as the "rationally necessary course of the World Spirit" (12), and "the working of Providence" (82), is perhaps the most explicit of post Enlightenment historians in his organicist beliefs. Leading romantic American historians of the nineteenth century, men like Bancroft, Prescott, Motley and Parkman, were less mystical in their language, but they share with Hegel the notion that history "was the unfolding of a vast Providential plan" (Levin 26).

The philosophy that underlies *Fools Crow* is similar to that of Parkman *et al* in that human events reflect divine intentions, but Blackfeet polytheism causes an important difference. To Hegel and American romantics the course of human history might not have always run smoothly from the perspective of individual men or peoples, but an omnipotent, omnibenevolent God was in control. The problem of the Blackfeet was that their tutelary diety, Feather Woman, had sinned against more powerful gods, and the tribe was being punished with her. Ultimately, however, she will be restored to grace, and the tribe with her.

The politics of *Fools Crow* might best be described as accommodational. Welch presents a number of viewpoints in the novel, but the most responsible and sympathetic leaders advocate compromising with the whites, chiefly on pragmatic grounds.

The most aggressive attitude is that of the renegades, Fast Horse, Owl Child and their band, Indians who had broken with the Blackfeet, and who harried white settlers, killing them, burning their homes, and stealing their horses. Owl Child's reaction to the encroachment of the whites and their herds of cattle is to kill as many of the *Napikwans* as possible before they can establish a foothold. "Some day, old man," he says to Three Bears,

> "a Napikwan will be standing right where you are and all around him
> will be grazing thousands of the whitehorns. You will be only part of the
> dust they kick up. If I have my way I will kill that white man and all his
> whitehorns before this happens . . . We will show you what real Pikunis
> do to these sonofabitch whites." (61)

What Owl Child says is consonant with the Blackfeet code of death before dishonor, and warfare as the proper way of settling foreign policy disputes. Although some romantic idealists among contemporary Americans like to think of Indians as sylvan pacifists, this is not, nor has ever been, the view Plains Indians held of themselves. As Vine Deloria points out in *Custer Died for Your Sins,*

> The Sioux, my own people, have a great tradition of conflict. We were the only nation ever to annihilate the United States Cavalry three times in succession. And when we have no one else to quarrel with, we often fight each other. . . . During one twenty-year period in the last century the Sioux fought over an area from LaCrosse, Wisconsin, to Sheridan, Wyoming against the Crow, Arapaho, Cheyenne, Mandan, Arikara, Hidatsa, Ponca, Iowa, Pawnee, Otoe, Omaha, Winnebago, Chippewa, Cree, Assiniboine, Sac and Fox, Potowatomi, Ute, and Gros Ventre. (29)

In *Fools Crow* Welch mentions battles between the Blackfeet, who pride themselves on being the scourge of the northern plains, and the Cree, Gros Ventre, and Crows. But those spokesmen in the novel who represent Welch's position (or the "implied" Welch, to use the formalist distinction) have a sense of *Realpolitik:* they realize that the whites are far too numerous, well armed, and technologically advanced to defeat. The logistical problems are impossible. The Indians have no source to resupply arms and ammunition other than what they can capture, and they must travel with their women and children, while the families of the Cavalry are out of reach of Indian attack. Accordingly, the voices of moderation counsel negotiation with the whites, preferably from a position of strength that is, before it is too late, while they still control valuable land. Rides-at-the-Door argues:

> The great war between the Napikwans far to the east [the Civil War] is over. More and more of the seizers who fought for Ka-ach-sino, the great grandfather, have moved out to our country. More will still come. If we take the war road against the whites, we will sooner or later encounter great numbers of them. Even with many-shots guns we couldn't hope to match their weapons . . . And so we must fend for ourselves, for our survival. That is why we must treat with the Napikwans. (177)

There is also an extreme position of accommodation, one that Welch seems to find as distasteful as extreme aggressiveness. White Man Dog reasons:

> His father was right and wise to attempt to treat with the Napikwans. But one day these blue-coated warriors would come, and White Man's Dog and the other young men would be forced to fight to the death. It

would be better to die than to end up standing around the fort, waiting for handouts that never came. Some bands, like the Grease Melters, had already begun to depend too much on the Napikwans. Ever since the Big Treaty they journeyed to the agent's house for the commodities that were promised to them. Most of the time they returned empty-handed. (93)

The politics of *Fools Crow* are clear: the Blackfeet must negotiate with the whites, but they must do it from a position of strength. To fight for a prolonged period would mean extermination for the tribe. To give in without driving a hard bargain would lead to starvation and humiliation. Welch is well aware that the Blackfeet did lose many people to starvation one winter shortly after the period covered in *Fools Crow*. He has written about that ordeal elsewhere. Nonetheless, the values of the Fools Crow are clear: the Blackfeet must cut the best bargain they can; they owe it to their children. The tribe must survive. Ultimately history will be on their side—Feather Woman will be returned to grace, and so will they.

Fools Crow is a familiar looking historical novel, more or less similar to Scott's Waverley novels. Like Scott, Welch writes about a romantic people whose wild, free way of life is over but not forgotten. In fact, the Blackfeet, like the Scots, are a warlike people who love nature, have little use for material possessions, live in the wilds, and are crushed and civilized by the less courageous but more numerous Anglo Saxons. Like the Blackfeet the Scots were tribal—*gentile* is the phrase Lukács uses—clans being the chief social unit (57). The appeal of the traditional historical novel is that it makes the reader long nostalgically for a way of life that has been destroyed.

In *The Heirs of Columbus*, Gerald Vizenor has written a very different type of historical novel, a postmodern version of the genre in which he abandons verisimilitude for absurdist fantasy. This may seem "unhistorical" to those who expect historical fiction to look like a Waverley novel, but Vizenor is just as interested in historical questions as Scott or Welch; he merely uses a different set of conventions to consider them.

In fact, *Heirs* is only partially a historical novel: the sections on Columbus, Pocahontas, and Louis Riel are based on history, but much of the novel fits more closely the conventions of other genres, in particular the murder mystery and utopian science fiction tale. However, Vizenor's ideas of history when contrasted with those of more traditional historical writers like Welch, serve to point up the literary nature of all historical writing.

In form *Heirs* is a romance, although the tone and conventions are those of comedy. To be more specific, it is a parody of a romance, even though it has a serious theme. Parodies of melodramas or romances—e.g., novels like Graham Greene's *Our Man in Havana* or Evelyn Waugh's *Scoop*, or films like *Airplane* or *Naked Gun 2 1/2*—utilize the form of romance, the plot structure pitting a group of heroes against villains, good guys aginst bad guys, culminating in a showdown, while retaining the conventions of comedy, the humorous tone and outlandish events.

In *Heirs* the heroes are Christopher Columbus and his Indian descendants, Anishinaabe from the White Earth Reservation in Minnesota, and their fellow tribesmen and allies. Columbus generated a good deal of interest among Indians as well as whites in his quincentenary year, and since negative treatments of Columbus by Indians have received a good deal of attention, it may be surprising to find that Vizenor makes Columbus not only sympathetic, but Indian.

Stone Columbus, descendant of the explorer, and radio talk show host, explains that "Columbus was Mayan . . ."

> "The Maya brought civilization to the savages of the Old World and the rest is natural," said Stone. "Columbus escaped from the culture of death and carried our tribal genes back to the New World, back to the great river, he was an adventurer in our blood and he returned to his homeland." (9)

This may seem preposterous in a historical novel, but actually it is not much more farfetched than what the reader is asked to swallow about Ivanhoe and his adventures with the Jewish Rebecca on the one hand or the mythical Robin Hood on the other. The main difference between *Ivanhoe* and *Heirs* is that Scott labors to retain what Henry James called "an air of reality" (14), even in Sherwood Forest, while Vizenor opts for the conventions of comedy, both tribal and western, which flout verisimilitude.

Samuel Eliot Morison, in his biography of Columbus, ridicules the claims earlier writers had made about the explorer's nationality—he was Portuguese, French, English, Greek, etc.—and adds what he considers the most preposterous hypothesis of all: "It only remains for some American patrioteer to come forward and claim that Columbus was really an Indian. . ."(6).

Vizenor is that "patrioteer," but his motive is hardly American chauvinism; rather he wishes to refigure Columbus for Indians, to defang the monster who enslaved Indians, and opened the door to their slaughter and subjugation. A major purpose of the novel, as Vizenor explains in the epilogue, is the domestication of Columbus, reclaiming him for Indians and rendering him harmless:

Columbus arises in tribal stories that heal with humor the world he

wounded; he is loathed, but he is not a separation in tribal conciousness.
The Admiral of the Ocean Sea is a trickster overturned in his own
stories five centuries later. (185)

The larger goal of *Heirs* is to depict a utopia in which the genes of the
survivor Columbus could be used to heal the rifts between Indian and Indian
(mixedblood and fullblood, tribal leaders and ordinary members) and Indian
and white.

Columbus becomes Indian when his Indian lover, Samana, liberates the
stories in his blood that had been passed down to him from his mother.

> He inherited the signature of survivance and tribal stories in the blood
> from his mother, and she inherited the genetic signature from maternal
> ancestors. (28)

Samana liberates Columbus's soul, and the stories in his blood,
through sex:

> Samana dove from the sterncastle into the shadows at the mouth of the
> river . . . Columbus removed his scarlet tunic and followed her in the water.
> That night he abandoned the curve of his pain in her hands and thighs and
> entered her maw to become a woman, a bear, a hand talker. . . . Overnight
> his discoveries reduced tribal cultures to the status of slaves; at the same
> time the stories in his blood were liberated by a tribal hand talker. (40, 41)

In retelling the story of Columbus in order to gain control over it for
tribal people, Vizenor's methods and conventions are very different from
those of a historical novelist like Scott, or a historian like Morison, but we
must remember that Scott and Morison also shape events to fit literary
patterns and political and philosophical preconceptions. Historians vigor-
ously protest that they are objective and bound by the truth, nonetheless it is
historians who have made the claim that Columbus was French, Greek or
German—not to mention that Shakespeare was Bacon or that slaves in the
ante-bellum South were better off than Northern workers.

These historians would argue that their claims are based on objective
historical evidence. Vizenor is more phenomenological; he advances the
Indian belief that the world exists in the imagination: "The New World is
heard, the tribal world is dreamed and imagined" (93) he puts it in one place;
"some tribal people would say that the real world exists and is remembered
nowhere else but in stories" (75), is the way he states it in another.

Samana makes her way to the headlands of the Mississippi River, and passes Columbus's "genetic signature" and the "stories in his blood" to his heirs, one of whom, Stone Columbus, is the protagonist of the book. Stone is a radio talk show host who helps found a utopian tribal colony called Point Assinka on Point Roberts in Puget Sound. The heirs of Columbus (others are Truman Columbus, Stone's grandmother, and Binn, his mother) declare Point Assinka a free state with "no prisons, no passports, no public schools, no missionaries, no television, and no public taxation . . ."

The colony finances itself through bingo, using the funds it generates to fund cures for wounded, deformed, and lonesome people. The cures are affected through genetic surgery. The process, "electrophoresis," involves radioactive genetic mutation, infusing the genes of the patients with the "genetic code of tribal survivance and radiance" (133), handed down through 5000 generations to Columbus, and so to his heirs.

The mystery in the novel revolves around the remains of Columbus and Pocahantas. One of the villains, Doric Miched, has acquired the casket that holds what is left of Columbus. Felipa Flowers, a "poacher" who liberates Indian artifacts from whites who have illicitly acquired them, uses shamanic magic to get the explorer's remains. She then tries to get the remains of Pocahantas, but is killed by Miched in the attempt. At the climax of the novel, Columbus, Pocahantas and Felipa are all buried on Point Assinka. Miched is never convicted of the murder, but is imprisoned for other crimes.

The other villain, the *wiindigoo*, or Evil Gambler, is adapted from Anishinaabe folklore. Vizenor depicts him as a blond water demon with a perfect smile who gambles with tribal members for their lives. Ice Woman freezes him solid, but he is thawed by "federal operatives" to punish the heirs. At the end of the book, the *wiindigoo* takes on the heirs in gambling game. If he wins the world will be destroyed. The *wiindigoo* loses his nerve, and instead of taking his turn, fades into the shadows. It is the showdown typical of romance; goodness prevails, evil is controlled.

Vizenor's political ideas may seem different from Welch's in that *Fool's Crow* ends with the Blackfeet living among whites in Montana, while *Heirs* ends with Vizenor's vision of a utopian separatist community. But both Vizenor and Welch are pragmatists who steer a middle course between confrontation and submission, advocating tribal basis of Indian life, and driving the best bargain one can with the whites that circumstances allow. *Fools Crow* is set in the past; Welch endorses the course the Blackfeet actually took. *Heirs* ends with a futurist fantasy which explores what might happen if tribal sovereignty were extended and bingo revenue greatly increased.

In his nonfiction works Vizenor makes it clear he avoids the extremes of the confrontational policies of AIM, which he detests and has fought for years, and the collusional corruption of tribal officials who get rich by playing footsie with white developers (*Crossbloods* xxvi).

Vizenor also takes the middle ground between right and left in white America when they argue about Indian matters. In *Crossbloods* he ridicules Ronald Reagan, who said:

> "Maybe we made a mistake in trying to maintain Indian cultures. Maybe we should not have humored them in wanting to stay in that kind of primitive lifestyle." (xxiii)

On the left Vizenor pillories the politically correct "romantics and culture cultists" who have

> homogenized tribal philosophies and transvalued tribal visions into counterculture slogans and environmental politics. (16)

For Vizenor, as for Welch, the most important aspect of Indian rights is tribal sovereignty.

Vizenor's political ideas are tied closely to his aesthetic ideas, which derive from Anishinaabe literature, particularly trickster tales. Vizenor's creed is stated in his first novel, *Darkness in Saint Louis Bearheart*. Third Proude Cedarfair, a "warrior diplomat," says:

> "Outwit but never kill evil . . . The tricksters and warriorclowns have stopped more evil violence with their wit than have lovers with their lust and fools with their power and rage . . ." (11)

Tricksters battle evil with wit and humor. The trickster is essentially comic, "a comic trope," "comic nature in a language game," is the way Vizenor puts it in *The Trickster of Liberty* (x). Comedy is communal; tragedy works in isolating the hero, separating him from his people. Comedy seals separations between people and peoples. The storyteller sends the trickster forth into the world to heal its rifts:

> The trickster is immortal; when the trickster emerges in imagination the author dies in comic discourse. To imagine the tribal trickster is to relume human unities; colonial surveillance, monologues, and racial separations are overturned in discourse. (x)

Vizenor combats evil through stories, comic stories like the trickster tales that were common to all Indian tribes. As Memphis the panther says in *Heirs*, these stories have "power to heal," (71) and the power to heal is comic.

In his fantasy Vizenor deals with a number of serious political issues for Indians: tribal sovereignty, ownership of tribal artifacts and human remains, and Indian gambling. With the flourishing of Indian gambling in recent years—bingo now generates millions of dollars annually for tribes, and casino gambling, with potentially higher revenues is just beginning—legal questions have arisen concerning the rights of tribes to be considered sovereign nations, outside the scope of state and federal laws. The United States government granted tribes sovereign status during the 18th and 19th centuries, withholding some of the prerogatives of citizenship. Today with tribal members holding full American citizenship, the legal questions are complex, and have not been fully ajudicated. Vizenor's utopia at Point Assinka—a tax-free sovereign country, financed by bingo—may seem fanciful, but it is merely an extension of the situation that could easily occur under current law on any reservation in the U.S. Many people, including Vizenor, worry about poor people squandering rent money, or becoming addicted to gambling, or even that the Mafia will take over bingo operations, but despite these dangers, Vizenor sees bingo as a boon for the Indian community, which has had little money coming in over the years. And, as Vizenor points out in his depiction of the *wiindigoo*, gambling is a very old tradition among Indians.

The status and ownership of Indian artifacts and remains is also a serious topic of this humorous novel. Anthropologists have acquired, by theft, purchase, or grave robbery, Indian remains and sacred objects, and kept them or delivered them to museums. Tribes have tried to regain the bodies and possessions of their ancestors, but have often been balked in the courts.

The incident in which Felipa Flowers dies while trying to "liberate" the bones of Pocahantas may seem fantastic, but the issue is serious. In *Crossbloods* Vizenor tells the story of a bulldozer operator in Iowa who dug up an unmarked cemetery, unearthing the remains of twenty-seven people. Twenty-six were reburied, but because of beads found with the remains of the twenty-seventh the state archeologist demanded that the bones be sent to him under state law. He got them (69).

Vizenor shares Welch's organicist conception of history, though Vizenor's supernatural forces are less anthropomorphic. In the case of *Fools Crow* Blackfeet deities influence the course of history. In *Heirs* there is no mention of a deity with a providential plan; history is working out of stories in the blood, stories passed from one people to another, from the Jews to the

Mayas, descendants of the Lost Tribe of Israel, to Columbus and his heirs among the Anishinaabe. Columbus first sensed the stories when he met Sephardic Jews in Europe before his voyage to the New World. Samana lured him to San Salvador with the idea of liberating the stories in his blood.

To Vizenor, stories are the way cultures come to terms with existence, how they make sense of the world around them. But stories are not simply produced consciously or unconsciously by societies; they belong to the realm of nature as much as culture. Vizenor extends Jung's ideas about narrative structures and archetypes being transmitted from one generation to the next; he describes how stories are actually transmitted from one generation to the next genetically.

> "The genome narratives are stories in the blood, a metaphor for racial memories, or the idea that we inherit the structures of language and genetic memories . . ." (136)

says Pir Cantrip, leading genetic researcher at Point Assinka.

Stories in the blood are linked to what Vizenor terms the "genes of survivance," a set of superior genes passed down from the ancient Mayans through Columbus to his heirs (170). The stories in the blood and the genes of survivance were the "new moities to heal" and Point Assinka "the first cross-blood nation dedicated to heal the wounded with genetic therapies" (144).

Since people are using genetic therapy to influence the course of history, this is a very different conception from most types of organicism, which posit some form of Providence as the controlling force behind history. However, the way Vizenor describes it, the genes seem to have their own agenda, and Cantrip and the other therapists are really following the mandate of the genes. In some ways Vizenor's ideas seem reminiscent of those of sociobiologist Edward Wilson, who argues that

> in a Darwinist sense the organism does not live for itself. Its primary function is not even to reproduce other organisms; it reproduces genes, and it serves as their temporary carrier. (3)

In conclusion, James Welch and Gerald Vizenor have written novels that appear to be radically different. Both however are historical novels, novels which not only describe historical events, but shape them in accordance with narrative, political and historical concepts In being aware of how Indian authors shape history when describing it, we can learn not only about the Indians of yesterday, but also of today.

ANNE MARIE DANNENBERG

"Where, Then, Shall We Place the Hero of the Wilderness?"

William Apess's Eulogy on King Philip and Doctrines of Racial Destiny

Between 1829 and 1836 William Apess was highly visible as an activist, lecturer, and author. A Methodist minister and mixed-blood Pequot, Apess was an outspoken advocate for Indian reform—education, christianization, temperance, and equal treatment under the law. Long a controversial figure in his native New England, Apess also briefly drew the eyes of the nation. Until just recently, however, Apess's writings were scattered in obscure repositories across the country and largely unknown to most contemporary scholars. Now, with the 1992 publication of Barry O'Connell's indispensable *On Our Own Ground: The Complete Writings of William Apess, A Pequot*, Apess's five published texts are widely available and are described as "the most considerable [body of writing produced] by any Native American before the 1840s" (xxxix). Largely due to O'Connell's broad-spectrum recovery of his work, Apess is becoming an important reference point amid efforts to retrieve occulted histories.

But despite the many vital contributions to Apess scholarship, there are still issues that make one worry. Even now, the most well-meaning recovery efforts are at times inflected by an Anglo-American view of history that carries a racial destiny—a version of the national creation story in which whites prevail, blacks are rescued from slavery, and Indians vanish. More specifically, since the early nineteenth century, the historical "fate" of Native

From *Early Native American Writing: New Critical Essays*. © 1996 by the Cambridge University Press.

Americans has been shaped by "vanishing American" ideology (the complex, pervasive nineteenth-century popular and scientific belief that indigenous Americans were a "dying race"). Accordingly, American Indians who resisted empire have been read as variants of the savage hero: noble and valiant but ultimately doomed. This tendency to view Native Americans as destined to vanish has thus far too readily framed our understanding of Apess's trajectory: Because the actual circumstances of his death were unknown until only very recently, the end of Apess's relatively short-lived prominence has been characterized as a "slide into anonymity" (O'Connell xxxviii), a mysterious disappearance from the textual record in 1838; and because the abolitionist movement is usually characterized as an antislavery movement rather than an antiracist movement, Apess's political project is understood to have been eclipsed by the emergence of broad-based support for abolitionism. Accordingly, both Apess and his reform efforts meet the Indian's "inevitable" fate; both are doomed by the natural course of history. Ironically, readings that cast Apess as a "doomed warrior" reaffirm the very ideologies he himself sought to fracture.

In his 1836 *Eulogy on King Philip*, Apess essayed his own reclamation project in memory of a colonial-era "villain," Metacomet, a Wampanoag leader known to the English as "King Philip". Throughout, Apess's *Eulogy* argues that our reading of the past determines our understanding of the present. Similarly, I argue that our construction of Apess's project in the *Eulogy* is critical to understanding Apess's place in American textual traditions.

≈≈≈≈≈≈≈≈

As its full title (*Eulogy on King Philip, as Pronounced at the Odeon, in Federal Street, Boston*) indicates, this 1836 text was originally presented as a lecture. Because it was Apess's last known writing, *Eulogy* is often presented as a sorrowful reminder of Apess's fate—regrettable, untimely, and unjust. O'Connell's preface to the *Eulogy*, for example, concludes with the elegiac assertion that "the *Eulogy* was [Apess's] final publication of himself to a society that briefly noticed and then forgot him" (276). But the *Eulogy* itself—arguably the most rhetorically complex of Apess's texts—challenges all assumptions on which such interpretation rests. To say that Apess was forgotten by society ignores the complex ideological machinery at play. Moreover, although Apess was in some ways separate and apart from the society to which he addressed his pleas for reform, he was in other ways very much part of it. Both Apess's lived experience and the *Eulogy*'s discursive intricacies suggest that "author" and "audience" are not so easily demarcated.

Although Apess presents a decidedly "Indian" self, that racialized self consistently defies a racial essence. Throughout, multiple discourses both shape his appeal for reform and constitute his textual identity. In *Eulogy*, Apess variously identifies himself as Pequot, (pan-)Indian, colored, Christian, male, (first) American, and embodiment of the Enlightenment notion of the "universal human"; he declares, "My image is of God; I am not a beast" (278). And like other overtly political texts advocating radical—perhaps revolutionary—social change (Jefferson's Declaration of Independence and King's "Letter from Birmingham Jail" may be parallels), Apess's *Eulogy* must confirm existing alliances, construct new ones, and, at the same time, reinforce the oppositions originally necessitating his plea. Definitive categories (racial, philosophical, religious, political, personal) disintegrate and coalesce by turns; throughout, they are at once applicable, useful, and contingent. In *Eulogy*, Apess is undeniably an Indian author addressing a non-Indian audience; he is simultaneously—as an advocate of Christian American Enlightenment humanism—a man and a Christian urging like-minded others to retrain their sights on shared goals. Thus, one cannot conclude that Apess adopted an alien discourse in order to address an alien audience. Although his audience in the Boston lecture hall in January 1836 was probably predominantly Christian and non-Indian, Apess's broader audience was far more diverse.

We do not know specifically what prompted Apess's presentation of the *Eulogy* at a Boston lecture hall, and there is no record of its sponsorship. Newspapers show that he lectured twice (January 8 and January 26, 1836); notices also promised Apess's "full view of the mission cause" (O'Connell 275). That he was both an Indian and a minister no doubt made Apess an authority on missionary efforts among Indians. Yet the *Eulogy*'s range far exceeds an assessment of evangelizing efforts. With the *Eulogy*, Apess makes a strong statement of cultural nationalism for Indian peoples and indicts whites' treatment of Indians both past and present. His message is social reform; his medium is history.

Introducing his subject, Apess pledges to "reveal the true character of Philip, in relation to those hostilities between himself and the whites" (278). To emend an Anglo-centered reading of colonial encounters between the Pilgrims and Native populations, particularly in regard to King Philip's War, Apess marshals "a mass of history and exposition" (289). Though he explicitly affirms an empirically accessible, objective truth that "wants no polishing whatsoever" (308), his handling of the "facts" suggests the quotidian business of historians to involve multiple provisional truths. He often introduces his evidence tentatively: Phrases such as "it was said" or "it appears that" or "[t]he history of New England writers says" or "as bar as we can learn by the records" (285–90) suggest that any single historical account is only one of many stories that must be told. But although Apess's counter-memory relies on the provisional nature of historical truths, his political goals necessitate firmer ground. Arguing a solid factual basis for his claim that Anglo aggression had been the ultimate cause of all hostilities from colonial times to his own, Apess proposes "one general law" for all (310)—a law presumably grounded in the truth his emended history reveals.

While the *Eulogy*'s surfaces treat history, its undercurrents address race. Whether he is speaking as revisionist historian, Indian activist, or Christian minister, Apess's aims are always political, and to wage politics in Apess's day was to struggle with racialist ideologies. The years when Apess published, 1829–36, are precisely those delimiting Andrew Jackson's presidency—key years for American expansion, critical years for the fate of indigenous populations. Between 1790 and 1830 the population of the western states (i.e., those west of the thirteen original states) rose from less than 3 percent to 28 percent of the total U.S. population, marking, according to Michael Rogin, "one of the great migrations in world history" (4). Continued expansion according to established patterns meant dispossession of the American Indian. Indicating the centrality of the "Indian question" in this period, Rogin maintains that "Indians had not mattered so much, in the history of Europeans in the English new world, since the colonial settlements. They would never matter so much again" (4). Jackson's 1830 Indian Removal Act requiring Indians' forced resettlement to lands west of the Mississippi River was bolstered by emergent doctrines of racial destiny—virulent discourses Apess knew well and perennially sought to undermine.

In his book on the origins of racial Anglo-Saxonism, Reginald Horsman marks 1815–50 as the period when white American society explicitly rejected American Indians (190). From the eighteenth-century flowering of interest in human origins to Apess's day, the History of the Human Race had gradually metamorphosed into the History of Human Races. The period's intellectuals attacked the Enlightenment belief in a common, inherently perfectable, and inalienably equal humankind, a belief that had explained observable, superficial differences in terms of environmental factors. Increasingly, scientists, social philosophers, historians, and charlatans cited arguments and empirical evidence as proof of innate differences among the "races of man." Anglo-Saxons—or "Anglo-Normans," as they were often designated in the South—were deemed patently superior to all other races. Although there was considerable disagreement among scholars as to just which human groups might claim to be Anglo-Saxons, by Apess's time the term "Anglo-Saxon" was popularly understood to mean white. All dark-skinned or "colored" peoples constituted the other, inferior races. Historical studies lauding the Anglo-Saxons' transcendent achievements throughout time began to be understood as a promise of things to come: Anglo-Saxons were destined to rule the world; other races must either bow or disappear. In the early nineteenth century, this certifiable racial destiny had begun to be used to rationalize social conditions and justify political policy.

As Horsman points out, emergent racialist thinking and the "eighteenth-century transatlantic view" that the Indian was a "fully improvable being" coexisted well into the nineteenth century, and Indians had "major defenders" among whites. But after 1830, neither the American masses nor their political leaders believed that Indians could ever be "enlightened" sufficiently to assimilate fully into American society (which, of course, presumed that Native peoples would desire assimilation). Horsman writes:

> Before 1830 there was a bitter struggle as those who believed in the Enlightenment view of the Indian as an innately equal, improvable being desperately defended the older ideals, but year by year the ideas of those who felt the Indians were expendable were reinforced by a variety of scientific and intellectual arguments. Indian Removal represented a major victory for ideas which, though long latent in American society, became fully explicit only after 1830. Political power was exercised by those who believed the Indians to be inferior, who did not wish them to be accepted as equals within American society, and who expected them ultimately to disappear. In shaping an Indian policy American politicians reflected the new ruthlessness of racial confidence . . . (190)

Any address by a Native American in 1836 would implicitly concern this "new ruthlessness." Apess's *Eulogy*, however, is more cynical than most. Apess argues that, except for formalized public discourse, the new ruthlessness differed little from the old. Strategically choosing a pre-Enlightenment period (the late colonial era) as his focus and then repeatedly comparing that period with his own, Apess obliterates any illusion that time has brought progress. His own experience had taught him how naive it would be to assume a direct correlation between Enlightenment rhetoric and enlightened practice. The *Eulogy* repeatedly reminds its audience that despite fluctuations in official policy, day-to-day Indian-white relations had changed little over time. Speaking of contemporaries who might be deluded by rhetoric sympathetic to Indians, Apess writes, "Although in words they deny it, yet in the works they approve of the iniquities of their fathers. And as the

seed of iniquity and prejudice was sown in that day, so it still remains. . . .
[T]he spirit of the Pilgrims yet remains" (287). Arguably, however, together
with Christian principles, Enlightenment ideals offered the best arsenal
against burgeoning anti-Indian thinking—perhaps the only tempering influence available in mainstream discourse. So, throughout the *Eulogy*, Apess
appeals to American Enlightenment values: inalienable human rights
sustained by a just system of laws, basic equality between human beings, a
confidence in human reason tempered by faith in divine providence.

In 1836 Boston, one of the remaining strongholds of Enlightenment
aspirations in the early nineteenth century as well as a site of early antislavery activism, Apess probably attracted an audience that favored egali-
tarianism and explicitly opposed racist practices. His pervasive sarcasm and
ironic barbs suggest that he took much support for granted. He both opens
and concludes his address with references to an Enlightenment—and abolitionist—shibboleth: liberty. "I appeal to the lovers of liberty," he states at
the outset (277). In closing, he asks that his "dear affectionate friends"
(308), "every friend of the Indians[,] . . . seize the mantle of Liberty" and
make war on "those corrupt and degrading principles that robs [sic] one of
all rights, merely because he is ignorant and of a little different color"
(307). By invoking liberty, Apess not only consolidates sympathies for a
commonly held value but also repudiates long-standing arguments for
Indian inferiority. According to Horsman, the earliest forms of Anglo-
Saxonist racialism (in the seventeenth and eighteenth centuries) celebrated
the superiority of so-called Anglo-Saxon institutions, but by the time Apess
was writing, Anglo-Saxonists focused not on superior institutions but
rather on superior blood.

American revolutionaries, notably Thomas Jefferson, drew on a
mythic construction of English history that framed Anglo-Saxon tribes as
the freedom-loving inventors of political institutions designed to preserve
"the natural rights of man"—rights on which all "men" had equal claims.
Separation from Britain could therefore be cast as a return to the supposed
purity of this mythic past (Horsman 9–24). In his study of the colonial era,
however, Apess examines a pre-Enlightenment context in which Indians
were generally believed incapable of—or, worse, indifferent to—forming
systems of government, and were considered devoid of any sense of rights
and attendant laws to safeguard them. The *Eulogy* refutes colonial charges
that Indian society was basically anarchic. Citing Roger Williams's writings
regarding Indian groups' strict geographical boundaries and disputes over
the use of hunting grounds, Apess concludes that "Indians had rights, and
those rights were near and dear to them" (288).

In other, pervasive references to indigenous political structures and social codes, he implicitly makes a case for cultural relativism, arguing, for example, that the Indians' avenging of the colonists' desecration of Indian graves and defacement of Indian monuments should be read not as an act of hostility but rather, "[a]ccording to the Indian custom," as "a righteous act" (282). With such examples, Apess invites his audience to read Indian "aggression" in Indian terms, as a defense of tradition-based, indigenous notions of rights and freedom. In Apess's reading, history shows that "the whites have always been the aggressors, and the war, cruelties, and bloodshed is a job of their own seeking, and not the Indians" (307). Moreover, he connects colonial hostilities with nineteenth-century frontier warfare, asserting that the wars arise "because the same spirit reigns there that reigned here in New England [in Philip's time]; and at present, there is no law to stop it" (307).

Revisions of the first colonists' view of Indian-white relations were not uncommon in Apess's day; many non-Indians, including both scholars and the public, had become critical of the early colonists' treatment of the "poor Indian." Such revisions, indeed, pervade the immensely popular "Indian plays" and romance novels of the period, all of them drenched in regret for the wronged, noble savage, whose fate was sealed by the purportedly inevitable course of human progress.

All such critiques of relations between savage and civilized, whether popular or scholarly, might be seen as continuing a lengthy tradition dating at least from the sixteenth century. Such treatments routinely catalogued the barbarities of so-called civilized nations and then queried just which human society rightly deserved the designation "savage." With this model in view, even Apess's most caustic inversions—for example, his painstakingly prefaced invocations of "white savages"—would not exactly shock his non-Indian audience. So Apess's innovation lies not primarily in his carefully documented exoneration of the "cursed memory" (284) of Philip, for whom he ultimately claims the distinction of being "the greatest man that ever lived upon the American shores" (290). Far more radically, Apess refuses the normalization of "extinction" by pointing out the ideological nature of American jurisprudence by contending that institutionalized racism—rather than so-called natural processes—threatened the Indian, and by urging political intervention to alter the supposed destiny of indigenous peoples in America.

Although there were certainly Indian-white wars in the 1830s, most removal was achieved without war. Likewise, in Philip's day, most real estate transactions between immigrant settlers and native peoples, although often grossly inequitable, were entirely within the legal parameters set down by Euro-Americans. Apess devotes a significant portion of the *Eulogy* to recounting details of Philip's "sales of lands" (290) and attendant court actions. Adducing evidence that Philip received unfair treatment in the "Pilgrims' court" (291), Apess adds, "And, indeed, it would be a strange thing for poor unfortunate Indians to find justice in those courts of the pretended pious in those days, or even since" (291).

As Apess argued his cause in New England, government agents were busily assisting frontier Indians in the exercise of their right to sign on the dotted line. As Michael Rogin has noted, the Jackson administration cloaked efforts to seize Indian lands in a "fiction of autonomous state and market processes" (223). Astutely, the *Eulogy* argues that "Indian rights" must be understood in Indian terms, for in New England as well as in the rest of the country, prevailing laws and customs marked a travesty of justice. Elaborating on the parallels between Philip's treatment under the law and the dynamics of Indian-white relations in his own day, Apess writes:

> Who stood up in those days, and since, to plead Indian rights? Was it the friend of the Indian? No, it was his enemies who rose—his enemies to judge and pass sentence. And we know that such kind of characters as the Pilgrims were, in regard to the Indians' rights, who, as they say, had none, must certainly always give verdict against them, as, generally speaking, they always have. (291)

Throughout, the *Eulogy* attempts to persuade so-called friends of the Indian that they must avoid the trap of thinking themselves powerless to change the course of "destiny."

Michael Rogin has called attention to the mutually reinforcing contradictions of Jacksonian rhetoric: While posturing as the benevolent parent and protector of the Indian, the federal government at the same time declared itself powerless to interfere with white settlers' usurpations—with the "natural course" of westward migration. But the government assured the people that even though such "natural processes" were afoot, the Great White Father, having his Indian children's best interests at heart, could be counted on to intervene and protect them. So the story went: Although the government could not eradicate the frontier settlers' greed, it could further Indians' best interests by convincing them that the only resource was to cede their lands. But in reality, Rogin argues, "Intruders entered Indian country only with government encouragement, after the extension of state law" (218–20).

Apess makes explicit reference to Jacksonian removal politics in referencing Jackson as the "president of the United States" who "tells the Indians they cannot live among civilized people" and in characterizing the president as saying, in effect, "we want your lands and must have them and will have them" (307). Burlesquing the paternal "protections" of the Jackson administration, Apess writes:

> You see, my red children, that our fathers carried on this scheme of getting your lands for our use, and we have now become rich and powerful; and we have a right to do with you just as we please; we claim to be your fathers. And we think we shall do you great favor, my dear sons and daughters, to drive you out, to get you away out of the reach of our civilized people, who are cheating you, for we have no law to reach them, we cannot protect you although you be our children. (307)

Thus, throughout his survey of the colonial encounter, Apess exposes the strange alchemy of the Europeans' Enlightenment claims to improve their inferiors and provide equal rights for equal citizens. He renders the first European colonists and their "rights" in terms of high irony: "those who came to improve our race and correct our errors, . . . those who are in the possession of [Philip's] soil, and only by the right of conquest" (277). Under existing laws, he contends, Indian rights amount to the "right" to relinquish rights and property. Eloquently affirming Philip's dire predictions, Apess writes:

> How deep, then, was the thought of Philip, when he could look from Maine to Georgia, and from the ocean to the lakes, and view with one look all his brethren withering before the more enlightened to come; and how true his prophecy, that the white people would not only cut down their groves but would enslave them. . . . Our groves and hunting grounds are gone, our dead are dug up, our council fires are put out, and a foundation was laid in the first Legislature to enslave our people, by taking from them all rights, which has been strictly adhered to ever since. (306)

Native peoples in his day, Apess concludes, remain "chained under desperate laws," just as they were "for nearly two hundred years" (306). Following precedents set in the colonial period, Apess declares, Philip's "few remaining descendants" (277) have been left to "drag out a miserable life as one chained to the galley" (306).

≈≈≈≈≈≈≈≈

As both imagery and explicit references in these passages demonstrate, Apess equates the treatment of native peoples with the more overt degradations of institutionalized slavery. Indeed, throughout, the *Eulogy* insists that there is more than a metaphoric link between these two forms of oppression and thus vehemently lays claim to the period's antislavery discourses.

From 1833 on, Apess's writings mark the kinds of connections between enslavement of African-Americans and the dispossession of American Indians that would be fully articulated by other activists and scholars only much later. Apess anticipates, for example, the analysis of contemporary historian Herbert Aptheker. Characterizing abolitionism as "the second successful revolutionary movement in the United States" (xi) (the American Revolution being the first), Aptheker writes: "The central commitment of the Abolitionist movement—its struggle against racism—was directed not only at enslavement but at all manifestations of the poison" (xiv). Patently, racism was as much a hallmark of European-Americans' relations with indigenous peoples as it was of their relations with Africans. Commenting on the relation between America's enslavement of blacks and its subjugation of Native Americans, Aptheker writes:

> Racism permeated slavery in the United States—characterized it, justified it, and sustained it. In another manifestation, in somewhat altered form, racism rationalized the genocidal policy practiced toward the indigenous population, the Native Americans. . . . To attack slavery, then, was to attack racism. (xiv)

From Apess's perspective, to attack racist policies toward Native Americans was to attack slavery. Congruent with historical analyses that view American abolitionism and the struggle for Indian rights as discrete social movements, it has been suggested that Apess's decline as a public figure resulted from the increasing momentum of an abolitionist movement that ultimately "relegated the plight of the American Indian to a secondary place in reform thinking" (McQuaid 623; see also O'Connell xxxix). But such analyses both reduce abolitionism and reinstantiate the discourses that separated African-Americans and Native Americans into distinct races. Apess did not merely appropriate abolitionist rhetoric for a separate Native American political agenda; rather, Apess *was*, in the truest sense, himself an abolitionist.

From his first publication to his last, racist attitudes toward Native

Americans are Apess's focus. Commencing with the 1833 publication of *The Experiences of Five Christian Indians of the Pequot Tribe*; or, *An Indian's Looking-Glass for the White Man*, however, Apess begins to examine parallels between the situations of Indians and Africans. (Notably, 1833 also marked the founding of the American Anti-Slavery Society.) Employing both Christian and Enlightenment rhetoric, Apess notes the lack of protections "in . . . persons and in property" for people of color "throughout the Union" and denounces those who "take the skin as a pretext to keep us from our unalienable and lawful rights" (156). With the chronicle of his role in the insurrection at Mashpee plantation, the 1835 *Indian Nullification of the Unconstitutional Laws of Massachusetts Relative to the Marshpee Tribe*; or, *The Pretended Riot Explained*, Apess reiterates the correspondences between economic exploitation of the Mashpees and enslavement of Africans. Presenting both historical and economic justifications to identify the oppression of Native Americans with that of Africans, Apess bitterly concludes: "It is a fine thing to be an Indian. One might almost as well be a slave" (188).

Although Apess clearly drew heavily on formalized abolitionist rhetoric in articulating such parallels, one need not assume that his ideas were borrowed from abolitionists. Apess's awareness of his own mixed biological heritage, his personal experience, and his social context could easily have suggested such equations. Census documents show that both Apess and his wife might themselves have been part African-American (O'Connell xxvii, fn. 17). Moreover, no doubt among his constituency in general, and certainly among the Mashpees with whom he lived and helped to organize an insurrection to demand legal rights, there was a great deal of intermarriage between Africans and Indians.

Additionally, the ongoing Seminole War provided a compelling backdrop for Apess's arguments implicitly advocating a joint black-red resistance. In that war—ultimately the longest and costliest "Indian war" in U.S. history—free blacks, escaped black slaves, and Seminole Indians fought side by side against American forces (Rogin 235ff.). No doubt, this protracted conflict would have revealed the many contradictions inherent in viewing the plight of African-Americans and the struggles of American Indians as separate issues. Indeed, a commander of government troops fighting the Seminoles at one point insisted, "This . . . is a negro, not an Indian war," an assessment that caused abolitionists to be blamed for the war (Rogin 238). With the hostilities in Florida, such strife was no longer framed as the familiar contest of savage against civilized; increasingly, such conflicts were framed, as in Thomas Hart Benton's words, as "the ravages of the colored races upon the white" (quoted in Horsman 205).

From the time of *Experiences* on, Apess's texts point out the analogous religious, juridical, and economic practices that underlay the dispossession and/or genocide of Native populations and the enslavement of Africans. Subordination of both groups, he realized was buttressed by complex moral arguments, by legal sleight of hand, by strong material incentives for certain segments of the population, and, increasingly, by scientific discourse. Although originally the "American savage" had been deemed a notch above the "African" in the Anglo-Saxonist vision of racial hierarchy, by Apess's time that slight advantage had been virtually erased. Americans had not only begun to doubt whether Indians could ever be "elevated" to the status of whites, but also speculated that indigenous peoples might in fact, be fated to move in the opposite direction. Georgia Governor George M. Troup's letter to then Secretary of War John C. Calhoun in 1824 demonstrates the perception that Indians would ultimately "devolve" to the level of blacks:

> [T]he utmost of rights and privileges which public opinion would concede
> to Indians, would fix them in a middle station between the negro and the
> white man; and that, as long as they survived this degradation, without the
> possibility of attaining the elevation of the latter, they would gradually
> sink to the condition of the former—a point of degeneracy below which
> they could not fall. . . . (quoted in Horsman 196)

Although intellectuals of predominantly northern European American heritage (self-identified Anglo-Saxons)—even those generally sympathetic to both abolitionism and Indian reform—might quibble over minute increments in the racial hierarchy, all agreed that when compared with themselves, Africans and Indians were undeniably alike: Both groups were inferior to Anglo-Saxons. For a host of reasons, then, Apess's work continually highlights the common legacy of people of color. The parallels between those identified as Native Americans and as African-Americans, in particular, are more vividly, more explicitly drawn with each new publication. In this regard, Apess's position indeed anticipates prominent black nationalist Martin R. Delaney's stance, progressive even in 1854: "[W]e [African-Americans and Native Americans] are identical as subjects of American wrongs, outrages, and oppression, and therefore one in interest" (214–15).

Because their ultimate goal—the eradication of American racism—was the same, abolitionism and Indian reform readily occupied the same rhetorical terrain. Like others more commonly considered abolitionists, Apess pleaded his cause by way of Judeo-Christian teachings and Enlightenment ideals as put forward in the Declaration of Independence. Apess's opening "appeal to the lovers of liberty" has a decidedly abolitionist ring. The *Eulogy* commences by chronicling an early-seventeenth-century incident in which thirty American Indians were taken captive by an English ship "to be sold for slaves among the Spaniards," an "inhuman act of the whites," Apess maintains, "which caused the Indians to be jealous forever afterward" (279). Thus he locates the historical roots of racial tensions between Europeans and American Indians in an actual attempt to enslave. Apess then implies that the colonial powers had forever after chronically confused enslavement with religious conversion; he states, "How they could go to work to enslave a free people and call it religion is beyond the power of my imagination and outstrips the revelation of God's word" (279). Further invoking Christianity as the ground for his broad-spectrum antislavery appeal, Apess tells the story of how the English, "those pretended Christians," captured and subsequently sold into slavery King Philip's ten-year-old son. Underscoring colonial hypocrisies, Apess asserts that the early European settlers would "on the Sabbath day . . . gather themselves together and say that God is no respecter of persons," even as they were "hating and selling their fellow men in bondage" (301). Proclaiming that "[he who would] advocate slavery is worse than a beast" surrounded by "the most corrupt and debasing principles in the world," Apess maintains that it was only violent resistance—including taking the lives of their own people—that saved Indians from the same fate as Africans. Apess contends:

> And there is no manner of doubt but that all my countrymen would have been enslaved if they had tamely submitted. But no sooner would they butcher every white man that come in their way, and even put an end to their own wives and children, and that was all that prevented them from being slaves; yes, *all*. (301)

Apess must have perceived in the burgeoning Abolitionist movement—a highly visible international movement with a sense of moral urgency, a movement with clearly defined goals, a movement bent on revolutionary intervention in the existing social matrix—a powerful ally for Indian reform. To link his own reform objectives with those of abolitionists, however, Apess needed to render his cause visible.

≈≈≈≈≈≈≈≈≈

In 1789 Henry Knox, secretary of war (and thus in charge of Indian affairs), pronounced New England Indians nonexistent:

> It is . . . painful to consider, that all the Indian tribes, once existing in those States now the best cultivated and most populous, have become extinct. If the same causes continue, the same effects will happen; and, in a short period, the idea of an Indian on this side of the Mississippi will only be found in the page of the historian. (quoted in Pearce 56)

Some forty years later, native historian William Apess—a mixed-blood survivor of the "extinct" Pequots—asserted the continuing presence of New England Native Americans. Congruent with Vanishing American ideology, non-Indians believed that the only authentic Indian was the "wild Indian" of the frontier. As James Madison stated on leaving office:

> Next to the case of the black race within our bosom, that of the red on our borders is the problem most baffling to the policy of our country. (quoted in Rogin 319)

Although blacks in contact with whites would always remain blacks, Indians mingling with whites ceased to be truly Indian. Indians who coexisted with whites either degenerated (becoming less Indian) or, in rare instances, assimilated (becoming less Indian). Either way, prolonged contact eroded true Indianness. Thus, for most New England non-Indians, Native Americans in their midst could no longer be considered "real" (noble) Indians, but merely degenerate "remnants" of an admirable—though quickly fading—past, living out the last days of their race in wantonness and squalor. Although, with free blacks, New England Indians were among the most despised people in New England (O'Connell lxii), their status was viewed differently from that of Indians on the frontier. Thus one of Apess's objectives was to demonstrate that "wherever there are any Indians" (307), the same legacy of colonial racism prevails. Focusing on the racialist dynamics of Indian-white relations "from Maine to Georgia," Apess's writings redraw the frontier as the color line, and in so doing lift the veil of invisibility that cloaks indigenous groups remaining east of the Mississippi.

To rephrase Apess's own question: Where, then, shall we place *this* hero of the wilderness? Arguably, Apess scholarship needs to move further in the direction suggested by Apess himself, needs to be examined outside the parameters of American exceptionalism, outside familiar plots of How the West Was Won. Clearly, the complexity of his political project has not yet been fully appreciated. To be sure, his Enlightenment discourse involves problematic language. With his assertions that Indians are *as good as* whites and that Indians ought to be acknowledged "as men and as Christians," he appears to concede to white males prior claims to the universal human subject. And although he forcefully advocates "rights" and "liberty" for indigenous peoples, it is unclear just what practices would fulfill his objectives—an ambiguity perhaps politically necessary.

Although as a political advocate and a cultural nationalist Apess appears to be without peer in his era, it is perhaps his role as historian that is most suggestive for contemporary scholars. O'Connell states, "The best modern histories of the encounters between New England Native Americans and the Anglo-Americans confirm the interpretive stance Apess takes" (276). But the *Eulogy*, like other Apess texts, goes beyond Indian-situated counter-memory; all his writings raise profound questions about the tensions between provisional and absolute truth and the implications of such questions for immediate political urgency. As an Indian, as a Pequot—a group whose extinction was decreed by law and subsequently transcribed by historians as fact—Apess was well aware that both law and history are ideologically invested cultural products. Yet he knew that without consensual truth, there would be little hope for implementation of "one general law" for all. The *Eulogy on King Philip* repeatedly reminds us that past and present stand in dynamic relation.

MARTHA L. VIEHMANN

"My People . . . My Kind":

Mourning Dove's Cogewea, the Half-blood *as a Narrative of Mixed Descent*

Gerald Vizenor, in his book *Earthdivers*, uses the term "mixed descent" as a symbolic category, moving beyond heredity to describe a strategy of discourse that promotes transformation. Bringing mixed descent to discourse undermines the modes of speech and thought that Vizenor calls "terminal creeds," that is, fixed, dogmatic beliefs or modes of expression that do not allow for ambiguity or change. The mixed-blood heroes of Vizenor's stories explode terminal creeds by their constantly shifting positions and discourses. Through figures that challenge boundaries, overturn expectations, and commit social offenses, and through narratives that break down genres and commit literary offenses, Vizenor opens a way for transformation. His concept allows for the expansion of mixed descent from a social and biological fact to a literary and cultural construct, thereby challenging readers to see mixed blood as a basis for a new literature rather than as a reason for questioning the "authenticity" of writings by Native Americans.

Vizenor's symbolic mixed descent is useful in understanding Mourning Dove, her novel, *Cogewea, the Half-blood: A Depiction of the Great Montana Cattle Range,* and her relationship to Lucullus McWhorter, the white amateur historian who collaborated with her to produce that text. An expanded conceptualization of mixed descent helps one appreciate the

From *Early Native American Writing: New Critical Essays.* © 1996 by the Cambridge University Press.

complexity of a novel that at first glance appears to be a simple Western romance. Moreover, following Vizenor and using mixed descent as a metaphor enriches interpretation of *Cogewea* by creating a central place for the collaboration between Mourning Dove and McWhorter within the analysis. Mourning Dove herself seems to have played with the freedom that the open-endedness of mixed descent provides. She apparently created a new persona to go with her pen name. In the discussion that follows, I use her family name, Christine Quintasket, when writing of her personal history and her pen name, Mourning Dove, when writing of the author.

Christine Quintasket was probably biologically and certainly metaphorically a woman of mixed descent. She lived in a transitional era and grew up in a household that embraced Okanogan traditions and accommodation to white society. Her parents bridged both worlds: Her father worked in the wage economy and continued traditional food-gathering practices, and her mother urged her daughter to learn Native medicinal lore and took her to the local Catholic church. As an adult, Quintasket served her people as a leader of Native women's organizations and as an activist, arbitrating disputes, encouraging fulfillment of agreements, and acting as an advocate for girls in trouble with white authorities (Miller, "Mourning Dove" 174, 176; Introduction xxv). In her upbringing and as a mediator for her people, Quintasket experienced mixed descent as a cultural condition.

In creating her persona as Mourning Dove the writer, Quintasket claimed for herself a European grandfather on her father's side. In reviewing the tribal rolls, one scholar finds no substantiation for this claim, and another finds evidence that suggests that her biological *father* was white. Whatever the facts, Mourning Dove's story resonates with the power of the ambiguities of cultural contact. By displacing the unfaithful white man one generation, she claims Joseph Quintasket as her only father, a role he in fact played. In addition, by claiming that Joseph was part white, Mourning Dove could rationalize the divergent sympathies in the Quintasket home. In her autobiographical writings, she emphasizes the role her mother played in promoting traditional education and the role of her father in encouraging formal schooling (*Mourning Dove* 27, 30–1, 43). By naming herself a mixed blood, she places herself in the position of her heroine, Cogewea, who creates contexts in which full bloods can rethink the divisions between the two cultures and between "pure" and "amalgamated" individuals. Through the persona of Mourning Dove, Quintasket creates for herself a transformative place in which she is a mixed blood yet has strong roots within the Okanogan community.

Within *Cogewea, the Half-blood,* the themes of biological mixed descent and cultural contact add tension to the romance plot. Cogewea's two suitors, Alfred Densmore, who is white, and Jim LaGranger, who is a half blood, represent divergent choices not only for the heroine but for all mixed bloods and Indians. Paralleling the romance are legends from Okanogan folkloric tradition, related by Cogewea's grandmother, that dwell on interactions between whites and Indians. Cultural contact produces the "issue," that is, the topic and the offspring, of mixed descent. It is the ever-present background for biological and symbolic mixed descent and a major analytical category in my approach to ethnic literature. Within the novel, Cogewea's status as a half blood, whose education has brought her additional contact with the white world, opens up both choices and challenges that her full-blood grandmother never faced. Moreover, Mourning Dove employs her knowledge of Native American and ranch life to rework a popular genre: She inserts Okanogan folklore, western tall tales, and a transformed image of the maligned "half breed" into the western romance, thereby altering its formula. Her incorporation of stories told directly by the grandmother is an example of Bakhtin's concept of the dialogic, as outlined in *The Dialogic Imagination*, which is, in turn, closely allied to Vizenor's idea of mixed descent. Both Vizenor and Bakhtin are interested in the breakdown of formulaic genres, the blurring of boundaries, and the power of humor and transformation as literary strategies. Mourning Dove transforms the western romance formula, creates a heroine based on a humorous figure from Okanogan folklore, and plays with the boundaries between Native and European American, between mixed bloods and full bloods to create a powerful novel that, in spite of its flaws, challenges conceptions of the half blood and of Native American literature.

Moreover, her editor, Lucullus Virgil McWhorter, further shaped *Cogewea* by adding sections in his distinctive literary style. The result of the collaboration of a white man sympathetic to his Native American neighbors and an Indian woman operating between the two cultures is a multivoiced text reflecting different approaches to the material and to the audience. A notable difference between Mourning Dove and McWhorter is that she has strong faith in the power of stories (or fiction) to sway readers to her point of view, whereas he places his faith in the power of historical facts. Where Mourning Dove included dramatic vignettes of western life and incorporated Okanogan folktales into the novel, McWhorter added footnotes and arguments against the Indian Bureau. His additions of notes, epigraphs, a photograph of the author, and an introduction describing her alter the reader's experience of the book. McWhorter's front and back matter also create a sort of "genetic map" that we may use to trace his additions to the main body of the text. In the novel proper, his inserted arguments can jolt the reader. The different voices, visions, and emphases that result from the collaboration reveal differences in the way the two chose to represent Native American culture as they demonstrate how mixed descent permeates every aspect of the text.

A Novel of Mixed Descent: Romance and Folklore in *Cogewea*

Cogewea passes an afternoon reading a western romance. Reading marks her as a heroine. She has leisure time during which she indulges in an activity that is emblematic of middle-class heroines; her comfortable location on the "veranda" (88) also attests to the leisure and spaciousness of her life. By contrast, Cogewea's Salish grandmother, having spent the morning weaving a basket, rests in her tipi, which lies in sight of the porch. Mourning Dove's juxtaposition implies that while Cogewea has adopted many aspects of the white world, the traditional ways of her Indian ancestry are literally still in view. The enduring presence of the grandmother, or *stemteemä*, in Cogewea's life provides an image that contrasts with and points up the failures of the romance Cogewea reads.

Mourning Dove's fictional character reads an actual book, Therese Broderick's *The Brand: A Tale of the Flathead Reservation* (1909). *The Brand*, like *Cogewea, the Half-blood*, is set in the Flathead region of Montana. Both books feature a protagonist of part Indian parentage and a romantic interest who is white. *The Brand* portrays Henry West, a young mixed blood, as a model hero; he possesses superhuman strength and outstanding moral character. He passes all the tests that demonstrate his worthiness of the affection of the refined eastern heroine, who is, of course, white. However, throughout the novel, Henry believes himself unworthy of Bess's affection because of his Indian blood. When first published, Broderick's novel was read as sympathetic to Native Americans because it shows that a man of mixed blood is capable of education and refinement (Rev. of *The Brand*). Broderick contrasts Henry's good character with occasional portraits of pathetic, impoverished full bloods, showing us just how far his half-blood mother's choice of a white rancher for a husband and of a Harvard education for her son can bring a descendant of Indians. At the end of the novel, Bess pledges her love to Henry West, vowing that she will forget that he is part Indian. Broderick asserts forgetting as the solution to the so-called Indian problem. However, events in the novel make it clear that "savagery," a word Broderick uses, still haunts the Wests. Furthermore, Bess ultimately gives in to her love for Henry only because she has fallen in love with the west itself;

it is her love of the land that brings her back to Henry. The power of the landscape overcomes the repulsion she felt when she witnessed West's violent attack on Dave Davis, the white suitor who proved unworthy. West's name links him to the landscape's power, as if to cement his association with the individualism embodied in the myth of the American frontier. It is the force of the land and the force of individuals' characters that prevail over race. *The Brand* implies that the west is the true home of vigorous, wholesome individualists like Bess and Henry. The Indians as a people will give way before them; the best of that race will merge with the white population, and the few full-blood hangers-on provide an outlet for Christian charity until they finally disappear for good. Although *The Brand* treats the themes of cultural contact and mixed descent, Broderick recoils from the implications of intermarriage by whitewashing her hero.

Mourning Dove uses Broderick's book to highlight the significance of mixed descent and its multifaceted repercussions. Cogewea's summary of *The Brand* distorts the book but gets to the heart of the problem in Broderick's portrayal of a mixed-blood hero. According to Cogewea, West "curses his own mother" for "branding" him with Native blood, marries the white heroine, and then "slaves for her the rest of his life" (91). Although Henry West neither curses his mother nor slaves for Bess, Cogewea's description underscores the assumption of white superiority that runs throughout the text. I begin my reading of Cogewea with the heroine's response to *The Brand* because Mourning Dove's novel is in part a response to popular images of Indians, images that she counters with her own, producing figures that arise from both popular romance and the experiences of an Okanogan woman. Mourning Dove creates her heroine in contrast to Henry West. In response to the struggle to negotiate a way of life between divergent worlds, Cogewea is cheerful and mischievous, like her namesake, the chipmunk, whereas West is consistently serious, even stoic, like the stereotyped noble Indian. Moreover, throughout *The Brand*, Henry remains consistently aware of the biological "fact" of his mixed blood. Even the closing call to forget race is a self-conscious turning away from biology. Broderick's emphasis on biology amounts to a form of determinism. Because of their Indian ancestry, Henry and Mrs. West are susceptible to "savage" reactions; their drive for vengeance consistently horrifies Bess, whom I take to represent the "civilized" norm in *The Brand*. Broderick draws scenes that suggest that in extreme situations, instinctual racial reactions break through the veneer of an acquired way of life. Race is apparently such a persistent influence on behavior that only denial, sheer force of will, and the love of the right woman serve to overcome its power.

Cogewea, on the other hand, can ignore race. For instance, at a basket social, she is flirtatious, as any young woman might be: She plays one suitor off the other, teasing Jim like the mischievous chipmunk of folklore. When Cogewea focuses on problems of race, her attention is on Native Americans as a group—the history of European-American injustice against them or the uncertainty of their future as a people. This is not the same as Henry West's concern for himself; drawn as an individualist, Henry mourns only his fate, not the fate of his people. Mourning Dove's attention to Indian *people* changes the terms of discourse from blood and biology to culture. She replaces the "facts" of biology with characters based on her own experience of mixed descent, thereby treating race as a story arising from a social context. Her full-blood Indians are dignified and forceful, not the inarticulate and helpless figures in Broderick's novel (figures that I suspect upset Mourning Dove at least as much as the morose Henry). Cogewea's grandmother is a living embodiment of the old ways, whose strength represents the continuing power of Native ways and beliefs. In contrast to her is Alfred Densmore, the self-serving and morally suspect white suitor, who represents the worst characteristics of American individualism. In between stands the heroine, negotiating a way between two apparently incompatible worlds.

Christine Quintasket's anger about the portrayal of Indians in books such as *The Brand* surely inspired her to write a novel of her own that attempts to bring to life the experience of an Indian woman in the early twentieth century. As she expressed it in an interview with the Spokane *Spokesman Review*, Quintasket was frustrated by the popular image of the stoic Indian, so she was determined to use her ability to write to describe the "true Indian character" (April 19, 1916, quoted in *Mourning Dove* xxi). In her writing, Mourning Dove draws on her education in both cultures. The yellowback novels, from which she learned to read, provide a model in the form of the popular romance, and the stories told by Long Theresa and other elders from the Colville reserve give her models for reshaping the melodramatic characters and plot. From the brief descriptions of reading in her autobiographical work and from accounts of collecting folklore in her letters, I infer that Quintasket found both methods of storytelling absorbing and so readily claimed both as "ancestors" for her own novel. Trusting in the power of stories to both reach and sway an audience, Mourning Dove revised the familiar western romance to show readers that Indians "'felt as deeply as whites'" (*Mourning Dove* xxi). Following the general plot lines of Broderick's novel, Mourning Dove drew on her own experience of life on the Flathead reserve and its ranches, thereby creating Indian characters and portraits of ranching that were more true to life than Broderick's.

In her writing, Mourning Dove also aimed to present and preserve some of the tribal folklore that influenced her and that, at the urging of McWhorter, she collected. *Cogewea* is perhaps the earliest work by an American Indian author that successfully combines fiction and folklore by using the folklore as a model for the protagonist's story. The romance plot overlaps with the stories recounted by the *stemteemä*, which warn of the dangers of intermarriage between Native women and white men. The reader early on knows that Alfred Densmore is false and the *stemteemä* correct in her suspicion that he will prove unfaithful. But Mourning Dove holds true to melodramatic form by bringing her heroine to the brink of disaster, thereby extending the parallel between legend and plot as long as possible. The stories related within the context of the novel reflect the main plot of the false love of the white man, or *shoyahpee*, for the Native woman, and they occupy a central place—literally and figuratively—in the novel. Through them, the reader gains insight into the true nature of the *shoyahpee* (meaning both Densmore and whites in general) and into the wisdom of the grandmother.

Mourning Dove also selects folkloric figures as models for her characters. In two stories that Mourning Dove collected but did not include in her novel, we see the chipmunk, called Cogewea, as a mischievous creature who is unable to keep out of trouble. Little Chipmunk, who lives with her grandmother, is sent to the lodge of Fisher and Skunk. She is to show herself to Fisher so that this good hunter will take her as a wife. But Chipmunk laughs at Skunk's bad smell, giving herself away to this undesirable mate. Fisher rescues her, but Chipmunk is again careless, putting them in danger. Mourning Dove makes her heroine a practical joker who herself brings Densmore to the ranch to tease her brother-in-law. Like the chipmunk of legend, Cogewea faces serious consequences because of her foolishness. The novel reaches its climax as Densmore and Cogewea run away to be married. When he discovers that the wealth attributed to her is only a cowboy's tall tale, he ties her up, leaving her helpless as he runs for the east-bound train. Only then does the heroine realize that she, too, has been led astray by lies. Like the Chipmunk, Cogewea gets into trouble because of her propensity for laughter and her disregard of her grandmother's advice.

In another story, the monster Owl Woman lures Little Chipmunk with lies, only to take out her heart. Densmore similarly steals Cogewea's heart with lies of love. Only time and the workings of spirit power restore the hearts of Cogewea and Little Chipmunk. Densmore's actions mimic those of the Owl Woman, but his true model is Coyote. Coyote, an important figure in Salish folklore, is the trickster responsible for shaping the world to suit humans, but he is also an antihero, consumed by insatiable desires and

constantly in trouble. Alfred Densmore inherits the negative characteristics of
Coyote. He is self-centered, greedy, and mendacious. Like Coyote, he conceals
his true identity. But the lies are always uncovered, so Densmore and Coyote
typically lose the prizes they seek. Like Fisher, Jim LaGranger is favored by the
grandmother, and he rescues Cogewea. Finally recognizing that the spirit
power urges her to do so, Cogewea gives her heart to Jim. When she is sure of
his love, she reveals the small fortune left by the father who deserted her and
her sisters. Densmore, in a cheap eastern boarding house, reads of his rival's
success and so, like Coyote, recognizes the extent of his loss.

Mourning Dove and McWhorter

On completing a draft of her book, Quintasket, discouraged by the
results, stowed the pages in the bottom of a trunk. At about this time, she
enrolled in a business school, hoping to improve her English, perhaps with
the aim of returning to her writing. She also must have spoken to friends
about her desire to write. On September 30, 1914, J. W. Langdon wrote to
her recommending that she contact Lucullus McWhorter to assist her in
preparing her book for publication (quoted by Fisher, Introduction v).
Quintasket eventually met McWhorter, and he provided a great deal of assistance with *Cogewea* and with the only other work she published in her life-
time, *Coyote Stories* (1933). McWhorter invited Quintasket to stay in his
home, where she revised the draft that he subsequently edited (Brown,
"Mourning Dove's Voice" 2). By 1919 the book was ready for publication,
but the paper shortage of World War I interfered. Hopeful of increasing the
appeal of the book, McWhorter made more changes to the text, which the
author did not see until it was published. Eventually he found a press, and
together Quintasket and McWhorter raised the necessary funds (Brown,
"Mourning Dove's Voice" 2; "Legacy Profile" 53–4). Because of his efforts,
the novel finally was published in 1927. As Quintasket wrote in 1933: "My
book of Cogeawea [*sic*] would never have been anything but the cheap
foolscap paper that it was written on if you had not helped me get it in shape"
(quoted by Fisher, Introduction xiii). But McWhorter's work with the manu-
script went beyond editorial corrections and suggestions. By adding sections
to *Cogewea*, McWhorter left his mark on the text, making it noticeably the
product of two collaborators.

McWhorter's various additions to the text reveal substantial differences
between his and Mourning Dove's appeal to white readers on behalf of
American Indians. Where Mourning Dove works with the power of stories,

McWhorter asserts the power of facts. Where she draws on romance and folklore, he draws on European-American conventions of biographical and historical writing. The photograph of Mourning Dove, McWhorter's prefatory remarks, and the footnotes all perform verifying functions. They assert that Mourning Dove is a real person, that she writes from actual experience of Native life, that some of the events are drawn from history, and that the descriptions of customs and events are accurate. McWhorter foresaw that doubt about the literary ability of an Indian woman would detract from *Cogewea*'s impact. His doubts proved true when an agency employee accused Mourning Dove of contributing only her name and photograph to the novel (*Mourning Dove* xi). In this instance, McWhorter's faith in the factual shows sensitivity to Mourning Dove's vulnerability as an author, even if all the verifying material was not enough to convince the most skeptical readers.

Some of McWhorter's additions reveal his apparent anxiety about readers' acceptance of the negative portrayal of Alfred Densmore and other white men. He includes factual items to show that whites have been unjust in their dealings with American Indians. Moreover, he seems to have viewed the book as a vehicle for the exposure of this injustice, for he described the book in a letter to J. P. McLean, saying that it "'is NOT fiction in the full sense of the word'" (quoted in Fisher, "Transformation" 119 n. 4). For McWhorter, the facts were essential. His own writings about Native Americans are historical and are concerned with expressing the Native point of view—a point of view essential for revealing the "truth" of historic events. Lucullus McWhorter's addition of attacks on the Bureau of Indian Affairs, of footnotes reiterating the tendency of white men on the frontier to abandon Native women, and of further examples of social injustices suffered by Native Americans as a group subtly change the stress of *Cogewea, the Half-blood*. The story becomes not simply the struggle of a young Okanogan woman to recognize her desire to live in affirmation of her tribal heritage. Under McWhorter's hand, the novel directly takes on the defense of all mixed-blood and full-blood Native Americans and urges the reform of the reader's feelings and of the social and governmental machinery that oppresses Native people.

Mourning Dove was concerned with this social struggle, yet she was content to leave the larger tale of oppression implicit in the story of an individual. Mourning Dove focuses on the wily Densmore's attempt to seduce Cogewea and steal her supposed wealth, a small-scale reenactment of the history of white-Indian relations. Using legends, Mourning Dove links the contemporary story to the tribal past, making the plot archetypal and the figures symbolic. McWhorter and Quintasket clearly agree on bringing to light the Native American view of race relations. They both see the importance of defending Indians and reforming social attitudes and structures. Her approval of his alterations attest to that. But McWhorter has less faith in the persuasive power of metaphor. Not content with the social implications of the novel, McWhorter, an amateur historian, inserts facts and verifying material into the romance.

Some of the polemical passages that stylistically appear to be McWhorter's have the unfortunate effect of weakening the portrayal of the villainous Densmore; they make him party to conversations that are inconsistent with his actions. To pave the way for Cogewea's critique of the Indian Bureau in chapter XVI, Densmore must feign interest in the future of the Indian tribes. The conversation is stilted, and the words ring false when spoken by this self-absorbed character. Despite this awkwardness, McWhorter's additions bring into high relief issues already implicit in the text.

As Dexter Fisher notes, the difference between McWhorter's stiff, rhetorical style and Mourning Dove's simplicity of expression highlights the importance of language in Cogewea's struggle to make a place for herself ("Transformation" 102-3). She is a mixed blood and an educated Indian, versed in the ways of two societies yet rejected by both. Cogewea's command of Salish, range slang, and proper English brings to life her indeterminate status. Her tendency to switch rapidly from one form of speech to another shows the moody character with which Mourning Dove endows her and her inability to choose between two different ways of life. Likewise, the passages in which Cogewea speaks up for her race—meaning the Indian people—contrast with Densmore's invocation of the individual. The novel sets up an opposition between the Native virtue of taking responsibility for the group and the Anglo-American virtue of individualism (which shades into the vice of greed). Polemics that I attribute to McWhorter keep the question of duty to one's people—indeed, of the Indian people's need for advocates—active in the text and underscore the opposition between white and Indian values.

The conclusion of the book sits squarely in the popular literary tradition of neat and happy endings: Cogewea and her sisters inherit fortunes, Cogewea marries Jim, and Mary, her younger sister, marries Frenchy, the sympathetic greenhorn who acts as a positive double for Densmore. McWhorter's additions qualify the romantic optimism of this ending, which should be qualified by the historical reality that Quintasket knew all too well. At her best, Mourning Dove transcends the limitations of the popular romance genre by adding sketches of cowboy and range life and by including the *stemteema*'s legends. With these, Mourning Dove adds the voices of range slang, tall tales, and an implicit Native American language that complicate the fixed form and enrich her work.

Folktale and Fact: The Story of Green-blanket Feet

Lucullus McWhorter also appended notes to the novel that explain Native words, verify historical references, and expand on injustice as a theme. The information establishes the authentic grounding of the book in Native American experience. The emphasis on authenticity gives us a context for the book, but it does not help readers grasp the literary workings of it. McWhorter's notes to the *stemteemä*'s story of Green-blanket Feet provide a good example. This is one of three tales that the grandmother relates; all of them are central to the novel, for they deal with European-Native contact and provide a mythic model for the fictional plot. By including the legend, Mourning Dove reworks the popular romance through the addition of folklore, and her use of the *stemteemä*'s voice contributes to the dialogism of the text. McWhorter's treatment of the legend in his foot-notes represents the collaborative aspect of mixed descent and demonstrates his own tendency toward a historical point of view.

In this chapter, Mourning Dove adopts the grandmother's voice and skillfully relates a pathetic story of a woman's losses. Green-blanket Feet marries a white man, bearing him two children. When the younger one is two years old, the man informs his wife that he is returning east with the chil-dren. She may come with him, never to see her people again, or she may remain. She chooses to go. As they travel, her husband treats her cruelly. Green-blanket Feet realizes that he wants his son and daughter but not her. She vows to escape with the younger, and, with the help of a loyal wolf-dog, she does. But on her return journey, she is captured by the Blackfeet, her people's enemy. The woman is enslaved and mistreated. In relating her tale, she reflects: "'Much of this hardship, I think, was because I had chosen a Shoyahpee husband instead of one of my own kind; that my child was half white. The Great Spirit must have been displeased with me'" (172–3).

Her words sum up the grandmother's intent in telling the story. To the *stemteemä*, white men are dangerous and bring suffering, so she hopes to dissuade Cogewea from accepting Densmore's attentions. Like Green-blanket Feet, Cogewea believes the lies of the *shoyahpee*; to him she loses her small savings (acquired through the lease of her allotment). Green-blanket Feet gains children and Cogewea money through contact with whites, and, in turn, they lose them. Green-blanket Feet eventually returns alone to her people with her feet wrapped in the last strips of the blanket her husband had given her. She finds comfort and gains a new name (Green-blanket Feet) that acknowledges her sufferings and her stamina. Likewise, Cogewea ends her suffering and her sense of failure for having been duped by Densmore when she heeds the "voice from the buffalo skull" (280).

Heeding this spirit power marks her reawakened respect for tribal traditions, a metaphoric return to her people. The green blanket is the legendary woman's last refuge and gives her a new identity. Cogewea finds refuge and begins a new stage in her life by accepting Jim. As a half blood, the son of a white man who abandoned his Native wife, Jim, like the blanket, is a legacy of the false *shoyahpee*. Jim and Cogewea are the inheritors and the issue of a history of suffering, yet their union is a positive event, covering the sad history with romantic happiness and promising a better future as it hints at the positive power of mixed descent.

The chapter in which the tale of Green-blanket Feet is related rates more notes than any other. Most of them define Okanogan words or describe Native customs and clarify events in the story. Note four is particularly helpful, for it describes the significance of Green-blanket Feet's acts when she escapes from the Blackfeet. McWhorter tells us that by touching the chief's sacred objects and mimicking their ritual use, she desecrates them, destroying their magic and humiliating the chief (293-4). McWhorter's remarks help give meaning to an otherwise mysterious action. Notes such as this show the benefits of the collaboration and the strength arising from the "mixed heritage" of the book.

However, the first note to the story of Green-blanket Feet is especially curious. Mourning Dove describes a suspenseful scene in which Green-blanket Feet plunges into a large badger hole to escape from her armed husband. McWhorter appends a note asserting that such large holes "are often met with in the loose desert soil" (293). Here and throughout the book, McWhorter reveals his anxiety that Mourning Dove's words be taken as true and shows his lack of faith in the power of stories. The note interrupts the scene, distracting the reader with facts. Instead of seeing Green-blanket Feet cowering in a hole, we see McWhorter hovering about the text like a nervous hen, trying to assure us that the words are true.

McWhorter's concern for veracity and detail also comes across in the last, lengthy footnote to the chapter. He begins by saying that "in the Stemteema's narrative of *Green-blanket Feet*, the author has purposely incorporated incidents connected with two or three different occurrences" (295). McWhorter then repeats the story as passed down through Green-blanket Feet's children. His tale can be as compelling as Mourning Dove's version, but his main concern seems to be factual accuracy, with names, places, and dates listed. He concludes with a few paragraphs about the fickleness of the Indian Bureau in dealing with children of mixed parentage. This information is not pertinent to the story of Green-blanket Feet or to Mourning Dove's reasons for relating it. Instead, it contributes to the arguments against the Indian Bureau and to the development of the broader theme of institutionally based injustice meted out to Native Americans, primary concerns of McWhorter. When McWhorter tells us that the author purposely connects several distinct occurrences, it is not clear whether he simply wants to set the story straight or if he truly appreciates Mourning Dove's artistry. By blending several tales of woe, Mourning Dove intensifies the pathos, building up to Green-blanket Feet's declaration of the Great Spirit's displeasure and her final warning to all Okanogan women to "shun the Shoyahpee. His words are poison! His touch is death." If the protagonist of the inserted tale has not made the point clear, the *stemteemä* repeats it, telling Cogewea that "the fate of Green-blanket Feet is for you; my grandchild unless you turn from him" (176). Where Mourning Dove relies on a character and narrator from a story within the story to express her theme, McWhorter adds an accumulation of facts to sway the readers.

Racing Race: The Social Context of Mixed Descent

In contrast to popular portrayals of half bloods as despicable and consumed by self-hatred, such as we find in *The Brand*, Mourning Dove goes to great lengths to show that mixed bloods exist mainly because white men took Indian wives and abandoned them and their children. These children are part of a Native community in contact with whites. Cogewea and her sisters are raised by their Okanogan grandmother and learn to speak English. Moreover, Cogewea appears both as a mixed blood and as an Indian. She refers to Native Americans as "my people" and to half bloods as "my kind." When she asserts her European-American heritage, she is clearly calling on the social rights she deems to be hers, challenging others to put democracy into practice. Cogewea's changing self-identification demonstrates that identity is contextual: Among whites, she is Indian; among Indians she is a "lowly breed"; among friends and family, she is a lively young woman. What at first glance appear to be inconsistencies resolve into a compelling portrayal of contextual identity.

The events of the Fourth of July celebration best illustrate Cogewea's shifting social identity. On this holiday, all gather together to celebrate. Cowboys join in the rodeo, Kootenais hold a powwow, and everyone races. Cogewea plans to compete with whites in the "Ladies" race. As Jim says, she hopes to "put it over them there high toned white gals who think they can beat the Injun gals a ridin'." Trying to choose between two good horses,

Cogewea decides to ride both: one in the "Ladies" race, the other in the "Squaw" race, saying, "If there's any difference between a *squaw* and a *lady*, I want to know it. I am going to pose as both for this day" (58–9). The conversation between Jim and Cogewea sets up chapter VII, "The 'Ladies' and the 'Squaw' Races," as a racial contest in which the "half-breed" heroine challenges the social distinctions between whites, Natives, and mixed bloods.

For the Fourth, Cogewea wears a blue riding habit and red, white, and blue ribbons in her hair. She is appropriately patriotic for the occasion, yet her long hair "streaming to the racer's back, lent a picturesque wildness to her figure" (62). The long, loose black hair attests to her Native ancestry even as it asserts her "wildness" and symbolizes the daring of her participation in a "whites-only" race. Cogewea's nerve earns her the jeers of the best non-Indian rider, Verona Webster, who loudly complains, "Why is this *squaw* permitted to ride? This is a *ladies* race!" The insult reiterates the linguistic and social distinctions that provide the moral undertone of this chapter. Cogewea and Verona, expert riders on well-matched mounts, run a close race. Near the end, Cogewea's bay pulls ahead of Verona's black. "Verona, maddened at the thought of being beaten by a presumptuous 'squaw,'" raises her quirt to strike Cogewea (63). Heroically, Cogewea dodges the blow and wrests the whip from her opponent. She strikes back, missing Verona but hitting the black. The bay pulls further ahead; Cogewea wins, and the men from Carter's ranch wildly cheer.

Quickly, Cogewea exchanges horses and goes to the Kootenai camp to "rent" Native dress (64). The costume is convincing; the judge takes her for a full blood and makes a lascivious remark in English, thereby clarifying the social distinction between "squaw" and "lady." Indian women receive none of the respect usually granted to white women. Once again, Cogewea's entrance in the race sparks the displeasure of the other contestants. One rider says, "You have no right to be here! You are half-white! This race is for Indians and not for *breeds!*" (66). The second race mirrors the first, ending in a close finish between Cogewea and the other favorite. Here, though, there is no violence, no resentment. The Indians take "winnings and losses alike . . . with stoic indifference" (67). The decorum at the end of the second race foreshadows the reconciliation between Cogewea and the full-blood Natives. Later, during the powwow, the Pend d'Oreille chief takes Cogewea as his partner for the friendship dance, and he gives her the pinto that his wife rode in the race. Her standing among Native peoples, shot down by the insulting remark about "breeds," is now restored.

In contrast, the "caucasians" maintain the insults and exclusion. After Cogewea wins the race with the Native women, she approaches the judge.

He is "anxious" to see her until he realizes that she speaks English and thus understood his lascivious remarks. The judge covers his embarrassment with strictly businesslike behavior, giving Cogewea the prize money for the second race. She then politely requests the prize for the first race. But she is told that to ride in both races is "irregular and will not be allowed" (67). "Because . . . she is a *squaw* [she has] no right to ride in the *ladies'* race" (68). Jim presses the point with the judge, to the official's discomfort and for the reader's edification: "I take it that the little gal bein' a *squaw*, she can't be a *lady!* Is that it? She's a waitin' to hear you say that. Tell these here people your 'cisin regardin' the character of the little gal" (69). The judge makes no response—it is unthinkable to state explicitly society's racist principles. Cogewea ends the dispute by tossing back the "tainted money" so that the "*racial* prizes" may go to full-blooded Natives and whites (70). The judge's ruling prevails but at the cost of his dignity.

Throughout the chapter, Mourning Dove uses quotation marks and italics to bracket the words "breed," "squaw," and "lady." She distances herself, Jim, and Cogewea from these terms to show that they are the words, in Bakhtin's phrase, of "public opinion." Bracketing the words, Mourning Dove makes clear that the social distinctions implied by the terms are the product of a white society that defines itself against an Other, in this case those of Native American descent. It is the interracial context that makes the word "breed" possible and that gives meaning to "squaw" and "lady." Through Jim we come to realize this, for he congratulates Cogewea on her riding while calling her a "squaw" without causing insult: "Her eyes sparkled at the compliment, for 'squaw' had not been intended as epithetical" (65). Between two friends of the same racial makeup, the social distinctions implied in the language do not obtain.

Throughout "The 'Ladies' and the 'Squaw' Races," Cogewea's identity shifts according to her social context. Mourning Dove's portrayal of contextual identity shows the isolation of those who are always in between. But this chapter also acknowledges the power of mixed descent. Because Cogewea is neither strictly "squaw" nor "lady," she is free to challenge these artificial distinctions. Although the white officials do not alter their dealings with Natives and mixed bloods, the confident white judge is left speechless, unable to assert his social power. The true hope for the transformative power of discourses of mixed descent is that readers will be affected. Such seems to be the goal of Mourning Dove, especially in this chapter that tells a simple, clear, and powerful story.

I have argued that Mourning Dove favors the use of story to sway readers, whereas Lucullus McWhorter favors history (in the form of verifying and verifiable elements). His frequent recourse to footnotes and the occasional polemical passages that appear to be in his hand show the editor's preference for the factual. McWhorter's preference for history adds a somber note to a text that is frequently light in tone. He reminds us that, for all the power of Mourning Dove's optimism, cultural contact between Europeans and Native Americans has deadly serious repercussions. The grandmother's historically based legends also place this grim view before the reader. The emphasis that both author and editor give to the story of Green-blanket Feet shows how the impulses of each can converge even though one values the story as an effective tale, whereas the other concerns himself with showing its relation to actual events and people.

The carefully constructed horse race chapter tells a compelling story simply and clearly. It is detailed enough to paint a picture but contains no unnecessary description. McWhorter finds no references worthy of a footnote. The chapter contains no allusions to Salish traditions or history, no Salish words, no apparent Native elements. Yet it is most assuredly about ethnicity and social identity. The chapter confirms Mourning Dove's faith in the power of story to address social issues as it raises questions about the necessary elements in authentic Native American literature.

The horse race scene poses a challenge to popular conceptions of ethnicity and social status, and the novel as a whole poses a challenge to popular literature. Mourning Dove maintains the stereotypes of the moral purity of the heroine, the false and base pretensions of the villain, and the undying loyalty of the hero, but she reshapes the racial and regional identity of the figures. *Cogewea, the Half-blood* thus moves the western romance into new realms that allow for the expression of a Native point of view and that alter the conventional alignment of the heroine with the forces of "civilization." The central place that Mourning Dove gives to folklore alters the romance framework even more significantly. The legends provide an element of dialogism, introducing a new voice and a new implied language (Salish) that push at the boundaries of the formulaic genre. The folklore provides more than a revision; it marks Cogewea as a narrative of mixed descent.

ARNOLD KRUPAT

Dead Voices, *Living Voice:*
On the Autobiographical Writing of Gerald Vizenor

*D*ead Voices, (1992) Gerald Vizenor's most recent novel is also, I believe, his most personal or autobiographical novel. Its protagonist, although not "really" the author, resembles him more nearly than the protagonists of any of Vizenor's other fictions; moreover, *Dead Voices* is a book centrally and explicitly concerned with the uses of stories for "survivance," a matter of considerable importance to Vizenor for some time. The origin or placement of stories—that is, whether they are "in the blood" or come from elsewhere —is not at issue here, as it was in *The Heirs of Columbus*; rather, the issue is whether stories can perform their healing function only as voiced or oral stories or whether they can retain their power—whether they can avoid simply becoming "dead voices"—when they are in written form. *Dead Voices* also takes up a number of other issues that Vizenor has addressed in his autobiographical or essayistic writing (the texts in which he speaks more or less in his "own" voice), such things, for example, as names and nicknames, pronouns, and the comparative political efficacy of the pen versus the sword or gun.

In this chapter I will be reading the "fictional" text *Dead Voices* as though it were in some measure "true." I will thus be blurring, far more than is inevitable, the generic line between the autobiography or personal essay and the novel, a line drawn on the Western epistemological distinction between "truth" and "fiction." I will mention some Western critical perspectives that might provide a rationale for such a reading, although it will be Native American perspectives on these matters from which I will

From *The Turn to the Native: Studies in Criticism and Culture.* © 1996 by the University of Nebraska Press.

draw my primary justification. The result should be an ethnocritical account of *Dead Voices*.

Just one word further: the fact that I situate *Dead Voices* in the context of Vizenor's autobiographical writing should not be seen as an attempt to peer into the psyche of its author. Although this does not strike me as an inherently disreputable practice, it is not a practice in which I am here engaged. As noted above, *Dead Voices* struck me as closer to Vizenor's autobiographical texts than to his novels, and thus I attempt to correlate these texts with *Dead Voices*.

Vizenor has published at least four autobiographical texts: "I Know What You Mean, Erdupps MacChurbbs: Autobiographical Myths and Metaphors," in 1976; the brief "self-portrait" (for Jane Katz's *This Song Remembers: Self-Portraits of Native Americans in the Arts*) titled "Gerald Vizenor, Ojibway/Chippewa Writer," in 1980; "Crows Written on the Poplars: Autocritical Autobiographies," in 1987; and the book-length *Interior Landscapes: Autobiographical Myths and Metaphors*, in 1990. I say "at least four," but this phrase could be replaced by "perhaps five or six or even more" if we include the abundantly self-referential essay "The Envoy to Haiku" and "The Tragic Wisdom of Salamanders," the latter with—as Vizenor himself notes—its "several autobiographical references" (personal communication), both published in 1993, or if we go back to 1984 and parts of Vizenor's *The People Named the Chippewa*. One could also say that Vizenor has published "only one" autobiography if we require autobiographies to be book-length texts (*Interior Landscapes*).

From a Western perspective, to read a novel as a type of autobiography, treating its protagonist as "really" or nearly speaking directly for its author, is to violate what Philippe Lejeune calls the "fictional pact" and thus apparently to confuse (to say "blur" here begs the question) genres traditionally kept distinct. A naive violation of this sort might lead one, in effect, to offer sociology or psychology where "literary criticism" should be. A more sophisticated violation of the "fictional pact" might follow Lejeune a bit further, to the point where one might justify an autobiographical reading of a fictional text by claiming its affinity with the curiously hybrid texts Lejeune calls "fictitious fiction[s]." These include, on the one hand, Gertrude Stein's *The Autobiography of Alice B. Toklas* and, on the other, certain dialogues of Plato and Jean-Jacques Rousseau's *Rousseau juge de Jean-Jacques* (Rousseau judge of Jean-Jacques), texts that offer what Lejeune calls "fictitious witness."

Dead Voices might be made to fit this latter category by following Lejeune's observations (he is, in turn, following Emile Benveniste) on the deictic rather than strictly referential nature of pronouns in autobiographical writing. And a fuller search of the expanding corpus of theoretical work on autobiography than I have attempted would, no doubt, provide other rationales for reading *Dead Voices* in relation to if not actually *as* autobiography. Let this serve, however inadequately, to provide a Western perspective on this matter.

But Gerald Vizenor is a Native American writer, so that we must also take into account indigenous views on these matters. Although we cannot hope to find traditional perspectives on such generic types as the novel or the autobiography, certainly there are Native views on narrative, the discursive modality we have already noted as centrally important to Indian peoples. What is curious to add is that many traditional Native narratives do not seem to divide along the lines of truth and fiction.

This is not to deny that Native Americans distinguish between stories they understand to be true and those they regard as false. The Plains peoples' customary practice that coup tales be told in the presence of people able to confirm or deny the veracity of the deeds being claimed is only one of several testimonies to their distinction between true and false. But, as Donald Bahr, an anthropologist whose work has been with the Akimel O'odham and Tohono O'odham (formerly Pima and Papago) peoples of the Arizona desert, wrote, "To my knowledge tribal societies do not have *fictions* in the modern sense of stories that people make up with no pretense or faith that the characters in the stories really lived or that the characters' actions really occurred" (47). Commenting on "Hohokam history" (the Hohokam were the ancestors of the Pima and Papago), Bahr has more recently noted, "All the stories or myths on this subject should be taken as good faith histories . . . offered by their tellers as *true*" (7, my emphasis). Robert Brightman noted of the Rock Cree people that stories they call *ācadōhkīwin*, stories of the ancient times, conventionally labeled "myth" by Westerners, "are generally said to be *true* accounts of events that transpired in an earlier condition of the world . . . the stories were relations of then contemporary events that were handed down successively through the generations" (7).

Here let me note in passing that the distinction between "history" and "myth," so important to the West, also seems to exist in Native cultures. But whereas the West bases its distinction between myth and history on a judgment of the fictionality or truthfulness of the narrative in question, indigenous peoples tend (I am unable to say whether this is a generalization that does indeed apply continent-wide, and I offer it for what heuristic use it may have) to make this distinction on the basis of the distance (earliness) or nearness (recentness) of the events narrated, very distant events having the aura of what we would call "myth" (though they are still "true") and more recent ones being responded to more nearly as history (also, but in no greater degree, "true").

Wendy Wickwire, who worked with Harry Robinson, a traditional Salishan storyteller of the Northwest (British Columbia), claims: "Harry never fictionalized stories. Indeed the very concept of fiction was foreign to him" (*Native Power* 20). This seems largely to be the case with what is known of other contemporary oral storytellers.

As it is for contemporary oral storytellers, so too may it be for at least some contemporary Native American writers. I offer, casually enough to be sure, an anecdote told by the linguist William Bright, who, as part of his work on an anthology that would be called *The Coyote Reader*, wrote to Peter Blue Cloud telling the poet of his interest in "the mythic Coyote." Blue Cloud sent back a postcard saying, "You sure Coyote is a myth?" (xix). In the same way, Clifford Trafzer, a mixed-blood Wyandot and former chair of the Department of Ethnic Studies at the University of California, Riverside, begins a recent essay called "Grandmother, Grandfather, and the First History of the Americas" with a quotation from the Okanagon writer Mourning Dove, who noted that stories about the Animal People "are not myths nor [sic] fiction; they are real history, true accounts of what happened near the Beginning when the World was very young" (474). In his essay, Trafzer generally supports Mourning Dove's view.

Thus the stories that Native Americans listen to and tell can be taken as "true" (i.e., they "really" happened, they are not "fiction"), no matter how improbable they may appear from a realistic perspective (e.g., the intervention of supernaturals). These stories, whomever they may actually tell of—gods, monsters, animals—and whenever they may actually have happened, are considered to be functionally relevant to present situations, bearing directly on the lives of presently existing people. Indeed, as Julie Cruikshank points out, there are very definitely "behavioral models in narrative" (344), some stories specifically offering ways to engage in the "cultural constructions of individual experiences" (339). Let me assemble just a few illustrations of this point from contemporary Native American oral performance and from contemporary Native texts.

In an important paper of 1984, the anthropologist Keith Basso described in detail the discursive practice of what he calls "Stalking with Stories" among the western Apaches. These Apaches use the narrative category of *'agodzaahi*, or historical tales, "to criticize[,] to warn[,] or to 'shoot'" (36) people who have behaved in a manner inappropriate to the Apache way. Basso tells of a seventeen-year-old Apache woman, recently returned home from boarding school, who attended a girl's puberty ceremony "with her hair rolled up in a set of pink plastic curlers" (39) even though "Western Apache women of all ages are expected to appear at puberty ceremonials with their hair worn loose" (39). Not to do so is not only disrespectful but potentially threatening to the ceremony's "most basic objectives, which are to invest the pubescent girl with qualities necessary for life as an adult" (40). Two weeks later, this young woman was present at a family birthday celebration. As Basso tells it, after the meal was over, the woman's grandmother narrated a version of a traditional historical story, said to have occurred sometime in the latter nineteenth century, about a forgetful Apache policeman. Immediately the young woman stood up and left the gathering. She left because, as the grandmother explained to Basso, "I shot her with an arrow" (40). And, indeed, this young woman understood the story to be "stalking" her; she recognized that the communally-agreed-upon moral of the story was not to behave too much like the "whiteman."

The story-arrow shot by the young woman's grandmother spoke literally of someone else, but as Basso notes, "every historical tale is also 'about' the person at whom it is directed" (39) and speaks directly to that person's behavior and sense of self. I emphasize Basso's account of the western Apaches' practice of stalking or hunting with words because Vizenor has independently invented the term *wordarrows*, and—a matter to which I will return—in his autobiographical writing he several times notes occasions on which he himself made the choice to hunt, or "stalk," with the pen rather than with the gun.

Cruikshank, to whom I have already referred, provides the fullest account of the way in which Native people—in particular, Native women— use traditional stories in the telling of their own lives. In her work with three Yukon Native elders—Angela Sidney, Kittie Smith, and Annie Ned— Cruikshank learned "how these women use traditional narrative to explain their life experiences" (2), how they combine "traditional narrative with individual experience to construct a coherent account" (xi) of their lives. Cruikshank adopts this "'bifocal' perspective" in the published text of Angela Sidney's life history by alternating chapters that "approximate a conventional Western understanding of life history and include events [Sidney] either experienced herself or heard about from older people" with "traditional narratives she also wanted to record as part of her life story" (29).

This is consistent with Melody Graulich's recent statement about Native Americans: "You claim who you are by the stories you accept as your own, the particular stories you tell and retell" (5). This would seem to be the case not only for contemporary Native oral storytellers but as well for many contemporary Native writers; Graulich's comment comes in an introduction to a book of critical essays on Leslie Marmon Silko. N. Scott Momaday, in *The Way to Rainy Mountain*, constructs his Kiowa identity, as is well-known,

in part by retelling the traditional stories of the Kiowas. Silko herself, in
Ceremony, wrote, "You don't have anything if you don't have the stories"
(2). Her autobiography, mixing "fictional" and "factual" discourse, is called
Storyteller. A very great many other writers might be mentioned here, but I
will quote only some lines by Simon Ortiz from a poem called "Survival
This Way":

> *We travelled this way,*
> *gauged our distance by stories*
> *and loved our children. . . .*
> *We told ourselves over and over*
> *again, "We shall survive*
> *this way." (168)*

Here we find, made explicit in the work of a contemporary Native American
writer, the linkage of storytelling to survival so important to traditional oral
cultures. This linkage has been important also to Gerald Vizenor, and it is
particularly important to him in Dead Voices, a story about stories that I
shall read as "true" in the sense that its stories, although they are about
someone else, also may speak of Vizenor himself. By telling these stories,
Vizenor in important measure accepts them as his own, thus—as I quoted
Graulich just above—claiming who he is.

Dead Voices begins in February 1982 and ends ten years later in February
1992. The first and last chapters are narrated by a lecturer at a California
university, a man known only as "Laundry Boy." He has been given this
nickname by the main character of the book, a Chippewa woman named
Bagese Bear, from the Leech Lake Reservation in Minnesota. Bagese tells
seven stories as she turns the cards of an Anishinaabe (Chippewa) card
game called "wanaki." Each of the cards pictures an animal, and according
to Laundry Boy, Bagese "explained that the players [of the wanaki game]
must use the plural pronoun *we* to share in the stories and become the creatures on the cards" (17). Bagese's insistence on the plural pronoun
is related to her insistence that "tribal stories must be told not recorded,
told to listeners but not readers, . . . heard through the ear not the eye" (6).
To Laundry Boy's early assertion that "written words are pictures," she
responds: "Printed books are the habits of dead voices. . . . The ear not the eye
sees the stories." To his rejoinder that "the eye hears the stories," she insists,
"The voices are dead" (18). Printed stories are nothing but "dead voices."
    As the narrator informs us, Bagese actually turned into a bear about a

year before the novel begins. It is to the absent Bagese that Laundry Boy addresses the final words in the book—"We must go on"—words that Bagese herself had several times pronounced. He offers these words in explanation of his decision to publish Bagese's wanaki stories despite his promise "not to publish what she told [him]" (6–7) and despite her warning that publication would kill the stories.

My very brief synopsis has sought to foreground the importance to *Dead Voices* of the apparent conflict between the oral and the textual transmission of stories, noting an attention to names, nicknames, and pronouns. All of these have been concerns of Vizenor's for a long time. I will deal with the subject of "writing the oral tradition," in Kimberly Blaeser's phrase, at considerable length below (this will also provide a segue to the issue of pens and swords or guns), but I turn here to a discussion of Vizenor's interest in names, nicknames, and pronouns.

In 1984, Vizenor published a text called *The People Named the Chippewa*, meditating on what it means to know oneself as *anishinaabe* or *anishinabeg* (plural) yet to be named—or, of course, misnamed—Chippewa. In a piece called "Native American Indian Identities: Autoinscriptions and the Cultures of Names" (1992), Vizenor continued his meditations on these matters, and in the recent *Manifest Manners* (1994), he speculates on how to name "Indians" in a "postindian" age, beginning the chapter "Ishi Obscura" with the words, "Ishi was never his real name" (126). (A few years ago, Vizenor also attempted to get the University of California at Berkeley to rename [Alfred] Kroeber Hall as Ishi Hall, an effort that so far has not met with success.) In 1985, he named Dennis Banks, of the American Indian Movement (AIM), "Dennis of Wounded Knee," then, in *The Trickster of Liberty* (1988), named him (the character in the novel may also refer to other Native politicos) Coke de Fountain. It appears likely that the author and media star Jamake Highwater appears in *The Trickster* as Homer Yellow Snow, and other examples of Vizenor's renamings of people might easily be added. Vizenor has also expended a great deal of imaginative energy on the names of the invented characters in his fiction: Inawa Biwide, Rosina Cedarfair, Griever DeHocus, Father Mother Browne, Belladonna Darwin-Winter Catcher, Transom Molte, and Justice Pardone Cozener, to mention only a very few. Examples of Vizenor's fascination with names and naming throughout his career could easily be multiplied; and I have already noted some of the curious names in *The Heirs of Columbus*.

Nicknames have also been of interest to Vizenor, who has engaged them from early to late in his work for what may be personal as well as political and esthetic reasons. His father, Clement Vizenor, horribly murdered before Vizenor was two, was known by the nickname Idee; his mother, who more than once abandoned him, was nicknamed Lovey (see *Interior Landscapes*). In *The People Named the Chippewa*, Vizenor approvingly notes Frances Densmore's attention to Chippewa nicknames (14), and in *Dead Voices*, the narrator learns the meaning of Bagese's name from her uncle, nicknamed Sucker; the name "means a tribal dish game in translation" (143), from *pagessewin* (bû´gese˝wĭn). Most recently, *Manifest Manners*, with reference to Matei Calinescu, nicknamed AIM activist Clyde Bellecourt "kitschyman" (154). Once more, many further examples could be listed.

In "The Ruins of Representation," in the new introduction to *Summer in the Spring*, and elsewhere, names and nicknames, Vizenor suggests, tell stories. In *Summer in the Spring*, for example, he wrote: "The stories of nature were heard in names. Place names and personal nicknames were communal stories. The *Anishinaabe* were never alone in their names, visions, and stories" (10). Pronouns, however, do not have the capacity of names and nicknames to tell stories, but what pronouns can and cannot do has been of concern to Vizenor generally and in his autobiographies most particularly, where he has for long wrestled with the issue of pronominal self-reference.

In 1976, in his first autobiography, "I Know What You Mean, Erdupps MacChurbbs: Autobiographical Myths and Metaphors," Vizenor rather unproblematically wrote of himself as "I," a practice he continued in the brief self-portrait "Gerald Vizenor" in 1980. By 1987, however, in "Crows Written on the Poplars: Autocritical Autobiographies," he quoted the 1976 text extensively but referred to himself in both the third and the first person, announcing, "The first and third person personas are me" (101). The reader is to place this enunciation in relation to a categorization of autobiographies as "wild pastimes over the pronouns" (101). It was in that same text that Vizenor—I believe for the first time (he has used the quotation on a number of other occasions)—quoted Georges Gusdorf's observation: "Through most of human history, the individual does not oppose himself to all others; he does not feel himself to exist outside of others and still less against others, but very much *with* others in an interdependent existence that asserts its rhythms everywhere" (107). *Interior Landscapes*, Vizenor's book-length autobiography of 1990, repeats the subtitle of the 1976 piece—*Autobiographical Myths and Metaphors*—and reassumes the relatively unproblematic use of the "I" as Vizenor revisits and also revises his life as previously published.

The recent essay "Shadow Survivance" contains Vizenor's fullest commentary on the subject of pronouns. Vizenor offers a virtual windstorm of quotations—from Francis Jacques, Anthony Kenny, Harold Noonan, and Mikhail Bakhtin—relating to pronoun usage. All of these are presented largely without comment, or they are glossed by sentences that intentionally and, often, all-too-successfully resist secure comprehension. In any case, although it is not clear what Vizenor might actually *mean*, what he forcefully *signifies* is his sense that pronoun usage, in particular the use of the first-person singular, is a very risky business.

In "Shadow Survivance," Vizenor quotes Gusdorf again (95), asserts that "first person pronouns have no referents" (20), and one time speaks of himself in the third person ("Gerald Vizenor edited *Narrative Chance*") (15). He quotes Bakhtin's notebook observation: "The *I* hides in the other and in others . . . to cast from itself the burden of being the only *I* (I-for-myself) in the world" (103). And he also quotes Kenny's question "Shall we say that 'I' is a demonstrative?" But whatever "I" is, Vizenor is wary of it:

> The first person pronoun has never been the original absence of the heard, not even as the absence or transvaluation in the silence of a reader. . . . The personal, possessive, demonstrative, relative and inter-rogative pronouns are translations and transvaluations, the absence of names, presence, and consciousness heard in tribal stories.
>
> The pronoun endures as twice the absence of the heard, and more than the mere surrogate signifier or simulation in tribal stories. (*Manifest* 97)

Denying to first-person pronouns the status of "original absence of the heard," Vizenor reserves that status for the noun in writing. In *Dead Voices*, he early on has Laundry Boy note that Bagese tricks demons "with *dead* pronouns" (16, my emphasis), and in a text of the following year, a new introduction to *Summer in the Spring: Anishinaabe Lyric Poems and Stories*, Vizenor speaks of "the ironic amusement of overstated personal pronouns" (10). And as he did in "Shadow Survivance" and "The Ruins of Representation," he here, one time at least, evades the most "overstated" pronoun of all, the "I," by writing of himself in the third person ("The editor and interpreter of the dream songs and stories in this book has heard songs and stories in anishi-naabemowin [the Ojibwa language], but he is not a primary speaker of a tribal language") (17–18).

The political dimension of Vizenor's hostility to the first-person singular becomes clear when we consider his remark, in *The People Named the Chippewa*, directed against some members of the American Indian Movement: "The new radicals frown, even grimace at cameras, and *claim the atrocities endured all tribal cultures in first person pronouns*" (130, my emphasis). How, then, is one to speak against "the atrocities endured by all tribal cultures" in a tribal or communal fashion? For Vizenor, the answer will come in *Dead Voices*, with the decision to adopt the first-person plural. But that decision requires first that he commit himself to fighting for the survivance of tribal people with the pen rather than—as the "new radicals" do—the sword or gun. Vizenor identifies himself as one whose weapon of choice is the "wordarrow."

It is in *Interior Landscapes*, in a chapter called, "Avengers at Wounded Knee," that Vizenor explicitly discovers and announces a turn away from the gun. The chapter describes Vizenor's attendance at a "historic meeting" (235) at Calico Hall on the Pine Ridge Reservation, in February 1973 during the AIM occupation, and his intense reaction to the presence in a small cabin of "more than a hundred tribal people from several tribes, from cities and reservations" (235). "I was obsessed," Vizenor wrote, "with a sense of spiritual warmth, and moved by the communal anticipation of the tribal people there" (235). He noted his deep response to "the sound of the drums, the drums, the drums"; then he went outside.

> I was liberated on the air, in the night sky, and said my name out loud, once, twice . . . I had been close to my own truth, the absolute truth of spiritual conversion that night; a few more minutes, hours, and my name might have been lost to the tribe behind a bunker at Wounded Knee. I might have raised my rifle to that airplane over the village in the morning; instead, my pen was raised to terminal creeds. (235)

Preserving his "name," Vizenor also preserves pronominal self-reference in the first-person singular. As I have tried to show, however, his dissatisfaction with an "I" that arrogates to itself qualities of autonomy, individuality and uniqueness—the qualities, of course, of the romantic and postromantic ego in the West—continues to grow.

Inasmuch as names and nicknames, by means of the stories they tell identify and link individuals to their communities, they have, for Vizenor a force and efficacy that pronouns cannot and do not have. Pronouns "endure," as we have noted, as "twice the absence of the heard"; in writing, as we have noted, they are marked by secondariness, and Vizenor's loyalties are to speech as primary and to nouns. This romantic position stands in rather uneasy tension with Vizenor's admiration, here and elsewhere, of a certain Derridaean poststructuralism or Lyotardian postmodernism for which writing is privileged over speech and for which names, inasmuch as they pretend to "natural" affinities with what they name, are acutely symptomatic of logocentric nostalgia.

This tension has a long and poignant history in Vizenor's work. For

Vizenor is deeply attracted to an orality traditionally associated with collective or "tribal" identities and ancestral homelands. But he is also absolutely and unsentimentally clear about the present necessity of writing the oral tradition in the diasporic solitude of the cities. As Elaine Jahner perceptively noted in 1985, "at the beginning of his career, Vizenor saw all writing as an act that destroys the life of the oral exchange," claiming as late as 1984 that printed stories alter tribal experience (in Blaeser in press). Nonetheless, Jahner continued, "over time he has come to a more accepting view of what writing is and can be" (in Blaeser in press)—provided, of course, that the writing be of the type that, in a phrase of Julia Kristeva's, "breaks out of the rules of a language censored by grammar and semantics" (in Hochbruck 98). Thus Vizenor's attempt to write the oral tradition, as Wolfgang Hochbruck shrewdly notes, "does not replace the monological form of colonial discourse with an equally monological romantic myth about what is or what is not Indian." For him, the oral tradition "has for the most part become one of many bits and pieces in a postmodern language game" (Hochbruck 93).

But this is not "only" a game; rather, like the wanaki game of *Dead Voices*, it is a chance at peace. As we have noted in *The Heirs of Columbus*, Vizenor wants—traditionally, romantically, or even in Sartrean left-modernist fashion—his postmodernist, fragmented oral writing to serve the unifying, communal-cohesive, and "healing" functions he associates with traditional orality. Just as Vizenor insists, in Robert Silverman's words, "that the trickster [can] be defined as compassionate rather than amoral and asocial, as Paul Radin described him," a "kind of necessary fiction" (15), so too must he insist that trickster discourse can be consistent functionally with an oral tradition that, both in the present and in the past, is marked by a certain groundedness (e.g., expectations are fulfilled rather than subverted, and ironies are of the satiric sort, focused and limited). This insistence, it seems to me, is also a necessary fiction. For all the wild and wonderful ironies and language games, *Dead Voices*, similar to *The Heirs of Columbus*, returns in the end to the old and moving values of communal cohesion and survivance. *Dead Voices*, like *The Heirs*, employs an apparently postmodernist manner in the interest of left-modernist or (neo-)humanist interests.

Indeed, *Dead Voices* concludes with the strongest defense Vizenor has yet provided of the necessity of writing the oral tradition in the urban post-Indian era in the interest of healing and survivance. In the remainder of this essay, I will try to show how he moves to this defense of written storytelling (a quite personal statement, it seems to me) with reference to the matters we have taken up thus far—names, nicknames, pronouns, pens, and guns—and, also, squirrels.

Having three times tried "I," and once "I" and "he" in his autobiographical writing, Vizenor, in *Dead Voices*, has Laundry Boy provisionally settle on "we," a move from metonymic to synecdochic self-reference. As I have shown elsewhere, this is a move quite typical of Native American writers of autobiography. My claim is that the shift from "I" to "we" in *Dead Voices* bears as much on Gerald Vizenor's sense of identity as it does on that of a fictional character nicknamed Laundry Boy.

The final words of *Dead Voices*, as I have said, are "We must go on." Spoken by Laundry Boy, these words are a quotation from Bagese, who has several times said "We must go on" (62, 135, 139ff) with reference to the importance of stories to the survivance of tribal people. But these words also refer to Samuel Beckett, whose conclusion to his novel *The Unnamable* serves as the first of three epigraphs to *Dead Voices*. And it is not Bagese or Laundry Boy but Gerald Vizenor who has seen to it that Beckett's words—"I can't go on, I'll go on"—echo in the novel, and it is Vizenor who has caused them to echo with a difference. For Bagese's "We must go on" transforms Beckett's first-person singular to the plural, as it also changes his auxiliary verb "will"—in contraction (in translation)—an enunciation of purpose or intention, to "must," an enunciation of necessity.

So we might say that *Dead Voices*, a story about stories, tells a tale of the hunt for pronouns, for some provisionally acceptable, pronominal "shadow writing" of the tribally *spoken* name or nickname. To speak of the hunt for pronouns in *Dead Voices* is once more to foreground the issue of Vizenor's commitment to word hunting rather than man or, as I want to show now, animal hunting. This commitment has been abundantly documented in Vizenor's autobiographical texts, in particular "Crows Written on the Poplars," in which Vizenor writes of himself in the third person, noting he "has pretended to be a hunter in his stories, . . . but he has never had to track an animal to the end, as he would to the last pronoun in his stories, to feed his families and friends" (105). Vizenor is commenting here on an incident that occurred in 1956 (or 1957); described in his first autobiography, "I Know What You Mean, Erdupps MacChurbbs," it is repeated in three of his four autobiographical texts. (It is omitted only from the brief 1980 account, "Gerald Vizenor.")

In "1956: In a Low Voice without Words," the penultimate section of "I Know What You Mean, Erdupps MacChurbbs," Vizenor tells of hunting a large red squirrel in the woods of Minnesota. His first shot shattered the squirrel's shoulder bone; a second shot "tore the flesh and fur away from the top of his skull"; a third "tore his lower jaw away"; and a fourth and final shot "shattered his forehead" (107). As this animal, "who wanted to live more than anything" Vizenor had ever known (107), finally died, Vizenor asked his forgiveness, wept, and sang "a slow death song in a low voice without words until it was dark" (108).

This moving story is central to "Crows Written on the Poplars," which is, at the outset, announced as "a mixedblood autobiographical causerie and a narrative on the slow death of a common red squirrel" (101). Vizenor quotes selected passages from the account of the killing of the squirrel in "Erdupps MacChurbbs" and comments on them, speaking of himself in the third person. Thus, for example, he wrote: "The slow death of the squirrel burned in his memories; he sold his rifles and never hunted animals. Instead he told stories about squirrels" (105–6). Refusing "to accept the world as a hunter" (106), Vizenor says that he became, instead, a "word hunter" (106).

He returns to the story of the squirrel in *Interior Landscapes* in the brief chapter called "October 1957: Death Song to a Red Rodent." Here he does not quote but slightly revises his earlier account, now suggesting that the "red squirrel *dared* Vizenor to hunt him" (168, my emphasis) and characterizing himself as an *urban* hunter (167–68). In some regards distancing himself from the squirrel—by referring to the animal as a "rodent, "by writing short, terse sentences, by interrupting the narrative with quotations, and by suggesting that the squirrel "dared" the hunter—Vizenor here also brings himself closer to the squirrel—by remarking, after the first shot, "I understood his instinct to escape; in a dream we reached up with *our* right paw" (168, my emphasis), and by stating, "I owe so much to that red squirrel who dared me to hunt him in the oaks, *who died in me*" (170 my emphasis). The chapter concludes: "I sold my rifle and never hunted to kill animals or birds again. The violent death of a wild animal caused by my weapon was a separation from the natural world, not a reunion. I would defend squirrels and comfort them in death; that would be the natural human response. I would not shoot an animal again unless my life depended on the hunt" (170).

The story of the hunting of the red squirrel reappears in *Dead Voices*. In the chapter dated June 1979, Bagese turns the third of the wanaki cards and says, "We are squirrels" (60). She then tells a story about a tribal hunter who "raised his small calibre rifle, took aim, and fired at a stout red squirrel" (64). And, in slow and detailed fashion, the story, as the reader has come to know it from Gerald Vizenor's autobiographies, unfolds again; only this time, the story is told from the point of view of the squirrel. Vizenor here imagines a literal conjunction, not a separation of the human and animal, but this union is possible only for Bagese, not for Laundry Boy.

In 1976 Vizenor, noting the "squirrels . . . eating without fear and jumping from tree to tree" ("I Know" 107), had written the sentence, "I was jumping with them but against them as the hunter" ("I Know" 107). He comments on this passage in 1987: "Here, in the last sentence, he pretends to be an arboreal animal, a romantic weakness; he was neither a hunter nor a tribal witness to the hunt. He was there as a mixedblood writer, in a transitive confessional, then and now, in his imaginative autobiographies" ("Crows" 105). Vizenor will no longer allow this sort of "natural" or "romantic" union with animals to himself or to Laundry Boy—although, as I have said, he does permit it to Bagese, very much a "tribal witness" (e.g., Bagese says, "We are squirrels out on a thin branch, and we run at dawn with the leaves" [Dead Voices 59]). Laundry Boy's connection to animals, his "reunion" with rather than "separation from the natural world" (Dead Voices 170), perhaps like Vizenor's own, must finally come through the adoption of Bagese's plural first-person pronoun in writing. (As when, for example, Bagese notes, "The plural pronoun we is used to be sure nature is not separated from humans" [Dead Voices 28]).

The "same" red squirrel, then, appears in the "same" story in Dead Voices, but with a difference, one that involves a name and a pronoun. For the red squirrel of Dead Voices is named (nicknamed?) Ducks, and Ducks is not male and pronominally referred to as "he" (as was the case in the earlier accounts) but is female and so is pronominally referred to as "she." (E.g., the first bullet "shattered the bone in her shoulder" [65].) Just as Gerald Vizenor, the young hunter, had done in his autobiographical accounts, so the hunter in Dead Voices "cried, and . . . sang a slow death song without words until it was dark" (67). But here Vizenor the word-hunter once again turns "autocritical," perhaps even indicating a dissatisfaction with or an incompleteness to his treatment of this part of his life in his earlier autobiographical writing. For Bagese (who, recall, is one with the squirrels) says, "The hunter wanted to believe that he was forgiven, but his stories were dead voices" (67).

In time, however, the hunter is forgiven after he tries to save a red squirrel hit by a car in the city. Such an event was, indeed, briefly mentioned in "Crows Written on the Poplars" (cf. 106), but it is expanded and given a very particular emphasis in Dead Voices as the hunter repeats, in the city, the actions he had once performed in the woods: "He stretched out beside the squirrel, touched his head and paws, and sang a death song" (68). "The hunter was forgiven at last in the city" (68).

Bagese shares Vizenor's view that the cities must become the sanctuaries for many tribal people because, as she says, "the tribes are dead" (134), having become "dead voices" (136). But she presents the case in her final monologue, dated January 1980: "There is nothing more to be done with our voices in the cities" (134). With a poignant, elegiac lyricism reminiscent perhaps of Beckett, she repeats the phrase "We must go on," although for her, the animals are now "in the eye and our voices are dead" (136), "our stories . . . removed with the animals" (137). If the only way the tribal voice can be heard in the city is textually (e.g., it can only be seen, not heard) and if stories in print are only dead voices, then we are at a tragic impasse. Twice more Bagese affirms, "We must go on" (139, 140). But she herself does not go on—rather, as we have noted, she becomes a bear, *makwa* the most powerful of animals to the Anishinaabe. But she cannot solve the problem of how to produce a living, healing voice in the interest of tribal survivance in the cities.

It remains for Laundry Boy to respond to Bagese, and his response, the replacement of Bagese's tragic story with a comic narrative of Native American survivance, is entirely consistent with Vizenor's regularly repeated sense of the function of the Native American writer today. Laundry Boy "waited a few more years and then decided that the stories [Bagese had] told [him] must be published" (143). Although he had initially agreed to refrain from publishing Bagese's stories, he changed his mind in a manner that parallels Vizenor's own thinking. With *Dead Voices*, Vizenor seems to have moved not merely to an acceptance of writing but to a firm defense of it. He has Laundry Boy conclude the novel with an address to Bagese: "Bagese, these published stories are the same as the wanaki pictures and stones that you placed in your apartment to remember the earth, the traces of birds and animals near the lake. I am with you in the mirror, and hold a stone in my pocket, the stone you left for me on the table, to remember your stories. We must go on" (144).

Referring to himself plurally, synecdochically, communally, and tribally, Laundry Boy accepts Bagese's stories about animals as his own and takes responsibility for publishing them in the interest of the people's survivance. We must go on, he says, echoing Bagese and altering Beckett to settle on the pronoun that Gerald Vizenor himself might choose; if not so good as a name or a nickname, the pronoun is at least the best choice available to a writer of stories in the oral tradition. *Dead Voices*, a novel and readable as "fiction" from a Euramerican perspective, may well, from a Native American perspective, also be read as autobiography, as a "true" account of Gerald Vizenor's experience as a mixed-blood writer, an account that documents an engagement and a trajectory that are not for him alone.

JEANNE ROSIER SMITH

Comic Liberators and Word-Healers:
The Interwoven Trickster Narratives of Louise Erdrich

From the first publication of *Love Medicine* in 1984, tricksters have played a central and pervasive role in Louise Erdrich's fiction. A family of tricksters wanders through *Love Medicine*, *Tracks*, and *The Bingo Palace*. The very existence of such a trickster "family" as Erdrich's rewrites a major tenet of a trickster tradition in which the trickster always travels alone. Erdrich's novels transgress trickster traditions in other ways as well, revising traditional myths, and in the cases of Fleur and Lulu, combining parts of several myths and pushing the limits of our conception of the trickster. Erdrich's tricksters can't be contained, whether in a body, in a prison, in a single story or novel, or as the expanded 1993 edition of *Love Medicine* suggests—even in a particular version of a novel.

Several of Erdrich's characters bear important resemblances to Chippewa trickster Nanabozho, and her work offers a trickster inspired view of identity, community, history, and narrative. As the community evolves, so do the novels' narrative forms. Indeed, the evolving narrative forms of *Love Medicine*, *Tracks*, and *The Bingo Palace* express the history of a Chippewa community in trickster terms that, far from reinforcing stereotypes of a vanishing tribe, emphasize variety, vibrancy, and continuance. Tricksters' ability to escape virtually any situation and survive any adventure makes them particularly appealing to an artist like Erdrich, who feels that Native American writers, "in the light of enormous loss, must tell the stories of contemporary survivors, while protecting and celebrating the

From *Writing Tricksters: Mythic Gambols in American Ethnic Literature.* © 1997 by The Regents of the University of California.

cores of cultures left in the wake of the catastrophe ("Where" 23). Through trickster characters and a trickster aesthetic, Erdrich attests to the personal and cultural survival of the Chippewa people.

In Erdrich's works, tricksters are central to the formulation of identity, the creation of community, and the preservation of culture. Through their courageous, outrageous stories, their transgressions not only of law and convention but also of flesh and blood, Erdrich's tricksters are, to borrow Gerald Vizenor's words, "enchanter[s], comic liberator[s], and word healer[s]" (*Trickster of Liberty* x). Erdrich's works convey a tricksterlike delight in the margin as a place of connection and transformation. Her novels focus our attention on these interconnections, not only between characters but also among the various stories and across the novels. The new and expanded version of *Love Medicine* heightens and reinforces the interconnections among the novels, while questioning the stability of the novel as a form. In keeping with Erdrich's aesthetic of interconnection, my discussion focuses first on the trickster's relationship to identity and then on the trickster inspired narrative structures that link family, the community, and the novels.

Trickster Identity: *Love Medicine* and *Tracks*

That tricksters inspire Erdrich's formulation of identity may appear at first a risky claim. After all, the trickster embodies paradox; his or her ever-shifting form seems to negate the possibility of any "stable" identity. Yet paradox is a part of Native American (and postmodern) conceptions of identity, and the shiftiness defines the trickster's identity. If aptly directed, Erdrich suggests, a trickster-inspired view of identity can be liberating and empowering. Traditionally, the Chippewa trickster Nanabozho is "the master of life the source and impersonation of the lives of all sentient things, human, faunal, and floral. . . . He was regarded as the master of ruses but also possessed great wisdom in the prolonging of life" (Densmore 97). As the "master of ruses," Nanabozho wields as his chief weapon the power of transformation. Nanabozho could "assume at will . . . a new form, shape, and existence"; he "could be a man, and change to a pebble in the next instant. He could be a puff of wind, a cloud fragment, a flower, a toad" Johnston 19–20). Using his transformational powers to escape from difficult situations and attack his enemies, Nanabozho's transformational ability implies control over his physical boundaries. It is the trickster's questioning of physical boundaries that is central to Erdrich's vision of identity based on connections to myth and community.

As I argue elsewhere in detail, Erdrich views identity as "transpersonal": a strong sense of self must be based not on isolation but on personal connections to community and to myth (see Smith). In *Love Medicine*, Erdrich translates the concept of a fluid, transpersonal identity in concretely physical terms: bodies become boundaries, outer layers that limit and define individuals. Characters flow out of their bodies and open themselves up to engulf the world. Even death does not contain them. Those characters gifted with Nanabozho's ability to control, or dissolve, their own physical boundaries have the strongest identities.

On the night of her homecoming at the beginning of *Love Medicine*, Albertine Johnson experiences a mystical merging with the northern lights as she lies in a field next to her cousin Lipsha. Her description shows how a physical connection to myth, community, and the landscape provides strength.

> Northern lights. Something in the cold, wet atmosphere brought them out. I grabbed Lipsha's arm. We floated into the field and sank down. . . . Everything seemed to be one piece. The air, our faces, all cool, moist, and dark, and the ghostly sky. . . . At times the whole sky was ringed in shooting points . . . pulsing, fading, rhythmical as breathing . . . as if the sky were a pattern of nerves and our thoughts and memories traveled across it . . . one gigantic memory for us all. (*LM* 37)

Albertine's vision of a vast, universal brain, of which her own face forms a part, expresses what William Bevis calls "transpersonal time and space" (585). Everything connects and interrelates in living, breathing patterns and rhythms that Albertine inhabits both physically and mentally.

Albertine's vision strikingly parallels one of Nanabozho, as described by the Chippewa writer Edward Benton-Banai:

> As he rested in camp that night, Waynaboozhoo looked up into the sky and was overwhelmed at the beauty of the ah-nung-ug (stars). They seemed to stretch away forever into the Ish-pi-ming (Universe). He became lost in the vast expanse of the stars. . . . Waynaboozhoo sensed a pulse, a rhythm in the Universe of stars. He felt his own o-day (heart) beating within himself. The beat of his heart and the beat of the Universe were the same. Waynaboozhoo gazed into the stars with joy. He drifted off to sleep listening to his heart and comforted by the feeling of oneness with the rhythm of the Universe. (56–57)

Like Albertine, Nanabozho in this story is lonely and confused. For both, the merging experience counteracts a sense of alienation and disconnectedness. Albertine's vision is powerful because it reestablishes her sense of connection to her home landscape, to her family (she holds Lipsha's arm and they float together), and, importantly, to Chippewa myth. Seeing the northern lights, Albertine imagines the sky as "a dance hall. And all the world's wandering souls were dancing there. I thought of June. She would be dancing if there were a dancehall in space" (*LM* 37). In Chippewa myth the joyful dancing of the dead in the afterworld creates the northern lights. Albertine's vision places June within a community, in a "dancehall in space," and reestablishes her own links to her culture. By reinforcing her transpersonal and mythic connections to her family, her community, and the natural universe, Albertine's physical merging into the cool, dark night intensifies her own sense of identity.

Albertine's single tricksterlike visionary experience is typical of Erdrich's technique; rather than assign a trickster identity to one particular character who has multiple trickster attributes, she emphasizes the trickster's multifaceted identity with an array of trickster characters. Nanabozho most clearly appears in *Love Medicine* in the magically flexible form of his namesake, Gerry Nanapush. As the novel's most conspicuous embodiment of the trickster, Gerry addresses Erdrich's central concerns by challenging the notion of fixed boundaries, both physically with his transformative powers and politically with his continual escapes from imprisonment by whites. Chippewa writer and critic Gerald Vizenor describes Nanabozho as a "comic healer and liberator" ("Trickster Discourse" 188). Gerry Nanapush fits both of these descriptions insofar as he represents Erdrich's concern with liberating and healing Chippewa culture from damaging white stereotypes. A thoroughly modern trickster, the two-hundred-and-fifty-pound Gerry squirms through prison walls and vanishes in thin air in *Love Medicine*, garnering his trickster reputation as a "famous politicking hero, dangerous armed criminal, judo expert, escape artist, charismatic member of the American Indian Movement, and smoker of many pipes of kinnikinnick in the most radical groups" (*LM* 341). Because it allows him to escape both literal and figurative confinement, the trickster's transformative power takes on political importance in *Love Medicine*.

Originally imprisoned because of a bar fight with a cowboy over a racial slur, Gerry ends up in jail because, as Albertine Johnson dryly observes,

> White people are good witnesses to have on your side, because they have names, addresses, social security numbers, and work phones. But they

are terrible witnesses to have against you, almost as bad as having Indians witness for you. Not only did Gerry's friends lack all forms of identification except their band cards, not only did they disappear (out of no malice but simply because Gerry was tried during powwow time), but the few he did manage to get were not interested in looking judge or jury in the eyes. . . . Gerry's friends, you see, had no confidence in the United States judicial system. (*LM* 201)

By placing her Nanabozho figure in such a conflict, Erdrich suggests the trickster's power to counteract and heal the wounds of racial injustice. Andrew Wiget points out that the ability to change form is an essential survival strategy against such restrictive forces: "Trickster is in the business of . . . insuring that man remains 'unfinished' by fossilized institutions, open and adaptable instead to changing contemporary realities" (21). Gerry keeps escaping, true to his proud slogan that "no concrete shitbarn prison's built that can hold a Chippewa" (*LM* 341). His face on protest buttons and the six o'clock news, he galvanizes the Chippewa community with his miraculous getaways, sailing out of three-story windows and flying up airshafts, which liberate him and by extension all Chippewas from the white world's effort to contain and define them.

The "unfinished" nature of the trickster provides an escape from essentializing definitions; however strong the mythic dimensions of Gerry's character, Erdrich carefully emphasizes his humanity as well. As Greg Sarris suggests, pinning a trickster identity onto Gerry would be just as confining as all of the stereotypes from which he snuggles to break free (130). With a deft sleight of hand, Erdrich shatters any static image of Gerry as trickster by showing the toll Gerry's public trickster role has taken as he awaits the birth of his daughter: "All the quickness and delicacy of his movements had disappeared, and he was only a poor tired fat man in those hours, a husband worried about his wife, menaced, tired of getting caught" (*LM* 168). Although he escapes from prison again in *The Bingo Palace*, his appearance in that novel makes over-romanticizing him impossible; physically diminished by years in a maximum security prison, Gerry's much-changed image on the television screen shocks his friend Albertine. Whereas the old Gerry "had absorbed and cushioned insults with a lopsided jolt of humor, . . . had been a man whose eyes lighted, who shed sparks," his gaze in a prison life documentary strikes her as hungry and desperate (*BP* 24–25). Erdrich's characterization of Gerry forces readers to consider both the mythic and the psychological dimensions of identity.

Given the fact that the trickster, as Vizenor explains, is a "teacher and healer in various personalities," Gerry's clownish, bumbling son, Lipsha, is clearly another of *Love Medicine*'s tricksters, deriving his healing "touch" from his mythical forebear ("People" 4). His uncle Lyman describes him as "a wild jack . . . clever and contriving as a fox," and, as a trickster in the youngest Chippewa generation, Lipsha represents the hope of cultural survival (*LM* 304). He goes on to become a central character in Erdrich's most recent novel *The Bingo Palace* (1994), in which he wavers (tricksterlike) between the luck and easy money of gambling and the fear that turning reservation lands into casino property will rob his community of its heritage and sense of identity.

In the title chapter of *Love Medicine*, Erdrich comically recasts the Nanabozho origin myth in the story of Lipsha's search for his parents. In the myth, when Nanabozho learns from his grandmother Nookomis that his mother had been stolen by a "powerful wind spirit" at his birth, he sets out on a long journey to find her and finally meets the great gambler, with whom he battles over the destiny of his people. At the tale's end, Nanabozho beats the gambler through trickery and returns to his people triumphant. The parallels to *Love Medicine* are clear. Like Nanabozho, Lipsha Morrissey first learns about his parents through his grandmother, Lulu Lamartine. Lipsha's mother, June, has also disappeared in a powerful wind (swept up in a North Dakota snowstorm), and after a search he finally meets his own trickster father, Gerry, and the traitorous King Kashpaw. The three gamble for King's car, and the father and son tricksters emerge victorious. Lipsha's repetition of Nanabozho's journey underscores the importance Erdrich places on cultural survival and suggests the danger betrayers like King pose to it. As with the Nanabozho myth, this poker game represents a struggle over the tribe's destiny, and by escaping from the police and winning King's car, Gerry and Lipsha outwit, if only for the moment, the internal and external forces that threaten to destroy the community. Erdrich's splitting of the trickster into two characters, the wandering Gerry and the homebound Lipsha, emphasizes the trickster's dual character as both marginal and central to the culture and underscores the trickster's multiple identity.

Although Gerry's mother, Lulu Lamartine, corresponds to Nanabozho's grandmother Nookomis, Lulu is also Erdrich's feminist revisioning of the trickster, sharing Nanabozho's physical flexibility, artful gambling, and sexual prowess. Like the trickster, Lulu can "beat the devil himself at cards." She brags, "I am a woman of detachable parts" (*LM* 115). Always the center of gossip for transgressing societal rules, Lulu even breaks the incest taboo, pursuing and catching her distant cousin Moses Pillager in a union that produces her trickster son, Gerry. Like Gerry, Lulu has a history of escape from government institutions; as a child she repeatedly ran away from her government boarding school (*LM* 68). When she escapes the schools for good, thanks to the clever letters of her trickster grandfather, old man Nanapush, she revels in the thought that "they could not cage me anymore" (*LM* 69).

Though she does not narrate her own story until *Love Medicine*, Lulu provides a vital link between *Love Medicine* and *Tracks* as the listener to whom old man Nanapush's narration in *Tracks* is addressed. Through his stories, Nanapush counteracts the Indian boarding schools' attempts at cultural erasure and recreates a family and a tribal history for Lulu. Lulu's nine children speak for the ultimate success of Nanapush's message, for she almost single-handedly repopulates the reservation, knitting the tribe into one big family through their many fathers (Van Dyke 20). Erdrich emphasizes this familial interconnectedness in her description of "Lulu's boys": "Their gangling legs, encased alike in faded denim, shifted as if a ripple went through them collectively. . . . Clearly they were of one soul. Handsome, rangy, wildly various, they were bound in total loyalty, not by oath but by the simple, unquestioning belongingness of part of one organism" (*LM* 118). Fostered by their trickster mother, the boys present a picture of a potentially competitive and explosive system of interrelationships unified and strengthened by a sense of unquestioning belongingness.

A transformer, Lulu possesses the trickster's ability to dissolve her physical boundaries and merge with and absorb her environment: "I'd open my mouth wide, my ears wide, my heart, and I'd let everything inside" (*LM* 276). Lulu questions even the possibility of imposing boundaries, and as with Gerry, her trickster qualities lead her to deliver a political message: "All through my life I never did believe in human measurement," she explains, "numbers, time, inches, feet. All are just ploys for cutting nature down to size. I know the grand scheme of the world is beyond our brains to fathom, so I don't try, just let it in. . . . If we're going to measure land, let's measure right. Every foot and inch you're standing on . . . belongs to the Indians" (*LM* 282). Though her sexual escapades win her a trickster's lowly reputation, Lulu's political awareness makes her a guardian of the culture. She warns the tribal council of selling land to the government for a "tomahawk factory [that] mocked us all. . . . Indian against Indian, that's how the government's money offer made us act" (*LM* 284, 283). By the end of *Love Medicine*, Lulu emerges as an "old-time traditional," a cultural leader whose outrageous behavior in no way lessens her influence (*LM* 363).

Uninhibited by social constraints, free to dissolve boundaries and break taboos, the trickster's position on the edges of culture makes her or his perspective inherently revolutionary. As an "animate principle of disruption," the trickster questions rigid definitions and boundaries and challenges cultural assumptions (Wiget 86). By emphasizing her characters' trickster traits, Erdrich turns stereotypically negative images into sources of strength and survival. Using Gerry's trickster characteristics to turn the threatening image of an escaped federal criminal into a symbol of human vitality and possibility, Erdrich also, through the resonance of the Nanabozho legend, transforms Lipsha's maladroit escape from home into a confirmation of personal and cultural identity. Finally, she makes us see Lulu not as the "heartless, shameless man-chaser" and "jabwa witch" that she is reputed to be, but as a woman of vibrancy and vision (*LM* 277, 322).

The oldest and most vocal of Erdrich's tricksters is old man Nanapush in *Tracks*, to whom Erdrich devotes over half of that novel's chapters. Nanapush has all the markings of a trickster: a joker, a healer, and a "clever gambler" who "satisfied three wives," he lives in a "tightly tamped box overlooking the crossroad" (*T* 38, 41, 4) Though of an earlier generation, Nanapush shares with Lulu and Gerry the circumstance of having escaped from confinement in a white world, and significantly, he associates this escape directly with being a trickster: "I had a Jesuit education in the halls of Saint John before I ran back to the woods and forgot all my prayers. My father said, 'Nanapush. That's what you'll be called. Because it's got to do with trickery and living in the bush'" (*T* 33). Erdrich's repetition of this pattern of indoctrination and escape indicates its importance as a trickster strategy for cultural survival.

Nanapush's tricksterlike skill as a mediator between worlds has led several critics to emphasize his adaptability. Certainly, survival depends upon adapting, yet in Erdrich's view adaptability can also lead to assimilation and even to a collapse of identity. Although Nanapush's knowledge of English makes him an authority within the tribe and a tribal representative to the government, his attitude toward his own bilingualism is deeply ambivalent. The trickster's transformational ability can only provide a useful model for identity when that fluid identity is firmly grounded in a sense of culture and place. For example, Nanapush's knowledge of American laws and language enable him to "reach through the loophole" and bring Lulu home from the government school (*T* 225). Yet Nanapush regards his own knowledge of written English warily, because he knows that adaptation to modern, western ways can mean the loss of cultural identity. As he observes, "We were becoming . . . a tribe of file cabinets and triplicates, a tribe of single-space documents, directives, policy. A tribe of pressed trees. A tribe of chicken-scratch that can be scattered by a wind, diminished to ashes by one struck match" (*T* 225). Adaptation without connection to one's home and culture undermines identity and threatens the community, as we see in Lyman Lamartine. Lyman's description of his own fragile identity in *Love Medicine* ironically fulfills Nanapush's prediction in *Tracks*. "I could die now and leave no ripple. Why not! I considered, but then I came up with the fact that my death would leave a gap in the BIA records, my IRS account would be labeled incomplete until it closed. . . . In cabinets of files, anyway, I still maintained existence. The government knew me though the wind and the earth did not. I was alive, at least on paper" (300). Reborn "out of papers," Lyman skillfully works his way up in the Bureau of Indian Affairs and goes on to build the very tomahawk factory that his mother, Lulu, had named a threat to traditional culture (*LM* 303).

Vividly illustrating this danger of adapting too completely, one Chippewa trickster tale recounts:

> One morning Winabojo got up early and went into the woods. He saw a great many men with clubs and asked what they were doing. They replied, "We are going to get the boy that your people wagered in the game; you had better join us or you will be killed." Winabojo decided to do this in order to save his family. When they attacked the village he was so eager that he went right to his own lodge and began to kill his family. He killed the old people and the two boys and was about to kill the baby girl when someone stopped him. Then he was like someone waking from a dream and felt very sorry for what he had done. (Densmore 99)

Winabojo identifies so completely with his enemies that he kills his own family without realizing it, a vivid warning against internalized oppression. The destruction of Lyman's tomahawk factory brings about a similar result when Lyman notices Marie Kashpaw's hands have been mutilated in a machine designed to reproduce the work of "a hundred Chippewa grand-mothers" (*LM* 310). Internalized racism sharply, if comically, colors Lyman's characterization of himself as "the flesh-and-blood proof of Nector Kashpaw's teepee-creeping" and his characterization of the activists in his community as "back-to-the-buffalo types" (*LM* 303). If such self-contempt and loss of identity is to be avoided, then the fluidity that allows the trickster to adapt to swiftly changing circumstances must spring from strong connections to community and culture.

One character so closely connected to the myths and old language of the traditional Chippewa that she remains at the margins of Erdrich's contemporary fictional world is Fleur Pillager, whose heroic fights to save

her land, unconventional dress and behavior, and mythic connections make
her a compelling female trickster figure. In addition to her pivotal role in
Tracks, Fleur appears as an itinerant healer and powerful medicine woman
in *The Beet Queen, Love Medicine*, and *The Bingo Palace*; she is the only character to appear in all four novels. That Erdrich revised *Love Medicine* to
include Fleur in her 1993 edition underscores Fleur's importance to the
series, connecting the novels through her marginal but powerful presence.
If Gerry and Nanapush are Erdrich's most traditional and widely recognized tricksters, Fleur represents Erdrich's most dramatic revision of the
trickster. With Fleur, Erdrich not only retells traditional myths but, like
Maxine Hong Kingston, reinvents and combines them. Fleur transgresses
traditional myths, combining elements of the wolf (Nanabozho's brother),
Misshepeshu the Water Monster, and the bear, making new combinations
that are necessary for survival.

As Gerry does with Lipsha in *Love Medicine*, Fleur shares the trickster's
role in *Tracks* with the verbose and socially central Nanapush, and like Gerry,
Fleur never narrates. As Bonnie Tu-Smith notes, whereas Nanapush's trick-
ster-outsider role is "sanctioned within the community" so that he "represents the communal voice" in the novel, Fleur escapes even the Chippewa
community's attempts to define her, dressing like a man and living alone in
spirit-inhabited woods (Tu-Smith, *All My Relatives* 131). Just as Gerry gains
fame for his outlaw status, Fleur in an earlier time achieves an equally mythic
reputation on the reservation and in nearby towns. "Power travels in the
bloodlines," Pauline says, and although Fleur is not a blood relative of
Nanapush, as his spiritual daughter she inherits his trickster traits along with
the mystical powers of her own Pillager line (*T* 31). Unconventional as she
is, Fleur displays traditional trickster behavior. She is sensual and skilled at
cards and, like Nanapush, Lulu, and Gerry, Fleur encounters and escapes
from a white world that attempts to define her too rigidly; she flees the small
town of Argus after being raped by the three white men whom she beats at
poker once too often. Like Lipsha's card game with King at the end of *Love
Medicine*, Fleur's poker game with the men at the butcher shop represents a
battle over the future of the tribe. By winning enough money to make tax
payments on her land, she saves herself and her family from starvation.

However, Fleur's tricksterlike pride and independence alone are not
enough to work miracles. She must journey, Nanabozho-like, to the afterworld to gamble for her second child's life, and ultimately she fails to save her
family's ancestral lands. As with Gerry, Erdrich uses Fleur's trickster traits to
show the mythic possibilities of real human beings and to emphasize the
importance of community to survival. Nanapush gives us a reason for Fleur's

failure that illuminates Erdrich's regard for community: "Power dies." Nanapush warns, "As soon as you rely on the possession it is gone. Forget that it ever existed, and it returns. I never made the mistake of thinking that I owned my own strength, that was my secret. And so I was never alone in my failures" (*T* 177). Human mythic strength, Nanapush suggests, demands community.

Lonely Tricksters: *The Beet Queen*

As if to reinforce the importance of community to a viable trickster identity, Erdrich introduces an alternative version of the trickster "family" in *The Beet Queen*. Karl and Mary Adare share many trickster traits, and even their estranged baby brother, Jude Miller, has "clever hands" (*BQ* 315). Yet in sharp contrast to the three novels set on the Chippewa reservation, this novel, set in the nearby town of Argus and containing mostly white characters, emphasizes the fragility of a trickster identity when not grounded in community and tradition.

The Beet Queen is only loosely connected to the tetralogy's other three novels. Albertine's introduction of Dot Adare in *Love Medicine* foregrounds Erdrich's concern with community and cultural heritage: "On my left sat Gerry Nanapush of the Chippewa Tribe. On my right sat Dot Adare of the has-been, of the never-was, of the what's-in-front-of-me people" (*LM* 155). Dot is *The Beet Queen*'s title character, and the has-been never-was people to whom she belongs become the novel's central concern. If *The Beet Queen* pays tribute to Erdrich's German-American heritage and to her family's butcher shop, it also allows Erdrich to undercut the notion of any one family or community as "central" to her fictional world. Clearly, her focus on the Chippewa community in three novels speaks for the importance of Chippewa history and culture to her own art, but her departure from this locale in *The Beet Queen* deliberately decenters the tetralogy and allows her to explore other aspects of trickster identity. In *The Beet Queen*, Erdrich investigates what holds together identity, family, and community by repeatedly examining their collapse.

The Beet Queen opens with the explosion of a family, each fragment hurtling in a different direction. A single mother driven to desperation by debt and responsibility, Adelaide Adare flies off in a carnival plane in the novel's opening scene, abandoning her three children at an "Orphans' picnic" (*BQ* 1O). As the sun sets and the children realize their mother is not coming back, young Karl and Mary finally agree to let a stranger take their hungry baby brother home. They soon separate; Mary ends up in Argus searching for relatives, while Karl drifts aimlessly on railway boxcars.

Forced at a carnival (the trickster's realm) to face the chaos of having no ties, Karl and Mary struggle to define themselves with trickster strategies. Yet without a mythic structure such as the Nanabozho tradition on which to draw, their search is alienating and terrifying. Even among her relatives, Mary always feels an outsider, eventually finding solace in her fortune-telling tarot cards, Ouija boards, and yarrow sticks. Mary and Karl both embody the trickster's androgyny; at fourteen the bisexual Karl is mistaken for a girl, and Celestine James notes that "if you didn't know [Mary] was a woman you would never know it" (*BQ* 214). Mary's childhood is marked by one miraculous accident, when her headfirst dive down a playground slide into a sheet of ice produces a "miracle," the likeness of Christ. Mary significantly sees not Christ's but Karl's face in the ice, which suggests his role as a double Christ-Satan figure in the novel, a suggestion that is later reinforced by Jude's recognizing Karl as "the devil" (*BQ* 82). Karl maintains a tricksterlike position in the church, practicing a double life in the seminary: "between the lines of sacred texts, I rendezvoused with thin hard hoboes who had slept in the bushes" (*BQ* 55).

Karl stands out as *The Beet Queen*'s most clearly developed trickster, turning his total loss of family into a fragile trickster identity. Karl becomes the trickster-as-con-man in his series of traveling salesman jobs; he meets lover Wallace Pfef while selling air seeders at a crop and livestock convention and later moves in with Celestine after trying to sell her a set of cheap knives. His rootlessness comes from having been torn away from his roots as a child, and he uses the trickster's wanderer identity to avoid human contact. Faced with the possibility of a genuine connection with Wallace, he is haunted by a fear of again losing physical (and psychological) reference to the world: "I suddenly had the feeling that had always frightened me, the blackness, the ground I'd stood on giving way, the falling no place" (*BQ* 106). His trickster identity—traveling light, no ties, no responsibility, no pain—relies on a lack of connections that leads eventually to his breakdown: "I made less and less sense too, until I made none at all. I was part of the senseless landscape. A pulse, a strip, of light. I give nothing, take nothing, mean nothing, hold nothing" (*BQ* 318). Karl's view of a "senseless landscape" contrasts sharply with the intense, historically grounded relationship to land evident in all of Erdrich's Chippewa novels. For the dispossessed, land becomes increasingly precious, but Karl remains oblivious to the landscape's history. In this novel, Erdrich shows the meaninglessness to which a lack of connection to culture and community leads. Despite Karl's collapse, Erdrich ends *The Beet*

Queen on a note of hope; Karl returns to Argus looking for Dot and finds Wallace. He is still a trickster, "disreputable, unshaven, unwashed, . . . hungry," and Dot notices his car is "backed into its parking place, ready for a smooth exit"; yet for the moment, he has reestablished the links (*BQ* 321, 338).

From the initial collapse of a family, the novel continually balances on the edge of connection and isolation, convergence and dispersion. The characters are all "marginal" in a small midwestern town: Karl is bisexual, Wallace is homosexual, Celestine is part Native American, Sita is mentally ill, Mary is just unusual, and Dot is a social misfit. Together, they form "a complicated house" like that of the spider who makes its web in baby Dot's hair (*BQ* 204). Their links are tenuous, even hostile, clustered as they are around their possessive love for Dot. "More than anything we had in common, Dot's spite drove Celestine, Mary, and me together," Wallace Pfef notes (*BQ* 301). In one of the novel's final scenes, Dot reenacts her grandmother Adelaide's flight at the fair as she boards the skywriter's plane. As the crowds leave the grandstand, Karl, Celestine, Mary, and Wallace remain: "They made a little group, flung out of nowhere, but together. They did not lower their eyes, but kept watching as above them Dot's name slowly spread, broke apart in air currents, and was sucked into the stratosphere, letter by letter" (*BQ* 328). This image captures both convergence (the little group flung together) and dispersion (Dot's name disappearing in air) and thus reflects the frailty and preciousness of human relationships. Unlike her grandmother, however, Dot returns and heads home with her mother—a final, powerful note of connection in a novel that repeatedly stresses loneliness and disconnection.

Chance and Design: *The Bingo Palace*

With its emphasis on strategy and luck, *The Bingo Palace* invokes the trickster more overtly than any other Erdrich novel and implies the trickster's centrality to contemporary community life. In *The Bingo Palace*, Erdrich plays with the possibilities of chance in narrative structure and community history, acting as trickster author in her orchestration of chance and design—from the characters' elaborate plans to the novel's own layout. The trickster's delight in "narrative chance" allows Erdrich to explore the future of a Chippewa community without containing or prescribing that future.

Unlike the dueling narrators of *Tracks* or the many-voiced narration in

Love Medicine, the narrative perspective in *The Bingo Palace* poises between individual perception and a group consciousness that emerges as the voice of communal history. Lipsha Morrissey is the novel's predominant (and only first-person) narrator, though he narrates less than half of the novel's twenty-seven chapters and his point of view is interspersed with that of eight others, including an innovative chorus. Lipsha's "I" is balanced most notably by the choral "we," which narrates four chapters, including the book's opening and closing segments. Partly the voice of gossip, the chorus is a (momentarily) unified communal voice that seems to have absorbed the tetralogy's previous three novels: it remarks about Lipsha's failures that "we wish we could report back different since he last told his story" (*BP* 7). In addition, the choral "we" implicitly links the chorus to the reader: "We don't know how it will work out, come to pass, which is why we watch so hard, all of us alike, one arguing voice. We do know that no one gets wise enough to really understand the heart of another, though it is the task of our life to try" (*BP* 6). The chorus's watching is analogous to reading. We might in fact look at reading (or writing) stories as an extension of gossip, of that curiosity we all have in others' lives. By keeping the stories going, the chorus keeps the community alive with its "one arguing voice," a phrase that suggests both unity and multiplicity.

Lipsha's role as trickster in *The Bingo Palace* emerges directly in relation to the choral voice, which defines the community by describing everything Lipsha is not:

> He was not a tribal council honcho, not a powwow organizer, not a medic in the cop's car in the parking lot. . . . He was not a member of a drum group, not a singer, not a candy-bar seller. Not a little old Cree lady with a scarf tied under her chin, a thin pocketbook in her lap, and a wax cup of coke, not one of us. He was not a fancy dancer with a mirror on his head and bobbing porcupine-hair roach, not a traditional. . . . He was not our grandfather, either, with the face like clean old-time chewed leather, who prayed over the microphone, head bowed. He was not even one of those gathered at the soda machines outside the doors, the ones who wouldn't go into the warm and grassy air because of being too drunk or too much in love or just bashful. He was not the Chippewa with rings pierced in her nose or the old aunt with water dripping through her fingers or the announcer with a ragged face and a drift of plumes on his indoor hat. (*BP* 9)

Like Morrison's *Sula*, Lipsha defines the community by his difference. As trickster, Lipsha fits nowhere in this community, yet his central narrative role suggests his importance to the community's future. As a narrative extension of *Tracks* and *Love Medicine*, *The Bingo Palace*'s mix of private and communal perspectives suggests a strong, vital, and unified (if arguing) community.

Lipsha shares his trickster role in *The Bingo Palace* with his uncle Lyman. The struggle between the two forms a pivotal tension in the book. As Lipsha remarks, their relationship, like his relationship to his heritage, cannot be sorted into separate strands of love and hate, jealousy and admiration. "Our history is a twisted rope and I hold on to it even as I saw against the knots" (*BP* 99). The novel's plot revolves around the two men and the one woman they both want, and a parallel struggle between preserving the land in traditional ways and selling out for a money-making casino project. Lyman is a classic trickster who always mixes his own selfishness with the good of the group: "a dark-minded schemer, a bitter yet shaman-pleasant entrepreneur who skipped money from behind the ears of uncle Sam, who joked to pull the wool down, who carved up this reservation the way his blood father Nector Kashpaw did, who had his own interest so mingled with his people's that he couldn't tell his personal ambition from the pride of the Kashpaws" (*BP* 5). As the tribe's leading entrepreneur, Lyman becomes a trickster creator whose plans can "bring the possibilities into existence" and generate badly needed revenue and jobs. Yet, sucked in by his own greed, he gambles away the tribe's loan money and his father's sacred pipe on his first night at a Las Vegas gaming convention, thereby threatening his community's future and traditions. As Nanabozho's struggle with the great gambler reminds us, the trickster's gambles can mean life or death for the community.

Lipsha's awareness of a new crisis facing the Chippewas, the challenge posed by casino gambling, forces him to consider with whom the spiritual future of the tribe lies. Although he senses his own role as the community's next healer and cultural guardian after Fleur Pillager, Lipsha wonders to himself if Lyman might be a more appropriate choice as Fleur's descendant: "Fleur Pillager is a poker sharp, along with her other medicines. She wants a bigger catch, a fish that knows how to steal the bait, a clever operator who can use the luck that temporary loopholes in the law bring to Indians for higher causes, steady advances" (*BP* 221). Despite the novel's repeated insistence on the inconstancy and fluidity of money, a "clever operator" like Lyman may be just what the tribe needs. Lipsha explains that the sides of casino debate are not clear cut: "It's more or less a gray area of tense negotiations. It's not completely one way or another, tradition against the bingo. You have to stay alive to keep your tradition alive and working" (*BP* 221).

As in *Tracks*, the community's survival balances on a dispute over land,

and again it is that land most sacred and vital to Chippewa traditions—
Fleur's plot on the edge of Lake Matchimanito. "Everybody knows bingo
money is not based on solid ground," Lipsha comments, yet despite its shiftiness, gambling is often a viable and necessary way of staying alive and maintaining ground (*BP* 221). After all, in *Tracks* Fleur earned enough money
playing poker to temporarily save her land, and in *The Bingo Palace* we learn
she has won back the land she lost at the end of *Tracks* in another poker game
(*BP* 145). By the end of *The Bingo Palace*, any attempt at human control over
land is clearly futile; Fleur's land eventually goes to Lyman's development
scheme. "Land is the only thing that lasts life to life," warns Nanapush in
Tracks, an edict echoed by Fleur in *The Bingo Palace* (*T* 33; *BP* 148). The land
itself becomes the ultimate trickster in *The Bingo Palace*, lasting life to life and
resisting human efforts to contain, order, and divide it. Just as Shawnee Ray
reminds Lyman and Lipsha that she is not theirs to argue over, the land itself
reminds them that it cannot be owned but will always slip from their grasp.
As the skunk says to Lipsha in a vision, "This ain't real estate" (*BP* 200). The
land's permanence reminds us of human impermanence, and the frailty of
our attempts to own the land. Lipsha muses,

> Sky, field, and the signs of human attempts to alter same so small and
> unimportant and forgettable as you whiz by. . . . Passing shelter belts
> and fields that divide the world into squares, I always think of the
> chaos underneath. The signs and boundaries and markers on the
> surface are laid out strict, so recent that they make me remember how
> little time has passed since everything was high grass, taller than we
> stand, thicker, with no end. (*BP* 234)

Like the trickster's balance of chance and design, the land's underlying chaos
and power is just barely contained under fragile, human-imposed structure.

The trickster's power lies in disruption of pattern, in an ability to
negotiate between the known and the inchoate, reminding us that all
human design is arbitrary. In *The Bingo Palace*, Erdrich constantly reiterates
the interplay between chance and design, both in her characters' attempts
to control their own lives and self-referentially in her own narrative structure. The novel is full of intricate plans, from Lulu's "small act" of sending
Gerry's picture to Lipsha, which hides a "complicated motive and a larger
story" (3), to the "house of pulled strings" that Lipsha imagines Zelda
constructing for those around her (14). to Shawnee Ray's elaborate patterns
and designs fashioned to bring her independence. Yet although the thought
of such human control is appealing, Erdrich emphasizes its drawbacks: in

the grip of a heart attack Zelda realizes she has wasted her life, and Shawnee Ray nearly loses her son in her ambition to win a dance competition.

Far from advocating random chance and chaos, however, Erdrich acknowledges maneuverability among the forces of fate. Between chance and design, chaos and order, the trickster operates. From his solitary jail cell, trickster Gerry Nanapush voices the novel's central dynamic: "He knew from sitting in the still eye of chance that fate was not random. . . . Chance was patterns of a stranger complexity than we could name, but predictable. There was no such thing as a complete lack of order, only a design so vast it seemed unrepetitive up close, that is, until . . . one day, just maybe, you caught a wider glimpse" (*BP* 226). Granted an authorlike perspective on the plot of his own life, Gerry senses his participation in a larger design, a feeling reiterated by Lipsha: "I will always be the subject of a plan greater than myself" (*BP* 21).

Although the book suggests design, Erdrich does not enclose plot or characters within that design. Rather, the plot of *The Bingo Palace* permits and even insists on chance and uncertainty. The novel, and the tetralogy, ends not with closure but with possibility. With the most ambiguous ending of the four novels, *The Bingo Palace* never resolves whether it is right or wrong to build the casino; Shawnee Ray, for the moment, chooses neither Lipsha nor Lyman; Gerry has apparently raced off with June's ghost, as the snow erases natural landmarks and finally obliterates boundaries between the living and the dead; Lipsha is left freezing to death (or not) with a baby in a stolen white car; and Fleur seems to have taken Lipsha's place on the road to death, and yet she "still walks," reminding others of her presence (*BP* 273). Fleur, as the tribe's history and its future, leaves her tracks on the snow, a gesture that links the saga's historically oldest and most recent books. Even after death, Fleur watches over the community from the lake: "We believe she follows our hands with her underwater eyes as we deal the cards on green baize, as we drown our past in love of chance, as our money collects, as we set fires and make personal wars over what to do with its weight, as we go forward into our own unsteady hopes" (*BP* 274). The novel ends in characteristic trickster fashion. Fleur's role as trickster at the end of *The Bingo Palace* reminds us of the uncontainability of her culture, of her history, and finally, of what the human mind can understand. Her bear's laugh can be heard on clear nights, but "no matter how we strain to decipher the sound it never quite makes sense, never relieves our certainty or our suspicion that there is more to be told, more than we know, more than can be caught in the sieve of our thinking" (*BP* 274). In *The Bingo Palace*, Fleur becomes the ghost in the machine, the fluid spirit, chance, chaos in the margins of our ordered minds that flashes out, in the novel's last words, "when we call our lives to question" (*BP* 274).

"The trickster's constant chatterings and antics remind us that life is endlessly narrative, prolific and openended," writes William Hynes, and Erdrich's trickster novels express just that ("Inconclusive Conclusions" 212). As Alan Velie reminds us, the trickster is "a figure created by the tribe as a whole, not an individual author" (131), and consequently every trickster narrative revises or comments upon the ones that have come before it, as Lipsha's journey to discover his parentage recasts the Nanabozho origin myth. The trickster could not exist without the community: he or she lives and breathes through stories told and retold and embodies the vulnerabilities and the strengths of the culture. The many voices of Erdrich's novels create life, community, and history through storytelling and express contemporary history in all of its complexity. Central to that history, and inspiring the life of the community, of Chippewa culture, and of Erdrich's narratives, is the trickster. Like Fleur's bear laugh, Erdrich's novels leave us with the sense that there is "more to be told, more than we know, more than can be caught in the sieve of our thinking."

Chronology

1762 *A Short Narrative*, the autobiography of Samson Occom (Mohegan).

1772 *Mr. Occom's Address to His Indian Brethren: On the day that Moses Paul, an Indian, was executed at New Haven, on the 2d of September, 1772, for the murder of Moses Cook*, by Samson Occom. 19 editions published over the next 30 years.

1774 *A Choice Collection of Hymns and Spiritual Songs Intended for the Edification of Sincere Christians, of All Denominations*, compiled by Samson Occom.

1827 "Journal of a Mission to the Western Tribes of Indians," by Hendrick Aupaumut. Written 1791.

1829 *A Son of the Forest. The Experience of William Apes, a Native of the Forest. Comprising a Notice of the Pequot Tribe of Indians. Written by Himself*, published by the author. (Pequot)

1831 *The Increase in the Kingdom of Christ* and *Autobiography*, by William Apes (variant spelling of Apess).

1833 *Experience of Five Christian Indians of the Pequod Tribe*, by William Apes. Includes "Experience of the Missionary's Consort, Written by Herself," by Mary Apess (variant spelling of Apes).

1834   *Life of Ma-ka-tai-me-she-kia-kiak or Black Hawk.* Autobiography of Sauk leader Black Hawk as dictated to interpreter Antoine LeClair; edited by Illinois journalist John B. Patterson.

1836   *Eulogy on King Philip, as Pronounced at the Odeon, in Federal Street, Boston,* by William Apes.

1841   *A Collection of Chippeway and English Hymns, for the Use of the Native Indians,* by Peter Jones (Missassaugua Ojibwe).

1847   *The Life, History, and Travels of Ka-ge-ga-gah-bowh: A Young Indian Chief of the Ojebwa Nation,* by George Copway (Ojibwe).

1850   *The Ojibway Conquest, a Tale of the Northwest by Kah-ge-ga-gah-bowh* and *The Traditional History and Characteristic Sketches of the Ojibway Nation,* by George Copway.

1851   *Running sketches of men and places, in England, France, Germany, Belgium, and Scotland,* by George Copway.

1854   *The Life and Adventures of Joaquin Murieta, the Celebrated California Bandit,* by John Rollin Ridge (Cherokee).

1858   *Indian Art and Indian History,* by George Copway.

1861   *History of the Ojibway Indians; with Especial Reference to Their Conversion to Christianity,* by Peter Jones.

1868   *Poems,* by John Rollin Ridge.

1872   *The Manners, Customs, Traditions, and Present Conditions of the Civilized Indians of the Indian Territory,* by Elias Cornelius Boudinot (Cherokee).

1883   *Life Among the Piutes: Their Wrongs and Claims,* by Sarah Winnemucca (Paiute).

1885   *History of the Ojibway People,* by William Whipple Warren (Minnesota Ojibwe).

1887   *History of the Ottawa and Chippewa Indians of Michigan,* by Andrew J. Blackbird (Ottawa chief).

1891   *Wynema: A Child of the Forest,* novel by Sophia Alice Callahan (Creek). Probably the first novel by a Native woman.

1893   *A Study of Omaha Music,* by Francis LaFlesche (Omaha).

1899   *Queen of the Woods (O-gei-meaw-kwee-mit-i-gwea-kei),* autobiography by Simon Pokagon (Potawatomi).

1900   *The Indian Problem, from the Indian's Standpoint,* by Andrew J. Blackbird.

1901-02 "Soft-Hearted Sioux," and "Trial Path: An Indian Romance," by Gertrude Simmons Bonnin (Sioux) published in *Harper's*; "Warrior's Daughter" published in *Everybody's* magazine.

1902   *Indian Boyhood,* autobiography of Ohiyesa (Charles Eastman, Dakota Sioux).

1904   *Red Hunters and the Animal People,* short stories by Charles Eastman.

1906   *Geronimo's Story of His Life,* as told to S.M. Barrett.

1910   *Poems of Alexander Lawrence Posey, Creek Indian Bard* (Creek/ Muscogee), collected and arranged by Mrs. Minnie H. Posey.

1916   *From the Deep Woods to Civilization: Chapters in the Autobiography of an Indian,* by Charles Eastman.

1921   *American Indian Stories,* biographies by Zitkala Sa (Dakota Sioux).

1925   *Wild Harvest: A Novel of Transition Days in Oklahoma,* by John M(ilton) Oskison (Cherokee).

1927   *Cogewea, the Half-Blood: A Depiction of the Great Montana Cattle Range* by Mourning Dove (Humi-she-ma/Christine Quintasket, an Okanogan).

1931   *Woodland Princess, a Book of 24 Poems*, by Natachee Scott Momaday
            (Kiowa/Cherokee).

1932   *Black Elk Speaks*, as told to John G. Neihardt.
            Wah'kon-tah: The Osage and the White Man's Road, by John Joseph
            Mathews (Osage).
            Dakota Texts, folklore collected by Ella Carr Deloria (Sioux/
            Dakota).

1933   *Coyote Stories*, by Mourning Dove.

1934   *Sundown*, novel by John Joseph Mathews.

1935   *Brothers Three*, novel by John Milton Oskison.

1936   *The Surrounded*, novel by D'Arcy McNickle (Salish/Kutenai).

1942   *Sun Chief; the Autobiography of a Hopi Indian*, by Don C. Talayesva
            (Hopi).

1953-54   *The Umbilical Cord*, poems, and *The Witch Deer: Poems of the
            Oklahoma Indian*, by Maggie Culver Fry (Cherokee).

1958   *Dead Letters Sent, and Other Poems*, by Maurice Kenny (Mohawk).

1962   *Two Wings the Butterfly; Haiku Poems in English*, by Gerald
            Vizenor (Chippewa).

1965   *Owl in the Cedar Tree*, novel by Natachee Scott Momaday.

1968   *House Made of Dawn*, novel by N(avarre). Scott Momaday
            (Kiowa/Cherokee).
            Escorts to White Earth: 1868-1968: 100 Year Reservation, by Gerald
            Vizenor.

1969   *House Made of Dawn* wins 1969 Pulitzer Prize.
            The Way to Rainy Mountain, novel by N. Scott Momaday.
            Custer Died For Your Sins: An Indian Manifesto, by Vine Deloria
            (Standing Rock Sioux).

1971   *Heaved From the Earth*, poems by Besmilr Brigham (Choctaw).

1972   *Seven Arrows*, novel by Hyemeyohsts Storm (Cheyenne/Crow).

1974   *Like Spirits of the Past Trying to Break Out and Walk West*, poems by Minerva Allen (Assiniboine).
        Angle of Geese and Other Poems, by N. Scott Momaday.
        Winter in the Blood, novel by James Welch (Blackfeet/Gros Ventre).
        Going for the Rain: Poems, by Simon Ortiz (Acoma Pueblo).
        Ascending Red Cedar Moon, poems by Duane Niatum (Klallum).
        The Owl's Song, novel by Janet Campbell Hale (Coeur d'Alene/Lakota).

1975   *Conversations from the Nightmare*, poems by Carol Lee Sanchez (Laguna Pueblo/Sioux), nominated by the American Academy of Poets for the Edgar Allan Poe Award.
        The Last Song, poems by Joy Harjo (Creek).
        The Blind Lion, poems by Paula Gunn Allen (Laguna Pueblo/ Sioux/Lebanese).
        Flow: Poems, by Joseph Bruchac (Abenaki).

1976   *To Frighten a Storm*, poems by Gladys Cardiff (Eastern Cherokee).

1977   *Ceremony*, novel by Leslie Marmon Silko (Laguna).
        Then Badger Said This, poems by Elizabeth Cook-Lynn (Crow/ Creek/Reservation Dakota).

1978   *Darkness in Saint Louis Bearheart*, novel by Gerald Vizenor.
        Back Then Tomorrow, short stories by Peter Blue Cloud (Mohawk).
        Wind From an Enemy Sky, novel by D'Arcy McNickle.

1979   *Calling Myself Home*, poems by Linda Hogan (Chickasaw).
        The Death of Jim Loney, poems by James Welch.
        The Good Message of Handsome Lake, poems by Joseph Bruchac.

1981   *There Is No Word For Goodbye*, poems by Mary Tall Mountain (Athabaskan), wins a Pushcart Prize.
        Lost Copper, poems by Wendy Rose (Hopi/Miwok), nominated

for the American Book Award.
Storyteller, novel by Leslie Marmon Silko.
Earthdivers: Tribal Narratives on Mixed Descent, by Gerald Vizenor.
Song of Heyoehkah, novel by Hyemeyohsts Storm.

1982   *Seasonal Woman*, poems by Luci Tapahonso (Navajo).
"The World's Greatest Fisherman," a short story by Louise
Erdrich, wins the first Nelson Algren Award.
Gorky Park, novel by Martin Cruz Smith (Pueblo/Yaqui).

1983   *The Woman Who Owned the Shadows*, novel by Paula Gunn Allen.
Harold of Orange, film and unpublished screenplay by Gerald
Vizenor.
Fightin': New and Collected Stories, by Simon Ortiz.

1984   *Love Medicine* and *Jacklight*, novels by Louise Erdrich (Turtle
Mountain Chippewa).

1985   *Iroquois Stories: Heroes and Heroines, Monsters and Magic*, by Joseph
Bruchac.
Inherit the Blood: Abbey of the Bear, poems by Barney Bush
(Shawnee/Cayuga Iroquois).
The Sun Is Not Merciful: Short Stories, by Anna Lee Walters
(Pawnee/Otoe).

1986   *The Sun Is Not Merciful: Short Stories*, wins 1986 American Book
Award.
Fools Crow: a Novel, by James Welch.
The Beet Queen, novel by Louise Erdrich.

1987   *Griever: An American Monkey King in China*, novel by Gerald
Vizenor.
The Jailing of Cecilia Capture, novel by Janet Campbell Hale.

1988   *Waterlily*, novel by Ella Carr Deloria.
Ghost Singer, novel by Anna Lee Walters.

1990   *Mean Spirit*, novel by Linda Hogan.
Trigger Dance, short stories by Diane Glancy (Cherokee).
The Power of Horses and Other Stories, by Elizabeth Cook-Lynn.

Lakota Woman, biography by Mary Brave Bird (Lakota).

1991   *Lakota Woman* wins 1991 American Book Award.
Monster Slayer: A Navajo Folktale, by Vee F. Browne (Navajo).
Landfill Meditation: Crossblood Stories, by Gerald Vizenor.
From the River's Edge, novel by Elizabeth Cook-Lynn.
Food & Spirits, Stories, by Beth Brant (Mohawk).

1992   *The Sharpest Sight*, novel by Louis Owens (Choctaw/Cherokee).
Red Square, novel by Martin Cruz Smith.
Grandmothers of Light: A Medicine Woman's Source Book, nonfiction by Paula Gunn Allen.

1993   *A Chief and Her People*, autobiography of Wilma Mankiller (Cherokee).
Monster Birds: A Navajo Folktale, by Vee F. Browne.
Dawn Land, novel by Joseph Bruchac.
The Lone Ranger and Tonto Fistfight in Heaven, short stories by Alexie Sherman (Spokane/Coeur d'Alene).
An Eagle Nation, poems by Carter Revard (Osage).

1994   *The Bone Game*, novel by Louis Owens.
Lightningbolt, novel by Hyemeyohsts Storm.
The Woman Who Owned the Shadows, novel by Paula Gunn Allen.
After and Before the Lightning, poems by Simon Ortiz.
The Woman Who Fell From the Sky, poems by Joy Harjo.
The Light People, novel by Gordon Henry (Chippewa).

1995   *Solar Storms*, novel by Linda Hogan.
Monkey Secret, novel by Diane Glancy.
Completing the Circle, biography by Virginia Driving Hawk Sneve (Lakota Sioux).

1996   *Indian Killer*, mystery by Alexie Sherman, wins the 1996 American Book Award.
Nightland, novel by Louis Owens.
Rose, novel by Martin Cruz Smith.
Pushing the Bear: A Novel of the Trail of Tears, by Diane Glancy.
Bad Boys and Black Sheep: Fateful Tales from the West, by Robert

Franklin Gish (Cherokee).
Tales of Burning Love, novel by Louise Erdrich.

1997   *Maria Tallchief: America's Prima Ballerina*, autobiography of Maria
        Tallchief (Osage/Scots-Irish), with Larry Kaplan.
        Remnants of the First Earth, novel by Ray Young Bear (Mesquakie
        Fox).
        Blue Horses Rush In, poems by Luci Tapahonso.

Contributors

HAROLD BLOOM is Sterling Professor of Humanities at Yale University and Professor of English at New York University. In 1987–88 he was Charles Eliot Norton Professor of Poetry at Harvard University. He is the author of *The Anxiety of Influence, Poetry and Repression*, and many other volumes of literary criticism. His forthcoming study, *Freud: Transference and Authority*, considers all of Freud's major writings. A MacArthur Prize Fellow, Professor Bloom is general editor of five series of literary criticism published by Chelsea House.

LAWRENCE J. EVERS teaches English at the University of Arizona. He has published many critical essays on Native American literature and is editor of Sun Tracks Press in Tucson. His most recent work, a translation, is *Wo'i Bwikam: Coyote Songs from the Yakui Bow Leaders' Society*.

KATHLEEN M. SANDS is professor of English at Arizona State University, Tempe. She is the author of *Escape From Paradise: Evil and Tragedy in Feminist Theology*, editor of *Charreria Mexicana: An Equestrian Folk Tradition*, and coeditor of *American Indian Women: A Guide to Research* and *American Indian Women, Telling Their Lives*.

ELAINE JAHNER is professor of English and Native American Studies at Dartmouth College. She has published extensively on cross cultural issues in literature and is editor of *American Indians Today: Their Thought, Their Literature, Their Art*, a special issue of *Book Forum*, and coeditor of the several volumes of *Lakota Belief and Ritual*.

285

LOUIS OWENS is Choctaw, Cherokee, and Irish-American. He is a professor of Literature at the University of California, Santa Cruz. His works include two novels, *Rainshadows* and *The Sharpest Sight*, and a critical study, *Between Two Fires: Understanding the American Indian Novel*.

KENNETH M. ROEMER teaches at the University of Texas, Arlington. He has published critical essays and reviews of Native American literature in many journals, including *American Indian Quarterly*. He is editor of *Approaches to Teaching Momaday's The Way to Rainy Mountain*.

JAMES RUPPERT is professor of English at the University of Alaska, Fairbanks. He has written extensively on contemporary Native American literature. His introduction to the life and work of D'Arcy McNickle is included in the Western Writers Series.

ARNOLD KRUPAT teaches American literature at Sarah Lawrence College. He is the author of a novel, *Woodsmen, or Thoreau and the Indians*; a study of Native American autobiography, *For Those Who Come After*; and coeditor of *I Tell You Now: Autobiographical Essays by Native Americans* and *Recovering the Word: Essays on Native American Literature*.

GREG SARRIS (Coast Mowok/Pomo/Jewish) was raised by a Pomo medicine woman in Santa Rosa, California. He currently teaches at the University of California, Los Angeles and is the author of *Grand Avenue, Keeping Slug Woman Alive: A Holistic Approach to American Indian Texts, Mabel McKay: Weaving the Dream*, and editor of *The Sound of Rattles and Clappers: A Collection of New California Indian Writing*.

CECILIA SIMS is a freelance writer from Belton, Missouri, and a graduate of Northeast Missouri State University.

A. LAVONNE RUOFF teaches English at the University of Illinois, Chicago. She is author of *American Indian Literatures: An Introduction, Bibliographic Review and Bibliography*, coeditor of *Redefining American Literary History*, and general editor of the *American Indian Lives* series published by the University of Nebraska Press.

JANET ST. CLAIR teaches English at Regis College in Denver, Colorado. Her critical essays have appeared in several journals and her scholarly focus is upon Native American women writers.

KIMBERLY M. BLAESER is a member of the Minnesota Chippewa Tribe and assistant professor of Native American Literatures in the English department at the University of Wisconsin, Milwaukee.

ROBERT DALE PARKER teaches at the University of Illinois at Urbana-Champaign. He is the author of *Faulkner and the Novelistic Imagination, The Unbeliever: The Poetry of Elizabeth Bishop*, and articles about D'Arcy McNickle.

ALAN VELIE teaches American Indian literature at the University of Oklahoma. He is editor of *American Indian Literature: An Anthology* and author of the critical volume *Four American Indian Literary Masters* and numerous articles on Shakespeare, folklore, and critical theory.

ROBERT ALLEN WARRIOR is professor of English at Stanford University where he established the program in Native American studies. An Osage, he has published many essays on Native American Literature and is the author of *Tribal Secrets: Recovering American Indian Intellectual Traditions*.

ANNE MARIE DANNENBERG is of Cherokee descent. She teaches at the University of California, Davis, and is completing a study of "Indianness" in the autobiographical works of William Apess, Sarah Winnemucca Hopkins, Charles A. Eastman, and Zitkala Sa.

MARTHA L. VIEHMANN completed her Ph.D. in American Studies at Yale University. She is currently adjunct professor of English at the University of Denver and is completing a critical study, *Writing Across the Cultural Divide*.

JEANNE ROSIER SMITH teaches American Literature at Seton Hall University. She is the author of *Writing Tricksters: Mythic Gambols in American Ethnic Literature*.

Bibliography

Aithal, S.K. "The Redemptive Return: Momaday's *House Made of Dawn*," *North Dakota Quarterly* 53:2 (Spring 1985): 160–72.

Allen, Minerva. *Like Spirits of the Past Trying to Break Out and Walk West*. Big Timber, Montana: Seven Buffaloes Press, 1974.

Allen, Paula Gunn. *The Blind Lion*. Berkeley, California: Thorp Springs Press, 1975.

———. *A Cannon Between My Knees*. Brooklyn, New York: Strawberry Press, 1981.

———. *Coyote's Daylight Trip*. Albuquerque, New Mexico: La Confluencia, 1978.

———. *Shadow Country*. Los Angeles: American Indian Studies Center Series, 1982.

———. *Star Child*. Marvin, South Dakota: Blue Cloud Press, 1981.

———. *The Woman Who Owned the Shadows*. New York: Spinsters Ink, 1983.

———. " 'Border' Studies: The Intersection of Gender and Color," *Introduction to Scholarship in Modern Languages and Literatures*. Joseph Gibaldi, editor. New York: Modern Language Association, 1992. 203–319.

———. "The Mythopoeic Vision in Native American Literature: The Problem of Myth," *American Indian Culture and Research Journal* I (1974): 1–13.

———. *The Sacred Hoop: Recovering the Feminine in American Indian Traditions*. Boston: Beacon Press, 1986.

Apes(s), William. *A Son of the Forest and Other Writings*. 1829. Amherst: University of Massachusetts Press, 1997.

———. *On Our Own Ground: Complete Writings of William Apess, a Pequot*. Amherst: University of Massachusetts Press, 1992.

———. *The Kingdom of Christ: A Sermon*. New York: G.F. Bunce, 1831.

———. *Eulogy on King Philip, as Pronounced at the Odeon in Federal Street, Boston*. 1836. Brookfield, Massachusetts: L.A. Dexter, 1985.

———. *Experience of Five Christian Indians of the Pequod Tribe*. Boston: William Apess, 1837.

———. *Indian Nullification of the Unconstitutional Laws of Massachusetts, Relative to the Marshpee Tribe: Or, The Pretended Riot Explained*. 1835. Stanfordville, New York: E.M. Coleman, 1979.

Barnett, Marianne. "Dreamstuff: Erdrich's *Love Medicine*," *North Dakota Quarterly* 56:1 (Winter 1988): 82–93.

Bataille, Gretchen M. Review of *Ancestral Voice* in *Choice* 27 (November 1989): 493.

Blicksilver, Edith. "Traditionalism versus Modernity: Leslie Silko on American Indian Women," *Southwest Review* 64:2 (1979): 149–60.

Bruchac, Joseph, editor. *Survival This Way: Interviews with American Indian Poets.* Tucson: University of Arizona Press, 1987.

———. *Smoke Rising: The Native North American Literary Companion.* Detroit: Visible Ink Press, 1995.

———. *Return of the Sun: Native American Tales from the Northeast Woodlands.* Freedom, California: Crossing Press, 1989.

Brumble, H. David, III. *An Annotated Bibliography of American Indian and Eskimo Autobiographies.* Lincoln, Nebraska: University of Nebraska Press, 1981.

Cook-Lynn, Elizabeth. *Seek the House of Relatives, Blue Cloud Quarterly* 29:4 (1983).

———. *Then Badger Said This.* New York: Vantage Press, 1977.

Craig, David M. "Beyond Assimilation: James Welch and the Indian Dilemma," *North Dakota Quarterly* 53:2 (Spring 1985): 182–90.

Danielson, Linda. "The Storytellers in *Storyteller*," *Studies in American Indian Literature* 2 (Fall 1989): 21–31.

DeFlyer, Joseph E. Review of *The Ancient Child* in *Choice* 27 (June 1990): 1679.

Deloria, Vine. *God Is Red: A Native View of Religion.* New York: Grosset & Dunlap, 1973. Golden, Colorado: Fulcrum Publishing, 1994.

———. *The Metaphysics of Modern Existence.* San Francisco: Harper & Row, 1979.

———. *Red Earth, White Lies: Native Americans and the Myth of Scientific Fact.* New York: Scribner, 1995.

Erdrich, Louise. *Baptism of Desire: Poems.* New York: Harper & Row, 1989.

———. *The Beet Queen.* New York: Holt, 1986.

———. *Jacklight.* New York: Holt, Rinehart, and Winston, 1984.

———. *Love Medicine.* New York: Holt, Rinehart, and Winston, 1984.

———. *Tracks.* New York: Henry Holt, 1988.

———. *The Bingo Palace.* New York: HarperPerennial, 1994.

———, with Michael Dorris. *The Crown of Columbus.* New York: Harper & Collins, 1991.

Evers, Lawrence J. "The Killing of a New Mexican State Trooper: Ways of Telling a Historical Event," *The Wicazo: A Journal of Indian Studies* 1:1 (Spring 1985): 17–25.

Flavin, Louise. "Louise Erdrich's *Love Medicine*: Loving Over Time and Distance," *Critique: Studies in Contemporary Fiction* 31:1 (Fall 1989): 55–64.

George, Jan. "Interview with Louise Erdrich," *North Dakota Quarterly* 53:2 (Spring 1985): 240–46.

———. Review of *Co-ge-wea. Tulsa Studies in Women's Literature* I:2 (1982): 217–21.

Harjo, Joy. *The Last Song.* Las Cruces, New Mexico: Puerta del Sol, 1975.

———. *She Had Some Horses.* New York and Chicago: Thunder's Mouth Press, 1982.

———. *What Moon Drove Me to This?* Berkeley: Reed and Canvas, 1978.

Hobson, Geary. *The Remembered Earth: An Anthology of Contemporary Native American Literature.* Albuquerque: University of New Mexico Press, 1981.

Hoffert, Barbara. Review of *Tracks* in *Library Journal* 113 (September 1, 1988): 182.

Hogan, Linda. *Calling Myself Home.* Greenfield Center, New York: Greenfield Review Press, 1979.

———. *Daughters, I Love You.* Denver: Loretto Heights College, 1981.

———. *Eclipse.* Los Angeles: UCLA American Indian Studies Center Series, 1983.

———, editor. *Frontiers: A Special Issue on Native American Women* 6:3 (1981).

Jahner, Elaine. "Allies in the Word Wars: Vizenor's Uses of Contemporary Critical Theory," *Studies in American Indian Literature* 9:2 (Spring 1985): 64–69.

———. "A Laddered Rain-Bearing Rug: The Poetry of Paula Gunn Allen," *Women and Western American Literature,* Susan Rosowski and Helen Stauffer, editors. Troy, New York: Whitson Press, 1982.

Lincoln, Kenneth. *Native American Renaissance.* Los Angeles: University of California Press, 1983.

———. *Indi'n Humor: Bicultural Play in Native America.* New York: Oxford University Press, 1993.

Mathews, John Joseph. *The Osages, Children of the Middle Waters.* Norman: University of Oklahoma Press, 1961, 1973.

———. *Sundown.* New York: Longmans, Green and Co., 1934. Norman: University of Oklahoma Press, 1988.

———. *Talking to the Moon.* Chicago: University of Chicago Press, 1945. Norman: University of Oklahoma Press, 1945, 1981.

———. *Wah'kon-tah: The Osage and the White Man's Road.* Norman: University of Oklahoma Press, 1932, 1968, 1981.

McFarland, Ronald E., editor. *James Welch.* Lewiston, Idaho: Confluence Press, 1986.

McKenzie, James. "Lipsha's Good Road Home: The Revival of Chippewa Culture in *Love Medicine,*" *American Indian Culture and Research Journal* 10:3 (1986): 53–63.

McNickle, D'Arcy. *Indian Man: A Life of Oliver LaFarge.* Bloomington: Indiana University Press, 1971.

———. *The Indian Tribes of United States: Ethnic and Cultural Survival.* London: Oxford University Press, 1962.

———, co-author with Harold E. Fey. *Indians and Other Americans: Two Ways of Life Meet.* New and revised edition. New York: Harper & Row, 1970.

———. *Native American Tribalism: Indian Survivals and Renewals.* New York: Oxford University Press, 1973.

———. *Runner in the Sun: A Story of Indian Maize.* Illus. by Allan Houser. Philadelphia: John C. Winston Company, 1954.

———. *The Surrounded.* New York: Dodd, Mead, 1936.

———. *They Came Here First: The Epic of the American Indian.* Philadelphia: J.B. Lippincott Co., 1949.

———. *Wind from an Enemy Sky.* San Francisco: Harper & Row, 1978.

Momaday, N(avarre). Scott, "The Man Made of Words," *Indian Voices: The First Convocation of American Indian Scholars.* San Francisco: Indian Historian Press, Inc., 1970.

———. *The Ancient Child.* New York: Doubleday, 1989.

———. *Angle of Geese and Other Poems.* Boston: David R. Godine, 1974.

———. *Colorado: Summer/Fall/Winter/Spring.* Illus. by David Muench. Chicago: Rand McNally, 1973.

———. *The Gourd Dancer* (poems with drawings by the author). New York: Harper

& Row, 1976.

———. *House Made of Dawn.* New York: Harper & Row, 1968.

———. *The Names: A Memoir.* New York: Harper & Row, 1976.

"Native American Authors Project," *The Internet Public Library.* Online: http://www.ipl.org/ref/native/ May 30, 1997.

Neihardt, John G. *Black Elk Speaks.* Lincoln: University of Nebraska Press, 1961.

Nelson, Robert M. "Snake and Eagle: Abel's Disease and the Landscape of *House Made of Dawn,*" *Studies in American Indian Literature* 1:2 (Fall 1989): 1–20.

"North American Native Authors Catalog," *The Internet Public Library.* Online: http://www.nativeauthors.com/ June 2, 1997.

Owens, Louis. "The 'Map of the Mind': D'Arcy McNickle and the American Indian Novel." *Western American Literature* 19:4 (Winter 1985): 275–83.

———. *Bone Game.* Norman: University of Oklahoma Press, 1994.

———. *The Grapes of Wrath: Trouble in the Promised Land.* Boston: Twayne, 1989.

———. *Nightland.* New York: Dutton, 1996.

———. *Other Destinies: Understanding the American Indian Novel.* Norman: University of Oklahoma Press, 1992.

———. *The Sharpest Sight.* Norman: University of Oklahoma Press, 1992.

———. *Wolfsong.* Albuquerque: West End Press, 1991.

Ortiz, Simon. *Earth Power Coming: Short Fiction in Native American Literature.* Tsaile, Arizona: Navajo Community College Press, 1983.

Purdy, John Lloyd. *Word Ways: The Novels of D'Arcy McNickle.* Tucson: University of Arizona Press, 1990.

Rabinowitz, Paula. "Naming, Magic, and Documentary: The Subversion of the Narrative in *Song of Solomon, Ceremony,* and *China Men,*" *Feminist Re-Visions.* Vivian Patraka and Louise Tilly, editors. Ann Arbor: University of Michigan Press, 1983. 26–42.

Rainwater, Catherine. "Reading between Worlds: Narrativity in the Fiction of Louise Erdrich," *American Literature* 62:3 (1990): 405–422.

Rose, Wendy. *Academic Squaw: Reports to the World from the Ivory Tower.* Marvin, South Dakota: Blue Cloud Press, 1977.

———. *Hopi Roadrunner Dancing.* Greenfield Center: Greenfield Review Press, 1973.

———. *What Happened When That Hopi Hit New York.* New York: Contact II Publications, 1983.

———. *Long Division, A Tribal History.* Brooklyn: Strawberry Press, 1976, 1982.

———. *Lost Copper.* Morongo Indian Reservation: Malki Museum Press, 1980.

Ruoff, A. LaVonne Brown. *Literatures of the American Indian.* New York: Chelsea House, 1991.

Ruppert, James. *D'Arcy McNickle.* Boise State University Western Writers Series; no. 83. Boise: Boise State University, 1988.

———. "Paula Gunn Allen and Joy Harjo: Closing the Distance Between Personal and Mythic Space," *American Indian Quarterly* 7:1 (1983): 27–40.

———. "Mediation and Multiple Narrative in Contemporary Native American Fiction," *Texas Studies in Literature and Language* 28:2 (1986): 209–255.

Sanchez, Carol Lee. *Conversations from the Nightmare.* San Francisco: Casa Editorial, 1975.

———. *Coyote's Journal.* Berkeley: Wingbow Press, 1981.

———. *Message Bringer Woman*. San Francisco: Taurean Horn Press, 1976.

———. *Morning Prayer*. Brooklyn: Strawberry Press, 1977.

———. *Time Warps*. San Francisco: Taurean Horn Press, 1976.

Sands, Kathleen Mullen. "Closing the Distance: Critic, Reader and the Works of James Welch," *Melus* 14:2 (Summer 1987): 73–85.

Scarberry-Garcia, Susan. *Landmarks of Healing: A Study of "House Made of Dawn."* Albuquerque: University of New Mexico Press, 1990.

Schubnell, Matthias. *N. Scott Momaday: The Cultural and Literary Background*. Norman, Oklahoma: University of Oklahoma Press, 1985.

Seyersted, Per. *Leslie Marmon Silko*. Boise State University Western Writers Series; no. 45. Boise: Boise State University, 1980.

Sharma, Sanjeev. "From Loneliness to Wedding Ring: Bridging Distances Through Ethnicity in *Winter in the Blood*," *Indian Journal of American Studies* 15:1 (Winter 1985): 25–31.

Silko, Leslie Marmon. *Almanac of the Dead*. New York: Simon & Schuster, 1991.

———. *Laguna Woman*. Greenfield Center: Greenfield Review Press, 1974.

———. *Ceremony*. New York: Viking Press, 1977.

———. *The Delicacy and Strength of Lace: Letters Between Leslie Marmon Silko & James Wright*. Anne Wright, editor. Saint Paul: Greywolf Press, 1986.

———. "Landscape, History, and the Pueblo Imagination," *On Nature: Nature, Landscape, and Natural History*. San Francisco: North Point Press, 1987. 83–94.

———. "The Man to Send Rain Clouds" and several other stories, *The Man to Send Rain Clouds*. Kenneth Rosen, editor. New York: Random House, 1975. 3–8.

———. *Storyteller*. New York: Seaver Books, 1981.

Slowik, Mary. "Henry James, Meet Spider Woman: A Study of Narrative Form in Leslie Silko's *Ceremony*," *North Dakota Review* 57:2 (Spring 1989): 104–20.

Swann, Brian, and Arnold Krupat, editors. *Recovering the Word: Essays on Native American Literature*. Berkeley: University of California Press, 1987.

Tall Mountain, Mary. *There Is No Word for Goodbye*. Marvin, South Dakota: Blue Cloud Press, 1982.

Trafzer, Clifford, editor. *Blue Dawn, Red Earth: New Native American Storytellers*. New York: Doubleday, 1996.

Tapahonso, Luci. *Seasonal Woman*. Santa Fe, New Mexico: Tooth of Time Press, 1982.

Trimble, Martha Scott. *N. Scott Momaday*. Boise, Idaho: Boise State College, 1973.

Velie, Alan R. *Four American Literary Masters: N. Scott Momaday, James Welch, Leslie Marmon Silko, and Gerald Vizenor*. Norman: University of Oklahoma Press, 1982.

Vizenor, Gerald. *The People Named the Chippewa*. Minneapolis: University of Minnesota Press, 1984.

———. *Crossbloods: Bone Courts, Bingo, and Other Reports*. Minneapolis: University of Minnesota Press, 1990.

———. "Crows Written on the Poplars: Autocritical Autobiographies," *I Tell You Now*, Brian Swann and Arnold Krupat, editors. Lincoln: University of Nebraska Press, 1987. 101–109.

———. *Darkness in Saint Louis Bearheart*. St. Paul, Minnesota: Bookslinger, 1978.

———. *Earthdivers: Tribal Narratives on Mixed Descent*. Minneapolis: University of Minnesota Press, 1981.

———. *Griever: An American Monkey King in China.* Normal: Illinois State University; New York: Fiction Collective, 1987.

———. *Interior Landscapes: Autobiographical Myths and Metaphors.* Minneapolis: University of Minnesota Press, 1990.

———, editor. *Narrative Chance: Postmodern Discourse on Native American Indian Literature.* Albuquerque: University of New Mexico Press, 1989.

———. *Woodarrows: Indians and Whites in the New Fur Trade.* Minneapolis: University of Minnesota Press, 1978.

Volborth, Judith Mountain Leaf. *Thunder Root: Traditional and Contemporary Native American Verse.* Los Angeles: UCLA American Indian Studies Center Series, 1978.

Warner, Nicholas O. "Images of Drinking in 'Woman Singing,' *Ceremony,* and *House Made of Dawn.*" *Melus* 11:4 (Winter 1984): 15–30.

Warrior, Robert Allen. *Tribal Secrets: Recovering American Indian Intellectual Traditions.* Minneapolis: University of Minnesota Press, 1995.

Welch, James. *The Death of Jim Loney.* New York: Harper & Row, 1979.

———. *Fools Crow.* New York: Viking, 1986.

———. *The Indian Lawyer.* New York: W.W. Norton, 1990.

———. *Riding the Earthboy 40: Poems.* New York: Harper & Row, 1975.

———. *Winter in the Blood.* New York: Harper & Row, 1974.

Wiget, Andrew. "His Life in His Tail: The Native American Trickster and the Literature of Possibility," *Redefining American Literary History.* A. LaVonne Brown Ruoff and Jerry W. Ward Jr., editors. New York: Modern Language Association, 1990. 83–96.

Wild, Peter. *James Welch.* Boise State University Western Writers Series; no. 57. Boise: Boise State University, 1983.

———. Review of *Fools Crow, New York Times Book Review* (November 2, 1986): 14.

Young Bear, Robert. *Winter of the Salamander: The Keeper of Importance.* San Francisco: Harper, 1980.

———. *The Invisible Musician.* Duluth, Minnesota: Holy Cow! Press, 1990.

———. *Black Eagle Child: The Facepaint Narratives.* Iowa City: University of Iowa Press, 1992.

Acknowledgements

"Words and Place: A Reading of *House Made of Dawn*" by Lawrence J. Evers from *Critical Essays on Native American Literature*, edited by Andrew Wiget, reprinted from *Western American Literature* 11 (1977): 297-320. Copyright © 1985 by Andrew Wiget.

"Alienation and Broken Narrative in *Winter in the Blood*" by Kathleen M. Sands from *Critical Essays on Native American Literature*, edited by Andrew Wiget, reprinted from *American Indian Quarterly* 4 (1978): 97-106. Copyright © 1985 by Andrew Wiget.

"An Act of Attention: Event Structure in *Ceremony*" by Elaine Jahner from *Critical Essays on Native American Literature*, edited by Andrew Wiget, reprinted from *American Indian Quarterly* 5 (1979): 37-46. Copyright © 1985 by Andrew Wiget.

" 'He Had Never Danced With His People': Cultural Survival in John Joseph Mathews's *Sundown*" by Louis Owens from *Native American Literatures*, Forum 2-3 (1990-91), edited by Laura Coltelli. Copyright © 1992 by SEU.

"Ancient Children at Play—Lyric, Petroglyphic, and Ceremonial" by Kenneth M. Roemer from *Critical Perspectives on Native American Fiction*, edited and compiled by Richard F. Fleck. Copyright © 1993, 1997 by Passeggiata Press.

"Textual Perspectives and the Reader in *The Surrounded*" by James Ruppert from *Narrative Chance: Postmodern Discourse on Native American Indian Literatures*, edited by Gerald Vizenor. Copyright © 1993 by the University of Oklahoma Press.

"The Dialogic of Silko's *Storyteller*" by Arnold Krupat from *Narrative Chance: Postmodern Discourse on Native American Indian Literatures*, edited by Gerald Vizenor. Copyright © 1993 by the University of Oklahoma Press.

"Reading Narrated American Indian Lives: Elizabeth Colson's *Autobiographies of Three Pomo Women* by Greg Sarris from *Keeping Slug Woman Alive: A Holistic Approach to American Indian Texts* by Greg Sarris. Copyright © 1993 by The Regents of the University of California.

"The Rebirth of Indian and Chinese Mythology in Gerald Vizenor's *Griever: An American Monkey King in China*" by Cecila Sims from *Bestia: A Yearbook of the Beast Fable Society*. Reprinted in *Critical Perspectives on Native American Fiction*, edited and compiled by Richard F. Fleck. Copyright © 1993, 1997 by Passeggiata Press.

"Alienation and the Female Principle in *Winter in the Blood*" by A. LaVonne Ruoff from *American Indian Quarterly*. Reprinted in *Critical Perspectives on Native American Fiction*, edited and compiled by Richard F. Fleck. Copyright © 1993, 1997 by Passeggiata Press.

"Fighting for Her Life: The Mixed-Blood Woman's Insistence Upon Selfhood" by Janet St. Clair from *Critical Perspectives on Native American Fiction*, edited and compiled by Richard F. Fleck. Copyright © 1993, 1997 by Passeggiata Press.

"The New 'Frontier' of Native American Literature: Dis-Arming History with Tribal Humor" by Kimberly M. Blaeser from *Genre* 25:4 (1994). Reprinted in *Native American Perspectives on Literature and History*, edited by Alan R. Velie. Copyright © 1994 by the University of Oklahoma Press.

"To Be There, No Authority to Anything: Ontological Desire and Cultural and Poetic Authority in the Poetry of Ray A. Young Bear" by Robert Dale Parker from *Arizona Quarterly* Vol. 50, No. 4 (Winter 1994). Copyright © 1994 by the Arizona Board of Regents.

"The Indian Historical Novel" by Alan Velie from *Genre* 25:4 (1994). Reprinted in *Native American Perspectives on Literature and History*, edited by Alan R. Velie. Copyright © 1994 by the University of Oklahoma Press.

"'Where, Then, Shall We Place the Hero of the Wilderness?': William Apess's Eulogy on King Philip and Doctrines of Racial Destiny" by Anne Marie Dannenberg from *Early Native American Writing: New Critical Essays*, edited by Helen Jaskoski. Copyright © 1996 by the Cambridge University Press.

"'My People . . . My Kind': Mourning Dove's *Cogewea, the Half-Blood* as a Narrative of Mixed Descent" by Martha L. Viehmann from *Early Native*

Index

Abolitionism, in *Eulogy on King Philip*, 212, 220–23
"Act of Attention: Event Structure in *Ceremony*, An" (Jahner), 35–44
Act of Reading, The (Iser), 73–74, 78–79, 80, 81
Ainsworth, Linda, 172
Alexander, Leighton, 104
"Alienation and Broken Narrative in *Winter in the Blood*" (Sands), 25–33
"Alienation and the Female Principle in *Winter in the Blood*" (Ruoff), 135–49
Allen, Paula Gunn, 152–53, 154, 155, 156–58
All My Relatives (Tu-Smith), 268
Almanac of the Dead (Silko), 71
American Indian Autobiography (Brumble), 103
American Indians and the Problem of History (Martin), 162
American Indian Women: Telling Their Lives (Bataille and Sands), 104, 105
American Poetry: The Nineteenth Century (Hollander), 2
Ancient Child, The (Momaday), 57–72
"Ancient Children at Play—Lyric, Petroglyphic, and Ceremonial" (Roemer), 57–72
Animals, Vizenor and, 255–57
Annotated Bibliography, An (Brumble), 115
Apess, William

Eulogy on King Philip, as Pronounced at the Odeon, in Federal Street, Boston, 211–25
The Experiences of Five Christian Indians of the Pequot Tribe; or An Indian's Looking-Glass for the White Man, 221
Indian Nullification of the Unconstitutional Laws of Massachusetts Relative to the Marshpee Tribe; or The Pretended Riot Explained, 221
Aptheker, Herbert, 220
Aspects of the Novel (Forster), 171
Attentiveness, in *Ceremony*, 35–44
Auden, W. H., 90–91
Auditory motifs, in *House Made of Dawn*, 8, 9–10, 12–13
Aupaumut, Hendrick, 84
Autobiographical Myths and Metaphors (Vizenor), 250
Autobiographies, 83–86
Autobiographies of Three Pomo Women, 97–99, 100–103, 106, 107, 108–26
Dead Voices, 243–57
Storyteller, 86–93
Autobiographies of Three Pomo Women (Colson), 97–99, 100–103, 106, 107, 108–26

Babcock, Barbara, 167

Bahr, Donald, 245
Bakhtin, Mikhail, 85–86, 87, 88, 91,
    229, 241, 250, 251
Banks, Dennis, 249
Barrett, S. A., 117
Barrett, S. M., 103, 104–5, 122
Basso, Keith, 246–47
Bataille, Gretchen, 104, 105
"Bear, The" (Faulkner), 59
Beckett, Samuel, 254, 257
Beet Queen, The (Erdrich), 268, 269–71
Ben-Amos, Dan, 44
Benton, Thomas Hart, 221
Benton-Banai, Edward, 261
Benveniste, Emile, 244
Bingo Palace, The (Erdrich), 259, 263,
    264, 268, 271–76
Black Eagle Child: The Facepaint
    Narratives (Young Bear), 175,
    178–80, 184
Black Elk Speaks (Neihardt), 162,
    197–98
Blaeser, Kimberly M., 161–73, 249
Bleich, David, 123
Blue Cloud, Peter, 246
Boas, Franz, 3
Booth, Wayne, 75
Boyd, Maurice, 64
Brand: A Tale of the Flathead
    Reservation, The (Broderick),
    230–31, 232, 239
Brant, Joseph, 198
Bright, William, 246
Brightman, Robert, 245
Broderick, Therese, The Brand: A Tale
    of the Flathead Reservation, 230–31,
    232, 239
Brumble, David H., 100, 103–4, 105,
    115
Buchen, Irving, 43

Calhoun, John C., 222
Ceremonial play, in The Ancient Child,
    65–71
Ceremony (Silko), 35–44, 70, 248

Chantway rituals, 7
    in House Made of Dawn, 12, 13
Chappell, Violet, 112
Christian, Chester, C., Jr., 112
Churchill, Ward, 162
Clifford, James, 92
Cogewea, the Half-blood: A Depiction of
    the Great Montana Cattle Range
    (Mourning Dove), 227–42
Colson, Elizabeth, Autobiographies of
    Three Pomo Women, 97–99,
    100–103, 106, 107, 108–26
"Comic Liberators and Word-Healers:
    The Interwoven Trickster
    Narratives of Louise Erdrich"
    (Smith), 259–76
Coyote, 17, 91, 133, 233–34, 246
Coyote Reader, The (Bright), 246
Coyote Stories (Mourning Dove), 234
Crane, Stephen, 75
Crapanzano, Vincent, 100, 116
Crossbloods (Vizenor), 207, 208
Crown of Columbus, The (Dorris and
    Erdrich), 71, 154, 155–56, 158–59
"Crows Written on the Poplars:
    Autocritical Autobiographies"
    (Vizenor), 244, 250, 254, 255, 256
Cruikshank, Julie, 246, 247
Cultural contact, in Cogewea, the Half-
    Blood: A Depiction of the Great
    Montana Cattle Range, 228–29,
    236–42
Cultural survival, in Sundown, 45–55
Custer Died for Your Sins (Deloria), 202

Dannenberg, Anne Marie, 211–25
Darkness in Saint Louis Bearheart
    (Vizenor), 207
Dead Voices (Vizenor), 243–57
"Dead Voices, Living Voice: On the
    Autobiographical Writing of
    Gerald Vizenor" (Krupat), 243–57
Delaney, Martin R., 222
Deloria, Vine
    Custer Died for Your Sins, 202

God is Red, 162
New and Old Voices of Wah'kon-tah: Contemporary Native American Poetry, 161–62
Dialogic Imagination, The (Bakhtin), 229
"Dialogic of Silko's *Storyteller*, The" (Krupat), 83–93
Dialogism, in *Cogewea, the Half-Blood: A Depiction of the Great Montana Cattle Range*, 229, 236–39, 242
Dialogue, 85–86
  Storyteller and, 86–93
Dickenson, Emily, 61
Donovan, Kathleen M., 69–70
Dorris, Michael
  The Crown of Columbus, 71, 154, 155–56, 158–59
  A Yellow Raft in Blue Water, 152, 153
"Dream of Purple Birds in Marshall, Washington, The" (Young Bear), 192
Dreiser, Theodore, 75
Drinnon, Richard, 162
Du Bois, W. E. B., 190

Earthdivers (Vizenor), 227
Edgarton, M., Jr., 112
Emergence journey, 6–7
  in *House Made of Dawn*, 8–10, 11–12, 15, 16, 17–18, 21
"Envoy to Haiku, The" (Vizenor), 244
Erdrich, Louise
  The Beet Queen, 268, 269–71
  The Bingo Palace, 259, 263, 264, 268, 271–76
  The Crown of Columbus, 71, 154, 155–56, 158–59
  Love Medicine, 152, 155, 156, 259, 260–63, 264–66, 267, 268, 269, 271, 273
  Tracks, 152, 154, 259, 265, 266–69, 271, 273, 274
Eulogy on King Philip, as Pronounced at the Odeon, in Federal Street, Boston (Apess), 211–25
Event, in *Ceremony*, 35–44
Evers, Lawrence J., 5–24
Evil, in *House Made of Dawn*, 13–15, 17, 20
Experiences of Five Christian Indians of the Pequot Tribe; or An Indian's Looking-Glass for the White Man, The (Apess), 221
Experiential transcendence, in *Griever: An American Monkey King in China*, 128, 131

Facing West: The Metaphysics of Indian-Hating and Empire Building (Drinnon), 162
Fantasies of the Master Race: Literature, Cinema and the Colonization of American Indians (Churchill), 162
Faulkner, William, 59, 62, 64, 66, 112
Female suffering
  mixed-blood women and, 151–59
  in *Winter in the Blood*, 135–49
Fight Back. For the Sake of the People— For the Sake of the Land (Ortiz), 162
"Fighting for Her Life: The Mixed-Blood Women's Insistence Upon Selfhood" (St. Clair), 151–59
Fisher, Dexter, 236
Fitzgerald, F. Scott, 70
Flaubert, Gustave, 195
Folklore. *See* Oral Tradition
Fools Crow (Welch), 196, 197–203, 206, 208, 209
Forster, E. M., 171
For Those Who Come After (Krupat), 103
Frantz, Frank, 50
Freud, Sigmund, 193
Frye, Northrop, 195, 196

Gearing, Frederick O., 184–85
Geertz, Clifford, 87

"Gerald Vizenor" (Vizenor), 250, 254
"Gerald Vizenor, Ojibway/Chippewa
    Writer" (Vizenor), 244
Geronimo's Story of His Life (Barrett),
    103, 104–5, 122
Ghost-Dance songs, 1–3
Gish, Robert F., 176
God is Red (Deloria), 162
Go Down, Moses (Faulkner), 64
"Grandmother, Grandfather, and the
    First History of the Americas"
    (Trafzer), 246
Graulich, Melody, 247, 248
Greene, Graham, 204
Gregorio, The Hand Trembler (Brumble),
    103–4
*Griever: An American Monkey King in
    China* (Vizenor), 127–34
Gusdorf, Georges, 250, 251

Hale, Janet Campbell, 152, 153–54,
    156, 157
Harmonic play, in *The Ancient Child*,
    57–72
Harold of Orange (Vizenor), 164, 167
*Harper's Anthology of 20th Century
    Native American Poetry* (Swann), 161
Hegel, Georg, 197
"'He Had Never Danced With His
    People': Cultural Survival in John
    Joseph Mathews's *Sundown*"
    (Owens), 45–55
Heirs of Columbus, The (Vizenor), 164,
    167, 168–69, 172, 196, 203–9,
    243, 249, 253
Hemingway, Ernest, 45
Henry, Gordon, 163, 167–68, 171, 172
    The Light People, 164–66, 167,
    169–70
Henry Esmond (Thackeray), 195
Historical Novel, The (Lukács), 195
History, 195–209, 245–46
    in *Cogewea, the Half-blood: A
    Depiction of the Great Montana
    Cattle Range*, 229–30, 234–36, 237,

238–39, 241–42
    in *Fools Crow*, 196, 197–203, 206,
    208, 209
    in *The Heirs of Columbus*, 164, 167,
    168–69, 172, 196, 203–9
    See also Humor
Hogan, Linda, *Mean Spirit*, 153, 158,
    162
Hollander, John, 2
Horsman, Reginald, 214–15, 216
House Made of Dawn (Momaday), 5–24,
    62, 66, 68–70
Humor, 161–73
    in *Harold of Orange*, 164, 167
    in *The Heirs of Columbus*, 164, 167,
    168–69, 172
    in *The Light People*, 164–66, 167,
    169–70
    in "Never Quite A Hollywood
    Star," 170–71
    in *The People Named Chippewa*, 171
    in "Report to the Nation:
    Claiming Europe," 166–67, 168,
    173
    in "Shadows at La Pointe,"
    171–72
Hynes, William, 276

"I Am a Sioux Brave, He Said in
    Minneapolis" (Wright), 185, 188,
    189, 190, 192
"I Know What You Mean, Erdupps
    MacChurbbs: Autobiographical
    Myths and Metaphors" (Vizenor),
    244, 250, 254–55, 256
Implied author, *The Surrounded* and,
    75–76, 77, 78, 79, 80
Implied reader, *The Surrounded* and,
    73–81
Inada, Lawson F., 91
*Indian Nullification of the
    Unconstitutional Laws of
    Massachusetts Relative to the
    Marshpee Tribe; or The Pretended
    Riot Explained* (Apess), 221

Interior Landscapes: Autobiographical Myths and Metaphors (Vizenor), 244, 250, 252, 255
Invisible Musician, The (Young Bear), 175, 176, 192, 193–94
Iser, Wolfgang, 73–74, 78–79, 80, 81
Ivanhoe (Scott), 204

Jackson, Andrew, 214, 218–19
Jacques, Francis, 250
Jahner, Elaine, 35–44, 253
Jailing of Cecelia Capture, The (Hale), 152, 153–54, 156, 157
James, Henry, 204
Jefferson, Thomas, 216
Jenkins, J. E., 50
Jump, Kenneth, 55
Jung, Carl, 133, 209

Kashaya Texts (Oswalt), 110–11
Katz, Jane, 244
Keats, John, 59
Kelsay, Isabel, 198
Kenny, Anthony, 250, 251
Knox, Henry, 223–24
Ko-sahn, 6
Kristeva, Julia, 253
Kroker, Arthur, 127, 132
Krupat, Arnold, 83–93, 99–100, 103, 104–5, 122, 243–57

Land, in *House Made of Dawn*, 5–7, 10, 11–12, 13, 16, 17–18, 19, 20, 21
Langdon, J. W., 234
Language
  in *Autobiographies of Three Pomo Women*, 109–13, 120, 121
  in *House Made of Dawn*, 5, 7–8, 11–12, 17, 18–19, 20–21, 22
Lawrence, D. H., 5
Leighton, Dorothea, 104
Lejeune, Philippe, 244
Liberty (Vizenor), 134

Life of Black Hawk (Patterson), 84
Lifton, Robert, 128, 131
Light People, The (Henry), 164–66, 167, 169–70
Long Theresa, 232
Lottinville, Savoie, 45–46
Love Medicine (Erdrich), 152, 155, 156, 259, 260–63, 264–66, 267, 268, 269, 271, 273
Lukács, Georg, 195
Lyotard, Jean Francois, 127
Lyric play, in *The Ancient Child*, 59–61, 71

McLean, J. P., 235
McNickle, D'Arcy, *The Surrounded*, 45, 73–81
McWhorter, Lucullus Virgil, 227, 228, 229–30, 233, 234–36, 237, 238–39, 241–42
Madison, James, 224
Manifest Manners (Vizenor), 249, 250
Martin, Calvin, 162
Mathews, John Joseph
  The Osages: Children of the Middle Waters, 46
  Sundown, 45–55
  Talking to the Moon, 46
  Wah'Kon-Tah: The Osage and the White Man's Road, 46
Mauss, Marcel, 87
Mean Spirit (Hogan), 153, 158, 162
Miller, Walter B., 184
"Mixedblood Metaphors: Identity in Contemporary Native American Fiction" (Owens), 163
Mixed descent
  Cogewea, the Half-Blood: A Depiction of the Great Montana Cattle Range as novel of, 227–42
  survival of women of, 151–59
Momaday, Navarre Scott, 171
  The Ancient Child, 57–72
  House Made of Dawn, 5–24, 62, 66, 68–70

The Names, 60
The Way to Rainy Mountain, 6, 59, 60, 62, 64, 67, 170, 247–48
Monkey (Wu Che'eng-en), 128, 130, 131, 133
Mooney, James, 1–2
Morison, Samuel Eliot, 204, 205
Mountainway (Wyman), 67
Mourning Dove, 246
    Cogewea, the Half-blood: A Depiction of the Great Montana Cattle Range, 227–42
    Coyote Stories, 234
    "'My People . . . My Kind': Mourning Dove's *Cogewea, the Half-blood* as a Narrative of Mixed Descent" (Viehmann), 227–42

Names, in *Dead Voices*, 249, 250, 252, 253, 254, 256, 257
Names, The (Momaday), 60
Narrated American Indian autobiography, 97–126
"Native American Indian Identities: Autoinscriptions and the Cultures of Names" (Vizenor), 249
Ned, Annie, 247
Neihardt, John, *Black Elk Speaks*, 162, 197–98
"Never Quite A Hollywood Star" (Revard), 170–71
New and Old Voices of Wah'kon-tah: Contemporary Native American Poetry (Deloria), 161–62
"New Frontier" of Native American Literature: Dis-Arming History with Tribal Humor, The" (Blaeser), 161–73
Nicknames, in *Dead Voices*, 249–50, 252, 253, 254, 256, 257
Noonan, Harold, 250
Norris, Frank, 75

O'Connell, Barry, 211, 212, 213, 220,

221, 224, 225
O'Connor, Kathy, 111
Odyssey, The, 200
On Our Own Grownd: The Complete Writings of William Apess, A Pequot (O'Connell), 211, 212, 213, 220, 221, 224, 225
Oral tradition, 245–48
    in *Ceremony*, 35, 40
    in *Cogewea, the Half-Blood: A Depiction of the Great Montana Cattle Range*, 232–34, 235, 236–39, 242
    in *Dead Voices*, 249, 253–57
    in *House Made of Dawn*, 5, 7–8, 11–12, 17, 18–19, 20–21, 22
    in *The Storyteller*, 88–90
    in *Winter in the Blood*, 25–33
    See also Autobiographies
Ortiz, Alfonso, 5
Ortiz, Simon, 88
    Fight Back. For the Sake of the People—For the Sake of the Land, 162
    "Survival This Way," 248
Osages: Children of the Middle Waters, The (Mathews), 46
Oswalt, Robert, 110–11
Our Man in Havana (Greene), 204
Owens, Louis, 45–55, 163

Panic Sex (Kroker), 127
Panic sex, in *Griever: An American Monkey King in China*, 127, 128, 132–33
Parker, Robert Dale, 175–94
Patterson, J. B., 84
People Named the Chippewa, The (Vizenor), 171, 244, 249, 250, 251
Petroglyphic play, in *The Ancient Child*, 61–65, 71
Peyote Cult, The (La Barre), 17
Place. *See* Sense of place
Play, in *The Ancient Child*, 57–72
Poetic authority, Young Bear and,

175–94
Poetry, 161
"Powwow" (Snodgrass), 185, 186, 187–88, 189, 190, 191, 192–93
Present, in *Winter in the Blood*, 25–33
Pronouns, in *Dead Voices*, 249, 250–52, 253, 254, 255, 256, 257

"Quail and His Role in Agriculture" (Young Bear), 193–94
Quintasket, Christine. *See* Mourning Dove

Rabinow, Paul, 92
Race, in *House Made of Dawn*, 8, 16–17, 23
Racism
    in *Cogewea, the Half-Blood: A Depiction of the Great Montana Cattle Range*, 227–42
    in *Eulogy on King Philip*, 211–25
Radin, Paul, 132, 133, 253
"Reading Narrated American Indian Lives: Elizabeth Colson's *Autobiographies of Three Pomo Women*" (Sarris), 95–126
Reagan, Ronald, 207
"Rebirth of Indian and Chinese Mythology in Gerald Vizenor's *Griever: An American Monkey King in China*, The" (Sims), 127–34
Red Antway (Wyman), 67
Regeneration Through Violence: The Mythology of the American Frontier, 1600–1860 (Slotkin), 162
Reichard, Gladys, 67
"Report to the Nation: Claiming Europe" (Revard), 166–67, 168, 173
Revard, Carter, 163, 172
    "Never Quite A Hollywood Star," 170–71
    "Report to the Nation: Claiming Europe," 166–67, 168, 173

Rights, in *Eulogy on King Philip*, 211–25
Robinson, Harry, 246
Roemer, Kenneth M., 57–72
Rogin, Michael, 214, 218, 221
Romance, *Cogewea, the Half-blood: A Depiction of the Great Montana Cattle Range* as, 227–42
"Ruins of Representation, The" (Vizenor), 250, 251
Ruoff, A. Lavonne, 135–49
Ruppert, James, 73–81

Said, Edward W., 123
St. Clair, Janet, 151–59
Salammbô (Flaubert), 195
Sands, Kathleen M., 25–33, 104, 105
Scarberry-Garcia, Susan, 62, 66, 70
Schubnell, Matthias, 62
Schwab, Gabriele, 106–7
Scoop (Waugh), 204
Scott, Walter, 195, 203, 204, 205
Sense of place, in *House Made of Dawn*, 5–24
"Shadows at La Pointe" (Vizenor), 171–72
"Shadow Survivance" (Vizenor), 250–51
Shakespeare, William, 70
Sidney, Angela, 247
Silko, Leslie Marmon, 175, 247
    Almanac of the Dead, 71
    Ceremony, 35–44, 70, 248
    "Skeleton Fixer," 88
    Storyteller, 86–93, 170, 248
    "Uncle Tony's Goat," 88
Silverman, Robert, 253
Sims, Cecilia, 127–34
Sitting Bull, 198
Slotkin, Richard, 162
Smith, Jeanne Rosier, 259–76
Smith, Kittie, 247
Snodgrass, W. D.
    "Powwow," 185, 186, 187–88, 189, 190, 191, 192–93
Southey, Robert, 84

Squirrels, Vizenor and, 255–57
*Summer in the Spring: Anishinaabe Lyric
    Poems and Stories* (Vizenor), 250,
    251
Sun Also Rises, The (Hemingway), 45
Sundown (Mathews), 45–55
Surrounded, The (McNickle), 45, 73–81
Survival humor. *See* Humor
"Survival This Way" (Ortiz), 248
Swann, Brian, 161

Talking to the Moon (Mathews), 46
Tedlock, Dennis, 88
Tewa World, The (Ortiz), 5
"Textual Perspectives and the Reader
    in *The Surrounded*" (Ruppert),
    73–81
Thackery, William Makepeace, 195
*This Song Remembers: Self-Portraits of
    Native Americans in the Arts* (Katz),
    244
"To Be There, No Authority to
    Anything: Ontological Desire and
    Cultural and Poetic Authority in
    the Poetry of Ray A. Young Bear"
    (Parker), 175–94
Tracks (Erdrich), 152, 154, 259, 265,
    266–69, 271, 273, 274
Trafzer, Clifford, 246
"Tragic Wisdom of Salamanders, The"
    (Vizenor), 244
Tribal humor. *See* Humor
Trickster, 253
    Coyote and, 17, 133, 233–34, 246
    Erdrich and, 259–76
    history and, 163–73
    Momaday and, 17
    Vizenor and, 127–34, 207, 260,
        262, 263–64
    See also Humor
Trickster, The (Vizenor), 249
"Trickster Discourse" (Vizenor), 262
Trickster of Liberty, The (Vizenor), 207,
    249, 260
Troup, George M., 222

Tu-Smith, Bonnie, 268

"Uncle Tony's Goat" (Silko), 88
Unnamable, The (Beckett), 254

Velie, Alan, 276
Vestal, Stanley, 198
Viehmann, Martha L., 227–42
Vizenor, Clement, 249–50
Vizenor, Gerald, 163, 170, 229, 263–64
    *Autobiographical Myths and
        Metaphors*, 250
    Crossbloods, 207, 208
    "Crows Written on the Poplars:
        Autocritical Autobiographies,"
        244, 250, 254, 255, 256
    Darkness in Saint Louis Bearheart,
        207
    Dead Voices, 243–57
    Earthdivers, 227
    "The Envoy to Haiku," 244
    "Gerald Vizenor," 250, 254
    "Gerald Vizenor,
        Ojibway/Chippewa Writer," 244
    *Griever: An American Monkey King
        in China*, 127–34
    Harold of Orange, 164, 167
    The Heirs of Columbus, 164, 167,
        168–69, 172, 196, 203–9, 243,
        249, 253
    "I Know What You Mean,
        Erdupps MacChurbbs:
        Autobiographical Myths and
        Metaphors," 244, 250, 254–55,
        256
    *Interior Landscapes: Autobiographical
        Myths and Metaphors*, 244, 250,
        252, 255
    Liberty, 134
    Manifest Manners, 249, 250
    "Native American Indian
        Identities: Autoinscriptions and
        the Cultures of Names," 249
    The People Named the Chippewa,

171, 244, 249, 250, 251
"The Ruins of Representation,"
250, 251
"Shadows at La Pointe," 171–72
"Shadow Survivance," 250–51
*Summer in the Spring: Anishinaabe
Lyric Poems and Stories,* 250, 251
"The Tragic Wisdom of
Salamanders," 244
The Trickster, 249
"Trickster Discourse," 262
The Trickster of Liberty, 207, 249,
260

*Wah'Kon-Tah: The Osage and the White
Man's Road* (Mathews), 46
Waugh, Evelyn, 204
Way to Rainy Mountain, The
(Momaday), 6, 59, 60, 62, 64, 67,
170, 247–48
Welch, James
Fools Crow, 196, 197–203, 206,
208, 209
Winter in the Blood, 25–33, 135–49
Western romance, *Cogewea, the Half-
Blood: A Depiction of the Great
Montana Cattle Range* as, 227–42
"'Where, Then, Shall We Place the
Hero of the Wilderness?' William
Apess's *Eulogy on King Philip* and
Doctrines of Racial Destiny"
(Dannenberg), 211–25

White, Hayden, 195, 196–97
Wickwire, Wendy, 246
Williams, Roger, 216
Wilson, Edward, 209
*Winter of the Salamander: The Keeper of
Importance* (Young Bear), 175,
185–87, 188–89, 190, 191–92
Women Who Owned the Shadows, The
(Allen), 152–53, 154, 155, 156–58
Woodard, Charles L., 58
"Words and Place: A Reading of *House
Made of Dawn*" (Evers), 5–24
Wright, James A., 91
"I Am a Sioux Brave, He Said in
Minneapolis," 185, 188, 189, 190,
192
Wu Che'eng-en, 128, 130, 131, 133

Yellow Raft in Blue Water, A (Dorris),
152, 153
Young Bear, Ray A.
*Black Eagle Child: The Facepaint
Narratives,* 175, 178–80, 184
"The Dream of Purple Birds in
Marshall, Washington," 192
The Invisible Musician, 175, 176,
192, 193–94
"Quail and His Role in
Agriculture," 193–94
*Winter of the Salamander: The
Keeper of Importance,* 175, 185–87,
188–89, 190, 191–92